Britain and World War One

Alan G.V. Simmonds

Routledge
Taylor & Francis Group

LONDON AND NEW YORK

First published 2012
by Routledge
2 Park Square, Milton Park, Abingdon, Oxon OX14 4RN

Simultaneously published in the USA and Canada
by Routledge
711 Third Avenue, New York, NY 10017

Routledge is an imprint of the Taylor & Francis Group, an informa business

© 2012 Alan G.V. Simmonds

British Library Cataloguing in Publication Data
A catalogue record for this book is available from the British Library

Library of Congress Cataloging in Publication Data
Britain and World War One / by Alan G.V. Simmonds.
    p. cm.
    Includes bibliographical references and index.
    1. Great Britain – History – George V, 1910–36. 2. World War,
1914–18 – Great Britain. 3. Great Britain – Social life and customs – 20th
century. 4. Great Britain – Economic conditions – 20th century. 5. World
War, 1914-1918 – Great Britain – Influence. I. Title. II. Title: Britain and
World War I.
    DA577.S56 2010
    940.3'41-dc22
        2011013427

ISBN: 978-0-415-45538-1 (hbk)
ISBN: 978-0-415-45539-8 (pbk)
ISBN: 978-0-203-80289-2 (ebk)

Typeset in Times New Roman
by Taylor & Francis Books

MIX
Paper from
responsible sources
FSC
www.fsc.org   FSC® C004839

Printed and bound in Great Britain by the MPG Books Group

In memory of Gwen Eggleston

Contents

Tables

Figures

Acknowledgements

The Publisher would like to thank the Imperial War Museum, The National Archives, Getty and Corbis for their permission to reproduce the images within this book.

Introduction

Writing a history of Britain's Home Front during the First World War is like trying to ride a bicycle backwards: the landscape looks enticing, but navigation is a constant challenge. Sensible historians have resisted the temptation. Some have preferred to settle in a quiet corner of historical scholarship, producing works of originality and importance on a diversity of specified topics, social, political and cultural, in an attempt to understand the war as it affected Britain's civilians. Though this corpus of academic endeavour has been vastly outweighed by military histories, it has, nonetheless, a lengthy pedigree that stretches back to the 1920s, and, since 1945, has been reinvigorated by the injection of fresh ideas and changing interpretations, occasionally overturning familiar debates. The work of historians during the 1960s and 1970s, for example, including Trevor Wilson, Cameron Hazlehurst and Zara Steiner (to name but three) placed an emphasis on diplomacy and high politics, reaching its apogee in the 1990s with the publication of John Turner's authoritative *British Politics and the Great War.*[1] By then research of women's wartime experiences, both civilian and military, was already flourishing, pioneered by Gail Braybon and powerfully reinforced by the writings of Angela Woollacott and Deborah Thom. The need to examine the social condition of the wartime population was championed in the 1980s by Jay Winter's seminal (and provocative) work, *The Great War and the British People* (first edition, 1985), whilst recent developments have revolved around specialist work on the arts in wartime and the reverberations of the conflict within British culture, as exemplified by Samuel Hynes's *A War Imagined* (1990) and George Robb's *British Culture and the First World War* (2002).[2] Such works have appeared amidst a blossoming number of publications on the voguish topic of war and memory, inspired perhaps by the publication of Paul Fussell's *The Great War and Modern Memory* (1975) and carried further by reassessments of the war's historical reputation as discussed in Dan Todman's excellent *The Great War: Myth and Memory* (2005), Brian Bond's thoughtful *The Unquiet Western Front* (2002) and Gary Sheffield's *Forgotten Victory* (2001).[3] In view of the range, quality and depth of all these contributions, perhaps it is not surprising that producing a general account of Britain's Home Front during the First World War is a nettle that historians have been reluctant to grasp.

Some authors have bravely attempted to marry the military side of Britain's war with aspects of the social, political and cultural, with varying degrees of success. John Bourne made light work of this 'total' history approach in his book *Britain and the Great War, 1914–1918* (1989).[4] Trevor Wilson's bulky tome *The Myriad Faces of War* (1986) courageously attempted to weave Home Front themes within an essentially military history, as did Malcolm Brown's use of letters, diaries and memoirs in the *Imperial War Museum Book of the First World War* (1991).[5] Without doubt, such books are of great value in addressing the question of the extent to which the military's demands for resources and manpower conditioned civilian life, industry, society and politics during the war. But perhaps they also reveal to other scholars in this field the perils of overambition.

Works that reduce military events to a backstage role owe much to Arthur Marwick's *The Deluge*, first published in 1965 and currently in its third edition.[6] Marwick broke new ground in many ways. He was one of the first historians to identify and highlight women's contribution to the war effort, and the first of his generation to view the war as a positive force. His thesis that the First World War had been the catalyst for social change and real advances in the condition of the poorer classes established a durable historiographical paradigm that held its ground until Gerard DeGroot published *Blighty* in 1996.[7] DeGroot's readiness to tackle cultural as well as social themes of the period was partly a recognition of how far the historical study of the Home Front had progressed since Marwick's day. But he also blew doubts over Marwick's grand thesis of war and social change, arguing that longer-term continuities in Britain's social and cultural life were equally important in determining how far the war changed the country and its people. As such, *Blighty* has proved invaluable in restoring Britain's Home Front during the 'Great War' to visibility amongst students and the book-buying public, while enticing fellow historians (including this one) into the field.

Since *Blighty*'s publication, the volume of work on the British Home Front has undoubtedly increased. Three of the most prominent subsequent works include Richard van Emden's and Steve Humphries's narrated compilation of civilian oral histories, *All Quiet on the Home Front* (2003): a book published to accompany a Channel 4 television documentary.[8] On the other hand, Ian Beckett's lavishly illustrated and highly useful account, *Home Front 1914–1918* (2006), based largely (but not exclusively) on documentary records from The National Archives, provides an important introduction to the subject.[9] Few of these tomes, however, touch the giddy cerebral heights of Adrian Gregory's *The Last Great War* (2008).[10] As a book principally intended for an academic readership, Gregory's work is a masterly piece of historical scholarship: intensively researched; brilliantly analysed; carefully and studiously written. Gregory succeeds in bringing broader and fresher dimensions to well-discussed topics, offering an 'interpretive synthesis' of the civilian experience of the First World War that invites readers to understand how and why the British people endured its seemingly unending hardships and upheavals. The result is a piece of Home Front social history that is in a class of its own.

Although this humble contribution lacks the analytical substance of Gregory's work, its intentions are different. This book also seeks to understand the nature of Britain's Home Front during the Great War, but interprets its task as one of presenting a more general account of British society at war by integrating and synthesizing existing research, exploring previously neglected areas whilst offering a broad-based introduction to the subject both for students and interested lay readers. Thus, in the pages that follow old themes are revisited alongside the occasional new perspective. The discussions on voluntary recruitment, family and society, women's work and cultural life hold no surprises for current scholars. Yet at the same time the book attempts to throw new light on areas that have not been fully accounted for in existing works. The domestic ramifications of wartime developments in technology and changes in industrial work practices have been given greater attention, as has the wartime housing crisis. Discussion of the wartime food question has been integrated with the effects of war and government policy on farming and rural societies, and an effort has been made to re-assess the political aspects of the war, an area of study that was once all the rage, but has since fallen out of favour.

In brief, then, *Britain and World War One* endeavours to wriggle between the broad-based approach of DeGroot and the intensive analysis offered by Gregory. By offering a thematic structure, whilst veering away from a specifically social history of Britain's First World War, its chapters are linked by a study of how the country geared itself for all-out conflict between 1914 and 1918, with its people and resources mobilized to defeat Germany and her allies, and of the impact this had on British polity, society and culture. While it aims to present a comprehensive account, this book is far from definitive and is inevitably shot through by the author's unwitting errors and oversights. All the same, it is important to emphasize how much of a shock the First World War was for the British people. Once the naiveties of 1914 had faded, both politicians and public alike were compelled to face the new actualities of twentieth-century warfare. In the process, deep tensions emerged between traditional and modern approaches to the conflict, tensions that were most sharply exposed with the growth of an aggressively interventionist state. As a result, Britain's wartime struggles brought about a much closer relationship between public opinion and political action that became central to the mass democracy that emerged after the Armistice. By then a new realism about the nature of industrialized warfare had been forced upon the nation. But it ensured that the British were better prepared mentally for the war that they did *not* want in 1939.

The assembly of this book has been a daunting and exhausting, but an ultimately enjoyable, experience and would not have been possible without the help of others. Thanks must go to the staff of the Imperial War Museum, The National Archives, the Brynmor Jones Library at the University of Hull, the Record Offices of West Sussex and East Yorkshire, and the City Archive in Hull, for their patience and professionalism. Special gratitude must also be acknowledged to Dr Stephen Sambrook of the University of Glasgow for his help and advice, Angela Matthews for taking the trouble to read and comment on earlier drafts, Eve Setch, my editor, for her support and patience in pushing through this project, the Routledge reader for constructive criticism and the students who studied my course, 'The Impact of the First World War in Britain', for asking awkward yet thought-provoking questions. Above all, my very special thanks must be reserved for Carin, whose unflinching help, support and encouragement through some difficult times has enabled this writer to see the task through to completion, instead of collapsing into a pile of tea-stained research notes.

Alan Simmonds
Department of History
University of Hull
March 2011

Notes

1 John Turner, *British Politics and the Great War: Coalition and Conflict 1915–1918*, London: Yale University Press, 1992.
2 J.M. Winter, *The Great War and the British People*, 1st edn, Basingstoke: Macmillian, 1985; see also 2nd edition, Basingstoke, Palgrave Macmillan, 2003; Samuel Hynes, *A War Imagined: The First World War and English Culture*, London: The Bodley Head, 1990; George Robb, *British Culture and the First World War*, Basingstoke: Palgrave, Macmillan, 2002, pp. 130–01.
3 Paul Fussell, *The Great War and Modern Memory*, Oxford: Oxford University Press, 1975; Dan Todman, *The Great War: Myth and Memory*, London: Hambledon, 2005; Brian Bond, *The Unquiet Western Front: Britain's Role in Literature and History*, Cambridge: Cambridge University Press, 2002; Gary Sheffield, *Forgotten Victory: The First World War: Myths and Realities*, London: Headline Review, 2002.
4 John Bourne, *Britain and the Great War, 1914–1918*, London: Edward Arnold, 1989.
5 Trevor Wilson, *The Myriad Faces of War: Britain and the Great War 1914–1918*, Cambridge: Polity Press, 1986; Malcolm Brown, *The Imperial War Museum Book of the First World War*, 1st edn, London: Sidgwick & Jackson, 1991; 2nd edition, London: Pan, 2002.
6 Arthur Marwick, *The Deluge: British Society and the First World War*, 1st edn, Basingstoke: Macmillan, 1965; 2nd edn, Basingstoke: Macmillan, 1991; 3rd edn, Basingstoke, Palgrave Macmillan, 2006.
7 Gerard DeGroot, *Blighty: British Society in the Era of the Great War*, Harlow: Longman, 1996.
8 Richard van Emden and Steve Humphries, *All Quiet on the Home Front: An Oral History of Life in Britain During the First World War*, London: Headline, 2003.
9 Ian F.W. Beckett, *Home Front 1914–1918: How Britain Survived the Great War*, London: National Archives, 2006.
10 Adrian Gregory, *The Last Great War: British Society and the First World War*, Cambridge: Cambridge University Press, 2008.

1 Summer's end

Britain's pre-war years are troublesome for the historian. Poised between the conclusion of one war in South Africa in 1902 and the onset of another in Europe 12 years later, the period has been historically labelled the 'Edwardian age', although perhaps this is stretching a point. Strictly speaking, the so-called 'Edwardian era' ended with the death of Edward VII in 1910 and the succession of his son, George V. But historians have understandably refrained from calling these years the 'Edwardian–Georgian age', preferring to associate this time with Britain's first twentieth-century male monarch, mainly in the interest of simplicity. This era is popularly remembered as one long, leisurely summer: an image nourished largely by the conspicuous consumption of Britain's wealthier classes, whose sumptuous abodes, weekend shoots and what Harold Nicolson called 'an unlimited addiction to food' set new standards in vulgar opulence.[1] Politically, the period was dominated by the Liberals, who won a famous landslide election victory in 1906 and formed the government that would take the country to war in 1914. Their main opponents, the Conservatives, still remained an electoral force. They won a second term of office in 1900 and, despite a mauling at the polls in 1906, had, by 1910, staged a remarkable political recovery and stood every chance of defeating the Liberals in 1914. Nevertheless, both parties, as products of an older, rigidly hierarchical and patriarchal political and social order, struggled with the rising demands from more representative groups – the industrial working classes and, of course, women. The upshot was a Britain that sank into what Elie Halévy described as an age of 'domestic anarchy': when Victorian liberal values collided with an ambiguous Edwardian modernity expressing itself most dramatically through social reform, constitutional change, industrial militancy and belligerent feminism.[2] Some commentators have suggested that such tensions pushed Britain towards major social upheaval by 1914, to be saved only by European conflict.[3] Subsequent studies are more sceptical.[4] If anything, Edwardian Britain was, according to H.G. Wells, suffering from a case of 'badly sprained optimism': anxious about itself, its status and its power in the new twentieth century.[5]

Society, class and Empire

Britain's aggregate population in 1911 (which at that time included the whole of Ireland) was approximately 45.2 million.[6] Although the pace of growth had slowed considerably, death rates per 1,000 head of population had decreased from 22.6 to 13.8 between 1871 and 1913. Average life expectancy had levelled at 52 for men and 55 for women, while the 1911 census recorded a marked rise in the proportion of the population who were aged 65 and over. Some of these changes were the result of improvements in housing, sanitation and nutrition, though the pattern varied widely across the regions and the social classes. Otherwise, the decline can be attributed to the spread of inoculation. Vaccination against smallpox had virtually eliminated the disease in England and Wales between 1871 and 1905, and mass outbreaks of typhoid and cholera had declined. New methods of treatment and isolation for victims of whooping cough, measles and scarlet fever were also becoming increasingly effective, although TB remained a constant scourge.[7] Falling death rates were matched by declining birth rates: from 32.4 births per 1,000 people between 1881 and 1890; to 29.9 between 1891 and 1900; and to 27.0 between 1900 and 1911.[8] Contemporary enquiries could find no single cause for this decline. In 1906, the Registrar-General estimated that 14 per cent of the fall in birth rates could be attributed to a rise in the age of marriage (it was reported that only half of the male population was married by the age of 30 in the early 1900s), 7 per cent to a decrease in illegitimacy rates, but 79 per cent to the 'deliberate restriction of child-bearing'.[9] Subsequent studies have highlighted rising living standards, family economics and subtle social and cultural changes. The fall-off in child mortality and increased education and literacy, with higher school fees for the upper and middle classes and the spread of compulsory state education for the working classes, meant that children were a drain on the family budget for much longer. Furthermore, the means of limiting family size were more accessible with the availability of contraceptives, reflecting perhaps a belief that large families were no longer quite respectable. However, smaller broods often led parents to make a greater emotional investment in their children. In the more progressive middle-class Edwardian families, it is possible to detect the emergence of an 'enhanced sense of the child', where childhood itself was seen as a complicated condition that possessed unique sensitivity and behaviour patterns requiring special understanding and treatment.[10]

Changes in Britain's population structure were further complicated by migration patterns. Approximately six million Britons sought a better life in foreign lands between 1871 and 1911, mainly to the dominion countries of Canada and Australasia. Replacing them were over one million Irish immigrants and 400,000 Jewish refugees, mostly from Eastern Europe. Immigration from the Empire countries was surprisingly negligible. The 1911 census reported that 4,000 people of Asiatic origin had moved to Britain; similarly 9,000 Caribbean immigrants had settled mainly in Merseyside and South

Wales. No doubt the influx of different races and nationalities added greatly to the cosmopolitan character of Britain's urban centres. But growing public disquiet over foreign émigrés pushed the Conservative government into establishing a Royal Commission on Alien Immigration in 1902, followed swiftly by the Aliens Act of 1905, granting power to refuse entry to those deemed to be criminals, paupers, insane or diseased: legislation that was not implemented by the succeeding Liberal government.[11]

A central feature of Edwardian society was social class. The modern concept of 'class' in Britain is seen largely as a product of nineteenth-century industrialization. During the latter years of the 1800s societal organization had become polarized into two dominant class groupings: the land and property-owning 'ruling class' which broke down into various subgroupings embracing the aristocracy, industrial and financial capitalists and professionals; and a 'property-less' working class, that again could be subdivided into skilled artisans, semi-skilled labourers, the unskilled and the poor. Movement within these structures was relatively uncommon. The majority of property-owners (including the ranks of the new provincial, professional and industrial bourgeoisie) failed to breach the walls of aristocratic society, while progress from the ranks of the very poor to the upper working classes was practically non-existent. Positions between (and within) the social classes could not just be identified through wealth but were also reinforced through institutions, culture, social mores and modes of behaviour, which provided much room for snobbery, rivalry and spatial separation to take root. Class distinctions could be expressed in the most mundane of personal habits, such as whether one washed in the evening or morning and in the bedroom, bathroom or scullery; ate luncheon and dinner or dinner and tea; spent one's leisure time at the pub, social club, music hall, theatre or opera house; or took holidays at the Cote d'Azur, Bournemouth or Blackpool.[12]

All the same, the Edwardian class structure was beginning to fray at the edges. This was partly aided by an unprecedented rise in the average Briton's standard of living. Real wages grew by just over 1 per cent annually between 1873 and 1913 (although this figure is disputed), and improvements in domestic agricultural production and the growth of cheaper food imports, particularly wheat from Canada and frozen meat from Australasia, sparked a marked fall in food prices by the 1890s.[13] Coupled with the growth of mass literacy and the creation of new opportunities in government services (specifically in teaching, clerical and low-grade administrative positions), the line between upper-working and lower-middle class could be more easily crossed, and even the landed classes were becoming more amenable to welcoming into their ranks a new middle-class metropolitan sect whose wealth was rooted in the City. Perhaps the blurring of social barriers was most evident in more humble manifestations, such as the Edwardian craze for cycling, which appealed to all classes and across the gender divide. Indeed, foreign observers were struck that, compared with European standards, the workers' 'Sunday-best' differed little from the everyday attire of the middle classes, with the bowler hat, of a kind worn by all but the most fashion-conscious of the upper and middle classes, becoming the most popular article of working-class male headgear and with the outward demeanour of many young working-class women increasingly resembling that of their middle-class counterparts in the 1900s.[14]

It was a belief in the virtues of empire, however, that united many Britons. Covering nearly ten million square miles of the world's habitable land surface, the British Empire in 1900 was at its peak, embracing the largely self-governing 'White Dominions' – Australia, New Zealand, Canada and later South Africa – and the Indian subcontinent, a land of 300 million people, encompassing a staggering diversity of regions and cultures, still ruled in some states by the remnants of an older royalty and in others by a handful of upper-class British administrators, aided by a network of Indian clerks and police, and held in place by the British and Indian armies. This was accompanied by a miscellany of smaller 'colonies', some located in Africa, as a series of minor regions pulled together in a single entity, as in Nigeria; old 'missionary' states such as Kenya, Tanganyika and Uganda; Victorian imperial 'creations' such as Rhodesia; and 'protectorates' such as Egypt (occupied to safeguard the Suez Canal, a vital trade route). This arrangement was reflected in the Far East in states such as Burma, Malaya, Hong Kong and Singapore and in older slave colonies in the West Indies. The Empire allowed the Edwardian economy to become highly specialized. British trade and manufacture focused its energies on exporting goods and services in exchange for commodities such as raw materials and food, which could be secured more cheaply and in larger quantities in other parts of the world. Thus food, drink and tobacco formed nearly half the country's imports by 1910, raw materials up to one-third, and manufactures nearly a quarter. On the other hand, 10 per cent of Britain's exports comprised of iron and steel (mostly in the form of railway rolling stock and infrastructure); coal (Britain was producing 287 million tons by 1913, 98 million of which went for export); and, most importantly, cotton.[15]

All this was supported by Britain's pivotal position in international trade and finance. Throughout the pre-war years the City of London stood at the centre of a worldwide network of banking, insurance and investment services. All national currencies were valued against sterling. Backed by the Gold Standard, a system through which the Bank of England guaranteed the pound for a prescribed weight of gold (a promise still made, but never kept, on English banknotes), sterling dominated international exchange. Import and export prices were set in sterling; settlements were made through British banks. Most of this financial trade was classed as 'invisible exports', which were crucial in keeping the national balance sheet in the black. Britain's economic strength was sustained further by the income accrued from her considerable overseas investments and by the domination of global trade routes by the British merchant marine, indisputably the world's largest trading fleet. The task of protecting this complex but vital system rested with the Royal

Navy, the most formidable floating military force in history, safeguarding British trade, securing the Empire and standing as the first line of defence against blockade and invasion.[16] For many Edwardian Britons, the Empire was a source of wealth, industry and employment, made Britain a leading world power, and helped to nurture a supreme self-confidence that often transmuted into attitudes of effortless superiority. It was much loathed by Britain's rivals, but also much coveted.

Facing decline

Yet Britain's international position was more precarious than it looked. One blow to national self-confidence was delivered by the protracted war in South Africa. British attempts to annex the goldfields in the republics of Transvaal and Orange Free State in 1899 had met with surprisingly effective resistance from the Boers (a nation of small farmers descended from early Dutch settlers), and the ensuing conflict cost Britain nearly 30,000 casualties and almost £200 million by the time peace was restored in 1902. Rising suspicions of administrative incompetence and fears over the country's social conditions were fuelled by revelations that large numbers of applicants for military service had been rejected as physically unfit.[17] This new sense of vulnerability was amplified by signs that Britain's long-held worldwide economic dominance was beginning to slide. Faced with competition from the rapidly growing new economies of Germany and the United States of America, Britain's percentage share of world manufacturing production was declining significantly – from 31.8 per cent in 1870, to 19.5 per cent in 1900; whilst her share of world trade fell from 35.8 per cent in 1883 to 28.4 per cent in just 17 years. The slippage was reflected most visibly in the growth of imported goods, which increased from 5.5 per cent of the country's balance of trade in 1860, to 17.3 per cent in 1880 and 25 per cent in 1900, casting doubts over Britain's claims to be the 'workshop of the world'.[18]

Explaining Britain's malaise began to preoccupy the Edwardian intelligentsia. *The Times* argued that the fault lay in the complacency of Britain's business leaders, who begrudged 'every penny spent in improvements' and extracted too much money for personal use. To be sure, Britain's sluggishness in developing the newer industries of steel, transport equipment, metal manufacture and chemicals was leaving the country well behind her major competitors.[19] On the other hand, militarists contended that the Army's shortcomings in South Africa were symptomatic of a general social malaise rooted in inadequate educational provision, the poor health and nutrition of the working classes and the politically partisan nature of government. Left-wing reformers pointed to the deep social fractures in Edwardian Britain that had been documented by Seebohm Rowntree's study of York, *Poverty: A Study of Town Life* (1902), which identified a 'poverty line' amongst working-class families; and L.G. Chiozza Money's exposures of the huge income disparities within Edwardian society.[20] Whatever the arguments, Britain's problems still needed remedies. The campaign for National Efficiency offered some solutions. Drawing its support from a range of political opinions, advocates of National Efficiency called for the introduction of coherent, efficient administration into national institutions and local authorities by reducing the interests of political parties and parliamentary government and encouraging the growth of an enlightened, apolitical bureaucracy. Such measures were essential to allow reforms in secondary education, particularly scientific and technical education, and improvements in working-class health and living conditions to be introduced with the aim of generating a more efficient workforce.[21]

Much of this assumed that the state should assume a much greater role in managing the country's social and economic affairs, though the lingering values of Victorian 'laissez-faire' would have ruled out any radical experiments. Even so, the notion of state intervention to facilitate social and economic improvements found a home in the mind of Joseph Chamberlain, Colonial Secretary, one time Mayor of Birmingham and father of Neville.[22] Chamberlain had watched how the German and American economies had grown successfully under the protection of import duties, and was convinced that these countries were exploiting Britain's more open 'free trade' policy to dump goods cheaply on her domestic consumers whilst undermining her manufacturing industries. Chamberlain thus advocated a policy of tariff reform. His aims were two-fold. As an imperialist, Chamberlain argued that, if duties were to be levied on all foreign imports, then empire countries would be exempt or given favoured status under a scheme he labelled 'imperial preference'. Such a policy would consolidate Britain's position as a world power by bringing her colonies together into a customs union that would safeguard home markets from foreign competitors and aid their own development. At the same time, Chamberlain hoped to prove to the working classes that their future welfare needs rested on the protection of home industries. Tariffs could well mean dearer food, but the income raised would be used to finance social welfare programmes, introduce old age pensions and guarantee future employment without the need to increase taxes.[23]

The controversy aroused by the two campaigns almost demanded a response from the Conservative (or 'Unionist') government, led by A.J. Balfour, yet it was difficult to occupy the middle ground. Chamberlain was a senior Cabinet member, and the Prime Minister was aware that the tariff reform campaign struck a chord with his backbenchers. But Balfour was also sympathetic to the cries of 'national efficiency' and the need for social reform. Thus, while official party doctrine clung to the principles of a nominal state, with low taxation and small government expenditures, Balfour adopted a flexible approach to domestic policy. Several nods were given in the direction of national efficiency by approving the Inter-departmental Committee on Physical Deterioration, which investigated the underlying social reasons for the Army's difficulties in finding suitable recruits for South Africa. Balfour also established a series of Cabinet committees, stuffed with scientists and business experts, designed to formulate policy free from political interference, the most famous being the Committee for Imperial Defence, which was retained when Balfour's government resigned from office in 1905. The mood was expressed most coherently in the passing of the 1902 Education Act, which placed the responsibility for local school provision into the hands of county and borough councils, making religious denominational schools eligible for funding from local taxation. Balfour also tried to placate the temperance movement and the brewing industry with the Licensing Act of 1904, which attempted to reduce the numbers of public houses by transferring licensing powers from magistrates to local quarter session courts, whilst granting compensation to landlords who surrendered their licence. Finally, Balfour responded to the sharp rise in unemployment following a short trade slump in 1905 by pushing through the Unemployed Workmen's Act, enabling local authorities to undertake public works projects as a way of helping the workless.[24]

While these measures allowed Balfour's government to tiptoe its way around the campaigns for reform, they could not insulate his administration from trouble. The new Licensing Act of 1904 infuriated the temperance movement. The Committee on Physical Deterioration, which reported shocking deprivation and levels of child mortality amongst the very poor, embarrassed the government with its recommendation to improve the 'eugenic health' of the nation, by giving the state powers to set up labour colonies for the poor.[25] The Education Act (later held to be one of Balfour's more enduring achievements) met with furious opposition from religious Nonconformists who objected strongly to the idea of having denominational schools, either Catholic or the Church of England, funded by ratepayers.[26] All these difficulties, however, were overshadowed by Chamberlain's tariff reform campaign, launched in May 1903 with a tub-thumping speech at Birmingham, a countrywide tour and the establishment of a Tariff Reform League.[27] Balfour's problem was that Chamberlain's arguments struck directly against the deeply rooted principle of free trade, an article of faith held by politicians across all parties. To its supporters, the abolition of import duties had underpinned Britain's laissez-faire economy. By eliminating state taxes on commerce, and taxing the wealthy to compensate for the losses in revenue, and by promoting international economic co-operation, free trade had furthered the cause of peace. Moreover it had brought cheap food to the working classes.[28] In an attempt to keep his government together, Balfour hedged his bets, expressing his sympathy for tariff reform whilst declaring himself a free-trader who did not share 'the loudly-expressed opinions of many who proclaim themselves of the same company'.[29] Nevertheless, his government was deeply split, with 17 of his 'free trade' MPs, including Winston Churchill, joining the Liberals in May 1904. While Balfour sought refuge in the relative calm of foreign policy and defence issues, his party was engulfed by a series of by-election defeats. At the end of 1905, Balfour's government collapsed.

The rise of the Liberals

Unionist difficulties presented the Liberals with an opportunity to regroup. Out of office since the 1890s, Liberalism had become more a matter of conscience than political consciousness. Traditionally, the party attracted support from the business and professional classes, artisans and religious Nonconformists (namely Methodists, Baptists and Congregationalists) and, increasingly after the franchise reforms of the later nineteenth century, the industrial working classes. But, as a political entity, the Liberal Party had few principles around which its followers could unite. After its near break-up following the deep disputes over Irish Home Rule and the vehement opposition waged by radical Liberals to the South African War, the need to defend free trade and cheap food, married to an enduring hostility to licensing reform and the Education Act, finally brought the Liberals together enough under their leader Henry Campbell-Bannerman to bring them to power in 1906. Their victory appeared to be a popular endorsement of a laissez-faire heritage.[30] Attempting to drag the party towards a more interventionist style of politics, however, were the so-called 'New Liberals'.

As part of a growing consensus for social reform, the 'New Liberals' were essentially an intellectual movement that formulated new policies for reforming Edwardian capitalism without disturbing its foundations. The movement had taken its inspiration from the writings of T.H. Green, an Oxford philosophy don, who argued in the 1880s that the Liberal creed of 'true liberty' could be achieved through a new 'political liberalism' that was not afraid to experiment with state intervention as political and social circumstances demanded.[31] In the hands of two of its leading protagonists (L.T. Hobhouse and J.A. Hobson), New Liberalism developed a coherent theory of state intervention, arguing that, if capitalism was equated with social improvement, then legislation applied in specific areas could guarantee provision of the basic conditions of life, whilst maintaining opportunities for individual initiative and private enterprise. In other words, a 'collectivist' state, which embodied the democratic will of the community, could help the poor to help themselves through dexterous state intervention in the interests of both economic efficiency and civilized society.[32] By harnessing its older individualist principles to the new modernizing forces of statist reform, New Liberals hoped to lasso the prosperous classes in Britain into bearing the costs of social reform without destroying their wealth, by arguing that a more healthy and contented working class would offer greater social stability and economic efficiency. Thus, Liberalism could hitch together both working-class and middle-class constituencies, ensuring fair play between them, offering progress without confrontation and, ultimately, government in the 'national interest'. Working out the policy details of New Liberal theory was left to groups like the Rainbow Circle, a gathering of Liberal socialist intellectuals who published widely in their journal *Progressive Review* and were supported by a sympathetic press that included the *Manchester Guardian* and the *Daily*

Chronicle. By 1906 the ideas of New Liberalism were well placed to occupy the centre ground of Edwardian politics.

Perhaps New Liberalism should be better understood as a response to the growing presence of organized labour. In pre-war Britain this could be seen on two levels. It was, first, most powerfully expressed through trade unionism. Originating as a movement of skilled artisans in the mid-nineteenth century, trade unions had since experienced spectacular growth in membership, touching four million by 1914 (embracing semi-skilled and unskilled workers in the process), and had become increasingly radical in their outlook. Despite the moderate stance of its umbrella organization, the Trades Union Congress (TUC), Edwardian unionism appeared to present a direct working-class challenge to the main channels of political activity.[33] Second, Labour's intellectual backbone was provided by groups like H.M. Hyndman's Social Democratic Federation, an avowedly Marxist organization dedicated to the overthrow of capitalism, and the Socialist League, whose principal member, the artist and thinker William Morris, placed socialism within an idealized pre-industrial, pre-urban medieval framework. Most notable of these groups, however, was the Fabian Society, a collection of busy left-wing thinkers who contended that socialism was achievable by patient argument and gradual transformation. Expressed through its principal exponents, Beatrice and Sidney Webb and the playwright George Bernard Shaw, Fabians gathered information, published tracts, channelled reports to government and permeated the political establishment with their ideas. Strongly technocratic in outlook, Fabians believed that an authoritarian yet benevolent state could successfully administer reform, efficiency and modernization. But such a 'top-down' approach was not easily digested within the wider labour movement.[34]

All the same, Labour's electoral performance had been disappointing. The Independent Labour Party had only one MP, James Keir Hardie, who had been elected to the Commons in 1900. A brighter future was promised with the formation of the Labour Representation Committee (LRC), which sought direct parliamentary representation through the election of its own MPs, and would eventually develop into a fully fledged Labour Party. For the time being, though, Labour's best hope of a parliamentary presence was an alliance with the New Liberals. Both were outraged at the Boer War, both argued for graduated taxes on income and land to fund social reform and both wanted better conditions at the workplace. In 1903 a secret electoral pact was agreed between the Liberal chief whip, Herbert Gladstone, and the LRC leader, Ramsay MacDonald, earmarking up to 40 constituencies in England and Wales where the Liberal candidate would withdraw in favour of Labour contenders. The plan was never foolproof; but for the Liberals it removed the threat of a split in the anti-Conservative vote, while Labourites received a share of the Liberal Party's financial resources and the opportunity to secure access to Parliament. Grandly labelled the Progressive Alliance, the agreement laid the ground rules for electoral co-operation through to 1914.[35]

It was soon clear that the first Liberal government's domestic policy was much informed by its contingent of 29 Labour MPs, as well as the sizeable number of New Liberals sprinkled along the backbenches and in the Cabinet. The government's obligations to the labour movement were acknowledged by the Trades Disputes Act (1906) which gave trade unions immunity from prosecution for damages resulting from industrial disputes. A Workman's Compensation Act (1906) expanded the compensation available for workplace injuries to six million employees. The government also passed a raft of child-welfare measures. Local authorities were allowed to give free school lunches to needy children in 1906, whilst the Children Act of 1908 established a system of juvenile courts and remand homes for children under 16 and outlawed the sale of tobacco to minors. The legislation on state-funded, non-contributory old-age pensions, introduced by Asquith in 1908, was universally popular, although, when set at five shillings a week, and payable only to the over-70s, it was clear that the government intended to minimize the state's financial obligations, whilst expecting the majority of applicants to opt for more beneficent schemes available through friendly societies and trade unions.[36] Yet by 1908 a dangerous gap had opened between the government's aspirations and its achievements. Home Secretary Herbert Gladstone's attempts to push through a bill limiting the miners' working day to eight hours floundered in the face of opposition from Liberal industrialists, fearful of its effects on profits and of state encroachment on the free market in labour. Attempts to overturn Tory measures on education, licensing reform and plural voting (preventing property-holders from voting in more than one constituency) were vetoed by the House of Lords. The Lords had always maintained that it was acting in the country's interests: rejecting badly drafted bills and weeding out flawed measures. But its actions appeared selective. Tory bills usually passed through the upper house without hindrance. To Liberals it was patently evident that Balfour was deploying the inherent Tory majority in the Lords to thwart their legislative programme in a way that was not possible in the Commons. When Campbell-Bannerman resigned due to ill health in April 1908, his successor, Herbert Henry Asquith, invited his party 'to treat the veto of the House of Lords as the dominating issue in politics'.[37] It was a prelude to a period of political upheaval not experienced since the 1830s.

Liberals in trouble

Asquith was ideal prime-ministerial material: superb in debates, adept at handling conflicting personalities and master of the written word. His known fondness for alcohol (a trait satirized by the music hall star George Robb, who sang, 'Mr Asquith says in a manner sweet and calm; another little drink won't do us any harm') and a quixotic obsession with the young socialite Venetia Stanley (to whom Asquith would write copiously, sometimes during Cabinet meetings) impinged little on his political nous.[38] Then again, Asquith's capabilities as Prime Minister were enhanced by a strong ministerial team, which included the erratic genius of Winston Churchill, foreign affairs specialist Edward Grey and the turbulent radical David Lloyd George, who had a reputation for fiery rhetoric, a skill for self-enhancement and an ill-concealed contempt for the aristocracy.[39] As Chancellor, Lloyd George's priority in 1908 was to deal with a growing fiscal crisis occasioned by the unexpectedly large expenditures on old-age pensions, the funding of further social reform measures and financing a naval arms race that was prompted when Germany attempted to outpace Britain in the construction of 'Dread-noughts', a new class of technologically advanced battleship launched by the Royal Navy in 1906. He responded with the famous 'People's Budget', delivered to the Commons in the spring of 1909.

Lloyd George's budget was less radical than was originally thought. Most of the revenue was found by increasing taxes on those earning over £3,000 a year, with a supertax on annual incomes over £5,000. Extra money was raised through taxes on beer, spirits and tobacco, new road fund licences for motor cars (then a luxury item), and a three-pence-per-gallon levy on petrol. But the sting was in the tail. Lloyd George proposed a 20 per cent tax on the unearned increase in the value of land sold without the owner having con-tributed to its appreciation, together with a half-penny-in-the-pound (0.21 per cent) duty on undeveloped land and minerals and a 10 per cent 'reversion' levy on the increased value of leasehold land when its letting period had ceased.[40] Lloyd George appeared determined to resolve his fiscal crisis by soaking the rich, rather than, as the tariff reformers would have preferred, by taxing foreigners. The bill passed through the Commons with an over-whelming majority. The Lords, however, egged on by Balfour, broke with precedent and rejected the bill by 375 votes to 75. The Lords' rebuff began a year of complex political manoeuvres. Asquith was compelled to call two general elections in 1910; lead the country's mourning for the death of the King; pursue a doomed attempt to settle matters through an inter-party con-ference; and persuade the new monarch to create enough new peers in the upper house to force through his government's measures. By the time their Lordships had accepted the budget, they had succumbed to a new Parliament Act, which prohibited interference with money bills passed by the Commons, whilst their powers of veto had been limited to the imposition of a two-year delay on any measure they found unpalatable. At the same time, the length of a parliament was reduced from seven years to five. The way was now clear for the introduction of social reform legislation, but the government had paid a heavy price. Its majority of 1906 had disappeared and, with the number of Liberal and Conservative MPs exactly equal in the Commons, Asquith was reliant on the votes of 42 Labour members and 84 Irish Nationalists to keep his government in power.[41]

Outside Parliament, serious problems had emerged in industrial relations. Between 1910 and 1913 a rash of strikes across the engineering, textile, mining and shipbuilding industries appeared to be symptomatic of an upsurge in working-class militancy that had, some commentators thought, revolutionary undertones. Statistics told their own story. Within a seven-year period, the number of industrial disputes rose from just 479 stoppages in 1906 to 1,459 by 1913. Numbers of working days lost through disputes increased from 2,150,000 in 1907 to an unprecedented 40,890,000 by 1912.[42] Unrest sprang from a number of sources. Some historians have highlighted the revolutionary motives residing in the ideas of Syndicalism, a derivative of Marxist theory that encouraged workers to take militant action, first to gain control of their industry, then to overthrow capitalist society and its political order.[43] But perhaps Keir Hardie was nearer the mark when he stated in Parliament that 'the workers have been crying out for a fuller share of life'.[44] The Board of Trade's enquiry in 1912 confirmed that the average 4 per cent rise in wages between 1905 and 1911 had lagged far behind the 11–12 per cent increase in the cost of living. And the subsequent erosion of living standards was inevitably felt more in working-class households than within more prosperous homes.[45] Yet the disputes exposed the government's lack of a coherent industrial relations strategy. If George Askwith, the Board of Trade's chief industrial conciliator, could broker deals when relations between management and workforce had collapsed, then Lloyd George would go his own way, often negotiating directly with unions (as seen in the railway strikes of 1907 and 1911) with promises of legislation to allay workers' grievances. Characteristically, Churchill chose confrontation, as witnessed in the deployment of troops to quell rioting Welsh miners at Tonypandy during 1911 and the despatch of gunboats and armoured cars to subdue striking dockers and merchant seamen in Liverpool.[46]

Even so, industrial conflict drove the government further towards interventionism. As President of the Board of Trade in 1908, Churchill, leaning heavily on a plan devised by his aide William Beveridge, tried to tackle the problem of short-term unemployment by the use of local 'labour exchanges' where a match could be made between unfilled vacancies and workers changing jobs, essentially lubricating the free market in labour.[47] In 1909 legislation was passed allowing the establishment of trade boards designed to protect low-paid workers in sweat-shop industries. Embroiled in a lengthy coal dispute in 1912, Parliament approved the setting up of District Boards to regulate local wage levels, whilst guaranteeing the miners a minimum wage. The principle action came with the passing of a vast National Insurance Act in 1911. Part Two (Churchill's plan) established a compulsory unemployment insurance scheme applying exclusively to workers in industries vulnerable to the vagaries of the economic cycle, or seasonal workers. Part One (Lloyd George's responsibility) was designed to protect a worker's family from poverty brought on by ill health. The scheme was directed primarily at breadwinners, invariably male, giving them the right to consult a doctor from a local panel of approved medics. The scheme provided sickness benefit for up to six months, excluding hospital treatment, and covered all those earning less than £160 a year, although the provisions did not stretch to wives and dependents. The act did, however, introduce maternity allowances and facilitated the free treatment of TB sufferers in special sanatoriums. It was characteristically a New Liberal measure: a state scheme for the alleviation of sickness, poverty and unemployment that made little use of the state. Instead, private insurance companies were brought in to manage and administer the scheme, while leaving other private interest groups (doctors, friendly societies and trade unions) free to work inside and outside the system.[48] It all pointed to an acknowledgement that industrial labour was becoming far more powerful than its Victorian predecessor. The Trade Union Act (1913), which granted unions the right to establish funds for political activity, hinted that two wings of the labour movement were converging, although with reports reaching the government forecasting a revival of industrial militancy in the autumn of 1914, doubts remained over whether 'labour' would decide to secure its progress through constitutional or unconstitutional means.[49]

The government also struggled to find a coherent response to the kicks it was receiving from the women's suffrage campaign. Centred mainly in Lancashire, Edinburgh and London, the movement had been building steadily since the 1860s. Important structural changes at the turn of the century saw many local organizations brought together under the National Union of Women's Suffrage Societies (NUWSS), led by Mrs Millicent Garrett Fawcett and intent on pursuing a 'constitutional' crusade of peaceful campaigning. A more militant wing, however, – the Women's Social and Political Union (WSPU) – led by Emmeline and Christabel Pankhurst, broke away from the movement in 1903 to conduct a much more radical agitation aimed directly at the government. Both organizations were right to highlight the inequities of a system that allowed women to vote in municipal elections and entitled them to serve on Poor Law Boards and county and borough councils, yet denied them a parliamentary vote.[50] But tactics divided the movement. The aggressive activities of the WSPU, nicknamed 'the suffragettes' by the *Daily Mail* in January 1909, undoubtedly raised the profile of women's suffrage with a campaign, towards 1914, that became increasingly militant.[51] The government's clumsy reaction often brought trouble upon itself. It delivered a propaganda coup to the WSPU with the force-feeding of imprisoned hunger-striking suffragettes. Then the subsequent attempt to recover the initiative with the Prisoners' Temporary Discharge Act in April 1913, which allowed offenders to be released on medical advice on condition that they resume their sentences once their health was restored, was dubbed by activists 'the cat and mouse act' and portrayed as punitive male repression.[52]

And yet, the harder the suffragettes pushed, the less progress they made. By 1912 public opinion was beginning to swing against them. WSPU meetings now attracted hostile crowds, and on several occasions campaigners sought police protection.[53] In Parliament those MPs sympathetic to the cause were alienated by suffragette violence, though some Liberals still recognized the merits of the women's case. Two private members' bills, introduced in 1910 and 1911, attracted cross-party support for abolishing the sex disqualification, but further progress was impossible without government support. In 1912

Asquith introduced an Electoral Reform Bill, which proposed universal suffrage but was ruled out by the Commons Speaker on a technicality.[54] Accusations of treachery were thrown at Asquith by the WSPU, but by now the impetus of the campaign had moved to the 'suffragist' NUWSS. Its membership had grown prodigiously from 13,161 in 1909 to 54,592 by 1914, helping the organization to transcend both class and political barriers to take on the trappings of a mass movement. By linking themselves with working-class organizations, the NUWSS had garnered pro-suffrage resolutions from a number of constituency parties, trades councils, trade union branches, Co-operative Women's Guilds and local authorities. Their success in cultivating a broad base of popular support was perhaps exemplified most clearly by the 'Pilgrimage' of 1913 when suffragists' marches along eight different routes across the country between 18th and 26th July culminated in a huge rally of 70,000 people in Hyde Park, central London. Such a large and peaceful display of support, shown 'respectful attention' by spectators, finally persuaded Asquith into meeting a deputation of suffragists soon after the Pilgrimage and signalling his readiness to support a women's suffrage bill in the next parliament. It was the tactics of persuasion based on a political and popular consensus that gave women's suffrage a sense of meaning and momentum in 1914. The war pushed the cause through a steadily opening door.[55]

Problems with the neighbours

The domestic troubles of the pre-war years can tempt the thoughts of historians. The enmities generated by a nation experiencing a deep restructuring of its social and political order provide plenty of material for those debating 'the Strange Death of Liberal England'. But it was the tensions within foreign affairs that proved a greater threat to national security. When the Liberals came to power in 1906 the prospects of a European war seemed unlikely. The fact that Britain became entangled in a disastrous continental conflict within eight years requires explanation. The problems lay not so much in Britain; her domestic troubles had little effect on the government's decision to go to war in 1914. It was the rapidly changing international circumstances that would ultimately force her hand.

In 1900, Britain's imperial position rested largely on the pursuit of two diplomatic imperatives. First, to safeguard the country's prosperity and status by protecting the Empire; second, to seek to maintain peace and stability in Europe by actively preventing the emergence of a dominant empire or nation-state that could impose its will on its neighbours and challenge British interests. Thus, for Britain, international order could be upheld by maintaining a 'balance of power' in Europe: an age-old diplomatic touchstone that was as viable in the twentieth century as it was in the nineteenth.[56] However, the rapid expansion of the British Empire in Africa and Asia during the late nineteenth century had strained relations with her two old imperial competitors, France and Russia, and Britain's struggles in the South African War (which was viewed with some relish by her rivals) laid bare the fact that she had become diplomatically isolated. Imperialists argued that the construction of a worldwide empire, policed by the Royal Navy, would make Britain virtually invulnerable. But the war had exposed the limits of Britain's capability in protecting her overseas interests, and her military resources were proving quite inadequate to defend the Empire from her international adversaries. Hence, after 1900, Britain sought to defend her territories by striking deals with nations who were neither friends nor potential enemies. By 1900 control of the seas around the Americas was ceded to the United States; and in 1902 Britain aimed at containing Russian expansion by signing an alliance with the rapidly growing Japan, with both countries pledging mutal assistance in a conflict with two other powers (ensuring that, when Japan went to war with Russia in 1905, Britain was not sucked in).[57] This still left the problem of Europe. Friction with France and Russia in the 1890s inclined Britain to cultivate friendly relations with Imperial Germany and her 'Triple Alliance' partners, Austria–Hungary and Italy, prompting speculation of her forging an alliance. Yet Germany, through a mix of indifference and arrogance, proved unresponsive to the idea, pushing Britain to agree an *entente cordiale* with France in 1904, symbolically brokered through the enthusiasm of Edward VII, whose liking of French culture (and French casinos) was well known.[58] The *entente* was not a military alliance. No obligations were imposed on either party. It was successful in easing imperial rivalries in Africa whilst moderating international tensions elsewhere. But this was not how it was seen in Germany.

Since announcing her presence on the European stage with unification in 1871, Germany had generated tremors that spread across the continent and the English Channel. The rapid growth of the German economy dwarfed that of her neighbours and, with the accession of Kaiser Wilhelm II in 1888, Germany sought to match her rising economic strength with an increasingly ambitious foreign and imperial policy aimed at elevating the Second Reich to 'great power' status. Britain was not ill-disposed to the new nation. The government accepted that, with the finest army in Europe, Germany would successfully counterbalance French and Russian power, whilst German imperial aspirations could be accommodated peacefully with British interests. Besides, Germany was one of Britain's best customers. Twenty per cent of all Germany's imports came from the British Empire, and German financial interests buoyed Britain's invisible earnings (most of Germany's merchant fleet was insured through London). Britain could live with a prosperous Germany, in spite of the large penetration of the British home market in manufactures; her passivity, however, was less than clear.[59] Hints that Germany was prepared to pursue a more aggressive foreign policy surfaced at several points. German attempts to acquire colonies in the Far East and Africa had given rise to a series of minor disputes over places like Samoa, Togoland and the Cameroons, and the Kaiser's highly publicized support for the Boers in South Africa in 1896 had done little to assuage British anxieties. Yet it was Germany's clumsy and provocative behaviour during the two Moroccan crises of 1905 and 1911 that brought matters to a head. Her bid to block French ambitions (which were fully endorsed by Britain) to incorporate Morocco into her North African empire represented to the Foreign Office a clear attempt to distance Britain from her new-found friend and presented a direct challenge to the *entente*.[60] A hardening of British attitudes ensued. A speech by David Lloyd George at the Mansion House, London, on 21st July 1911 warned that, if Britain was treated 'as if she were of no account in the Cabinet of nations, then ... peace at that price would be a humiliation intolerable for a great country like ours to endure'. The Germans took offence; British forces were placed on a war footing.[61]

The diplomatic stand-off with Germany left a deep scar on British policy and attitudes. On the one hand, German action drove Britain closer to France. One of Edward Grey's first moves as the Liberal Foreign Secretary was to open 'military conversations' with France (without informing the Cabinet).[62] On the other hand, German behaviour pushed Britain to reconcile her differences with another old adversary, Russia. To the astonishment of observers, Grey, in 1907, agreed a 'convention' with Russia that settled long-standing imperial disputes over Afghanistan, Tibet and Persia and secured the Indian border from Russian threats, leaving British military planners to refocus their attention on ways of supporting France in the event of a European war.[63] This, perhaps, was appropriate, for Anglo-German relations were at their most fraught over the strength of their respective navies. The German government's decision to embark on a programme of naval expansion was first recognized in 1902 by Lord Selborne, First Lord of the Admiralty, as a direct challenge to British naval supremacy. Possessing the world's largest fleet, Britain's quantitative lead was unassailable. But, with the launch of the technically superior HMS Dreadnought in 1906, her qualitative lead was weakened. Once Germany had perfected the technique of building her own Dreadnoughts her government pledged itself to building four such 'capital ships' each year for the period 1908–09 to 1911–12, posing a direct challenge to British superiority. Britain's naval dominance depended on the maintenance of a 'two-power standard', namely, having a fleet capable of resisting a threat from an alliance of two European powers. Her only effective response, therefore, was to outbuild Germany. Fears of a German navy consisting of 17, possibly 21, Dreadnoughts by 1912 drove the Admiralty to lobby the government to sanction the annual construction of eight Dreadnoughts. Faced with a divided Cabinet and Admiralty reports of the German build-up that were clearly exaggerated, Asquith compromised by fixing the immediate number of Dreadnoughts to four a year, with a promise to build four more if circumstances changed. When Germany's allies, Austria–Hungary and Italy, began building their own Dreadnoughts, Britain increased her production to eight.[64]

Asquith's decision was accompanied by a raucous campaign against all things German led by Lord Northcliffe's *Daily Mail* and right-wing journals such as Leo Maxse's *National Review*. In the *Sunday Observer*, edited by the brilliant J.L. Garvin, a campaign was launched for the building of eight Dreadnoughts, asserting the view that Britain's Navy stood alone between Germany and her securing of international hegemony.[65] Certainly, a culture of Germanophobia, typified by the pre-war novels, Erskine Childers's *Riddle of the Sands* (1903) and William Le Queux's *The Invasion of 1910* (1906), fed a public appetite for fantasies of Teutonic espionage and occupying armies, and suspicion of Germany ran like a plume of smoke through the corridors of the Foreign Office. In a lengthy and illuminating memorandum in January 1907, Eyre Crowe, a Foreign Office senior clerk, argued that, *inter alia*, German policy was driven by hostility towards Britain, the breaking up of her Empire and 'consciously aiming at the establishment of a German hege-mony at first in Europe, and eventually in the world'.[66] Other Foreign Office officials agreed, including the two permanent chiefs, Charles Hardinge and Arthur Nicolson, though Thomas Sanderson begged to differ. Grey was not at odds with Crowe's view, but the Foreign Secretary was more inclined to favour conciliation and mediation as a way of managing the German threat and, together with the German Chancellor Bethmann-Hollweg, strove hard to improve relations.[67]

Some turned a deaf ear to anti-Germanism. Popular authors such as A.A. Milne and P.G. Wodehouse satirized the cult mercilessly, and liberal newspapers like the *Manchester Guardian*, under the editorship of C.P. Scott, and the *Daily News* under A.G. Gardiner, were highly critical of the rabble-rousing activities of the Tory press.[68] Yet perhaps the most significant antidote to Germanophobia was Norman Angell's pacifist polemic, *The Great Illusion* (1910). Published at the height of the naval panic, Angell's work argued that, through the growth of trade and financial links, all the industrialized national economies had become increasingly interdependent. War would thus trigger a collapse in credit, bring international business activity to a halt and generate mass unemployment with widespread starvation. Faced with social break-down and economic ruin, no belligerent country could thus afford to wage a protracted conflict.[69] Niall Ferguson has suggested that there was more to Angell's book than is normally supposed.[70] But there is no denying the book's popularity. It sold over two million copies between 1910 and 1913, ran into numerous editions and was translated into 25 languages. Its success persuaded Angell to lead a 'New Pacifism' movement whose message was grounded in economic logicality rather than in vague moralistic or emotional appeals. But the popular impression Angell created was far removed from any rational analysis. If Britons were flexing themselves for a conflict with Germany before 1914, it was on the understanding that any war would be nasty, bloody, but, above all, short.

Besides, between 1912 and 1914 many Britons anticipated that a conflict would erupt in Ireland rather than in Europe. Since its incorporation in 1801, Ireland had been the neglected child of the United Kingdom family. It had not experienced the economic progress seen in other parts of the union, and

Anglo-Irish relations had not been helped by English insensitivity to the needs of the Irish people (as witnessed in the British government's mishandling of the potato famine between 1845 and 1849).[71] As a result, the cause of Irish nationalism had continued to grow throughout the nineteenth century (peppered by violent outrages) and by 1910 was powerfully represented by the parliamentary presence of the 82 Irish Nationalist MPs. For some Liberals, greater autonomy for Ireland had a moral appeal; yet a consensus had been hard to find. Gladstone's two Home Rule Bills of 1886 and 1893 had left the party deeply divided. The triumph of 1906 had allowed the Liberals to conveniently ignore the Irish Question. But the elections of 1910 left Asquith's administration dependent for its survival on the support of the Irish Nationalist MPs, who fully utilized their position in pushing for a new Home Rule Bill, comforted by the fact that the Lords would not reject it.

Opposition to Home Rule now switched to Ulster, a collection of counties in the north-east of Ireland populated by a mix of Catholics and Protestants whose Scottish ancestors had migrated to the province in the sixteenth century. Protestant Ulster had much to lose from Home Rule. The province had prospered economically during the nineteenth century in contrast to the rural south. Moreover, the possibility of an independent Ireland raised the prospect of Ulster falling under the jurisdiction of a Catholic-dominated government in Dublin. Fearing for its independence, Ulster Protestantism, under the pugnacious leadership of Edward Carson, became increasingly militant. Some 471,000 Ulster men and women signed a 'solemn league and covenant' in September 1912 pledging themselves 'to use all means which may be found necessary' to defeat Home Rule. In January 1913 the Ulster Unionist Council set up the Ulster Volunteer Force (UVF) of some 100,000 men. Across the province drilling, manoeuvres and paramilitary training were stepped up. Ulster rifle clubs and Orange Order lodges made plans to be placed under military command. Nationalists responded accordingly. The 'Irish Volunteers' were formed as a paramilitary force to oppose the UVF. Secret organizations such as the Irish Republican Brotherhood (forerunner of the Irish Republican Army – IRA) and pro-independence groups like Sinn Fein prepared to move against the North.[72] These gloomy auspices were made more toxic by the intervention of Andrew Bonar Law, the Conservatives' newly appointed leader, who, at a rally held in Blenheim Palace in July 1912, unwisely hitched his party to the Ulster cause.[73]

In the spring of 1914, when the Liberals' Home Rule Bill was about to go back before the Commons following its rejection by the Lords, a possible compromise emerged. After months of secret talks, Asquith proposed that Ulster be excluded from Home Rule for six years, after which it would revert to the jurisdiction of Dublin. Both sides rejected it. Carson referred to the proposal as 'a sentence of death with a stay of execution for six years'; nationalists demanded that Home Rule had to apply to the whole of Ireland.[74] Back in Ulster, however, matters were moving beyond the government's control. Following reports of 20,000 illegally smuggled rifles being landed at

Larne, Bangor and Donaghee, Churchill, First Lord of the Admiralty, and Seely, Secretary of State for War, planned to move troops to guard strategic points in Ulster and send naval warships into Irish waters in an attempt to prevent any gunrunning by the UVF, while preventing Carson from establishing a provisional government. The plan floundered when 58 cavalry officers stationed at the Curragh outside Dublin refused to move against Ulster. On 4th July 1914, the Army Council estimated that there were over 200,000 armed volunteers in Ireland, warning the Cabinet that, if the whole of the British Expeditionary Force, the Special Reserve and the Territorial Army were deployed to maintain order in the event of civil war, 'we should be quite incapable of meeting our obligations abroad'.[75] A further attempt to break the deadlock through an all-party conference chaired by the King at Buckingham Palace floundered again over the Ulster question. Despite these setbacks, Asquith decided to press ahead with the bill and its exclusion clauses. When the finer details of Ulster partition were being discussed at a Cabinet meeting on 24th July, Grey interrupted with news of Austria's ultimatum to Serbia following the assassination of Archduke Franz Ferdinand, heir to the Austrian throne, in Sarajevo, Bosnia on 28th June 1914.

The lamps go out

Reports of another European crisis caused little alarm in the Cabinet. The Balkans were the most unstable part of the continent. Two wars in 1912 and 1913 had successfully overturned Turkish dominance in the region, resulting in the emergence of new independent kingdoms in Bulgaria, Serbia, Albania and Bosnia, as well as a more assertive Greece and Romania. The region was still bubbling with tensions in 1914.[76] Austria's annexation of neighbouring Bosnia in 1908 had fuelled enormous Serbian resentment; Serbia's territorial gains as a result of the conflicts of 1913 had alarmed Austria, already struggling to contain the rise of Serb nationalism within its borders. Ideally, this could have been kept as a local affair. But both countries had powerful friends. Austria was in alliance with Germany, keen to pursue an ambitious imperial policy in the region as a gateway to the Middle East. Serbia, as a Slav nation, could look to Russia (in alliance with France) for support if threatened. When it emerged that the Archduke had been murdered by a Slav nationalist, Gavrilo Princip, Austria, with the tacit support of her ally, resolved to make war on her troublesome neighbour.[77] If attacked, Serbia would inevitably appeal to Russia for military backing, a move that would bring a confrontation with Germany and threatened to drag France into any conflict. If France went to war with Germany, Britain could be drawn in. Not for the first (or last) time, a Balkan crisis threatened to drag Europe into war. Grey's instincts were to prevent war, although not at all costs. If this failed, then it was imperative that France should not be abandoned if she were attacked. This left some awkward questions, however. Without any formal treaty obligations, should Britain remain aloof from the crisis? Could the

Cabinet be persuaded to enter a European conflict if British interests were not directly threatened? Could the government count on public support if Britain went to war? How these issues were settled shaped the British experience of the July crisis in 1914. In a week fraught with tension, Britain's passage to war journeyed through four untidy phases.

The first was laced with feelings of mild optimism. Fixing his attention primarily on Germany, Grey attempted to set up a four-power conference, in partnership with the Reich, in an attempt to secure a peaceful resolution to the crisis. Grey could be forgiven for adopting this line of thought. As Churchill recalled, after the second Moroccan crisis, relations between Britain and Germany had improved. The two countries combined their diplomatic efforts to settle the Balkan conflicts of 1912–13, and the level of 'personal goodwill and mutual respect' gave rise to hope that the two powers 'might together bring the two opposing European systems into harmony'.[78] Grey felt that war between the continental powers could be avoided by means of an international conference, essentially a reversion to the diplomacy of the 'Concert of Europe', when potentially dangerous European crises were averted by talks across the negotiating table. However, to Grey's intense dismay, Germany, along with Austria–Hungary, in a telegram of 28th July, rejected the conference proposal, but not the idea of mediation. The rebuff threw matters into confusion. Without the prospect of a peace conference, Grey hoped that Austro-Russian 'conversations' in St Petersburg would provide a favourable outcome.[79] But it was soon evident that Germany's tacit support had given Austria the confidence to declare war on Serbia, after the rejection of her infamous ultimatum. That day, Austrian artillery shelled the Serbian capital, Belgrade.

This was the prelude to a second phase in the crisis. In a telegram received on 30th July the German Chancellor, Bethmann-Hollweg, mooted the idea that 'a general neutrality agreement between England and Germany' could be approved if Germany promised to honour French territory, even if she were defeated in war, though no guarantees were offered on the acquisition of French colonies or on the question of Belgian neutrality. Grey was having none of it. It was clear that German policy was not addressing the avoidance of conflict, but trying to keep Britain away from what was, for the Germans, a risky two-front war. For Grey, Bethmann-Hollweg's 'bribe' meant abandoning France and accepting any deal strictly on Germany's terms. Asquith described it as 'a rather shameless attempt on the part of Germany to buy our neutrality'.[80] If Britain was to remain neutral, it had to be unconditional. But Britain's next move was far from certain. It was clear that she was unable to influence the unfolding developments in Europe, but the rapidly evaporating peace now threw open the question of British support for France. Here, confusion reigned. Although the *entente* did not suggest any military obligations, closer co-operation between the British and French armies had been in place for some time. Furthermore, plans agreed between 1912 and 1913 had brought the French and Royal Navies to an understanding that, in the event of a military confrontation with Germany, France would deploy her fleet in the Mediterranean, while the British would assume responsibility for defending the Channel coast. Grey had long insisted that Britain would stand by France in the event of war. He warned the German Ambassador, Lichnowsky, on 29th July that, in the event of a Franco-German war, 'it would not be practicable to stand aside and wait for any length of time'.[81] Yet, puzzlingly, at the same time Grey informed Cambon, the French Ambassador, that Britain was 'free from engagements and we should have to decide what British interests require us to do'.[82] British hesitancy was confirmed when the Cabinet decided on 1st August not to despatch a British Expeditionary Force to help France face a German invasion.[83]

In this third phase of the crisis, it became clear that the source of Grey's ambivalence lay in a Cabinet that was, in Churchill's words, 'overwhelmingly pacific'.[84] Led somewhat loosely by Lloyd George (a staunch anti-war advocate, but whose position was weakening by the day), at least three-quarters of the Cabinet were against going to war, with four Cabinet members ready to resign. Arthur Ponsonby, a backbench spokesman, claimed at one point that nine-tenths of the party were anti-war. Grey's stance on the war was supported by Viscount Richard Haldane, the Lord Chancellor; the future propagandist Charles Masterman; an increasingly bellicose Churchill; and Asquith, who joined the list more for the sake of party unity. The Conservatives were also divided. Bonar Law felt that Britain should honour her obligations to France, although he confessed that 'it was not easy to be sure what the opinion of his whole party was'.[85] The parliamentary Labour Party, however, was unanimously opposed. Keir Hardie and Arthur Henderson published an anti-war manifesto and marshalled a mass rally of supporters to be held at Trafalgar Square on 2nd August. The wider public mood was difficult to judge.[86] The idea of going to war for the sake of a murdered foreign aristocrat would, to many, have seemed puzzling, a mood perhaps reflected in the remark of Cabinet member John Burns: 'Why four great powers should fight over Serbia no fellow can understand.'[87]

By the time the Cabinet gathered for its meeting on the afternoon of Sunday 2nd August, the crisis was moving towards its climax. Ministers contemplated noxious circumstances. It was clear that Europe was at war. Following Austria's moves on Belgrade, Russia, on 30th July, had mobilized her army in defence of Serbia. At 6 p.m. the following day Germany, after the Tsar's refusal to desist from all military measures, declared war on Russia. France, under her treaty obligations and fully aware of the dangers she now faced, ordered full mobilization of her army. On 1st August, Germany, reacting to spurious reports of frontier violations, declared war on France. The outbreak of European war now placed the British government's dilemma in full view. Consensus was elusive. To Asquith, the anti-war mood in his party and the country appeared to be very strong. Labour's peace rally drew a crowd of around 10,000.[88] Asquith confided to Venetia Stanley 'a good ¾ of our party in the H. of Commons are for non-interference at any price'. Grey, on the other hand, had long trumpeted the dangers to Britain of a German-dominated Europe and advocated that the government had to honour its moral commitment to France if she were invaded.[89] The implications were clear. If France succumbed to Germany, if Germany was prepared to inflict war on Europe, then Britain had to resist. Along with his allies, Asquith, Haldane and Churchill (who found the prospect of war quite delicious), Grey threatened resignation if the Cabinet refused to support his view. Asquith, in private correspondence, clarified the government's dilemma. Under the terms of the *entente*, British military support for France remained optional; nevertheless, she could not stand by while French independence was in peril. However, the moment his Cabinet authorized the despatch of an army to the continent, the government would surely collapse. The only obligation for military action was in the defence of Belgium, whose neutrality Britain had guaranteed under a treaty of 1839. Whatever the misgivings over joining a European war, Britain could not allow Belgium to be 'utilized and absorbed by Germany'.[90]

On 1st August the question of defending Belgian neutrality was not an immediate issue; that it became so was the outcome of German rather than British policy. German war strategy had been framed by the Franco-Russian alliance. The German High Command had always feared a war with two enemies. Germany could not enter a long war if she was outnumbered by French and Russian forces. Her only chance was to secure a quick victory by knocking out France in the west before Russian troops could invade from the east. Thus, under plans first formulated by General Alfred von Schlieffen (later modified by Moltke) in the event of war, the German army's first priority was to advance on France via Belgium.[91] On 2nd August the German government presented a demand to the Belgian government for a right of passage through its territory. The Belgians refused and King Albert appealed to George V for support on 3rd August. Britain's position remained ambiguous. A precedent for inaction could be found in Gladstone's position in 1870 when Belgian territory was threatened by the Franco-Prussian war. Then it was decided that the treaty obligation fell collectively upon all the signatory nations (Prussia, Austria, France and Russia) rather than an individual power. Asquith appeared to confirm this on 29th July when he told the King that Britain's position on Belgian neutrality was 'one of policy rather than legal obligation'.[92] However, the difference, as Grey recollected, was that Germany had now become a far more powerful entity. If 'the evil' of a violation into Belgium was accommodated by her guarantors, her neutrality would vanish, making her 'the satellite and serf' of her larger neighbour.[93]

The stance of the 'anti-war party' in the Cabinet began to soften. Cracks in their argument had already appeared before the Cabinet met on 2nd August when a number of anti-war ministers, following a gathering at Lloyd George's official residence, reaffirmed their opposition to the war 'but that in certain events we might reconsider [the] position, such as the invasion wholesale of

Belgium'.[94] Their position was weakened further following the realization that to continue opposing the conflict risked breaking up the government in favour of a Conservative-dominated administration committed to war. Grey had already indicated (on 1st August) his intention to resign if the Cabinet agreed a policy of non-intervention; Asquith was ready to join him. For the pacifists, staying out of a European conflict was plausible if Britain remained a safe haven for liberal principles and democracy. But was that now possible with the massing of German troops on the Belgian border and the pleas of the Belgian monarch for help? The Cabinet's reservations about war evaporated. Lloyd George rescinded his decision to resign; most of the Cabinet's 'anti-war party' joined him.[95] For Grey there was really no alternative. Having gained Cabinet support to inform the French that Britain would not tolerate the German fleet using the Channel for 'hostile operations', the price of Britain not entering the war appeared to be heavier than if she did.[96] In the event, Belgium was the instance, not the reason, for Britain's entry into the First World War. As Grey later pointed out to an American correspondent:

> The issue for us was that, if Germany won, she would dominate France; the independence of Belgium, Holland, Denmark, and perhaps Norway and Sweden, would be a mere shadow: their separate existence as nations would really be a fiction; all their harbours would be at Germany's disposal: she would dominate the whole of Western Europe, and this would make our position quite impossible. We could not exist as a first-class State under such circumstances.[97]

German troops crossed the Belgian border on 4th August. At midday the Cabinet issued an ultimatum to Germany to remove her troops from Belgian territory by midnight (11 p.m. British time). That evening in the Cabinet room in Downing Street, Grey, Asquith, Lloyd George and others waited in vain for the German reply. When Big Ben struck 11, Churchill immediately despatched his action telegrams to the fleet; Anglo-French naval plans were put into operation; and the Army was mobilized. Asquith reflected, 'the whole prospect fills me with sadness, we are on the eve of horrible things'.[98]

Asquith's sadness could not disguise his sense of relief. In Ireland civil strife appeared imminent following the Army's attempt to disrupt a gunrunning operation by the Irish Volunteers in Dublin on 26th July, which had resulted in troops opening fire on an attacking crowd, killing three. Two armies, nationalist and unionist, appeared destined to fight. But the sudden outbreak of war in Europe quickly overshadowed all domestic concerns. Home Rule was passed by Parliament but suspended until a year after the resumption of peace; Protestant volunteers now turned their aggression towards Germany. One war had saved Asquith's government from another. He remarked to his friend J.A. Pease, 'the one bright spot in this hateful war was the settlement of Irish civil strife and the cordial union of forces in Ireland in aiding the government to maintain our supreme national interest', adding, on the point of tears, 'Jack, God moves in a mysterious way his wonders to perform'.[99] And yet, doubts remained. Did Britain need to fight? Had the outbreak of war concealed rather than cured the political, industrial and social tensions of Edwardian Britain? Such questions hung unanswered as the country erupted in a fever of patriotism and moral outrage at Germany's behaviour, and government ministers expected that a naval blockade of Germany would hasten her economic collapse, starve her population into submission and force an early end to hostilities. Grey confidently told Parliament that 'If we are engaged in a war ... we shall suffer but little more than we shall suffer if we stand aside'.[100] Famous last words?

Notes

1 Harold Nicolson, *Small Talk*, London: Constable, 1937, p. 73.
2 Elie Halévy, *A History of the English People in the Nineteenth Century*, vol. VI, *The Rule of Democracy 1905–1914*, London: Ernest Benn, 1932, p. 441. (See also part III.)
3 George Dangerfield, *The Strange Death of Liberal England*, St Albans: Granada, 1934, 1970 edn; for further discussion of the Dangerfield thesis, see Arno J. Mayer, 'Domestic Causes of the First World War', in Leonard Krieger and Fritz Stern, eds, *The Responsibility of Power: Historical Essays in Honor of Hajo Holborn*, New York: Doubleday, 1967, pp. 286–300; Michael R. Gordon, 'Domestic Conflict and the Origins of the First World War: The British and the German Cases', *Journal of Modern History*, vol. 46, no. 2, June 1974, pp. 191–226.
4 David French, 'The Edwardian Crisis and the Origins of the First World War', *International History Review*, vol. IV, no. 2, May 1982, pp. 207–22; Charles More, *Britain in the Twentieth Century*, Harlow: Pearson, 2007, pp. 22–28; see also Michael Bentley, *The Liberal Mind 1914–29*, Cambridge: Cambridge University Press, 1977; John Grigg, 'Liberals on Trial', in Alan Sked and Chris Cook, eds, *Crisis and Controversy: Essays in Honour of A.J.P. Taylor*, London: Macmillan, 1976; C.W. White, 'The Strange Death of Liberal England in Its Time', *Albion*, vol. 17, 1985, pp. 425–47; David Powell, *The Edwardian Crisis: Britain 1901–1914*, London: Macmillan, 1996.
5 H.G.Wells, *The Wife of Sir Isaac Harman*, London: Macmillan, 1914, p. 259.
6 B.R. Mitchell, *British Historical Statistics*, Cambridge: Cambridge University Press, 1988, pp. 15–17.
7 *Seventy-Third Annual Report of the Registrar-General of Births, Deaths and Marriages in England and Wales (1910)*, Cmnd 5988, London: HMSO, 1912, pp. xxxviii–xli; B.R. Mitchell, *British Historical Statistics*, op. cit., pp. 57–58; Jose Harris, *Private Lives, Public Spirit: Britain 1870–1914*, Harmondsworth: Penguin, 1994, pp. 50–60; Peter Clarke, *Hope and Glory: Britain 1900–1990*, Harmondsworth: Penguin, 1997, p. 40.
8 N.L. Tranter, *Population and Society, 1750–1940: Contrasts in Population Growth*, Harlow: Longman, 1985, p. 59.
9 *Sixty-Ninth Annual Report of the Registrar-General of Births, Deaths and Marriages in England and Wales (1906)*, Cmnd 3833, London: HMSO, 1908, p. xiv; also National Birth Rate Commission, *The Declining Birth Rate: Its Causes and Effects*, London: Chapman & Hall, 1916, p. 21.
10 Jose Harris, *Private Lives, Public Spirit: Britain 1870–1914*, op. cit., p. 47. See also Suzanne Buckley, 'The Family and the Role of Women', in Alan O'Day, ed.,

The Edwardian Age: Conflict and Stability 1900–1914, Hamden, Connecticut: Archon, 1979, p. 135; J.A. Banks, *Victorian Values: Secularism and the Size of Families*, London: Routledge, 1981, pp. 98–99, 106–07; M. Anderson, 'Households, Families and Individuals', *Continuity and Change*, vol. 3, 1988, pp. 424–25.

11 Theo Barker and Michael Drake, *Population and Society in Britain 1850–1950*, London: Batsford, 1982; E.A Wrigley and B.S. Schofield, *The Population History of England, 1541–1871: A Reconstruction*, London: Edward Arnold, 1981; Jose Harris, *Private Lives, Public Spirit: Britain 1870–1914*, op. cit., p. 44.

12 Jose Harris, *Private Lives, Public Spirit: Britain 1870–1914*, op. cit., pp. 6–11.

13 T.R. Gourvish, 'The Standard of Living 1890–1914', in Alan O'Day, ed., *The Edwardian Age: Conflict and Stability 1900–1914*, op. cit., p. 13; see also Charles Feinstein, 'What Really Happened to Real Wages? Trends in Wages, Prices, and Productivity in the United Kingdom, 1880–1913', *Economic History Review*, New Series, vol. 43, no. 3, 1990, pp. 329–55; Peter Clarke, *Hope and Glory*, op. cit., p. 9.

14 Jose Harris, *Private Lives, Public Spirit: Britain 1870–1914*, op. cit., p. 10.

15 See E.J. Hobsbawm, *Industry and Empire*, Harmondsworth: Penguin, 1982, p. 251.

16 Peter Clarke, *Hope and Glory*, op. cit., pp. 12–13.

17 Peter Warwick, ed., *The South African War*, Harlow: Longman, 1980.

18 See Peter Cain, 'Political Economy in Edwardian England: The Tariff-Reform Controversy', in Alan O'Day, ed., *The Edwardian Age: Conflict and Stability 1900–1914*, op. cit., pp. 35–59. See also Nicholas Crafts, 'The British Economy', in Francesca Carnevali and Julie-Marie Strange, eds, *20th Century Britain: Economic, Cultural and Social Change*, 2nd edn, Harlow: Pearson, 2007, pp. 7–25.

19 *The Times*, 17th April 1912; see also Peter Cain, 'Political Economy in Edwardian England: The Tariff-Reform Controversy', op. cit., p. 36.

20 Seebohm Rowntree, *Poverty: A Study of Town Life*, London: Macmillan, 1902; L.G. Chiozza Money, *Riches and Poverty*, London: Methuen, 1905, p. 42; Peter Clarke, *Hope and Glory*, op. cit., p. 42.

21 G.R. Searle, *The Quest for National Efficiency 1899–1914: A Study of British Politics and Political Thought*, London: Ashfield, 1990; G.R. Searle, 'Critics of Edwardian Society: The Case of the Radical Right', in Alan O'Day, ed., *The Edwardian Age: Conflict and Stability 1900–1914*, op cit., pp. 82–83; Martin Pugh, *The Making of Modern British Politics, 1867–1945*, 3rd edn, Oxford: Blackwell, 2002, pp. 99–102.

22 Richard Jay, *Joseph Chamberlain: A Political Biography*, Oxford: Clarendon, 1981.

23 See E.H.H. Green, *The Crisis of Conservatism: The Politics, Economics and Ideology of the British Conservative Party 1880–1914*, London: Routledge, 1995; Alan Sykes, *Tariff Reform in British Politics 1903–13*, Oxford: Clarendon, 1979; Martin Pugh, *The Making of Modern British Politics, 1867–1945*, op. cit., pp. 101–03; Peter Cain, 'Political Economy in Edwardian England: The Tariff-Reform Controversy', op. cit.; Peter Clarke, *Hope and Glory*, op. cit., pp. 19–28.

24 A general evaluation of Balfour's government can be found in David Brooks, *The Age of Upheaval: Edwardian Politics 1899–1914*, Manchester: Manchester University Press, 1995, pp. 42–89; see also John Ramsden, *An Appetite for Power: A History of the Conservative Party since 1830*, London: Harper Collins, 1998, pp. 190–221; Martin Pugh, *The Making of Modern British Politics, 1867–1945*, op. cit., pp. 101–03.

25 *Report of the Inter-Departmental Committee on Physical Deterioration*, Cmnd 2175, London: HMSO, 1904, pp. 16–18.

26 *The Times*, 15th October 1902; see also J.K.B. Munson, 'The Unionist Coalition and Education, 1895–1902', *Historical Journal*, vol. 20, no. 3, 1977, pp. 607–45.

27 *The Times*, 16th May 1903.
28 David Brooks, *The Age of Upheaval*, op. cit., pp. 63–64; Peter Clarke, *Hope and Glory*, op. cit., p. 25.
29 National Archives (hereafter 'NA'), Cabinet papers (hereafter 'CAB') 37/65/47, 1st August 1903.
30 David Brooks, *The Age of Upheaval*, op. cit., pp. 90–112.
31 T.H. Green, *Lectures on the Principles of Political Obligation*, London: Longmans, 1895; see also Martin Pugh, *The Making of Modern British Politics, 1867–1945*, op. cit., p. 108.
32 L.T. Hobhouse, *Liberalism*, London: L. Williams & Norgate, 1911; see also Stefan Collini, *Liberalism and Sociology: L.T. Hobhouse and Political Argument in England 1880–1914*, Cambridge: Cambridge University Press, 1979; J.A. Hobson, *The Crisis of Liberalism: New Issues of Democracy*, London: P.S. King, 1909, p. xii.
33 Peter Clarke, *Hope and Glory*, op. cit., p. 97; see also H.A. Clegg, A. Fox and A. F. Thompson, *A History of Trade Unions since 1889*, vol. I, *1889–1910*, Oxford: Oxford University Press, 1964.
34 Andrew Thorpe, *A History of the British Labour Party*, 2nd edn, Basingstoke: Palgrave, 2001, pp. 5–7; Henry Pelling, *The Origins of the Labour Party 1880–1900*, Oxford: Oxford University Press, 1965; Jon Lawrence, *Speaking for the People: Party, Language and Popular Politics in England, 1867–1914*, Cambridge: Cambridge University Press, 1998; A.M. McBriar, *Fabian Socialism and English Politics, 1884–1918*, Cambridge: Cambridge University Press, 1962; M. Bevir, 'Fabianism, Permeation and Independent Labour', *Historical Journal*, vol. 39, no. 1, 1996, pp. 139–96.
35 Martin Pugh, *The Making of Modern British Politics*, op. cit., pp. 115–18; see also Andrew Thorpe, *A History of the British Labour Party*, op. cit., pp. 7–15.
36 Michael Bentley, *The Climax of Liberal Politics: British Liberalism in Theory and Practice, 1868–1918*, London: Arnold, 1987; G.R. Searle, *The Liberal Party: Triumph and Disintegration, 1886–1929*, Basingstoke: Macmillan, 1992; David Brooks, *The Age of Upheaval*, op. cit., pp. 90–108.
37 Cited in Walter L. Arnstein, 'Edwardian Politics: Turbulent Spring or Indian Summer?', in Alan O'Day, *The Edwardian Age: Conflict and Stability 1900–1914*, op. cit., p. 71.
38 S.E. Koss, *Asquith*, New York: St Martin's Press, 1976; Roy Jenkins, *Asquith*, London: Papermac, 1994; Cameron Hazlehurst, 'Herbert Henry Asquith', in John P. Mackintosh, ed., *British Prime Ministers in the Twentieth Century*, vol. I, *Balfour to Chamberlain*, London: Weidenfeld & Nicolson, 1977, pp. 78–117; Michael and Eleanor Brock, eds, *H.H. Asquith: Letters to Venetia Stanley*, Oxford: Oxford University Press, 1982.
39 For accounts of Winston Churchill's early career, see Keith Robbins, *Churchill*, Harlow: Longman, 1992, pp. 28–57; Roy Jenkins, *Churchill*, Basingstoke: Macmillan, 2001, part 2; Paul Addison, *Churchill on the Home Front, 1900–1955*, London: Pimlico, 1993. For Lloyd George, see John Grigg, *Lloyd George: The People's Champion, 1902–11*, London: Methuen, 1978; Martin Pugh, *Lloyd George*, Harlow: Longman, 1988.
40 Bruce K. Murray, *The People's Budget, 1909–1910: Lloyd George and Liberal Politics*, Oxford: Clarendon, 1980.
41 Walter L. Arnstein, 'Edwardian Politics: Turbulent Spring or Indian Summer?', in Alan O'Day, *The Edwardian Age: Conflict and Stability 1900–1914*, op. cit., pp. 72–78; David Powell, *The Edwardian Crisis: Britain 1901–1914*, op. cit., pp. 39–67; Neal Blewett, *The Peers, the Parties and the People: The General Elections of 1910*, London: Macmillan, 1972.
42 Henry Pelling, *A History of British Trade Unionism*, London: Macmillan, 1976, pp. 293–94; David Powell, *The Edwardian Crisis: Britain 1901–1914*, op. cit.,

pp. 117–28; S. Meacham, 'The Sense of an Impending Clash: English Working-Class Unrest before the First World War', *American Historical Review*, vol. LXXVII, 1972, pp. 1343–64; R. Church, 'Edwardian Labour Unrest and Coal-field Militancy, 1890–1914', *Historical Journal*, vol. 30, no. 4, 1987, pp. 841–57.

43 Bob Holton, *British Syndicalism 1900–1914: Myths and Realities*, London: Pluto, 1976; R. Price, 'Contextualising British Syndicalism, c.1907–c.1920', *Labour History Review*, vol. 63(3), 1998, pp. 261–76.

44 Hansard, *Parliamentary Debates*, Fifth Series, vol. XXXVIII, cols 487–534, 8th May 1912.

45 See *Report of an Enquiry by the Board of Trade into Working-Class Rents and Retail Prices Together with the Rates of Wages in Certain Occupations in Industrial Towns of the United Kingdom in 1912*, Cmnd 6955, London: HMSO, 1913, pp. xxxi–lvi; NA, CAB 37/110/63, 'Labour Unrest', 14th April 1912.

46 David Powell, *The Age of Upheaval*, op. cit., pp. 126–27; Paul Addison, *Churchill on the Home Front, 1900–1955*, op. cit., pp. 140–51.

47 Paul Addison, *Churchill on the Home Front, 1900–1955*, op. cit., pp. 140–51.

48 See Bentley B. Gilbert, *The Evolution of National Insurance in Britain*, London: Joseph, 1966; Peter Clarke, *Hope and Glory*, op. cit., pp. 59–60.

49 The miners, railway and transport workers unions had agreed to co-ordinate their actions through a 'Triple Alliance' in 1914. See Lloyd George, *War Memoirs*, London: Nicholson & Watson, 1933, p. 1141; G.A. Phillips, 'The Triple Industrial Alliance in 1914', *Economic History Review*, vol. XXIV, 1971, pp. 55–67; David Powell, *The Edwardian Crisis; Britain 1901–1914*, op. cit., pp. 117–28.

50 See Jill Liddington and Jill Norris, *One Hand Tied Behind Us: The Rise of the Women's Suffrage Movement*, new edn, London: Rivers Oram, 2000, pp. 142–215.

51 Martin Pugh, *The March of the Women: A Revisionist Analysis of the Campaign for Women's Suffrage 1866–1914*, Oxford: Oxford University Press, 2000, ch. 8, 'The Anatomy of Militancy'.

52 For an example of the authorities' treatment of hunger-striking suffragette prisoners, see NA, Home Office files (hereafter 'HO') 144/1558/234191, 'Disturbances: Miss Sylvia Pankhurst, Suffragette, 1913–20'; see also HO 45/10695/231366; HO 45/10700/236973, 'Disturbances: Suffragette Meetings, Outrages etc., 1912–13'.

53 See NA, HO 45/10689/228470, 'Disturbances: Meeting in Wales Attended by Lloyd George, 1912'; *Daily Mirror*, 23rd September 1912; see also Martin Pugh, *The March of the Women*, op. cit., pp. 224–52.

54 Martin Pugh, *The March of the Women*, op. cit., pp. 136–43.

55 Martin Pugh, *The March of the Women*, op. cit., pp. 253–83.

56 *The Times*, 8th April 1914; see also G.P. Gooch and Harold Temperley, *British Documents on the Origins of the War 1898–1914*, vol. III, *The Testing of the Entente, 1904–6*, London: HMSO, 1928, Appendix A, Memorandum by Mr Eyre Crowe, 1st January 1907, pp. 402–03; J.A.S. Grenville, 'Foreign Policy and the Coming of War', in Donald Read, ed., *Edwardian England*, London: Croom Helm, 1982, pp. 162–80; Gordon Martel, *The Origins of the First World War*, 3rd edn, Harlow: Longman, 2003, pp. 41–47.

57 Hew Strachan, *The First World War*, vol. I, *To Arms*, Oxford: Oxford University Press, p. 14; Ian Nish, *The Anglo-Japanese Alliance: The Diplomacy of Two Island Empires, 1894–1907*, London: Athlone, 1966; Zara S. Steiner, 'Great Britain and the Creation of the Anglo-Japanese alliance', *Journal of Modern History*, vol. 31, 1959, pp. 27–36.

58 Paul M. Kennedy, 'German World Policy and the Alliance Negotiations with England, 1897–1900', *Journal of Modern History*, vol. 45, 1973, pp. 605–25; Gordon Martel, 'The Limits of Commitment: Rosebury and the Definition of the Anglo-German Understanding', *Historical Journal*, vol. 26, no. 3, 1983, pp. 387–404;

Zara S. Steiner and Keith Neilson, *Britain and the Origins of the First World War*, 2nd edn, Basingstoke: Macmillan, 2003, pp. 30–32.

59 Paul Kennedy, *The Rise of Anglo-German Antagonism, 1860–1914*, London: Allen & Unwin, 1980; Zara Steiner and Keith Neilson, *Britain and the Origins of the First World War*, op. cit., pp. 44–83.

60 Viscount Grey of Falloden, *Twenty-Five Years 1892–1916*, vol. 2, London: Hodder & Stoughton, 1925, pp. 31–72; James Joll and Gordon Martel, *The Origins of the First World War*, 3rd edn, Harlow, Pearson, Longman, 2007, pp. 61–62; Gordon Martel, *The Origins of the First World War*, op. cit., pp. 64–65; Michael Dockrill, 'British Policy during the Agadir Crisis of 1911', in F.H. Hinsley, ed., *British Foreign Policy under Sir Edward Grey*, Cambridge: Cambridge University Press, 1977, pp. 271–87.

61 *The Times*, 22nd July 1911; Keith Wilson, 'The Agadir Crisis, the Mansion House Speech, and the Double-Edgedness of Agreements', in Keith M. Wilson, *Empire and Continent: Studies in British Foreign Policy from the 1880s to the First World War*, London: Mansell, 1987, pp. 89–109.

62 Zara Steiner and Keith Neilson, *Britain and the Origins of the First World War*, op. cit., pp. 210–11.

63 Zara Steiner and Keith Neilson, *Britain and the Origins of the First World War*, op. cit., pp. 90–91.

64 Peter Padfield, *The Great Naval Race: The Anglo-German Naval Rivalry, 1900–1914*, London: Hart-David, MacGibon, 1974; see also Paul Kennedy, op. cit., pp. 291–440; Michael Howard, 'The Edwardian Arms Race', in Donald Read, ed., op. cit., pp. 145–61; Zara Steiner and Keith Neilson, *Britain and the Origins of the First World War*, op. cit., pp. 51–63; Phillips Payson O'Brien, *British and American Naval Power: Politics and Policy, 1900–1936*, Westport, Connecticut: Praeger, 1998, pp. 73–97; Paul Haggie, 'The Royal Navy and War Planning in the Fisher Era', *Journal of Contemporary History*, vol. 8, 1973, pp. 113–32.

65 A.J.A. Morris, *The Scaremongers: The Advocacy of War and Rearmament 1896–1914*, London: Routledge, 1984, pp. 1–9; 164–84; 203–23; Keith Robbins, *Politicians, Diplomacy and War in Modern British History*, London: Hambledon, 1994, pp. 125–47, see also ch. 7.

66 G.P. Gooch and Harold Temperley, *British Documents on the Origins of the War 1898–1914*, vol. III, *The Testing of the Entente, 1904–6*, London: HMSO, 1928, Appendix A, Memorandum by Mr Eyre Crowe, 1st January 1907; Keith Wilson, 'The Question of Anti-Germanism at the British Foreign Office before the First World War', *Canadian Journal of History*, vol. 18, 1983.

67 G.P. Gooch and Harold Temperley, *British Documents on the Origins of the War 1898–1914*, vol. VI, *Anglo-German Tension: Armaments and Negotiation 1907–12*, London: HMSO, 1930, Appendix V, 'Extract from Minutes of the Committee of Imperial Defence at a meeting of May 26 1911', pp. 781–87.

68 Niall Ferguson, *The Pity of War*, Harmondsworth: Penguin, 1998, pp. 5–6; Keith Robbins, *Politicians, Diplomacy and War in Modern British History*, op. cit., p. 97.

69 Norman Angell, *The Great Illusion: A Study of the Relation of Military Power in Nations to their Economic and Social Advantage*, London: Heinemann, 1910; see also Howard Weinroth, 'Norman Angell and *The Great Illusion*: An Episode in pre-1914 Pacifism', in *Historical Journal*, vol. 13, no. 3, 1974, pp. 551–74.

70 Niall Ferguson, *The Pity of War*, op. cit., pp. 21–23; see also A.J.A. Morris, *The Scaremongers: The Advocacy of War and Rearmament 1896–1914*, op. cit., p. 266.

71 K. Theodore Hoppen, *Ireland since 1800: Conflict and Conformity*, Harlow: Longman, 1999.

72 David Powell, *The Edwardian Crisis: Britain 1901–1914*, op. cit., pp. 141–52; David Brooks, *The Age of Upheaval*, op. cit., pp. 142–50; Alan O'Day, 'Irish

Home Rule and Liberalism', in Alan O'Day, ed., *The Edwardian Age: Conflict and Stability 1900–1914*, op. cit., pp. 113–43.

73 *The Times*, 28th July, 1912.

74 Cited in David Powell, *The Edwardian Crisis: Britain 1901–1914*, op. cit., p.149.

75 NA, CAB 37/120/81, 'A Memorandum by the Military Members of the Army Council on the Military Situation in Ireland', 4th July, 1914.

76 See James Joll and Gordon Martel, *The Origins of the First World War*, op. cit., pp. 12–45; D.W. Sweet, 'The Bosnian Crisis', in F.H. Hinckley, ed., *British Foreign Policy under Sir Edward Grey*, Cambridge: Cambridge University Press, 1977.

77 W. Jannen Jr, 'The Austro-Hungarian Decision for War in July 1914', in Samuel R. Williamson Jr and Peter Pastor, eds, *Essays on World War I: Origins and Prisoners of War*, New York: Brooklyn College Press, 1983; R.J.W. Evans, 'The Hapsburg Monarchy and the Coming of War', in R.J.W Evans and Hartmut Pogge von Strandemann, eds, *The Coming of the First World War*, Oxford: Oxford University Press, 1988.

78 Winston Churchill, *The World Crisis 1911–1918* (1931), Harmondsworth: Penguin, 2007, pp. 87–88.

79 See Viscount Grey of Falloden, *Twenty-Five Years 1892–1916*, op. cit., pp. 161–75; see also Michael Ekstein, 'Sir Edward Grey and Imperial Germany in 1914', *Journal of Contemporary History*, vol. 6, no. 3, 1971; Herbert Butterfield, 'Sir Edward Grey in July 1914', *Historical Studies*, vol. V, 1965.

80 Viscount Grey of Falloden, *Twenty-Five Years 1892–1916*, op. cit., p. 177. See also Keith Wilson, ed., *Decisions for War 1914*, London: UCL Press, 1995, pp. 190–91.

81 Keith Wilson, ed., *Decisions for War 1914*, op. cit., p. 190.

82 Zara S. Steiner and Keith Neilson, *Britain and the Origins of the First World War*, op. cit., pp. 239–40.

83 See S.J. Valone, 'There Must Be Some Misunderstanding: Sir Edward Grey's Diplomacy of August 1st, 1914', *Journal of British Studies*, vol. 27, 1988, pp. 405–24.

84 Winston Churchill, *The World Crisis*, op. cit., p. 99.

85 Zara S. Steiner and Keith Neilson, *Britain and the Origins of the First World War*, op. cit., p. 246.

86 See Adrian Gregory, *The Last Great War: British Society and the First World War*, Cambridge: Cambridge University Press, 2008, pp. 16–25, for a fuller discussion.

87 Cited in Colin Nicolson, 'Edwardian England and the Coming of the First World War', in Alan O'Day, *The Edwardian Age: Conflict and Stability 1900–1914*, op. cit., p. 157.

88 Trevor Wilson, *The Myriad Faces of War*, Oxford: Polity Press, 1986, p. 28.

89 Trevor Wilson, 'Britain's "Moral Commitment" to France in August 1914', *History*, vol. 64(212), 1979, pp. 380–90.

90 The Earl of Oxford and Asquith, *Memories and Reflections 1852–1927*, London: Cassell, pp. 6–9; Trevor Wilson, *The Myriad Faces of War*, op. cit., p. 31.

91 Hew Strachan, *The First World War*, London: Simon & Schuster, 2003, pp. 43–45.

92 Zara S. Steiner and Keith Neilson, *Britain and the Origins of the First World War*, op. cit., p. 239.

93 Viscount Grey of Falloden, *Twenty-Five Years 1892–1916*, op. cit., p. 208.

94 Diary of J.A. Pease, 2 August 1914, cited in Cameron Hazlehurst, *Politicians at War, July 1914 to May 1915*, London: Jonathan Cape, 1971, p. 66.

95 Stephen Koss, *Asquith*, op. cit., p. 159.

96 The Earl of Oxford and Asquith, *Memories and Reflections 1852–1927*, op. cit., p. 8; Winston Churchill, *The World Crisis*, op. cit., pp. 100–01; Zara S. Steiner and Keith Neilson, *Britain and the Origins of the First World War*, op. cit., pp. 250–53.

97 Sir Edward Grey to Mr Barclay, 4th August 1914, in G.P. Gooch and Harold Temperley, *British Documents on the Origins of the War 1898–1914*, vol. XI; J.W. Headlam Morley, *The Outbreak of War*, p. 328.
98 Cited in Stephen Koss, *Asquith*, op. cit., p. 160.
99 David French, 'The Edwardian Crisis and the Origins of the First World War', op. cit.
100 Hansard, *Parliamentary Debates*, Fifth series, vol. LXV, col. 1823.

2 For King and Country

The onset of war caught some of the London public in festive mood. *The Times* reported that thousands were stranded owing to the suspension of services on the major railway routes over the bank holiday weekend, whilst large crowds dressed in their holiday apparel gathered in Trafalgar Square, along Whitehall and outside the gates of Buckingham Palace, forcing the King to appear no less than three times on the balcony as they chanted 'we want war'.[1] Lloyd George, writing in 1938, remembered 'the warlike crowds that thronged Whitehall and poured into Downing Street ... multitudes of young people concentrated in Westminster demonstrating for war against Germany'.[2] The many reports of flag-waving crowds, queues forming outside army recruitment offices and young men marching with toy rifles have, until recently, led historians to believe that Britons in 1914 universally greeted the war with rampant enthusiasm.[3] Subsequent studies have tended to undermine this picture. Some anecdotal evidence of popular reactions outside London do cast doubts on the accepted view. In the Sussex coastal town of Littlehampton, a popular tourist resort, it was recorded that the outbreak of war quelled the bank holiday merriment to a level of 'underlying suspense and subdued enjoyment'.[4] In the same manner, at the other end of the country in Newcastle the Revd James Mackay, a Methodist minister, recorded in his diary for 5th August, 'Weeping women everywhere. There are no great demonstrations of enthusiasm. Everyone feels the awfulness of the situation and a becoming gravity prevails.'[5]

As such, some writers have suggested that the general reaction to the war was more nuanced and complex than previously assumed. Cheering crowds in central London were an inaccurate gauge of the national mood, which in other places was more restrained. Historians have discovered hidden agendas amongst the accounts of widespread bellicosity. Politicians, for example, exaggerated their memories of war fever amongst the British public to cover their guilt at leading the country into a disastrous conflict; in reality, the provincial crowds that cheered did so to support their local army units as they marched for France. The multitudes in London during August 1914 consisted more of interested spectators ('audience crowds' in the opinion of one observer) than vociferous supporters.[6] Moreover, the historical focus on the pro-war demonstrations has been too impressionistic and ignores the sizeable voice of pacifist opinion, spread across a number of religious and political groups, which was calling for British neutrality.[7] The evidence is compelling enough to persuade us that the people's fervour of August 1914 has been exaggerated. Even so, the absence of popular resistance to the conflict suggests that many Britons accepted the war as necessary and, by implication, endorsed the politicians' resolution. This was to prove critical in the tough days to come and as the country faced up to its first emergency of the war.

Calamity beckons ...

The crisis took several forms. Potentially the most perilous was the breakdown in the world's foreign-exchange markets and the subsequent paralysis in international trade, which had gripped the London financial market two days after Austria–Hungary and Serbia had ceased diplomatic relations. Heavy selling of securities had already begun on the Vienna bourse in mid-July as domestic and foreign investors sold their stocks and bonds for cash. By the 29th fear of imminent hostilities prompted similar heavy sales of securities across the major European stock exchanges, spilling over onto Wall Street in New York. On 31st July the growing sense of panic hit the London markets. The first to feel the pressure were the 'jobbers' firms, whose trading in stocks and shares was largely financed by borrowed money. After being engulfed by orders to sell stock from their clients, some jobbers found that the market value of their portfolios had slumped below their original purchase value, leaving them heavily in debt, forcing many into bankruptcy.[8] In a bid to prevent a collapse in the market, the authorities agreed to close the Stock Exchange until further notice. Matters were compounded by the parallel crisis emerging in the foreign-exchange markets, which threatened the financial position of the London Accepting Houses.[9] As institutions greasing the wheels of international commerce by accepting and guaranteeing bills of exchange, Accepting Houses (which were later to become better known as 'investment' or 'merchant' banks) played a central role in foreign trade. Bills of exchange were essentially cheques or 'IOUs' passed from buyer to seller in international markets whose value could be realized if subsequently sold to an Accepting House which bought them using short-term loans from the major joint-stock banks. 'Accepting' a bill in this manner virtually guaranteed its value and not only ensured that sellers received their money, but also meant that the bill could be sold on at a profit or used as collateral for further bank loans or credit. The problem in 1914 was that once the international trade in securities had broken down, the supply of bills to the Accepting Houses dried up, leaving many unable to meet their liabilities to the banks.[10]

The joint-stock banks, however, deepened the crisis. Anticipating a full-scale European war, the banks feared a widespread withdrawal of funds by panicking investors. As a considerable portion of their assets now lay in unrealizable bills, the banks, in the interests of protecting both their deposits and their depositors, promptly stopped lending money. All short-term loans to the Accepting Houses were foreclosed and foreign credit was severely curtailed, leaving the City's Accepting Houses incapable of financing international trade and depriving the government of its main source of funding the war and purchasing essential food supplies. Facing ruin, the Accepting Houses turned to the Bank of England to accept their bills of exchange, effectively draining the Bank's own cash deposits straight into the coffers of the joint-stock banks. The crisis then shifted a gear. Investors (then and now) have traditionally used their cash assets to buy gold as the only safe way of retaining their capital value in a financial crisis. However, the banks, also anxious to hang on to their gold reserves, opted to pay customers in the form of Bank of England notes. Alarmed investors, concerned for their savings, and holidaymakers reliant on funds to see them through the bank holiday weekend, immediately took the notes to the Bank of England to exchange for gold, forming long queues along Threadneedle Street over the final weekend of peace. Struggling to stem the run on its reserves, the Bank hastily raised interest rates from 3 to 4 per cent on 30th July; the following day rates were increased to 8 per cent; by 1st August rates peaked at 10 per cent. But in just three days the Bank of England lost 16 per cent of its pre-July reserves, nearly £6 million.[11] Writing to his wife, Churchill bemoaned that the City was in chaos, world credit was at a standstill and that it was impossible to borrow money or sell shares.[12]

Fear of war and the crisis in international trade brought on a sharp downturn in the economy. For the first time since the days of Napoleon, Britons were faced with an acute shortage of money. Shoppers stopped buying, exports weakened and companies began laying off workers. By the end of August, nearly 500,000 employees were either unemployed or on short-time working, with the cotton, furniture and storage trades (all export-led industries) being the hardest hit.[13] Britain's merchant marine was also affected as ships, fearing capture or sinking, either stayed in harbour or were prevented from sailing as insurance companies refused to cover their passage through war zones, or charged exorbitant premiums for cargoes. The danger this posed to food imports fuelled steep rises in retail prices (in the region of 15 per cent according to the Board of Trade) and sent the British public into an orgy of panic-buying (mainly by the wealthy), with outbreaks of looting and riots on Tyneside and in Bedfordshire. Grocers across the country were recording nearly eight days' business in one day, with the more unscrupulous traders seeking to profit further by withholding supplies.[14]

Calamity beckoned; yet the government was not wholly unprepared. In the summer of 1914 the Committee of Imperial Defence produced a War Book, running to 11 chapters, setting out, in meticulous detail, the administrative measures required by each government department in the event of a major conflict.[15] This weighty tome, which had been gestating in numerous sub and *ad hoc* committees under the guidance of Sir Charles Ottley and Captain

Maurice Hankey since 1911, was intended to co-ordinate the actions of the 'home' ministries with the mobilization plans of the armed forces. But it was far from foolproof. It ignored the role of the Cabinet in directing the war effort, contained no plans for mobilizing and managing the country's industrial and manpower resources and encompassed only the first few days of war.[16] However, the government was quick to recognize the danger zones. Fears of food riots, civil strife and industrial unrest led the Cabinet to retain two divisions of the British Expeditionary Force (BEF) for preserving public order after the bulk of the Army was sent to France on 6th August. The Metropolitan Police, under plans drawn up by the War Office in 1913, was despatched to guard warehouses, abattoirs, flour mills and bakers.[17] Such actions were supported by the passing of the first instalment of the Defence of the Realm Act (DORA) on 8th August, giving the government power to court-martial any citizen giving information and assistance to the enemy and the right 'to secure the safety of any means of communication, or of railways, docks and harbours'.[18]

Asquith also moved smartly to appoint a series of *ad hoc* committees to enact emergency procedures. This committee culture was a convenient way of reassuring the public that the government was responding to major problems, without directly involving the state. Committees came in two types: Cabinet Committees, consisting mainly of ministers supported by their civil service and civilian advisers; and Advisory Committees, comprised of outside experts. Essentially, Cabinet Committees distributed the government's workload whilst formulating policies for Cabinet approval. Advisory Committees explain themselves, as in the case of the Consultative Agricultural Committee, or they were more informal bodies established to implement Cabinet directives. Committees grew rapidly: there were 20 on 20th August and 38 by 1st January 1915.[19] Of these, four are perhaps worthy of note. First, under a Parliamentary Act of 1871, the government oversaw the everyday running of the railroad system by appointing a Railway Executive Committee. As a temporary measure requiring parliamentary approval every seven days, the committee was staffed almost entirely by the general managers of the larger companies, which allowed the government to manage the network through professional expertise. Lines, locomotives, rolling stock and staff now came under 'the service of the state', co-ordinating the movement of food supplies, troops and stores.[20]

At the same time an Admiralty Advisory Committee on Trade Diversions became operational, issuing daily reports on the safety of sea-lanes and the handling capacity of ports in order to prevent congestion at southern and south-western docks caused by shipping being diverted from the east coast for fear of enemy action.[21] This was supported by the government's plan to insure British shipping against war risks. The 'Huth-Jackson' scheme (named after its originator, Frederick Huth-Jackson, governor of the Bank of England), was designed to overcome shipowners' difficulties in finding, and affording, insurance for their vessels, crews and cargoes. Enacted on 3rd August, the scheme offered generous terms. The government promised to underwrite 80 per cent of the insurance risks on shipping, thus keeping the British merchant fleet at sea and facilitating the free flow of food imports, whilst insuring cargoes at reasonable premiums. A state insurance office was established in London, led by a board of experts appointed to administer the scheme's operation. British shipping recovered remarkably. By the end of 1914 cargo rates had quadrupled, older derelict ships were being restored to operation and labour shortages ensured that the wages of officers and seamen rocketed.[22]

Food supplies were another priority.[23] In August 1914, Asquith established the Cabinet Committee on Food Supplies, chaired by Home Secretary Reginald McKenna.[24] The committee's remit was simple enough: prevent food supplies from reaching Germany and protect the national food store. On 8th August, McKenna pushed through Parliament the Unreasonable Withholding of Foodstuffs Act, giving the Board of Trade authority to requisition the stocks of retailers suspected of hoarding supplies.[25] More controversial, however, was McKenna's order, made on 12th August under the authority of the Admiralty, to compel all British ships carrying food to enemy countries to unload their cargoes at British ports, even if their shipments had originated in a neutral country. The move was quickly curtailed when American grain-owners, suspicious that Britain sought to drive down prices, threatened to terminate all supplies forthwith. The country's heavy dependency on American grain ensured quick compliance. More successful, however, was the committee's entry onto the world markets to secure supplies previously imported from Germany and Austria. In mid-August it had drawn up purchasing contracts for supplies of sugar on the New York market, as well as large supplies of Argentine (and later Australian) beef 'on Government account', and the securing of other commodities, including timber from Scandinavia and supplies of chemicals, colours and dye-stuffs.[26]

This still left the crisis in the financial markets. The near-collapse of international trade and finance had caught the government off guard. Global economic crisis was something that had not been considered by the compilers of the War Book, and the commentator Hartley Withers was correct in his remark that 'the fleet was ready and the Expeditionary Force was ready. The financial machinery was not.'[27] Lacking a strategy, the government was forced to rely on the advice of a small coterie of trusted experts, including Sir George Paish, editor of *The Statist*, and a young J.M. Keynes, to shape its rescue plan. Paish had the greater influence a series of conferences between 31st July and 6th August, a Cabinet Committee of seven ministers and officials from the Bank of England and the Treasury, chaired by Lloyd George, agreed a policy based largely on a Paish memorandum of 1st August that aimed to restore confidence in the financial markets. First, the committee introduced a one-month moratorium on all bad debts incurred by the banks and finance houses. Second, the committee authorized the turning of postal orders into legal tender and the swift issue of 'Treasury' bank notes (called

Bradburys, since they bore the signature of Sir John Bradbury, Permanent Under-Secretary to the Treasury) in order to relieve the pressure on the gold reserves. To allow time for these measures to be arranged, the bank holiday was extended to three days.[28] Confidence had largely returned when the banks re-opened on 7th August. Yet other issues remained. Despite Lloyd George's offer to underwrite their losses on bad loans, the banks' reluctance to give short-term credit was threatening to push the economy deeper into recession as companies struggling with their cash flows began to lay off workers. It was not until the Chancellor bullied the banks with the promise of greater government regulation that a loosening of credit supply ensued. By November, Lloyd George had moved to restore foreign trade by promising the Accepting Houses enough government money to help them generate new business, whilst Treasury guarantees to underwrite 75 per cent of the debts owed by hostile powers to British merchants and manufacturers helped to revive confidence in international commerce.[29]

Did this represent a reappraisal of the Liberal government's laissez-faire values? Not necessarily. Throughout the crisis Lloyd George maintained that the government's aim was to soften the immediate effects of the war by stabilizing the financial system enough to restore normality to trade and finance: a policy summarized by Lloyd George's concluding remarks at a Treasury conference of businessmen, bankers and 'traders' on 4th August that the government had endeavoured 'to enable the traders of this country to carry on business as *usual*'.[30] This was more than a frantic cry for the country not to panic in a moment of crisis. Lloyd George was, perhaps subconsciously, alluding to a pre-war strategy that, as David French has argued, envisaged Britain taking on the role of back-seat driver in the event of a European conflict. If the 'Triple Entente' were to thwart Germany's quest for continental domination, then it would be Britain's allies, with their mass conscript armies, who would bear the brunt of the fighting. For her part, Britain, through her powerful Navy, would enforce an economic blockade, protect her international trade from enemy action, allow British traders to capture German markets and enable British banks to finance the allied war effort while her traders supplied her belligerent friends with munitions and other essential supplies. Britain's contribution to the land war would be limited to sending a small professional army to France. Essentially, 'Business as Usual' was a neat, tidy box of assumptions designed so that the government could fight a laissez-faire war. Rooted in the policies deployed to defeat Napoleon a hundred years earlier, the effectiveness of Business as Usual necessitated the safeguarding of Britain's economic strength and was dependent on a short war, to minimalize its effect on her economy. That meant, as Hankey had insisted in 1913, that Business as Usual would work only if the conditions of economic life in Britain remained tolerable and 'tremendous drains on our labour supply' were avoided.[31] A man about to upset all these calculations was Field Marshal Lord Kitchener, appointed by Asquith as Secretary of State for War on 5th August.

Kitchener's call

Asquith knew that his choice was politically risky.[32] Kitchener, by his own admission, was ignorant of Europe, England and the British Army.[33] But, as the architect of famous British victories in Sudan and South Africa, the Field Marshal commanded huge public support, and his military background kept him detached from party ties and brought a sense of national unity right to the centre of government.[34] Above all, however, Kitchener was a realist. Echoing the discussions of the War Council, Kitchener, on his second day in office, told the Cabinet that the war would be expensive, would last at least three years and would require a million-strong army in the field. Accordingly, on 6th August, Kitchener called for 100,000 new recruits; the following day Asquith sought parliamentary approval for the recruitment of half a million men for the Army, with further calls made on three occasions during August and September 1914 for an additional 100,000. By 12th November an increase of one million men had been authorized and would henceforth be known as the 'New Armies'.[35] They were to be trained as a new force of 'regular' soldiers, established to supplement the professional troops of the British Expeditionary Force (comprising 247,432 men, constituted in 1906 under the reforms initiated by R.B. Haldane),[36] but set apart from the country's part-time reservists, the Territorials, whom Kitchener dismissed as a 'Town Clerk's army'.[37] 'I prefer men who know nothing', Kitchener told Violet Asquith, 'to those who have been taught a smattering of the wrong thing'.[38] Kitchener's new force would thus be enlisted and trained according to the needs of this war, unencumbered by tradition, to be despatched when and where it was needed and composed entirely of volunteers.[39]

Kitchener's disdain for the Territorials was misplaced. The 'Saturday night soldiers', though poorly equipped and trained, still represented a sizeable force of some 268,777 officers and men, many of whom were mobilized for home defence in the first weeks of August 1914. Furthermore, in the County Associations – ensembles of local worthies and dignitaries who were responsible for recruiting and equipping local Territorial units – there lay a ready network of organizations proven to be of immense value in gathering new recruits, as Kitchener quickly realized when, on 7th August, he instructed the Associations to raise new units to replace those volunteering for overseas service.[40] By now, however, the response to Kitchener's call for volunteers was overwhelming. In the first week of August a total of 8,193 men across the country were attested for army service, averaging 1,640 men a day. On Sunday 9th August a further 2,433 enlisted. After that the figures rose steadily: 43,764 in the week of 15th August; 66,310 in the week ending on the 29th. Numbers peaked between 30th August and 5th September, when a total of 174,901 men were recruited, with 33,304 enlistments recorded on one day.[41] What the *Manchester Guardian* termed 'a rush to the colours' took the War Office aback. Army recruitment before 1914 had averaged fewer than 100 men daily across the country; now some recruitment offices confessed to being 'buried alive' with recruits.[42]

The men who walked into the recruiting stations during the early weeks of the war did so for differing reasons. Some historians contend that men joined the Army to escape the drudgery and humdrum existence of work and everyday life. The excitement of travelling overseas, relatively unknown to many young working-class men at the time, must have been an enticing alternative to a mundane job in a shop, factory or office. Understanding hard graft and boredom may explain the resilience of the ordinary British soldier, but not necessarily why he enlisted.[43] All the same, substantial numbers of men who joined the colours were almost certainly driven by enthusiasm, naivety and expectations of a short war. In a letter to his family, the soldier-poet Julian Grenfell enthused, 'I adore war. It's like a big picnic without the objectlessness of a picnic ... one loves one's fellow man so much more when one is bent on killing him.'[44] University student Godfrey Buxton signed up convinced that Germany would be defeated by 7th October, when he was due back at Cambridge. Captain Philip Neame, VC, who was stationed in Gibraltar when war broke out, was 'only too anxious to be at the front' before the fighting was over.[45] However, evidence also suggests that volunteering for reasons of patriotism or a sense of duty should not be under-estimated. The protection of 'plucky little Belgium', defence of the Empire and words like duty and honour had a resonance for this wartime generation. Men and women talked openly of loyalty to their country. A.J. Gosling, a cobbler, felt that the war was a 'just one', which England 'had declared ... to uphold her honour and freedom and rights of small nations to live'.[46] Another volunteer spoke 'of a minor battle' taking place within him. 'I had no thirst for war, and I loathed the thought of having to kill someone. Yet I felt that I owed a duty to my country.'[47] Similarly, recruitment rates were heavily influenced by news of overseas events. For example, the jump in enlistments during the last two weeks of August 1914 was attributed to the infamous 'Amiens dispatches', reporting on the Army's retreat from Mons, that appeared in *The Times* between 25th and 31st August.[48] And further surges were recorded following news of German atrocities and the sight of forlorn Belgian refugees landing on English shores.[49]

Other historians have explained 'the rush' as an expression of values and practices within the Edwardian education system that conditioned young men into a militaristic culture, idealizing war.[50] Many who enlisted into the officer ranks in 1914 were drawn from public schools where the option of military drill was provided for in the Education Code of 1875, and Haldane's army reforms included the establishment of Officer Training Corps in over 150 schools and 20 universities across the country. Edwardian upper-class schoolboys were familiar with the demands of elementary military training and the public school itself, with its hierarchical prefectorial system and notions of teamwork and prize-giving, was soaked in educational *mores* that loosely reflected army life.[51] War was a matter of honour, glory, courage and self-sacrifice: principles which permeated the games-playing ethos of English public schools, embodying the maxims of 'Muscular Christianity', an ideal propagated by Thomas Arnold, headmaster of Rugby in the 1830s, that valued physical health and fitness over intellectual prowess.[52]

This emphasis on games and team sports was designed to foster the development of manliness, where strong will and good character, and a healthy mind and body assumed a singular importance. Team sports were especially valuable in developing the qualities of discipline, self-sacrifice, leadership and a readiness to place your own interests below those of others, virtues suited both to the playing-field and the battlefield. For the poet Henry Newbolt, a propagandist for public school education, playing cricket developed military qualities that could be easily deployed in combat. His poem 'Vitai Lampada' had a schoolboy rallying his team as a tail-end batsman, employing the same formula to encourage his troops as they fought the raving Dervish in the Sudan. War, in this context, was a 'greater game', played to a set of rules, fought by gentlemen, representing a utopian ideal within a dystopian setting.[53] Thus, it has been argued that a class of young men saw the war as an opportunity to test their courage, whilst satisfying their primal yearnings for adventure and emotional fulfilment. Death in battle was not something to be feared. 'To die young, clean, ardent', wrote H.A. Vachell, 'to die swiftly, in perfect health ... saving others from death ... is not that cause for joy rather than sorrow?'[54] Others may have followed the poet Rupert Brooke's belief that the war would rescue them from a society that had become staid and sedate. Brooke thanked God 'Who has matched us with His Hour,/ And caught our youth, and wakened us from sleeping,/ ... / To turn, as swimmers into cleanness leaping,/ Glad from a world grown old and cold and weary'.[55]

Such ideals were not necessarily confined to upper-class youth. In one respect, the idea of war as an adventure was encouraged by a variety of boys' magazines and cheap literature, aimed at middle- and working-class children. Novels relating tales of derring-do, usually set in some far corner of the Empire, became enormously popular between 1880 and 1914, their stories published in instalments through affordable weekly magazines like *The Boys' Herald* ('A Healthy Paper for Manly Boys') and the *Boy's Own Paper*, with contributions from Jules Verne, Rider Haggard, Talbot Baines Reed and G.A. Henty. Each had a weekly circulation of around 50,000 and were read (so it is claimed) by approximately two-thirds of British schoolboys.[56] Working-class school children were also taught the values of loving one's country and reverence for the Empire, often rammed home with a cast-iron disciplinary code that emphasized notions of obedience and authority: instruments of social control that channelled youthful boisterousness into a militaristic framework, while elevating ideas of duty to a higher national cause.[57] Organizations such as William Smith's Boys' Brigade, formed in Glasgow during 1883, tried to instil 'manly' instincts in slum-dwelling teenage males by introducing them to team games. Smith's organization was militarist in tone, with drum and bugle bands, uniforms and pill-box hats, and a membership of approximately 150,000 by 1914.[58] Accompanying it was an array of youth organizations, all combining religion, athleticism and military discipline. Organizations such as the Duty and Discipline Movement, the Church Lads' Brigade and the Lads' Drill Association combined a Christian message with patriotism, teamwork and mutual help.[59] The most successful of these groups, the Boy Scouts, founded in 1908 by Robert Baden-Powell, attempted to cultivate physical fitness and group loyalty 'in boys from the slums', insisting that every lad 'ought to learn how to shoot and obey orders'.[60] Baden-Powell insisted that his motives were imperial rather than military. Boy Scouts were to be 'the frontiersmen of the Empire', and the underlying message of the manual *Scouting for Boys* emphasized the importance of equipping boys with the skills to survive in the wild. Scouts were organized into small patrols and encouraged to be self-reliant, whilst being 'ready to face danger and always keen to help each other'. Nevertheless Scouts, with their rituals, badges and banners, came almost ready-made for army life when the need arose.[61]

How far such cultures helped to spread military values in pre-war Britain is highly conjectural. If newly enlisted officers and humble squaddies entered the trenches with an idea of war as a destiny or adventure, then it is probably likely that many others did not. DeGroot asserts that 60 per cent of British adolescents fell outside the influence of a youth movement before 1914 and, unable to afford their subscriptions, the poorest families had little affinity with the aims and activities of these societies and resented their attempt to exercise some form of authoritarian control over their lives.[62] Besides, by 1914, some working-class men cared less for duty and honour than the struggle to avoid destitution. The onset of a severe trade slump and rapidly rising unemployment at the start of the war has been cited as a major factor in stimulating recruitment. Board of Trade figures indicated that unemployment rates amongst trade union members rose from 2.8 per cent to 7.1 per cent between the end of July and late August 1914, with rates of short-time working increasing to 26 per cent of the active labour force during August and September. Rates of male employment fell by 10 per cent in the same period.[63] Few across the social classes escaped the pain of economic hardship, but it was often the urban unskilled workers who were hit hardest and provided the Army with its most fruitful source of recruitment, as they did before the war.[64] In Birmingham nine-tenths of this class of unemployed men were reported as having enlisted in September, while, across the country, recruitment of former employees in the so-called 'shrinking' industries was greater than that of those from firms prospering from the conflict.[65] Then again, the numbers of unemployed men who volunteered for armed service were far outweighed by those who chose not to.[66]

All this suggests that the early-war 'rush to the colours' was a phenomenon more complex than hitherto supposed. The idealists and enthusiasts probably did account for the heavy recruitment rates experienced in the first week of the war, yet Adrian Gregory has suggested that the era of mass recruitment began when news of the BEF's fighting retreat from Mons made the British realize that the war had 'turned serious' and their country was facing a desperate fight for national defence. Hence, what began as a politicians' and diplomats' war declared for reasons of economic security and European hegemony became a struggle for national unity, civilization, liberty and for the protection of Britain's Empire and her essentially Victorian way of life. The threat to all of this was a powerful reason for men to enlist, but it proved insufficient to satisfy the Army's ever-growing need for recruits.

Both the government and army authorities quickly discovered that enthusiasm alone would not create the army that Kitchener required; persuasion was also needed. This produced two initiatives. The first was perhaps the most inspired idea of the war. Mooted originally in the War Office but popularized by Lord Derby, the notion of 'Pals Battalions' successfully embodied the powerful forces of peer pressure and civic pride. Groups of men, linked by a common bond of professional, recreational or educational ties, were encouraged to join up together in units that combined a strong sense of local identity with group solidarity, along with an opportunity to exploit alternative loyalties for which to fight other than 'King and Country'. At a time of deep social class divisions, it was perhaps a comfort to volunteers that they would not go into combat alongside other social groups. The fellowship of the Cheshire Pals, for example, enabled men to fight beside their 'socialist comrades'.[67] The first recognizable Pals unit, the 'Stockbrokers', some 1,600 strong, was formed on 21st August in the City of London.[68] Yet the movement had its deepest roots in Northern England, particularly Merseyside, where Lord Derby's first appeal for men in the clerking and commercial trades met with a strong response, with four units being formed in one week. Units were formed that became part of Great War folklore: the Hull Pals, the Accrington Pals, the Grimsby Chums, the Manchester Pals, the Oldham Comrades and the Birmingham Battalion. Elsewhere, the Pals movement faltered. In Scotland, only Glasgow displayed any enthusiasm; and Pals units were scarce in Wales, with brigades formed in Cardiff, Swansea and the Rhondda, but far less prominent in the north-west region.[69] The Pals, however, were a victory for the art of thinking on one's feet, and Derby took enough of the credit to warrant his appointment as the government's Director-General of Recruiting in 1915.

A second initiative was the creation of the Parliamentary Recruiting Committee (PRC) on 27th August 1914. The PRC was essentially an apolitical body with a mission to invigorate the recruitment campaign by employing the resources and expertise of the constituency organizations of the main political parties in a drive to persuade, cajole, browbeat, harangue and humiliate men into joining the Army. Jointly presided over by Asquith, Bonar Law and the Labour Party leader Arthur Henderson, the committee was made up of 32 members, including 11 Conservative, seven Liberal and four Labour MPs, a motley gang of party officials, and Sir Henry Rawlinson, Director-General of Recruiting at the War Office.[70] Like the single cell dividing, the PRC quickly fragmented. By the autumn of 1915 it had broken down into a number of local Joint Parliamentary Committees and five separate subcommittees – Householders' Return and Inquiries; Finance; Publications; Meetings; and Publicity – all co-ordinated by a General Purposes Committee. The PRC also inspired the creation of separate, non-related committees, such as the Scottish Recruiting Committee and Labour Recruiting Committee, established jointly by the TUC's parliamentary group, the General Federation of Trade Unions and the Labour Party.[71]

Reluctant recruits now had nowhere to run. In its search to discover how large the reservoir of potential volunteers was, the committee authorized, in October 1914, the setting up of a Householders' Return: a vast postal canvass, co-ordinated by Sir Jesse Herbert at the National Liberal Club, of eight million letters distributed through party agents to every family on the electoral register. Each householder was required to supply their local council with details of the names and numbers of all males aged between 19 and 35 years 'residing in this house', detailing for each his marital status (with any children), height, occupation and a statement declaring his willingness to enlist. Party canvassers collected any forms that had not been returned after five days. Names of potential recruits were then collected together as 'good papers' and passed on to local recruiting officers.[72] Thenceforth, the PRC's efforts diversified. Outdoor recruitment rallies were most favoured. They were cheap to organize ('I have the Union Jack and a bell', remembered one enthusiast. 'I ring the bell and wave the Jack. A crowd is immediately gathered.')[73] and required a simple platform strategically erected in a town or market square, playing field or street corner. Meetings would usually be preceded by a march, led by military bands (the most successful was Lieutenant W.J. West's Highland Pipe Band which toured the country from Cornwall to Northumberland between 1914 and 1916), and accompanied by motor cars or buses adorned with bunting, recruitment posters and slogans together with soldiers and an array of guns and wagons. At the meeting, recruiting officers, medics and magistrates were on hand to 'enrol recruits on the spot'.[74]

Indoor meetings, however, were seen as equally valuable. Lantern Lectures, delivered in local halls and designed for 'large numbers of people [who] were quite ignorant as to the causes of the war and the need for men' proved popular.[75] Most spectacular were the gatherings at large city-centre theatres addressed by a famous politician or personality, such as Horatio Bottomley ('the tribune of the people'), who regularly spoke to audiences of 20,000, praising the British Empire, damning Germany and spraying insults on both pacifists and politicians who did not support the war and on young men who shrank from enlisting.[76] There was also the recruitment meeting masquerading as a music hall concert. Such events were often glamourized by leading performers: Harry Lauder, for example, a former Scottish miner turned comedian; and Vesta Tilley and Edith Bracewell, both of whom specialized in reciting stirring patriotic songs, followed by a walk amongst their adoring audiences singling out potential new recruits.[77]

But the PRC's central thrust was focused through recruitment pamphlets and posters. In March 1915 the committee published a catalogue recording 35 sets of pamphlets and leaflets to be distributed by its constituency workers. Pamphlets 1, 1A and 1B detailed the terms of enlistment, pay and allowances for new recruits; no. 2 reproduced a Bernard Partridge cartoon showing Liberty comforting Belgium; no. 5 reported speeches by leading politicians. Others included patriotic song sheets, appeals for more men and a great deal of atrocity propaganda. Posters covered much the same ground. The PRC issued approximately 150 designs on a hundred distinct subjects.[78] Some, such as the face of Lord Kitchener, complete with eyes and finger pointing directly at the viewer, were to achieve almost iconic status. Otherwise they followed a few well-defined themes. Many early posters relied on simple patriotism: 'Rally round the Flag! Fight for King and Empire'; 'Lend your strong right arm to your country'. Other messages played on generating hatred for the enemy by exploiting real events, such as the German navy's bombardment of Scarborough in December 1914. Later the messages became quite crude, exploiting stories of German troops' mistreatment of Belgian civilians, with one carrying Kitchener's assertion: 'The Germans act with the same barbarous savagery as the Sudan Dervishes'. Another technique played on emotional blackmail. 'Why are *you* stopping HERE when your pals are out THERE?' demanded one design; 'You're proud of your pals in the Army of course! But what will your pals think of YOU?' exclaimed another. More controversial was the depiction of a family man seated in his armchair, son at his feet and daughter on his knee, looking shamefaced at the viewer as his offspring ask, 'Daddy, what did YOU do in the Great War?' The message was most effective when the appeal was addressed through women, with the well-known image of a proud-looking mother and daughter gazing at a line of departing troops and the caption 'Women of Britain say – *GO!*'[79]

The PRC's output was prodigious. During its 16-month existence its publicity department issued 54 million posters and 5.8 million leaflets and pamphlets; organized 12,000 meetings; and arranged 20,000 speeches: an advertising campaign on a scale never previously reached.[80] These efforts were complemented by a plethora of smaller organizations, such as the Imperial Maritime League, which held 1,000 meetings in rural locations during the first six months of 1915, and the National Union of Women's Suffrage Societies, who were keen to use their large and well-organized resources 'to help our country through this period of strain and sorrow'.[81] Others indulged in more direct methods of recruiting, ranging from ritual humiliation, such as Penrose Fitzgerald's campaign advising women to distribute white feathers to young men seen on the street not wearing a uniform (a constant scourge), to landowners threatening their tenantry with eviction if their menfolk refrained from enlisting. Mr Rogers-Jenkins, 'a well-known South African', however, adopted a press-gang recruiting method, driving about London in a chauffeur-driven car picking out 'unemployed men and idlers' and forcibly bundling them to the nearest recruitment station. Rogers-Jenkins was said to have netted 174 recruits in one week.[82]

Even so, despite the PRC's huffing and puffing, its effect on recruitment rates remains questionable. Once the surges of August and September had dissipated, overall enlistment rates declined. Official figures for October 1914 recorded that 136,811 men had enlisted, but this was a considerable fall from the peak achieved in September. November showed a recovery, when 169,862 men enlisted, yet in December figures fell to 117,860. Another brief rise, to 156,290, was recorded in January 1915, but February was disastrous – 87,896.[83] Records showed 113,907 enlistments in March 1915; in April, 119,087; and in May, 135,263. By June numbers had slipped to 114,679; to 95,413 in July; and to 71,617 in September. The next two months showed a slight improvement, with the recruitment of 113,285 and 121,793, respectively; but by December the numbers had slumped to 55,152.[84] This was not necessarily a cause for alarm. The War Office calculated that monthly recruitment rates averaged 145,101 men between August 1914 and December 1915, more than enough to compensate for the average monthly losses of 23,287.[85] The decline was puzzling, but the reasons were plain enough. A decisive factor in constraining recruitment was financial. On the one hand, many married men in particular were reluctant to enlist for fear of leaving their families in severe hardship. Though the government revived the system of 'Separation Allowances' in August 1914, which allowed wives and dependants to claim cash benefits to compensate for the loss of a breadwinner to the armed forces, its administration was inefficient, and payment levels had remained unaltered since the South African War. Any additional benefits had to be drawn from charitable organizations and local support agencies.[86] On the other hand, the economy had begun to recover by October on the back of increased government orders, particularly for armaments, textiles and clothing. Rising wages and the prospect of full-time employment far outweighed, for many workers, the dangerous and poorly paid business of soldiering.[87]

Otherwise, considerable numbers of men were deterred from military service by reports of poor treatment of recruits and shortages of food, sleeping quarters and other basic facilities.[88] Men were either being enlisted in the Reserve and then sent home until they could be accommodated, or were billeted in local private houses, hired buildings, schools and hostels.[89] The composer George Butterworth's experiences were perhaps typical. After enlisting in the Duke of Cornwall's Light Infantry, he was sent to camp at Bodmin, arriving 'after dark':

> There we were met by a sergeant and marched up without delay to the Barracks. Our reception there was not encouraging; at the gate we were presented with one blanket, and told that the sleeping accommodation was already over-full, and that we must do as best we could in the open. Some 20 of us accordingly stationed ourselves under a small group of trees. Food was the next question ... nothing was provided for us. Luckily the canteen was still open, and by dint of much pushing we managed to secure a tin of corned beef and bottled beer.[90]

Attempts by the War Office to control the flood of volunteers made matters worse. Minimum height requirements and age limits for new recruits were increased in mid-September, leading to the rejection of some 10,000 men who had already enlisted. In October height requirements and age limits were again altered, eventually settling at a minimum height of 5ft 3ins and a maximum age of 40 years in July 1915, which threw open the possibility of recruiting 'Bantam' units of small men who made smaller targets for enemy bullets.[91] The fluctuating standards gave rise to a national whisper that volunteers were no longer needed, a rumour fully denied by the government.[92]

But the crisis in recruitment was symptomatic of a deeper malaise in Britain's early war effort. For all the carefully laid plans, Kitchener had thrown a well-aimed spanner in the workings of Business as Usual. Ministers were not ready to meet the demands of a large-scale army. Only 70,000 of the 795,000 rifles in stock had been retained on mobilization; the Army's reserves of heavy artillery were sufficient for a five-division, rather than a 50-division, army. At home, barrack space was available for only 175,000 soldiers and uniforms were in short supply. Recruits to the New Armies in 1914 dressed in a combination of khaki, civilian clothing and blue serge tunics borrowed from the Post Office; drilled with sticks or antique rifles; and deservedly earned the soubriquet, 'the ragtime infantry'. Moreover, it was clear, by the spring of 1915, that Business as Usual was failing. The naval blockade had not brought Germany to her knees; the BEF was heavily outnumbered in France; and High Command was complaining of a munitions shortage. By the principles of its pre-1914 strategy, Britain was fighting the wrong war.[93] Cabinet Secretary Maurice Hankey later recalled:

> The government had no national plan for an expansion of the Army, or for its armament. None of the problems had been worked out or thought of at all – exemption from military service of skilled or unskilled labour, machine tools, raw materials, and national industrial mobilisation generally. Consequently ... there was no basis for programme making or for estimating future requirements and supplies ... . In order to avert future chaos both in military recruitment and industrial policy the government had no option but to intervene more systematically on the Home Front: which meant raising the spectre of conscription.[94]

The road to conscription

Compelling men by law to join the armed services was a question not easily decided. The War Office regarded the issue as relatively straightforward. Although total enlistments in the New Armies at the end of 1915 had touched 2.5 million, Kitchener, in a Cabinet memorandum of October, admitted that the flow of voluntary recruits was beginning to run dry. Major Western Front engagements at Loos and the campaign against the Turks in Gallipoli had incurred very heavy casualties, and Kitchener estimated that a regular influx of 35,000 men were needed just to maintain the Army's current strength.[95] However, in making its demands, the Army failed to account for the fact that the real argument for conscription was logistical: any decision needed to be balanced with the labour requirements of the munitions industries and would force the government into formulating a comprehensive strategy on manpower. But this did not form the parameters of the debate. Even if the military case for conscription was undeniable, the issue touched some raw political nerves.

The problem lived in two dimensions. Ideologically, Liberals argued that the decision to fight for one's country was the most fundamental of all human freedoms and, as such, should remain one of individual conscience, however noble the cause or dangerous the foe. Besides, voluntary recruitment was a clear expression of the principles of liberty and individual freedom that had long provided a bulwark against religious and political despotism.[96] On the other hand, Conservatives argued that the moral terms of the conscription debate had been altered by the war itself. While Liberal notions of individual liberty were exquisitely laudable, Britain was plainly embroiled in a struggle for survival; therefore individual freedom had to be subsumed in the national interest for as long as the emergency continued. Democracy needed defending and, in such circumstances, the individual interest had be subordinated to the greater needs of state and nation. Writing in *The Times*, Lord Derby urged:

> It is the duty of every man in this crisis to offer his services to the State, and for the State definitely to allot him his position, whether it be in some branch of His Majesty's forces or in the munition works, or in one of the indispensable industries of this country ... it must be the State and not the individual which decides a man's proper place in the machinery of the country. In other words, if the nation had to apply its whole strength to the achievement of victory, conscription would ensure that the national effort was built upon a principle of equality of sacrifice. Thus liberty had to be surrendered in the short term, so that its long-term future could be secured.[97]

The ideological divisions ensured that there was little political consensus on conscription. The pre-war activities of the National Service League had revealed a powerful current of (largely conservative) public opinion favouring conscription, although with a membership that peaked at 100,000 the League's claims were dubious.[98] Even so, by the spring of 1915 a vociferous campaign for compulsion was gathering strength, with most of the noise coming from its two leading crusaders, Lord Milner (chairman of the League), amplified by Viscount Northcliffe in his *Daily Mail* and *The Times*, who argued provocatively that the anti-conscriptionists were placing their own principles over the greater national interest.[99] By contrast, the anti-conscriptionists were organized in four camps: Liberals who had yet to lose their faith in voluntarism, but nevertheless recognized the need for some form of statutory measure on manpower; the left-wing of the Labour Party; a number of pacifist organizations, like Fenner Brockway's No Conscription Fellowship, which resisted compulsion in all its forms; and the more formidable opposition of the trade unions, whose hostility arose from a fear that military compulsion would lead inevitably to industrial conscription and the loss of workplace rights.[100]

These fractures drove into the heart of Asquith's new and fragile all-party coalition government, formed following the political crisis in May 1915 (of which more later). Broadly, conscription split Asquith's Cabinet along party lines. Not surprisingly, the Conservatives favoured compulsion, but with varying degrees of fervour. Lords Lansdowne and Curzon wanted its immediate introduction and, together with Walter Long, were openly lobbying for conscription by August 1915. Amongst the Liberals on the other hand, Lloyd George and Churchill had no objection, but Grey, Runciman and McKenna were actively opposed, along with the majority of Liberal and Labour MPs. Kitchener was more equivocal on the issue, preferring to support voluntarism, but more perhaps out of loyalty to the Prime Minister.[101] Asquith's own position on conscription has been endlessly debated. Some historians have labelled him a die-hard voluntarist.[102] More accurate perhaps has been the assertion that, whilst Asquith undoubtedly remained sympathetic to the voluntary principle, he had no *a priori* objection to compulsory military recruitment, but was acutely aware of the dangers it posed both to the unity of his government and to national harmony. If conscription was to be introduced, then it had to be carried by political agreement, and public consent, with a demonstration that its need had been proved beyond doubt.[103] To this end, Asquith tried to harness the controversy by initiating a series of deft political manoeuvres.[104]

Asquith's first move was the National Register. Styled as a nationwide audit of the country's manpower, the register required all British citizens between the ages of 16 and 65 to make themselves known to the government. Taken on 15th August 1915, and administered through a small army of volunteer helpers, the register, in its report issued a month later, estimated that, of the five million men who were of military age, nearly 1.5 million were eligible for military service, taking into account those who were married (and unlikely to volunteer) and those who worked in essential occupations.[105] Kitchener immediately exploited the register's findings in calling for weekly recruiting levels to be increased to 35,000.[106] But, with volunteering rates hovering around 19,000, this would be impossible without conscription, and the War Minister's authority in these matters had declined considerably. This informed Asquith's second initiative, the establishment of a War Policy Committee to address the question of manpower resources and army requirements. Unfortunately, the committee proved as indecisive as the Cabinet: its official report, delivered in early September 1915, contained three different opinions. The first recommended freezing the Army at its current size and relying on voluntary recruitment to replace the casualties; the second advocated the immediate introduction of conscription;[107] the third, singularly signed by Arthur Henderson (the Coalition Cabinet's only Labour member), offered Asquith a way through the impasse. Henderson argued that, if conscription was indeed necessary, it could be made palatable to the working classes if it was accompanied by a number of government guarantees: electoral reform; a removal of inequalities 'in our present system'; and new taxes on luxuries, unearned income and war profits, together with a pledge that compulsion would be terminated at the end of the war. Henderson concluded:

> Our aim must be to handle the situation so that compulsion, if it comes, comes by the action of the people themselves. On the alternative of conscription or defeat they will be united again. But they cannot be brought to that alternative suddenly, or apart from the conviction that it is a military necessity. They must have time. And if the time is spent in a final endeavour, made after the most solemn appeal and on a full and reasoned statement of our obligations to our Allies, to meet those obligations voluntarily, I believe that one of two results will follow. Either conscription will be accepted without serious injury to the nation, or it will prove to be unnecessary.[108]

This was enough for Asquith to give voluntarism one last stand. In September 1915 the Prime Minister attempted to silence his critics by appointing Lord Derby, an avowed pro-conscriptionist, as Director-General of Recruiting at the War Office. Derby confessed that he felt 'somewhat in a position of a receiver who was put in to wind up a bankrupt concern' and saw his task as exposing, once and for all, the failures of voluntary recruiting.[109] To this end, Derby announced in October an ingenious scheme whereby all men between the ages of 18 and 41 were to 'attest' a willingness to volunteer for army service if called on by the government. The 'attested' men would then be divided into two groups, single and married, and each subdivided into 23 groups according to age, to be called up in strict order as and when required. Asquith sweetened the pill by pledging in November that attested married men would not be summoned until all the single men had been called.[110] The attestation lists would then be compared to the National Register. If sufficient numbers were raised to meet the needs of the Army, voluntarism would be preserved; if not (as Henderson had indicated), then compulsion would be necessary. This was not quite conscription; but neither was it volunteering.[111]

Derby's report, presented to the Cabinet on 15th December, was disappointing to the voluntarists. Married men, encouraged by the 'Asquith pledge', had attested in larger numbers than single men, many of whom were hardly likely to offer themselves for volunteering if they were to be treated unequally. Hence, of the 2,179,231 available bachelors, according to the National Register, nearly half had ignored the calls to attest. Allowing for medical rejections, Derby estimated that the scheme had produced only 343,386 single men for the military, a tally well below the prescribed minimum of 500,000.[112] Although 103,000 single and 112,000 married men had enlisted during the period of the scheme, this had failed to reverse the downward trend in recruitment, and the reopening of attestation on 10th January 1916 only confirmed that voluntarism had run its course. Asquith was caught. If his pledge to married men was to hold, then all single men had to be called and, given Derby's findings, this would be impossible without compulsion. Under the shadow of threatened resignations by some of its senior members, Asquith's Cabinet, on 28th December, approved the outlines of a Military Service Bill which was presented to Parliament on 5th January 1916.[113] The Military Service Act, imposing conscription on all single men between the ages of 18 and 41, became law on 27th January 1916. The measure did not apply to Ireland.

Even then, the Army's recruitment troubles continued. When the War Office began to conscript single men aged between 19 and 30 in March 1916, in addition to the 'attested Derbyites' signed up during the last week of January, Chief of Imperial General Staff William Robertson reported that, of the 193,891 men called up, 57,416 (approximately 30 per cent) had failed to appear.[114] While this could be attributed to the inaccuracies in the National Register and maladministration by the Area Recruiting Officers, it meant that the Army was still short of 66,000 men at a time when the Allies were planning major offensives at the Somme and Salonika. Consequently, in April, the War Office called up the first of Derby's married groups alongside all 18-year-olds who were ordered to report for duty on their nineteenth birthday. This was subsequently followed by the passing of the second Military Service Act in May 1916, which made all men between the ages of 18 and 40, single or married, liable for military service. 'The opposition to it', Lloyd George remembered later, 'was of quite a trivial nature'.[115]

Dissenters

In spite of the threatened uproar from Liberal and Labour ranks, much of the political damage was contained. The Cabinet remained intact – only Sir John Simon resigned – and Arthur Henderson stayed in the government after receiving Asquith's assurances that industrial conscription would not be introduced, and a promise that a parliamentary conference would be convened to address the question of electoral reform. In the Commons, those 160 Liberal MPs who declared themselves against conscription chose to abstain rather than vote against the government.[116] The Labour Party kept up its opposition to the bill, although its MPs, following the recommendations of the national conference in January 1916, declined to agitate for its repeal.[117] As an appeasing gesture to the anti-conscriptionists, Asquith permitted the insertion of an exemption clause in the Military Service Bill that allowed men to appeal against the call-up on grounds of personal hardship or ill health, as

Figure 2.1 Reluctant recruits. Men enlisted under the Derby scheme, *c.* 1916

fathers of young dependent children, as being engaged on essential war work, or on the ground of 'conscience'. The passage of conscription had been a messy affair, and it was not over yet.

Under the legislation all individuals who sought exemption from the call-up had to appear before their local Military Service Tribunal, a body staffed by magistrates, municipal officers and chosen citizens, alongside a War Office Adviser or military representative. While not convened as courts of law, tribunals were still subject to strict regulation, and all hearings were held in public. Furthermore, the normal rules of evidence did not apply in tribunal hearings: opinion and gossip were admissible.[118] Applicants, if successful, would be granted an exemption certificate, which could be either absolute or conditional. Those whose cases were rejected had the right to appeal, firstly with the local tribunal, but ultimately to a Central Appeals Tribunal at the Home Office in London. Theoretically impartial, the tribunals still attracted criticism. They were staffed largely by elderly members whose strident views occasionally hindered their capacity to make just and objective decisions. The tribunals were also overworked. Charles Messenger has argued that no fewer than 750,000 claims for exemption were submitted during the first six months of 1916: a workload that invariably restricted the tribunals' ability to consider each case carefully, resulting in the vast majority of cases being rejected.[119] Conversely, the tribunals were accused of being too liberal in granting exemptions. Between 1st March 1916 and 31st March 1917, 779,936 men won exemptions from military service, while only 371,500 were compulsorily enlisted: a rate less than that achieved under the voluntary system, and still insufficient for the Army's requirements.[120]

It was, however, the so-called 'conscientious objectors' who would give the authorities their biggest headache. Matters were complicated partly by the failure of the legislation to define the term 'conscience', but this was nevertheless widely interpreted as an objection that rested on 'religious or moral convictions'.[121] Difficulties also arose when objectors could not be identified as one homogenous category. All were opposed to war, but the scale of their resistance differed in intensity. One group, seen by historians as the 'alternativists', refused any work that fell under military control, but were prepared to undertake alternative civilian duties. Tribunals often granted this group exemption from the call-up on condition that they worked in non-military occupations. Their case was usually referred to the Pelham Committee, a Board of Trade body appointed in April 1916 which acted as a conscientious objectors' labour exchange, matching individuals to industries with acute labour shortages, usually munitions, agriculture or docks and harbours, but with army pay rates and no separation allowances.[122] A second, larger group were identified as 'non-combatants': men who accepted being conscripted into the Army, but would refuse to undergo any weapons training, or any related combat duties. Many were sent into a new army unit, the Non-Combatant Corps (NCC), established in March 1916, for service in Britain and France in construction or field engineering, with others deployed as medical and sanitary orderlies, stretcher-bearers and ambulance drivers, all part of army service units, but kept well away from the fighting.[123] Others, who had either ignored the tribunals, or whose appeals had been rejected and were under army arrest facing court-martial and imprisonment, came under the jurisdiction of the Home Office's Brace Committee, which oversaw their employment in forestry, agriculture and road-repair, working in harsh conditions like those of the soldiers in France. Men who were unfit for manual duties were placed in 'work centres' set up in redundant prisons at Warwick and Wakefield, and later at Dartmoor. Any non-combatant conscientious objectors convicted of indiscipline, or in breach of the Home Office's conditions, under the terms of Army Order X issued in May 1916, and Army Order 203 (1916), could be court-martialled, sentenced and returned to a civilian prison. It was estimated that 6,000 men were classed as non-combatants between 1916 and 1918.

This left the 'absolutists': men who refused to apply for exemption, accept tribunal verdicts, or undertake any form of military service. Approximately 1,500 in total, absolutists caused considerable difficulties for the Army. Technically they were seen as conscripts, and their refusal to don uniforms, sign forms or undergo medical examinations placed them at the mercy of military law. In France this ranged from Field Punishment No. 1, 28 days' detention, to court-martial and two years' imprisonment, whilst 34 absolutists received death sentences, later commuted to ten years' penal servitude.[124] Undeterred, some absolutists took their protests into prison, refusing all offers of compromise, facing a cycle of arrest, trial and further incarceration. Some were subjected to acts of brutal ill-treatment including force feeding, mock execution and routine beatings. Seventy-one objectors died as a result of injuries sustained during imprisonment.[125]

Between 1916 and 1918, some 16,500 men registered as conscientious objectors under the terms of the Act. Some 6,000 had their appeals upheld, and nearly 5,000 were granted immunity from combat.[126] History has been kinder to conscientious objectors than their contemporaries. Derided as 'conchies' by the public, vilified by the press, hated by soldiers, mocked in the music halls, the current 'heroic' reputation of conscientious objectors obscures the fact that they represented just one-third of a per cent of all those who were eligible for military service in the Great War.[127] Yet the government's handling of the 'conchies' was symptomatic of its increasing entanglement in the national war effort. After all the early excitement, the unrelenting demands of war put paid to the Business as Usual strategy and dragged ministers to the realization that this conflict would not be won by boundless enthusiasm and patriotic spirit. The country needed to be mobilized as the military had been for all-out war, with a much more systematic use of the state than had hitherto been anticipated. Nowhere was this need greater than in the organization of industrial labour and the production of munitions.

Manpower

Manpower shortages were one of the more formidable hurdles that the government had to overcome during the war. Balancing the demands of the armed services with the needs of industry was a question never fully resolved and was the source of constant tensions between government departments and Army High Command, who often assumed that their needs took priority over the claims of others. The problem was first brought sharply into view by the recruitment drive of Kitchener's New Armies which had pulled in around 120,000 men from skilled trades by 1915, threatening armaments production. Lloyd George, as Minister of Munitions, was reduced to pleading with the Army High Command for their return, while his civil servants hastily devised more formalized arrangements for the drafting of skilled men back into the civilian labour force. The passing of the conscription acts in 1916 allowed the government, in theory at least, to take hold of the problem, but even this failed to reconcile the continuing squabbles for labour between the armed forces, the Ministry of Munitions and the Board of Trade. Asquith attempted a further solution by forming, first, the Cabinet Committee for the Co-ordination of Military and Financial Effort and, subsequently, the Cabinet Committee on the Size of the Army. Neither of these was very effective, however, and, in August 1916, Asquith attempted to place the problem on a more systematic footing by setting up the Manpower Distribution Board under the chairmanship of Austen Chamberlain. Yet Chamberlain, too, found himself being sucked into departmental disputes. From the outset he was too easily persuaded by the Army Council's incessant demands for men and he never resolved the long-running disputes between the War Office and the Munitions Ministry over badging. The War Office was certain that badges giving skilled men exemption from military service were being issued indiscriminately. In response, Edwin Montagu (who had succeeded Lloyd George as minister in the summer of 1916) maintained that indiscriminate conscription was depriving war industries of essential labour. In any event, the ministry was managing to bat away army claims on its workforce with conspicuous success. Defending its interests in the Military Service Tribunals, the ministry managed to save around 1.4 million men from military service by November 1916: a number that swelled to approximately two million by April 1917. The badging system was modified four times between 1916 and 1917. It eventually emerged as a more formal Certified Occupations Scheme, which was essentially an official list of trades and occupations that were deemed critical to the war effort on the Home Front. The list was further overhauled in February 1918, when a more detailed Schedule of Protected Occupations was published, increasing the numbers of men officially excused from the call-up to 2.3 million by the end of October 1918.

Yet this settled only one side of the problem. Lloyd George, when he became Prime Minister in 1916, was convinced that the solution to the manpower issue lay in better administration. Shying away from the notion of industrial conscription, he authorized the establishment of a new National Service Department, led by Austen's half-brother Neville Chamberlain, with a remit to launch a national voluntary scheme of enrolment for industrial work. As Director-General for National Service, Chamberlain was expected to create a more flexible response to the government's manpower needs, but, as a former Lord Mayor of Birmingham, he was ill-prepared for the quagmire of Whitehall bureaucracy. Chamberlain's inexperience created a whiff of incompetence around him, and his capabilities were questioned when he launched the National Service Scheme (basically a variation on the Derby Scheme) on 6th February 1917 in London. The aim was to encourage all males between 18 and 61 to enrol for war work, even if already employed on essential civilian duties. National Service Committees, formed from local council worthies, were appointed to publicize the campaign and direct all those who attested to Labour Exchanges. However, by the end of March 1917 only 206,000 out of the anticipated half-million had registered, of whom only 92,489 were subsequently processed by the employment exchanges. Of those, 50 per cent were already in protected trades, and only 388 were eventually directed into war work. Some localities failed to register any impact. In spite of all Chamberlain's expectations, the scheme failed to live up to its initial promise. The source of the failure lay in two critical errors. First, on appointment Chamberlain clumsily proclaimed himself as 'a dentist to the nation ... extracting teeth with as little inconvenience to the victim as possible and providing a reasonably satisfactory set of artificial ones', while speaking naively of constituting 'an industrial army', with civilians working as troops under the power of a government ready to direct them according to circumstances. Talk of compulsion succeeded in alienating the very workers Chamberlain was trying to attract. But this was compounded by his second error in failing to ease labour shortages by using powers under the Defence of the Realm Act (DORA) to forcefully move women and juveniles out of non-essential trades into war-related industries. Lloyd George quickly lost faith with Chamberlain, but the Director-General could rightly claim that the Prime Minister was undermining him. Chamberlain was never granted the powers he needed, and his post lacked the authority of a parliamentary office. He complained that he had never been given 'a scrap of paper appointing me' and that no direction was given as to where his duties began and ended. His task was further complicated by uncertainties over what industries could be categorized as of national importance and those that were non-essential. This oversight became all too evident when 30,000 'scheduled' agricultural workers were called up in 1917 just when food supplies were being threatened by the German U-boat campaign; furthermore, the removal of 1,005 semi-skilled men under the age of 23 from steel foundries greatly undermined productive capacity at a critical stage of the war. Chamberlain resigned in August 1917, nursing a life-long enmity towards the Prime Minister.

A more systematic approach was achieved under Chamberlain's successor, Auckland Geddes. As the head of a new Ministry of National Service, Geddes assumed responsibility for both army recruitment and labour distribution. Under DORA he gained additional authority to close non-essential industries if necessary and re-assign their workforces to essential war work. A more comprehensive List of Reserved Occupations was finally compiled, together with a new Priority List for employment exchanges. Finally, Geddes became a member of the Cabinet War Priorities Committee, allowing manpower requirements to be considered more accurately in relation to the demands of the Western Front and thus enabling a more harmonious working relationship between those ministries competing for labour. With these mechanisms in place, Geddes could manage and revise manpower resources according to circumstances. The new management scheme reached its climax under the terms of the Military Service (No. 1) Act passed in February 1918, giving the government power both to cancel exemption certificates granted on occupational grounds and to streamline enlistment procedures.

The new regime's major victim was the Army. Its continual arguments for more men had been weakened by the battlefield failures at the Somme, Passchendaele and Cambrai. On the War Priorities Committee, Geddes, giving priority to the agricultural, munitions and shipbuilding industries, argued that he could spare just 100,000 for the Army out of the 3.5 million men of military age in Britain. To make matters worse, when the Cabinet Committee on Manpower reported in December 1917, the Army's claims for an extra 1.3 million recruits were placed behind the requirements of the Admiralty and the needs of ship and tank construction. The Army was also compelled to make its own savings on manpower by scaling down the size of the Home Army, reducing the number of cavalry units and forming smaller divisions. Nevertheless, when the German Spring Offensive was launched in March 1918, pushing the Allies back some 40 miles on the Western Front, the new measures began to work in the Army's favour. Geddes passed the Military Service (No. 2) Act in April, raising the upper age limit for recruits to 50, and made amendments to the Revised Schedule of Protected Operations, raising the minimum exemption age to 23 in those trades protected by the legislation. Conscription was even extended to Ireland, with promises of Home Rule. The new system of manpower administration, though never flawless, at least gave the government the upper hand in managing its scarce labour resources, even if ministerial competition was never subdued. All the same, the system was just about enough to give Britain the men she needed to squeeze victory from catastrophe on the Western Front, with more than a little help from the growing presence of an American army in France. The experience taught future wartime governments some important lessons: government by improvization has its uses, but also its limitations; do not become ensnared between the needs of war and the protection of liberal freedoms when faced with a dangerous enemy; do assume effective control over manpower at the outset; and do not allow inter-departmental rivalries to impede policy making. The experiences of this war left the administrations of the early 1940s much better prepared.

References

History of the Ministry of Munitions, vol. VI, part II, 'The Control of Industrial Manpower 1917–18'.

Gerard DeGroot, *Blighty: British Society in the Era of the Great War*, Harlow: Longman, 1996, pp. 92–106.

Peter Dewey, 'Military Recruiting and the British Labour Force During the First World War', *Historical Journal*, vol. 27, no. 1, 1984, pp. 199–223.

Keith Grieves, *The Politics of Manpower, 1914–18*, Manchester: Manchester University Press, 1988, chs 3–7.

Robert Self, *Neville Chamberlain: A Biography*, Aldershot: Ashgate, 2006, pp. 53–63.

The Times, 22nd January 1917.

John Turner, *British Politics and the Great War*, London: Yale University Press, 1992, pp. 165–70.

Notes

1 *The Times*, 4th August 1914.
2 David Lloyd George, *War Memoirs*, new edn, vol. I, London: Odhams Press, 1938, p. 39.

3 See Arthur Marwick, *The Deluge: British Society and the First World War*, 2nd edn, Basingstoke: Macmillan, 1991, p. 349.

4 *Littlehampton Observer*, 5th August 1914; *West Sussex Gazette*, 6th August 1914.

5 Cited in Malcolm Brown, *1914: The Men Who Went to War*, Basingstoke: Pan Macmillan, 2005, p. 52.

6 Cited in Adrian Gregory, *The Last Great War: British Society and the First World War*, Cambridge: Cambridge University Press, 2008, p. 13.

7 See Adrian Gregory, *The Last Great War*, op. cit., pp. 9–39; see also Niall Ferguson, *The Pity of War*, London: Penguin, 1999, ch. 7; C. Kit Good, 'England Goes to War 1914–15', unpublished PhD thesis, University of Liverpool, 2002; Hew Strachan, *The First World War*, vol. I, *To Arms*, Oxford: Oxford University Press, 2001, pp. 103–10.

8 See Niall Ferguson, *The Ascent of Money*, London: Penguin, 2009.

9 NA, Treasury papers (hereafter 'T') 172/163, part 2, 'The Emergency Financial Measures of 1914', W.R. Fraser.

10 NA, T 171/92, Letter, George Paish to David Lloyd George, 1st August 1914.

11 *The Times*, 31st July 1914; 1st August 1914; 2nd August 1914. See also R.S. Sayers, *The Bank of England 1891–1944*, Cambridge: Cambridge University Press, 1976, appendix 3; 'Sir John Clapham's Account of the Financial Crisis in August 1914', E. Victor Morgan, *Studies in British Financial Policy, 1914–25*, London: Macmillan, 1952, ch. 1; David French, *British Economic and Strategic Planning 1905–1915*, London: Allen & Unwin, 1982, pp. 90–91; NA, T 172/163, part 2, 'The Emergency Financial Measures of 1914', (n.d.).

12 From David French, *British Economic and Strategic Planning 1905–1915*, op. cit., p. 91.

13 NA, Cabinet Papers (hereafter 'CAB') 37/120/100, 'Unemployment Due to the War', 28th August 1914.

14 NA, CAB 1/11, 'Notes by Sir M. Hankey', n.d.; Sir J.A. Hammerton, ed., *A Popular History of the Great War*, vol. I, *The First Phase: 1914*, London: Fleetway House, n.d., ch. 3; David French, 'The Edwardian Crisis and the Origins of the First World War', *International History Review*, vol. IV, no. 2, May 1982, pp. 207–21; Richard van Emden and Steve Humphries, *All Quiet on the Home Front*, London: Headline, 2003, p. 16; Adrian Gregory, *The Last Great War*, op. cit., pp. 28–29.

15 NA, CAB, 15/5, 'War Book', 1914 edn, chs 1–11.

16 See David French, *British Economic and Strategic Planning 1905–1915*, op. cit., ch. 2, 5; David French, 'The Rise and Fall of Business as Usual', in Kathleen Burk, ed., *War and the State: The Transformation of British Government, 1914–1919*, London, Allen & Unwin, 1982, pp. 14–19; Sokolov Grant, 'The Origins of the War Book', *Journal of the Royal Services Institute*, vol. 117, 1972.

17 NA, CAB 22/1, 'Minutes of the War Council', 6th August 1914; Gerard DeGroot, *Blighty: British Society in the Era of the Great War*, Harlow: Longman, 1996, p. 58.

18 Arthur Marwick, *The Deluge: British Society and the First World War*, op. cit., 2nd edn, pp. 76–77; Sir J.A. Hammerton, ed., *A Popular History of the Great War*, op. cit., pp. 71–72.

19 NA, CAB 42/2/2, CID Paper 2145B: List of Committees Appointed to Consider Questions Arising During the Present War, 1st March 1915; see also L. Margaret Barnett, *British Food Policy During the First World War*, London: Allen & Unwin, 1985, p. 21.

20 *The Times*, 5th August 1914; Trevor Wilson, *The Myriad Faces of War*, Cambridge: Polity Press, 1986, p. 215.

21 NA, CAB 1/11, 'Miscellaneous Records: Notes by Sir M. Hankey', n.d.; David French, *British Economic and Strategic Planning*, op. cit., pp. 88–89.

22 NA, CAB 1/11, 'Miscellaneous Records: Notes by Sir M. Hankey, n.d.; NA, CAB 16/29, 'Report and Proceedings of the Standing Sub-committee of the

CID on the Insurance of British Shipping in Time of War', 12th May 1914; NA, CAB 2/3, Minutes of the 127th Meeting of the CID, 21st May 1914; David French, *British Economic and Strategic Planning 1905–1915*, op. cit., pp. 67–69; Sir J.A. Hammerton, ed., *A Popular History of the Great War*, op. cit., p. 69.

23 See David French, 'The Edwardian Crisis and the Origins of the First World War', *International History Review*, vol. 4, no. 2, 1982.

24 *The Times*, 5th August 1914.

25 W.H. Beveridge, *British Food Control*, Oxford: Oxford University Press, 1928, p. 7.

26 NA, CAB 1/11, 'Miscellaneous Records: Notes by Sir M. Hankey', n.d.; NA, CAB 17/102B, 'Report on the Opening of the War by the CID Historical Section', 1st November 1914; David French, *British Economic and Strategic Planning 1905–1915*, op. cit., pp. 88–90, pp. 101–2; see also ch. 7.

27 Hartley Withers, *The War and Lombard Street*, London: Smith, Elder, 1915, p. 32.

28 NA, T 171/92, 'Sir George Paish to Lloyd George', 1st August 1914; NA, T 170/55, 'Conference Between the Chancellor of the Exchequer and Representatives of the Bankers and Traders', 4th August 1914; see also R.S. Sayers, *The Bank of England 1891–1944*, op. cit., pp. 34–7; E. Victor Morgan, *Studies in British Financial Policy, 1914–25*, op. cit., pp. 12–15; David Lloyd George, *War Memoirs*, op. cit., pp. 63–66; Kathleen Burk, 'The Treasury: From Impotence to Power', in Kathleen Burk, ed., *War and the State*, op. cit., p. 87.

29 NA, T 172/163, part 2, 'The Emergency Financial Measures of 1914' (W.R. Fraser, n.d.); David Lloyd George, *War Memoirs*, op. cit., pp. 66–70; David French, *British Economic and Strategic Planning 1905–1915*, op. cit., pp. 93–95.

30 NA, T 170/55, 'Conference Between the Chancellor of the Exchequer and Representatives of Bankers and Traders', 4th August 1914; emphasis as in document. See also David French, *British Economic and Strategic Planning 1905–1915*, op. cit., p. 92; David French, 'The Rise and Fall of Business as Usual', op. cit.

31 David French, *British Economic and Strategic Planning 1905–1915*, op. cit., p. 34.

32 See H.H. Asquith, *Memories and Reflections, 1852–1927*, vol. II, London: Cassell, 1928, p. 24.

33 See Ian Colvin, *The Life of Lord Carson*, vol. III, London: Gollancz, 1934–36, p. 79.

34 Peter Simkins, *Kitchener's Army*, Barnsley: Pen and Sword, 2007, pp. 31–38.

35 NA, War Office papers (hereafter 'WO') 163/44, Minutes of the Meeting of the Military Members of the War Council, 10th and 14th August 1914; Viscount Reginald Esher, *The Tragedy of Lord Kitchener*, London: John Murray, 1921, p. 35; Peter Simkins, *Kitchener's Army: The Raising of the New Armies*, op. cit., pp. 38–40; Charles Messenger, *Call-to-Arms: The British Army 1914–18*, London: Cassell, 2006, pp. 94–95.

36 David G. Chandler and Ian Beckett, *The Oxford History of the British Army*, Oxford: Oxford University Press, 1994, p. 211; Peter Simkins, *Kitchener's Army*, op. cit., pp. 6–19; Gerard DeGroot, *Blighty*, op. cit., pp. 24–26.

37 Viscount Grey of Falloden, *Twenty-Five Years, 1892–1916*, vol. II, London: Hodder & Stoughton, 1925, p. 287.

38 Violet Bonham Carter, *Winston Churchill as I Knew Him*, London: Eyre, Spottiswood & Collins, 1965, p. 319.

39 Stephen Koss, *Asquith*, New York: St Martin's Press, 1976, p. 169; Winston Churchill, *The World Crisis 1911–1918*, London: Penguin Classics, 2007, p. 126; Viscount Grey of Falloden, *Twenty-Five Years, 1892–1916*, vol. 2, 1925, op. cit., pp. 286–88.

40 Ian Beckett, 'The Territorial Force', in Ian Beckett and Keith Simpson, eds, *A Nation in Arms: A Social Study of the British Army in the First World War*,

Manchester: Manchester University Press, 1985, p. 130; Peter Simkins, *Kitchener's Army*, op. cit., pp. 39–46; Charles Messenger, *Call-to-Arms*, op. cit., ch. 3.

41 NA, WO 73/97, General Monthly Return of the Regimental Strength of the British Army, part III, May–Aug. 1914; NA, WO 73/98, General Monthly Return of the Regimental Strength of the British Army, part III, Sept.–Dec. 1914; NA, CAB 21/107, 'Recruiting in England'.

42 *The Manchester Guardian*, 6th August 1914; NA, WO 159/18, War Office Memorandum, 4th September 1914; NA, T 1/11662/17287/14, Memoranda: War Proposals Committee, Aug.–Oct. 1914; David Silbey, *The British Working Class and Enthusiasm for War, 1914–1916*, London: Frank Cass, 2005, p. 25.

43 Adrian Gregory, *The Last Great War*, op. cit., p. 31; Gerard DeGroot, *Blighty*, op. cit., pp. 47–48.

44 Cited in Jon Stallworthy, *Anthem for Doomed Youth: Twelve Soldier-Poets of the First World War*, London: Constable, 2002, p. 25.

45 Max Arthur, *Forgotten Voices of the Great War*, op. cit., p. 16.

46 Imperial War Museum (hereafter 'IWM'), 81/14/1, Gosling, A.J. (Papers), 1914–18.

47 David Silbey, *The British Working Class and Enthusiasm for War, 1914–1916*, op. cit., p. 108.

48 *The Times*, 25th–31st August 1914; see also Peter Simkins, *Kitchener's Army*, op. cit., p. 64; Adrian Gregory, *The Last Great War*, op. cit., p. 32.

49 Peter Simkins, *Kitchener's Army*, op. cit., p. 64; Adrian Gregory, *The Last Great War*, op. cit., p. 32. See also the comments of Private F.B. Vaughan, in Max Arthur, ed., *Forgotten Voices of the Great War*, London: Ebury Press, 2003, pp. 16–18.

50 See Anne Summers, 'Militarism in Britain before the Great War', *History Workshop Journal*, vol. 2, 1, 1976, pp. 104–23.

51 See Geoffrey Best, 'Militarism and the Victorian Public School', in Brian Simon and Ian Bradley, eds, *The Victorian Public School: Studies in the Development of an Educational Institution*, Dublin: Gill & Macmillan, 1975, pp. 129–46; Gerard DeGroot, *Blighty*, op. cit., p. 32.

52 T.W. Bamford, 'Thomas Arnold and the Victorian Idea of a Public School', in Brian Simon and Ian Bradley, *The Victorian Public School*, op. cit., pp. 68–71.

53 W.J. Reader, *At Duty's Call: A Study in Obsolete Patriotism*, Manchester: Manchester University Press, pp. 83–100; 'Athleticism: A Case Study of the Evolution of an Educational Ideology', in Brian Simon and Ian Bradley, *The Victorian Public School*, op. cit., pp. 147–67; Gerard DeGroot, *Blighty*, op. cit., pp. 31–36.

54 Cited in Gerard DeGroot, *Blighty*, op. cit., p. 36.

55 Rupert Brooke, 'Peace' (1914), from Jon Stallworthy, *Anthem for Doomed Youth*, op. cit., p. 16.

56 W.J. Reader, *At Duty's Call*, op. cit., pp. 27–30; John Springhall, 'Building Character in the British Boy', in J.A. Mangan and James Walvin, eds, *Manliness and Morality: Middle-class Masculinity in Britain and America, 1800–1940*, Manchester: Manchester University Press, 1987, p. 64; Gerard DeGroot, *Blighty*, op. cit., pp. 38–39.

57 Richard van Emden and Steve Humphries, *All Quiet on the Home Front*, op. cit., pp. 4–5; David Silbey, *The British Working Class and Enthusiasm for War, 1914–1916*, op. cit., pp. 50–54.

58 W.J. Reader, *At Duty's Call*, op. cit., p. 77; John Springhall, *Sure and Steadfast: A History of the Boys' Brigade, 1883–1983*, London: Collins, 1983.

59 W.J. Reader, *At Duty's Call*, op. cit., p. 77.

60 J.M. Mackenzie, 'The Imperial Pioneer and Hunter and the British Masculine Stereotype in Late Victorian and Edwardian Times', in J.A. Mangan and James Walvin, *Manliness and Morality: Middle-class Masculinity in Britain and America, 1800–1940*, op. cit., p. 176.

61 Lord Baden-Powell of Gilwell, *Scouting for Boys: A Handbook for Instruction in Good Citizenship*, revised edn, London: Horace Cox, 1908, pp. 256–80; T.H.E. Travers, 'Technology, Tactics and Morale: Jean de Bloch, the Boer War, and British Military Theory, 1900–914', *Journal of Modern History*, vol. 51, no. 2, June 1979, pp. 264–86; W.J. Reader, *At Duty's Call*, op. cit., p. 77; Zara S. Steiner and Keith Neilson, *Britain and the Origins of the First World War*, 2nd edn, Basingstoke: Macmillan, 2003, pp. 168–70.

62 Gerard DeGroot, *Blighty*, op. cit., pp. 40–42.

63 Adrian Gregory, *The Last Great War*, op. cit., p. 31.

64 See William Linton Andrews, *Haunting Years: The Commentaries of a War Territorial*, London: Hutchinson, 1930, pp. 11–13.

65 David Silbey, *The British Working Class and Enthusiasm for War, 1914–1916*, op. cit., pp. 82–103.

66 Adrian Gregory, *The Last Great War*, op. cit., pp. 31–32.

67 Peter Simkins, *Kitchener's Army*, op. cit., p. 83; Randolph S. Churchill, *Lord Derby: 'King of Lancashire'*, London: William Heinemann, 1959, p. 187; *Manchester Guardian*, 7th October 1915; Adrian Gregory, *The Last Great War: British Society and the First World War*, op. cit., pp. 78–79.

68 Peter Simkins, *Kitchener's Army*, op. cit., p. 83.

69 Ian Beckett, 'The Nation in Arms, 1914–18', in Ian Beckett and Keith Simpson, *A Nation in Arms*, op. cit., pp. 7–12; J.M. Winter, *The Great War and the British People*, 2nd edn, Basingstoke: Palgrave, 2003, pp. 30–33; Peter Simkins, *Kitchener's Army*, op. cit., pp. 82–100; Hew Strachan, *The First World War*, op. cit., p. 160.

70 British Library (hereafter 'BL'), Add. Mss. 54192, A, Minutes of the Parliamentary Recruiting Committee, vol. I, 'Minutes of Preliminary Meeting of the Parliamentary Recruiting Committee', 27th August 1914, p. 1; Letter, R. Humphrey Davies, 4th May 1967; Roy Douglas, 'Voluntary Enlistment in the First World War and the Work of the Parliamentary Recruiting Committee', *Journal of Modern History*, vol. 42, no. 4, December 1970, pp. 564–85.

71 BL, Add. Mss. 54192, Minutes of the Parliamentary Recruiting Committee, op. cit., Minutes of meetings, 28th–31st August 1914; Roy Douglas, op. cit., pp. 575–76.

72 BL, Add. Mss. 54192, A, op. cit., Minutes of meetings, 28th–31st August 1914; Minutes of Meetings of General Purposes Committee, 21st October 1914; 26th October 1914; *The Times Recruiting Supplement*, 3rd November 1914; *The Times*, 11th November 1914; Roy Douglas, 'Voluntary Enlistment in the First World War and the Work of the Parliamentary Recruiting Committee', op. cit., p. 572; Basil Williams, *Raising and Training the New Armies*, London: Constable, 1918, pp. 16–17; W.J. Reader, *At Duty's Call*, op. cit., p. 113; Peter Simkins, *Kitchener's Army*, op. cit., p. 62.

73 Alec John Dawson, *How to Help Lord Kitchener*, London: Constable, 1914, p. 50; W.J. Reader, *At Duty's Call*, op. cit., p. 118.

74 NA, WO 106/367, 'Parliamentary Recruiting Committee: Meetings Sub-Department Report, March 1916', W.J. Reader, *At Duty's Call*, op. cit., pp. 118–19.

75 NA, WO 106/367; 'Parliamentary Recruiting Committee: Meetings Sub-Department Report, March 1916'.

76 W.J. Reader, *At Duty's Call*, op. cit., pp. 117–18. See also A.J.P. Taylor, *English History 1914–1945*, Oxford: Oxford University Press, 1975 edn, p. 20; A.J.P. Taylor, 'Politics in the First World War', in *Essays in English History*, Harmondsworth: Penguin, 1976, p. 224.

77 W.J.Reader, *At Duty's Call*, op. cit., p. 117; see also 'Kitty Eckersley, Mill Worker', in Max Arthur, *Forgotten Voices of the Great War*, op. cit., pp. 14–15. This topic is discussed further in Chapter 8.

78 W.J. Reader, *At Duty's Call*, op. cit., p. 115.

79 Philip Dutton, 'Moving Images? The Parliamentary Committee's Poster Campaign 1914–16', *Imperial War Museum Review*, 1989, pp. 43–58; W.J. Reader, *At Duty's Call*, op. cit., pp. 113–14. See also Chapter 8.

80 Basil Williams, *Raising and Training the New Armies*, op. cit., p. 16; NA, WO 106/367, 'Parliamentary Recruiting Committee: Meetings Sub-Department Report, March 1916'.

81 Gerard DeGroot, *Blighty*, op. cit., p. 66.

82 Peter Simkins, *Kitchener's Army*, op. cit., p. 124; W.J. Reader, *At Duty's Call*, p. 119. See also 'Rifleman Norman Demuth', 'Private S.C. Lang' in Max Arthur, *Forgotten Voices of the Great War*, op. cit., p. 19 and p. 62 respectively.

83 *Statistics of the Military Effort of the British Empire During the Great War*, London: HMSO, 1922, p. 364; NA, CAB 21/107, 'Recruiting in England', 13th April 1916.

84 *Statistics of the Military Effort of the British Empire*, op. cit., p. 364; NA, CAB 21/107, 'Recruiting in England'.

85 NA, WO 161/82, 'Armies Home and Abroad; Statistical Abstract', 1920; David Silbey, *The British Working Class and Enthusiasm for War*, op. cit., p. 27.

86 Peter Simkins, *Kitchener's Army*, op. cit., p. 106.

87 Peter Simkins, *Kitchener's Army*, op. cit., pp. 108–9.

88 NA, WO 162/26, 'Letters on Recruits, 1914, Telegram of 1st September to Commanders of Recruitment Centres'; NA, WO 159/18, 'Copy of Telegram Despatched by the War Office (A.G.2.B), 4th Sept. 1914'; *Statistics of the Military Effort of the British Empire During the Great War*, op. cit.; 'Supply Services During the War: Note by the Quartermaster-General to the Forces (the late General, Sir J.S. Cowans)', p. 833.

89 Peter Simkins, 'Soldiers and Civilians: Billeting in Britain and France', in Ian Beckett and Keith Simpson, *A Nation in Arms*, op. cit., pp. 169–71.

90 BL, 10823 k 28, George Butterworth (1885–1916), *Diary and Letters*, London and York: privately published, 1918, pp. 19–20.

91 NA, CAB 21/107, 'Recruiting in England', op. cit., Ian Beckett, 'The Nation in Arms', op. cit., pp. 8–9; Peter Simkins, 'Soldiers and Civilians', op. cit., pp. 105–06; J.M. Osborne, *The Voluntary Recruiting Movement in Britain, 1914–16*, New York: Garland, 1982, pp. 73–105; *Manchester Guardian*, 27th November 1914.

92 Parliamentary Recruiting Committee, *Leaflets of the Parliamentary Recruiting Committee*, London: HMSO, 1914–16, 28th October 1914.

93 Hew Strachan, *To Arms*, op. cit., p. 1067; David French, *British Economic and Strategic Planning*, op. cit., pp. 118–19.

94 NA, T 181/50, 'Royal Commission on the Private Manufacture of, and Trading in, Arms, Annex II, Pre-war Orders', Sir M. Hankey, May 1935; David French, *British Economic and Strategic Planning*, op. cit., pp. 127–28.

95 NA, CAB 37/135/15, 'Recruiting for the Army', 8th October 1915; Charles Messenger, *Call to Arms*, op. cit., p. 131.

96 See Viscount Esher, 'The Voluntary Principle', *National Review*, September 1910, pp. 41–47; John Rae, *Conscience and Politics: The British Government and the Conscientious Objector to Military Service 1916–1919*, Oxford: Oxford University Press, 1970, pp. 5–6; David French, *British Economic and Strategic Planning*, op. cit., p. 128; Edward David, ed., *Inside Asquith's Cabinet: From the Diaries of Charles Hobhouse*, London: John Murray, 1977, pp. 184–85.

97 *The Times Recruiting Supplement*, 3rd November 1915.

98 Anne Summers, 'Militarism in Britain before the Great War', op. cit.; Gerard DeGroot, *Blighty*, op. cit., p. 27.

99 John Rae, *Conscience and Politics*, op. cit., p. 8.

100 See Denis Hayes, *Conscription Conflict*, London: Sheppard Press, 1949, ch. 18; NA, CAB 27/2, 'Committee of Imperial Defence: War Policy 1915;

Supplementary Memorandum: Memorandum by Mr A. Henderson, Sept 7th 1915', pp. 25–29; NA, CAB 37/134/5, A.H., 'Manpower and Conscription', 7th September 1915.

101 R.J.Q. Adams and Philip Poirier, *The Conscription Controversy in Great Britain 1900–18*, Ohio: Ohio State University Press, 1987, pp. 93–118.

102 See Trevor Wilson, *The Downfall of the Liberal Party, 1914–1935*, London: Collins, 1966, p. 73; A.J.P. Taylor, 'Politics in the First World War', in A.J.P. Taylor, *Essays in English History*, op. cit., pp. 218–54; Lord Beaverbrook, *Politicians and the War 1914–1916*, London: Oldbourne, 1960.

103 *Hansard Parliamentary Debates*, 5th series, vol. LXXV, 2nd November 1915, cols 521–22.

104 See R.J.Q. Adams, 'Asquith's Choice: The May Coalition and the Coming of Conscription, 1915–16', *Journal of British Studies*, vol. 25, no. 3, 1986, pp. 247–63; R.J.Q Adams and Philip Poirier, *The Conscription Controversy in Great Britain 1900–18*, op. cit., pp. 106–07. See John Gordon Little, 'H.H. Asquith and Britain's Manpower Problem, 1914–15', *History*, vol. 82, no. 267, 1997, pp. 397–409.

105 See 'Report on Recruiting by the Earl of Derby, K.G., Director-General of Recruiting', Cmnd 8149, London: HMSO, 1916, pp. 5–6; Peter Simkins, *Kitchener's Army*, op. cit., pp. 144–48; Keith Grieves, *The Politics of Manpower, 1914–18*, Manchester: Manchester University Press, 1988, pp. 21–2.

106 See NA, CAB 37/135/15, 'Recruiting for the Army', October 1915.

107 NA, CAB 37/134/9, 'War Policy Committee Report', 8th September 1915.

108 NA, CAB 37/134/5, A.H., 'Manpower and Conscription', 7th September 1915.

109 Stephen Koss, *Asquith*, op. cit., p. 199; *London Star*, 6th October 1915, cited in R.J.Q. Adams, 'Asquith's Choice', op. cit., p. 254.

110 See Charles Messenger, *Call to Arms*, op. cit., pp. 131–32; *Hansard Parliamentary Debates*, 5th series, vol. LXXV, 2nd November 1915, col. 524.

111 Peter Simkins, *Kitchener's Army*, op. cit., pp. 150–56. See also *The Times*, 16th October 1915; NA, PRO 30/57/73, 'Circular from Lord Derby October 1915'.

112 NA, CAB 37/139/41, 'Report on Recruiting by the Earl of Derby, K.G., Director-General of Recruiting', Cmnd 8149, London: HMSO, 1916, pp. 5–7; Randolph S. Churchill, *Lord Derby, 'King of Lancashire'*, London: Heinemann, 1959, pp. 194–98.

113 NA, CAB 41/36/56, 'Conscription for Military Service', 28th December 1915; NA, CAB 41/37/1, 'The Military Service Bill', 1st January 1916.

114 David Lloyd George, *War Memoirs*, op. cit., p. 438; Peter Simkins, *Kitchener's Army*, op. cit., p. 158.

115 David Lloyd George, *War Memoirs*, op. cit., p. 439.

116 *Hansard Parliamentary Debates*, 5th series, 27th January 1916, vol. LXXVII, cols 1251–55, 1038–42.

117 *The Times*, 28th January 1916; John Rae, *Conscience and Politics*, op. cit., pp. 37–39.

118 See John Rae, *Conscience and Politics*, op. cit., ch. 6. See also I. Slocombe, 'Recruitment into the Armed Services During the First World War: The Work of the Military Tribunals in Wiltshire 1915–18', *Local Historian*, vol. 30, no. 2, 2000, pp. 105–23.

119 Charles Messenger, *Call to Arms*, op. cit., p. 136.

120 *Statistics of the Military Effort of the British Empire*, pp. 364, 367.

121 See www.nationalarchives.gov.uk, 'First World War: Conscientious Objectors and Exemptions from Service, 1914–18'.

122 See www.ppu.org.uk/learn/infodocs/cos/st_co_wwone.html.

123 John Rae, *Conscience and Politics*, op. cit., pp. 192–93; Charles Messenger, *Call to Arms*, op. cit., p. 137.

124 John Rae, *Conscience and Politics*, op. cit., pp. 201–05; Charles Messenger, *Call to Arms*, op. cit., pp. 137–38; Howard Marten, in IWM, *The First World War Remembered*, op. cit.

125 John W. Graham, *Conscription and Conscience: A History 1916–1919*, London: Allen & Unwin, 1922, pp. 322, 347–52.

126 *General Annual Reports of the British Army for the Period from 1st October 1913 to 30th September 1919*, Cmnd 1193, London: HMSO, 1921, p. 9; Charles Messenger, *Call to Arms*, op. cit., p. 136.; John Rae, *Conscience and Politics*, op. cit., p. 71.

127 John Rae, *Conscience and Politics*, op. cit., p. 71. See also the comments by Dick Read, quoted in Charles Messenger, *Call to Arms*, op. cit., p. 142. A popular music hall song, 'The Conscientious Objector's Lament', written by Gitz Rice in 1917 and sung by Alfred Lester, set out to ridicule conscientious objectors with the refrain 'Send out the Army and the Navy, send out the rank and file, send out the brave old Territorials, they'll face the danger with a smile. Send out the boys of the Old Brigade, who made old England free, send out me brother, me sister and me mother, but for Gawd's sake don't send me.'

3 The industry of conflict

Even though the British public were slow to realize it, by the end of 1914 it was clear that this was a different kind of war. After nearly a century of relative peace in Europe, Britain's experience of continental warfare was confined to memories of Napoleon's campaigns and the bloody experiences of the Crimea, while the South African conflict provided few lessons for the war that was unfolding on the Western Front. Here the BEF faced an enemy that was not just superior in guns and munitions, but ready to deploy new and technologically sophisticated weaponry that both amazed and appalled British soldiers, yet soon led to demands that they be armed in much the same way. This then would be as much a war of technology and scientific innovation as it was of raw firepower. For Lloyd George, this required nothing less than the mass mobilization of the country's industrial and technical resources to be managed by a new ministry with new methods and a tightly controlled industrial workforce. Such a state-driven system challenged old practices and attitudes, and acute tensions were to emerge between government and people as the country adapted to a different reality. The new strategies were certainly innovative in outlook and approach, although their more distant consequences were far from clear.

Early war predicaments

For much of the pre-war era the Army had been left playing second fiddle to the Navy in the procurement of armaments, new munitions and wireless technologies. Kitchener admitted to Walter Runciman, President of the Board of Trade, that equipping the BEF had been 'not much more difficult than buying a straw hat at Harrods'.[1] Estimates of the Army's requirements in 1914 relied mainly on the recommendations of the War Office's 1904 'Mowat' Committee and the Army Council's calculations of 1913, which saw the BEF despatched to France with shell reserves approximating to 29 million rounds and 795,000 rifles, enough for four major battles in the expected short war.[2] Yet, by the time the war of movement on the Western Front had settled into 'positional warfare', the Army's stock of shell rounds had shrunk to just three million and, though its 'shrapnel' shells (hollow iron canisters that shot out a profusion of small lead balls across a large area on detonation) had proved effective in cutting barbed wire, Sir John French, Commander-in-Chief of the BEF, insisted that shifting the Germans out of their deep dugouts required more heavy guns and greatly increased supplies of high-explosive ammunition.[3] Alongside these weapons of siege warfare came all the accoutrements of trench life: barbed wire, sandbags, wooden duckboards, corrugated iron for shelters, shovels and picks, flare pistols, light machine guns and trench mortars.

Predictably, this brought new stresses on the War Office. As the Army's traditional armaments supplier, its early policy was to centralize production at the Royal Ordnance Factories at Woolwich, the Royal Gunpowder Factory at Waltham Abbey and the Royal Small Arms Factory at Enfield Lock, with larger orders being contracted to a few trusted firms, principally Vickers, Armstrong, Cammell-Laird and the Coventry Ordnance Works.[4] War Office officials also streamlined the placing of new contracts, with fresh orders being passed directly to the managers of the Ordnance Factories and the larger armament firms, instead of being processed through Whitehall, and munitions firms being given the freedom to subcontract any work to smaller outfits if orders went beyond their productive capacity. The entire process was lubricated by a Treasury cash guarantee of £20 million which indemnified companies against the financial losses incurred as a result of expanding their plant and buildings and converting machinery to arms manufacture.[5] Consequently, the Royal Factory at Enfield doubled its rifle production from a weekly total of 700 in August 1914 to 1,500 by January 1915.[6] And total output of munitions across all manufacturers increased 90 per cent between August and October 1914, 186 per cent by January 1915 and 388 per cent by March.[7]

It was not enough. One difficulty lay in the War Office's obligation to supply two armies at once. Raising and equipping the New Armies generated constant pressure on production, yet their immediate needs were forsaken in favour of steering the bulk of ordnance production, at Sir John French's insistence, to the BEF in France. By November 1914, Kitchener's first New Army had only 30 per cent of the rifles it required and 11 per cent of its field guns, while two of the BEF's three corps had only sufficient ammunition for one day's combat.[8] War Office conservatism did not help. Kitchener's efforts to boost supplies by placing orders with firms outside the traditional suppliers met with opposition from his officials, and new innovations in weaponry were dismissed as impractical. Motor manufacturer Herbert Austin's offer to mass-produce lorries and military transport vehicles for the Army was dismissed as unnecessary, and his factories were hastily turned over to shell making, working to designs drawn on a scrap of War Office notepaper.[9]

In other respects, however, the War Office was a victim of circumstances. Turning half the country's existing shell-producing machinery over to manufacturing high-explosive shells took at least ten weeks, and some firms were reluctant to undertake expensive alterations to their plant and facilities for producing *materiel* that was far removed from their usual business, with no guarantees of orders beyond a few weeks of production. There were also doubts over the capacity of Britain's industries to meet the new demands. Vickers's deliveries of high-explosive shells were delayed for five months because of shortages in machine tools, raw materials and technical expertise. Workshop capability in gauge making, for example, crucial in the production of gun fuses, was extremely limited in Britain. Few British firms were able to manufacture fuses with accuracies down to three-thousandths of an inch and this often left shell production reliant on an uninterrupted supply from the USA.[10] Labour shortages added to War Office woes. As early as December 1914 armaments firms were complaining that production levels had been affected by the loss of men to the Army. By June 1915 two Royal factories and sixteen private firms engaged in munitions manufacture were short of 14,000 skilled workers. In July four-fifths of munitions-making equipment was in use for only a single shift, and even in December 750 presses and other machines lay idle. Out of the 38,806,046 rounds of all calibres on order, only 1,972,558 (including 800 of the 2,338 18-pound shells) had been delivered. Across-the-board shortages ranged from rifles (12 per cent) to machine guns (55 per cent) and high explosives (92 per cent).[11] Clearly, increasing orders for munitions was not the same as taking deliveries, and many of the War Office's targets had been fixed without sufficiently harnessing industrial capacity to meet the new orders. The War Office's performance had its merits, but its shortcomings in meeting new wartime demands fuelled the impression that its structure, policy and methods belonged to the old world of war.

Lloyd George's interest

The War Office's struggle with munitions supply made it a target for a growing body of detractors. Elements of the press talked openly of a government department devoted exclusively to armaments production. Meanwhile Lloyd George, increasingly scathing of War Office bureaucracy, in particular of Master-General of the Ordnance Stanley von Donop's failure to tell firms about the Treasury's financial support for expanding their munitions-making facilities, successfully badgered Asquith into establishing a Cabinet Committee on Munitions (chaired by a reluctant Kitchener) to monitor supplies.[12] By February 1915, Lloyd George was calling for powers to compel companies into munitions production, with controls over industry and labour – a plan that was part of his grand strategy, first aired in a 15-page Cabinet memorandum, 'Some Further Considerations on the Conduct of the War'.[13] Kitchener simply regarded Lloyd George's interference as a crude attempt to grasp power, and the simmering tensions between the two from October 1914 to May 1915 ensured that the administration of munitions supply came to resemble a two-ringed circus. The rapid demise of the Cabinet's Munitions Committee inspired Lloyd George to launch another attempt to control armaments policy by persuading Asquith in March 1915 to set up a Treasury

Munitions of War Committee, ostensibly to strengthen the armaments industry and clear the deficits in shell deliveries. With Lloyd George as chairman, the body assumed wider powers to issue contracts and initiate policy, noticeably excluding Kitchener from its membership. Kitchener reacted by setting up a War Office Armaments Output Committee (AOC) with a remit to secure additional resources for munitions production. Lloyd George then attempted to incorporate the AOC as the executive arm of his own committee, making its status as a War Office body less tenable. An administrative stand-off thus ensued. The Chancellor's committee could modify War Office policy as it saw fit, but the War Office could veto the Chancellor's committee's work by refusing to sign any contracts that it had negotiated.[14]

Yet it was Kitchener's initiatives that would have a more lasting impact. The first was the establishment of co-operative groups. One of the drawbacks in shell production was the inability of many smaller firms to manufacture complete shells. Most, however, could make individual components. So, in January 1915 the Board of Trade and the Engineering Employers' Federation argued that production could be increased if contracts for parts manufacture could be offered to smaller enterprises who could then pool their machine tools, expertise and manpower with other firms within a defined region, all working on a co-operative basis. The practice was first tried in Leicester and its success encouraged the AOC to develop the regional system into a national network of small-scale armaments production. By May, 2,500 firms were working on War Office contracts under this arrangement.[15] Kitchener's second initiative was to co-opt outside experts. His appointment of the barrister-cum-scientist Lord Moulton to chair a committee on explosives in November 1914 was a notable success and the practice was continued under the authority of Allan M. Smith, of the Engineering Employers' Federation, drafted in as the secretary of the Armaments Committee. The appointment of George Macauley Booth as chairman of this body was equally important in applying the Leicester co-operative system on a national scale.[16] However, frictions arose when Sir Percy Girouard (a former soldier who had served with Kitchener in South Africa) was brought onto the Committee in the early spring of 1915. Girouard disliked Booth's regional system, arguing instead that issuing large contracts to major firms was a better way of boosting output. Booth was reluctant to give way and the resulting compromise saw British munitions production divided into two zones, one operating under the Girouard system and the other on a co-operative basis. This arrangement would subsequently become an integral part of the Ministry of Munitions.[17]

New ministry, new methods

The new ministry was brought into being following the 'Shells Scandal' of May 1915 and Asquith's subsequent decision to reform his government as an all-party coalition (see Chapter 4). With Lloyd George in charge, the Ministry of Munitions was of its time and for its time. Its existence had no precedent; neither was it replicated during the Second World War. Through his memoirs Lloyd George conjured an institution full of buzz and hum, innovation and achievement, although the minister was always inclined to borrow ideas and fashion them to his own purposes. Kitchener's policy of recruiting prominent businessmen was shamelessly exploited. From the outset, Lloyd George stuffed the ministry's management with business entrepreneurs, the so-called 'men of push and go'. Only one appointment was made from within the government, that of the distinguished physician Dr Christopher Addison from the Board of Education. Otherwise men were recruited who could improvise in a crisis. Within three months over 90 had been enlisted with a wide range of skills and backgrounds, including Samuel Hardman Lever, a Merseyside detergent manufacturer; Eric Geddes, deputy general manager of the North-Eastern Railway; Lord James Stevenson, distiller of Johnny Walker whisky; Sir Ernest Moir, builder of docks and harbours; William Beveridge (a man who was credited with an 'unrivalled knowledge of labour problems'); as well as businessmen recruited from the coal, shipbuilding, machine tools (Alfred Herbert in Coventry) and armaments industries.[18]

The practice was continued in the construction of the ministry's internal organization. One of George Booth's innovations was to structure the ministry around four principal departments: Engineer Munitions, Munitions Supply, Explosives and the Secretariat. Munitions Supply was further divided into subsections: Artillery Production (led by Geddes); Artillery Ammunition (led by G.H. West); while Booth took responsibility for organization and labour. In July 1915 the ministry acquired the War Office's Trench Warfare Department, responsible for manufacturing grenades, poison gas, flame-throwers and mortars. Geddes's section was split into smaller divisions for rifles and machine guns, with a new section for artillery under Charles Ellis. By July 1916, Munitions Supply had mutated into ten sections and formed its own supply department, together with a research and development section.[19] The ministry's manufacturing strength was based in 12 distinct regions, each with its own area office providing weapons specification and allocating labour and supplies of raw materials. Arms contracts were managed by local Munitions Committees, answerable to a higher tier of management boards formed of unpaid businessmen deemed to be sufficiently knowledgeable of local conditions and capabilities to make justifiable decisions. Even so, the image of a smoothly functioning, well-oiled administrative machine is misleading. The ministry lacked any central co-ordination. As it grew in response to constantly shifting imperatives, each department and regional office was encouraged to find its own way. Staff were recruited piecemeal, in line with the mounting responsibilities that the ministry was obliged to shoulder. Few, if any, staff records were kept; there was no clear system of making appointments, or proper grading, and no clear principles in fixing rates of pay. By 1918 the ministry's staff totalled over 25,000, with women making up more than 60 per cent of its workforce.[20] When Churchill became minister in 1917 he found:

> The growth of the Ministry of Munitions had far outstripped its organization ... . The two gifted Ministers who had succeeded [Lloyd George], Mr Montagu and Dr Addison, had dealt with the needs as they arose, shouldering one responsibility after another, adding department to department and branch to branch, without altering in essentials the central organization from the form it had assumed in the empirical and convulsive period of creation. I found a staff of 12,000 officials organized in no less than fifty principal departments each claiming direct access to the Chief, and requiring a swift flow of decisions upon most intricate and interrelated problems.[21]

The ministry's policy was neatly summarized by one Treasury official as 'all of everything'.[22] Initially production continued to be channelled through the existing armaments industry, dominated on one side by Vickers, which built ships and naval supplies at Barrow-in-Furness and manufactured guns at Erith, Crayford, Dartford and Birmingham, with further production facilities provided by its associate firm, the Armstrong Whitworth Company, based on Tyneside, with additional plants in Manchester. On the other side there was a scattering of government arsenals, dockyards and naval bases across the country, some of which had supplied Nelson's navy and Wellington's army. The most renowned of these was at Woolwich Arsenal, a seventeenth-century establishment which grew during the First World War into a labyrinth of laboratories, small-arms manufacturers, shell-filling, gun and carriage factories, and chemicals and fuse workshops, sprawling across a five-mile site south of the Thames, employing 28,000 women, 4,200 men and 6,500 children.[23]

Primarily, however, the ministry's production strategy functioned on three levels: increasing the output of heavy artillery and high-explosive shells; stimulating the development of industries critical to the war effort; and intensifying programmes of scientific and technological innovation. Lloyd George's intentions during his year as minister were informed by a conference with army chiefs and representatives of the French War Office at Boulogne in June 1915 where the ministry's expansion programme was fixed in line with the growth of the Western Front army.[24] 'Gun Programme A', aimed at a force of 50 divisions, envisaged a target of 8,881 guns of all calibres, both existing and new, of which 7,240 were to be fully operative by March 1916. This was revised upwards in July 1915, when the War Office began planning for a 70-division army. 'Gun Programme B' accordingly raised its requirement of heavy guns to 641 60-pounders, 458 6-inch howitzers, and 316 8-inch and larger howitzers. In August, Lloyd George increased these targets still further. 'Gun Programme C' aimed for a 100-division army, with 920 60-pounders, 980 6-inch howitzers and 925 larger howitzers by December 1916. Ministry officials estimated that the ammunition programme would require 400 tons of high explosives a week in July 1915, a figure that was expected to rise to 7,000 tons by 1917.[25]

This entailed a wholesale shift in Britain's industrial methods, financial practices and attitudes. In the Commons, Lloyd George insisted that the peacetime doctrines of economy and sound finance in defence spending no longer applied. Wartime armaments manufacture would be geared towards expanding supply, rather than meeting demand, supported by loans and advances on capital that were now exempt from Treasury approval, with expense no object. The swamp of borrowed money enabled arms deals to be struck with engineering companies with an eye to meeting medium- and long-term targets, allowing firms to turn their plant and machinery over to the manufacture of heavy guns and high-explosive shells without fear of incurring swingeing losses if their contracts were not renewed. Booth's co-operative scheme was adapted to help increase the capacities of the principal armaments manufacturers by entrusting the production of gun components to smaller local firms. Vickers, for example, farmed out the production of its 6-inch howitzer carriages to a network of smaller engineering concerns in Manchester, dividing the manufacturing process into three parts. While Vickers undertook the making of the gun and its mechanism, other firms produced the sights and carriages, employing their individual expertise, machinery and labour, but all sharing the necessary machine tools.[26]

Figure 3.1 Shell inspection, *c.* 1917

The new regime solved some problems, but created others. The grumbling of some local manufacturers over the supervising and scrutinizing of finished products and overcoming union restrictive practices that constantly impeded production led the ministry to initiate National Factories where manufacturing, supervision, inspection and labour could be brought together under one management. The first such experiment took place in May 1915, when a National Shell Factory was established near Leeds to produce light and medium-sized shells. Here an autonomous management board took responsibility for everyday affairs, while financial policy, purchase of plant and equipment and staff salaries lay in the hands of Whitehall, with the entire enterprise being owned by the state.[27] The innovation quickly took root. Between 1915 and 1916 a complex of National Shell Factories was established, each designed to produce light and medium-calibre quick-firing and breech-loading shells and mortars. This was followed by Lloyd George's decision to shift the manufacture of heavy artillery shells to state-sponsored National Projectile Factories, managed by staff seconded from the major commercial arms firms. Six were built in Glasgow, of which three were managed by Beardmore's, a local engineering company. A further two were located in Sheffield; one in Birtley, near Gateshead (run by Armstrong's); one in Dudley, in the West Midlands; one at Hackney Marshes in London; one in Nottingham; and another in Lancaster, administered by Vickers.

The shells produced in these establishments were then shipped to National Filling Factories (designed to load shells with explosive material and run on lines similar to the National Shell Factories), the largest of which was situated at Georgetown near Glasgow, with others scattered around the British Isles, including 34 in England, and six in Dublin. This tentacle-like growth in British armaments manufacture was augmented first by four National Cartridge Factories focused on the production of rifle ammunition (traditionally the responsibility of the Royal Small Arms Factory at Enfield) and second by aeroplane manufacture centred at Royal Aircraft Factories in Farnborough and Shepherd's Bush in London.[28] By 1918, a total of 250 factories were under ministry supervision, along with another 20,000 'controlled' establishments, representing a new industrial infrastructure where outputs counted more than costs.[29]

Perhaps the real drama of the National Factories was seen in the production of industrial chemicals. Changes in the chemical constituents of shell propellants and explosives had led to a growing demand for raw materials that had been previously imported. Cordite, for example, used as the main propellant in high-explosive shells and machine-gun bullets, was a jelly-like material composed of nitroglycerine, gun cotton and acetone, bought primarily from the United States of America and Germany before 1914. Similarly, the chemical production of trinitrotoluene (TNT – a new material for the British) required coal, ammonium nitrate (a chemical salt commonly used as agricultural fertiliser) and saltpetre (potassium nitrate or potash), which had previously been imported from Europe and South America.[30] The manufacture of such substances necessitated an industrial refining and distillation infrastructure on a vast scale, so the government was driven to concentrate production across a number of HM Factories devoted solely to the production of explosive materials. TNT and phenol manufacture, for example, was undertaken by government establishments in West Gorton, near Manchester, and Hackney Wick in London. Acetone was produced at a wood-distillation factory in Kings Lynn.[31] By far the largest undertaking was at Gretna, which occupied a 12-mile site straddling the English/Scottish border, between Longtown and Dornock, adjacent to the Solway Firth. Initiated in May 1915, the Gretna factory was mainly responsible for the production of cordite RDB (research department formula B), known locally as 'Devil's Porridge'.[32] The plant employed 20,000 (mostly women) workers and consisted of four production sites, two townships, an independent water-supply system consisting of a reservoir and filters, and several water pumping stations. The factory had its own railway network with 125 miles (200 km) of track and 34 railway engines, its own power station to provide electricity for the factory and townships, a telephone exchange that could handle 2.5 million calls by 1918, a bakery and a laundry. Production peaked in 1917, with 800 tons of cordite produced in one week: a total that exceeded the combined operations of all other plants in Britain.[33]

The production of munitions on such a scale placed enormous strains on the British economy. Shortages of glycerine – an essential ingredient in the manufacture of soap, margarine, candles and cattle feed – were already being reported towards the end of 1915. The demand for nitrates, a vital constituent in agricultural manures, was threatening food supplies, and government requisitioning of distilleries for alcohol production hit the drinks trade. The enforced diversion of the country's supplies of sulphuric acid for the production of high explosives affected the paper, paint, leather and bleach powder industries.[34] Elsewhere, the demand for munitions halted the pre-war decline in the coal, shipping, iron and steel industries. In Dundee, the Scottish jute industry more than made up for its loss of exports with army demands for sandbags and sacks for transporting food. Birmingham jewellers turned to the production of fuses and anti-gas apparatus. Cycle-makers devoted their attention to fuses and shells; pen-makers adapted their machines to manufacture cartridge clips. By 1917, munitions had become the mainstay of Britain's industrial economy. Never was Churchill's comment that 'the whole island was an arsenal' more apt.[35]

The necessity of innovation

National Factories effectively filled the gaps in Britain's armaments industry. They allowed the government greater flexibility and control over munitions production. Gun and artillery programmes could be adjusted according to circumstances. Productive capacities for medium-sized guns increased by 380 per cent in the ministry's first year, while output of heavy guns grew by 1,200 per cent. By contrast, production of lighter weaponry shrank by 28 per cent.[36] National Factories also lent the ministry more scope to manage prices and regulate the costs of materials through central purchasing. Lloyd George looked upon them as models of modernization (adopting the latest manufacturing techniques, working with new power sources, deploying newer and more efficient management practices), while taming trade union interference.

All the same, the ministry was still hostage to circumstances. The firing of over 1.5 million shells during the week-long bombardment before the Battle of the Somme in July 1916 exposed failure rates of up to 30 per cent through faulty fuses and inadequate filling methods. Reports of design flaws in 25 per cent of its guns and heavy artillery demonstrated how far the ministry's rapid expansion programme favoured a production culture that emphasized quantity over quality. Short-cuts taken in inspection routines, and the rapid conversion of engineering companies to shell production using mostly unskilled labour, showed how much was still to be learnt.[37] And the ministry was as much surprised as the Army by Germany's first use of poison gas at Ypres in April 1915. British gas supplies in 1915 rested solely on supplies of chlorine imported from the United States of America. In response, the Royal Society hastily set up a War Committee comprising several offshoots dealing with chemical and trench warfare, which forwarded confidential reports to the government on chemical warfare, while sponsoring research in major university science departments and encouraging the ministry to bring in other firms (such as the United Alkali Company) to manufacture phosgene and mustard gas.[38]

Britain's lack of expertise in some basic warfare technologies was also revealed in the supply of optical munitions. Some parts of the industry were in robust health before 1914, with firms such as the Glasgow-based Barr & Stroud acquiring a considerable domestic and international reputation.[39] But on the whole the industry struggled to meet wartime demands.[40] Shortfalls in supply were made glaringly evident when the government appealed for private donations of field glasses, gun sights and other optical instruments in the newspapers.[41] In November 1915 all unsold optical instruments, in private or commercial hands, were commandeered. Negotiations were even opened with the German government (using a Swiss intermediary) to exchange British supplies of rubber for optical instruments, securing 30,000 binoculars by the end of 1915, with further supplies being secured from the United States of America.[42] Ministry intervention brought variable success. The output of rifle sights was expanded successfully, but only because the materials demanded were relatively small and well-adapted to pre-war production methods. Increasing binocular manufacture suffered through the lack of machine capacity and technical expertise.[43] Nevertheless the abrupt cessation of imports of high-quality optical glass from Germany (in August 1914, 60 per cent of supplies came from Jena) did create dangerous shortages, with only one firm, Messrs Chance Brothers of Birmingham, able to supply just 10 per cent of British needs.[44] In July 1915 the Royal Society's Advisory Council for Scientific and Industrial Research and the Ministry of Munitions' Optical Munitions and Glassware Department (OMGD) took overall responsibility for glass production and immediately offered Chance Brothers the promise of state finance and a guaranteed market to push the company into increasing its glass production to 120,000lbs annually. Chance embarked on a large-scale expansion of its premises. New investment in its machinery and plant (at a total cost of £40,000) increased annual output to around 70,000lbs by November 1916; output touched 92,000lbs by 1918, assisted by heavy investment in Chance's research laboratories, although difficulties in securing domestic supplies of essential raw materials, particularly potash, were never resolved.[45]

Two lessons could be drawn from the government's management of the optical munitions problem. The first was that, when pushed, the state was highly useful as an agency of industrial modernization. The ministry actively promoted greater usage of the latest machinery and production techniques across all the industries that it managed. Ninety-five per cent of the machinery in the new munitions factories was electrically powered, which in turn stimulated demand for more generating capacity, with closer integration of municipal power plants that foreshadowed the post-war establishment of the national grid. The ministry also supported the deployment of improved production methods across the engineering, iron and steel and shipbuilding industries, with greater use of arc furnaces replacing older Bessemer processes. Many shipyards were persuaded to introduce the more efficient pneumatic and electrical tooling, whilst the spread of standardization helped to simplify working practices: methods that crossed over into munitions manufacture with the introduction of automatic and semi-automatic lathes. Many of these innovations also found their way into the larger sectors of British industry, allowing many firms scope for economies in labour and new levels of efficiency in production.[46]

The second lesson taught how far British battlefield technologies lagged behind that of her enemies. Britain lacked Germany's closely co-ordinated links between the state and scientific research. State funding of science in Britain before 1914 was negligible, a result partly of the peculiarly anti-scientific bias in English education and the absence of scientists in high politics. Research tended to be financed through private industry and the science departments of major universities, with only scant attention given to military needs. Furthermore, war challenged notions of the 'neutrality' of science, creating tensions between the needs of the wartime state and intellectual constructs of greater understanding and human advancement. Nevertheless, Britain possessed a considerable reservoir of scientific and technological expertise and, despite widespread public indifference, the exigencies of war reinforced the sense of cohesion amongst her scientists and generated confidence in the belief that Germany's lead in military technology could be successfully challenged. This, however, would not be possible without state support.[47]

The ministry's Munitions Inventions Department (MID), set up in August 1915, was the culmination of a series of *ad hoc* attempts by the Army and the War Office to deal with the growing number of ideas for new munitions that had been flowing from front-line troops and the general public almost from the moment the BEF landed in France. It formed part of a triangle of similar sections – along with the Admiralty's Board of Invention and Research, and the Air Inventions Committee – which came into existence in May 1917.[48] Led by Ernest Moir, a well-known civil engineer, the MID consisted of a panel of 20 scientists and engineers whose main brief was to examine new suggestions, develop potentially viable propositions and conduct a programme of original research.[49] On his appointment, Moir let it be known that he 'was open to suggestions of all kinds', which opened the door to a deluge of crackpot ideas and half-baked designs. The trick, however, as Lloyd George confided to Moir, was to 'try to form your own judgement even upon the rubbish: that very often what appeared to be a wild notion contained a germ of a valuable idea'.[50] Many of the suggestions received were of little practical use. Perhaps the most eccentric was the Heat Ray, a device that fired lethal electric beams in the direction of the enemy, invented by a radio ham employed in naval intelligence.[51] Other ideas ranged from the insertion of rubber tubes into soldiers' socks to warm their feet during trench duty by breathing out through the tubes, to a proposal to manufacture bullets with lateral grooves to help snipers cut barbed wire, and to training flocks of cormorants fitted with explosives to swoop on surfaced submarines or, alternatively, to peck away the mortar on the chimney of the Krupps armaments factory in Essen. One inventor forwarded a process to produce gold from quicksilver. There were also suggestions for constructing shells from earthenware, cast-iron or concrete, filled with a myriad of glass fragments, beer bottles and darts, or for discharging electrically charged snuff on enemy soldiers to bring on their death by shock or sneezing.[52]

Some suggestions, however, were apparently more useful. The use of giant ladies' fans, for example, like fly swatters on long sticks, to blow back German gas attacks, initially dismissed as ludicrous, was given serious consideration, though how close these implements came to being deployed on the front line is open to doubt.[53] Successful practical ideas included designs for bomb throwers, gun-sights, devices that aided signalling and machine-gun efficiency, height and range finders and the production of smoke bombs, as well as improvements in cameras used for aerial photography and for the manufacture of an aluminium-compound internal combustion engine, designed by Henry Ricardo, complete with six cylinders, an improved ignition system, a fan-driven exhaust and an anti-stalling governor, which was incorporated into later versions of the tank. In all, the ministry received nearly 48,000 inventions and ideas between August 1915 and March 1919, of which about one-twelfth were considered worthy of detailed investigation. More than 200 were eventually adopted for service or approved for extensive field trials.[54]

The whole point of MID activity, however, was the pursuit of the probable over the possible. Of the 'high' technologies that it aided during the war, much has been written. In some cases, such as field telephony and wireless communication, the needs of war accelerated developments that had been progressing before 1914.[55] This is equally true of aircraft technology. At the time of the establishment of the Royal Flying Corps in 1912, aeroplanes were rudimentary and dangerous machines constructed of wood and cloth, lacking in armaments, and primarily intended for reconnaissance. Pilots would fly into combat either unarmed or equipped with a revolver or a Winchester repeater rifle. By 1918, however, aircraft had rapidly evolved into fighter aeroplanes and tactical and strategic bombers, dragging British aviation from a relatively backward cottage enterprise to a highly organized industry dominated by the Sopwith and de Havilland companies, with engines developed in harness with the car manufacturers, Rolls Royce and Sunbeam.[56] Other inventions, such as the tank, were borne from the circumstances of war. Tank development was extremely rapid. From its early manifestation in 1915, based on a design for a caterpillar-tracked farm tractor, the early 'Mark I' prototypes, armed with a small gun and capable of cutting through barbed wire, first saw action on the Somme a year later and subsequently progressed to the more sophisticated 'Mark V' tanks that fought at Cambrai in 1917. But the tank's chronic technical limitations were well known. They were notoriously difficult to drive and crews suffered greatly from heat exhaustion and carbon monoxide poisoning, and the Army was never fully convinced of their usefulness in battle.[57]

It was, though, the men in the trenches who experienced the more immediate effects of technological invention. Part improvisation, part inspiration, these 'low' technologies were often hastily devised in response to the new war weaponry that afflicted the ordinary soldier on a daily basis. Ideas were legion and often developed through unorthodox and irregular channels in an atmosphere, as Christopher Addison remarked, of 'agonised urgency'.[58] But perhaps three of the most mundane, and yet the most enduring, stand out. One triumph of improvisation was the Stokes trench mortar. The Army's need for small tactical mortar weapons to match the German's 'horribly effective' *Minenwerfer* had attracted several designs (mainly from soldiers) for crude mortars made from water pipes and ration tins. A more sophisticated trench howitzer firing 50lb bombs then followed, along with a 4-inch light mortar made from empty naval shells and fired from rifles, and the Vickers 1.57-inch mortar, which fired a bomb shaped like a toffee apple.[59] British trench weaponry was eventually transformed by the Stokes mortar, a weapon designed by Wilfred Stokes, chairman of an Ipswich engineering firm, which consisted of a 3-inch cylinder that propelled a small bomb launched by a firing pin as it dropped to the bottom of the tube. Mounted on an adjustable bipod, Stokes's mortar was made up of six small components for easy transportation and could be manufactured by firms that were not adapted to producing high-explosive shells. Stokes had difficulty persuading a sceptical War Office to take his early prototypes seriously. But an improved version submitted to the Ministry of Munitions Trench Warfare Department (TWD) in August 1915 was endorsed and Stokes's mortar finally entered service in March 1916. Over 11,400 Stokes mortars had been manufactured by the end of the war.[60]

Another necessary success was the gas mask. The high casualty rates caused by German gas attacks in 1915 hastened the War Office into creating a new chemical Central Laboratory led by William Watson, head of the physics department at Imperial College. Early efforts at protection consisted of a cloth covering of the nose and mouth soaked in a solution of bicarbonate of soda or, more commonly, urine. This was quickly replaced by gauze pads soaked in castor oil and held in place by tapes tied around the head, and later improved by a gauze veil impregnated with hyposulphite, devised by J.S. Haldane. Greater protection was subsequently gained by Watson's 'hypo helmet', basically a grey flannel hood soaked in a solution of glycerine, hyposulphite and bicarbonate of soda and fitted with two mica eyepieces (later replaced by celluloid) and a rubber mouthpiece.[61] Soldiers referred to these contraptions as 'the goggle-eyed booger with the tit'.[62]

Gas masks, however, evolved rapidly. In the autumn of 1915, S.J.M. Auld, a chemist from Reading University, introduced a PH helmet, consisting of thicker material impregnated with alcohol, glycerine, caustic soda and a solution of sodium phenate-hexamine and a mouthpiece with a one-way valve and two glass eyepieces. Yet this, too, was soon succeeded by a device concocted by B. Lambert, a professional chemist, which guarded against a greater range of gasses. Lambert's invention was essentially a small tin cylinder containing absorbent soda lime permanganate granules which cleansed the toxic air as it was being inhaled by the soldier. This acted as a respirator that was placed on the front of a close-fitting waterproof fabric mask with celluloid eyepieces, a nose clip and a tube of rubber connected to the filter box. The mask was made up of 35 separate components, while the finished product was manufactured to a high standard of perfection to prevent leaks and fatal injury to the wearer. The 'small box respirator', introduced in 1917, was to become the standard gas mask for the British Army in both the First and Second World Wars.[63]

But the unsung hero of British trench technology was the steel helmet, nicknamed 'tin hats', 'trench hats' or 'battle bowlers' by the troops. Photographs of the peaked caps worn by smiling Tommies on their way to France in 1914 suggest that there was little inkling of what was to come, and early attempts to limit the proliferating rates of head wounds caused by shrapnel and debris amounted to little more than silk necklets that covered the skull and neck. By the late summer of 1915, War Office officials, drawn to adapt the French army's *Casque Adrian*, prompted an initial order of 500 helmets. But when tests revealed their limited capability, the decision was taken to design a specifically British version. In the late summer the inventor John Leopold Brodie developed a prototype steel helmet, modelled on armour from the fifteenth century, spherically shaped like a deep soup bowl, with a short, softer-metal ring around the edge. Further versions followed. Type A followed Brodie's original design, with the top slightly flattened and a metal ring of 50mm added to the side and 40mm to the front, and manufactured from manganese steel. Type B, on the other hand, had a slightly larger sphere and narrower rings, 25mm at the front and back and 35mm at the sides, and was forged from manganese fluid steel. When the first batches were sent to France in September 1915, Type A was preferred because of its stronger armour. By March 1916 over 270,000 had been produced and these succeeded in lowering the number of head injuries by 75 per cent. Even so, a new steel rim was added to the Type B, transforming it into a Mark 1 helmet, which was then covered with a mix of sand and paint for camouflage. A padding composed of leather, felt and rubber studs was later added, giving greater comfort and security for the wearer.

Though the new helmet was cheap and easy to produce, it raised two problems for the TWD: how to fashion a steel helmet hard enough to resist high-velocity shrapnel and projectiles; and how to manufacture the new helmets in sufficient quantities. Manufacture of original Type A 'Brodies' was a comparatively simple matter and production rates reached 850 daily before the War Office ordered improvement. The use of hardened manganese steel, developed by the Hadfields company in Sheffield, was an advance. The new Mark 1 helmet weighed 2lbs and was capable of resisting shrapnel travelling up to speeds of 750ft per second, and occasionally 900ft per second, or a mile in six seconds. Whilst this type of steel was more costly and slower to produce, its superior qualities encouraged Army High Command to demand increasing supplies of the new type. Following a conference between the steel makers and ministry representatives in November 1915, Beardmore, an experienced manufacturer of armour, and a number of steel rolling firms in Glasgow and Wolverhampton were contracted to produce the plate and stampings for the new helmet. The Sheffield Munitions Committee also requisitioned the silver-plating trades (whose business had been badly hit by the war) to deploy their presses into helmet manufacture, with lining and fittings being undertaken by the Army and Navy stores. There were now three sources of supply. Wolverhampton contractors were expected to supply 25,000–30,000 weekly; the Sheffield group undertook output at a similar rate; and the Glasgow firm's rate of production was estimated at 45,000 weekly. The first 300,000 were delivered by mid-March 1916, and delivery of the first million helmets was completed for the start of the Battle of the Somme. By the end of the war, production totals touched seven and a quarter million.[64]

Labour

At whatever level the ministry functioned, nothing was possible without settling the labour question. As the shift from civil to war-related industrial production took hold, so the character of the British workforce changed significantly. The numbers in civil employment fell from 19,440,000 to 17,060,000 (down by 12 per cent) between 1914 and 1918, while those employed in the metal trades grew from 1,804,000 to 2,418,000 (by 34 per cent) in the same period. Similarly, people working in government establishments (arsenals, national factories and dockyards) increased from 76,000 to 277,000. The war also provided fertile ground for trade union expansion, with virtually full employment being reached after 1915 and price inflation high enough to keep workers anxious about wages. Total trade union membership grew by 57 per cent during the war (approximately 39 per cent of the total workforce), gaining strength in areas that had been union strongholds before 1914, especially coal mining, metals and engineering, printing, railways and textiles, where overall densities of union membership rose from 29.2 per cent to 55.5 per cent. Union membership among white-collar workers rose from 11.6 per cent to 24.2 per cent between 1911 and 1921, while the numbers of manual workers joining trade unions rose by 57.6 per cent between 1914 and 1918.[65]

From the outset, Britain's working classes demonstrated remarkable constraint and commitment to the war. Trade union leaders quickly declared an 'industrial truce'; strikes were immediately curtailed; demands for improved pay and working conditions were postponed; and exorbitant wage claims were held in check.[66] Moreover, British workers retained a deep sense of patriotism throughout the conflict, conditioned to an extent by an education system that emphasized the virtues of empire and a belief in Britain's worldwide economic and moral supremacy. Yet labour still presented a package of unknowns for the government. Britain's social and political elite were largely ignorant of working-class life and culture. Many middle- and upper-class Britons (and the right-wing press) regarded the labouring classes as essential for taking care of the everyday functions of modern life, but with habits and attitudes that were difficult to gauge and occasionally turbulent. Strikes or public expressions of grievance during wartime were thus seen as selfish and unpatriotic or, even worse, potentially revolutionary.[67]

This view was partially reflected in Lloyd George's tendency to associate less with trade union leaders than with self-made businessmen. Like him, they possessed energy and dynamism; like him they had escaped their origins through hard work and a sharp mind; like him they held a healthy scepticism towards over-educated civil servants and administrators who clogged the mechanics of the war effort. Industrial magnates presented Lloyd George with fewer problems than trade union leaders. Industrialists were not accountable to their shareholders in the way that trade union leaders were answerable to their members. Union leaders drew their strength from the combined wishes of their membership, and the collective interest they served was potentially formidable. With employers, the reverse was true. Capital would willingly defer to state authority if it was not wantonly provoked. Too many concessions to labour, however, could place the state at the mercy of popular will.[68]

Such attitudes fostered the assumption amongst ministers that industrial workers could be treated as a single entity, with trade union leaders acting as one voice for the entire workforce. Yet any idea of working-class unity was never tenable. Those union leaders who bargained with Lloyd George tended to represent an industrial elite of skilled workers, whose long years of apprenticeship and training had placed them at the top of the workplace hierarchy: a position that was jealously guarded behind a wall of restrictive practices, superior wage rates and industrial privileges.

Less-skilled workers, who could be engaged in a diversity of occupations, from machinists to unskilled labourers, whose pay and conditions varied considerably and whose representation was concentrated in the General Unions, were repeatedly excluded from negotiation. Ministers thus bargained with more 'specialist' unions, such as the Amalgamated Society of Engineers

Table 3.1 Changes in male employment, July 1914–July 1918

	Numbers employed, July 1914	*Numbers employed, July 1918*	*Contraction (-) or expansion (+) per cent since July 1914*	*Numbers enlisted since July 1914*	*Percentage enlisted since July 1914*
Industry					
Building	920,000	440,000	− 52.2	430,000	46.7
Mining	1,266,000	1,016,000	− 19.7	448,000	35.3
Metals	1,634,000	1,824,000	+ 11.7	681,000	41.6
Chemicals	159,000	162,000	+ 1.9	85,000	53.4
Textiles	625,000	411,000	− 34.2	292,000	46.7
Clothing	287,000	183,000	− 36.2	170,000	59.3
Food, Drink & Tobacco	360,000	243,000	− 32.5	221,000	61.3
Paper	261,000	156,000	− 40.2	135,000	51.8
Wood	258,000	168,000	− 34.9	136,000	52.7
Other Trades	393,000	253,000	− 35.6	180,000	45.8
Total (Private Industry)	6,163,000	4,856,000	− 21.2	2,778,000	45.1
Government Establishments	76,000	257,000	+ 238.2	53,000	69.4
Agriculture (permanent labour)	800,000	589,000	− 26.4	281,000	35.1
Local Authorities	496,000	340,000	− 31.5	182,000	36.7
Civil Service	244,000	192,000	− 21.3	107,000	43.9
Other Occupations*	2,831,000	1,846,000	− 34.8	1,495,000	52.8
Grand Total	10,610,000	8,080,000	− 23.8	4,896,000	46.1

* includes transport, printing and commerce
Source: Adapted from *History of the Ministry of Munitions*, vol. VI, part I, ch. III

(the most prominent – and most awkward) who, as representatives of skilled workers, invariably struck agreements in their own self-interest, and frequently at the expense of other equally essential workers.[69] For ministers, anxious to secure sweeping workplace agreements in the midst of war, the inclination to deal with a few, in the hope that they spoke for the many, was a mistake that would rebound on them.

Such distortions in ministerial attitudes towards the industrial workforce ensured that Lloyd George's expansionist munitions policy would be achieved through the containment of labour rather than the management of capitalism. This would not be easy. Labour was a scarce resource. Many skilled men had enlisted and shortages, especially in the skilled engineering trades, had begun to be felt only a month into the war. In December 1914, Armstrong needed 4,150 skilled workers; Vickers required 1,676.[70] By June 1915 two government factories and 16 private firms engaged in munitions work were short of 14,000 skilled workers. By the middle of 1915 mining had lost 21.8 per cent of its workforce; iron and steel 18.8 per cent; engineering 19.5 per cent; electrical engineering 23.7 per cent; shipbuilding 16.5 per cent; small-arms manufacturers 16 per cent; and chemicals and explosives 23.8 per cent.[71] This unexpected emergency led Asquith to sanction negotiations with Army authorities in France to release skilled workers from the ranks. In January 1915, on the insistence of George Booth and Llewellyn Smith, the War Office published a Circular Memorandum to recruitment officers listing occupations exempt from the call-up.

Vickers, however, offered an emergency solution in September 1914, when the company began issuing its skilled employees with a wartime service badge emphasizing their importance in munitions production and protecting them from social and moral pressures to enlist. Churchill was sufficiently impressed to apply the scheme to Admiralty contractors in October, and by December the 'badging' system had received full Cabinet endorsement. Even so, badging was never seen as a complete solution to resolving labour shortages, despite the system being continually refined and extended throughout the war.[72] At the same time, the government was compelled to manage the competing needs of the Army, industry and agriculture. Conscription helped. But, in the event, the government adopted two ways of dealing with the manpower problem: manipulating industrial working practices to release more men for the front; and organizing labour through central state planning (see Chapter 2 text box, Manpower).

Government attempts to siphon off more men for the military through tampering with industrial working practices began and ended with 'dilution' and 'substitution', namely the replacement of skilled by less-skilled workers in the production process.[73] The principle could be applied across a number of industries. However, it was engineering that appeared almost ready-made for such measures. Prior to 1914, manufacturing methods in many workshops were dominated by the centre lathe, a finely tuned, specialized machine capable of many separate operations worked by a highly skilled, fully trained and apprenticed (invariably male) worker. At the outbreak of war this method was already being broken up to a degree, with centre-lathed work being handled by less-skilled but more specialized operatives, namely millers, planers, borers and slotters. The pressures of war production accelerated the development of single-purpose machines that increasingly replaced the skills previously demanded of their operators. The upshot was the development of the more modern type of universal turret and semi-automatic capstan lathes, expensive machines that worked with a huge equipment of standardized tools, capable of being operated either by a skilled man or by one of the newer grades of semi-skilled workers. The job still required the services of a fully skilled employee, but as long as the machine was to be used for repetition work (performing a run of identical operations), the amount of skill required for its operation was relatively small.[74]

This meant that the working process could be divided into smaller and simpler constituent parts, allowing the complexities of skilled engineering work to be surrendered to mass-production techniques, with the element of skill transferred to the machine, and the skilled artisan's job 'diluted' by employing less-skilled operatives. Assembling the Lee-Enfield rifle, for example, consisted of producing 131 distinct parts, including the butt; hand-guards, rear and front; fore-end; body; barrel; bolt; nose cap; guard; butt plate; magazine case; and magazine platform. Forging the barrel alone comprised 85 machining tasks, involving the manufacture of 1,310,000 components and over 15,000,000 separate operations.[75] The promise of higher outputs, cheaper wage rates and a more flexible workforce proved irresistible for the government and employers alike. For skilled workers, assailed by the threat of military service and the potential destruction of their jobs, dilution was grudgingly accepted, but on the understanding that it would be dropped once peace had been restored.

Dilution, however, was a live wire. The Trades Union Congress (TUC) was berated on the subject by a finger-wagging Lloyd George at its conference in September 1915. At a packed meeting of workers in Glasgow in December the minister's speech was heckled into silence by a noisy and aggressive audience, forcing him to deploy the powers of DORA to prevent reports of the meeting being leaked to the press.[76] Negotiation, not lectures, offered a chance of progress. In November 1914 the management at the Vickers plant in Crayford, following a dispute over the use of female 'diluters', formulated an agreement with its engineering unions allowing unskilled workers to be employed throughout the plant, but only on repetitive work, and only for the duration of the war. All the same, Vickers's attempt to extend the agreement to its other works, with additional curtailments on restrictive practices, floundered in the face of grass-roots opposition. The War Office's reluctance to intervene led the Board of Trade, in January 1915, to appoint Sir George Askwith, a veteran negotiator of pre-war industrial disputes, to chair a Production Committee, bringing together the Engineering Employers' Federation (EEF) and the Amalgamated Society of Engineers (ASE) to sign a Shells and

Figure 3.2 Doing their bit. Young women making shells at Vickers Ltd, *c.* 1915

Fuses Agreement in March, limiting the use of dilution solely to the armaments industry until the end of the war.[77]

This gave Lloyd George an opportunity to tie some loose ends. Agreement was still needed to extend dilution across all war industries, and the question of curbing restrictive practices and working-to-rule and the settlement of wage disputes had yet to be fully addressed. Lloyd George toyed with the idea of dealing with such problems by introducing industrial conscription. But imposing state controls on the free movement of labour was a step too far, raising the spectre of 'Prussianism' in the eyes of the public, and the government was warned that it would be faced 'by factories full of sullen workers supported by a riotous and rebellious proletariat'.[78] Lloyd George thus arrived at a two-stroke solution. The first was to draft an amendment to the Defence of the Realm Act (DORA). Guided by one of four reports produced by Askwith's production committee, Lloyd George introduced legislation granting the government powers to requisition any factory or machinery for munitions production, to coerce private manufacturers into undertaking government work and to compel their employees to work on government contracts.[79]

This coincided with Lloyd George's efforts to push the recommendations of Askwith's committee still further by convening a conference at the Treasury in March 1915 with major trade union leaders, where it was agreed to outlaw strikes, accept compulsory arbitration in workplace disputes and allow dilution. Eventually the so-called Treasury Agreements were reached with 35 unions, but they were never fully accepted by the shipbuilding unions, while the ASE negotiated a separate deal. The Miners' Federation refuted the new arrangements in their entirety.[80] The new order was subsequently codified by the Munitions of War Act of July 1915, which enshrined the Shells and Fuses and Treasury Agreements in law, while introducing the leaving certificate, which, in prohibiting employers from taking on new workers unless they possessed the certificate signed by their former company, effectively prevented employees from changing jobs in search of higher wages. Without the certificate, workers were forced into a six-week unpaid wait for a new job (the notorious Clause VII of the Act), while employers were given free rein to use the certificate as a character reference. Workers had the right to appeal to a Munitions Tribunal, but seeking improved pay and conditions was not considered suitable grounds for leaving a job.[81] On paper, at least, the balance of power within industrial Britain had tilted decisively towards the government. Unions had surrendered many of their basic rights. In return, they received a rather nebulous assurance from Lloyd George that he would limit excessive profiteering by firms working on government contracts. But this excluded the many companies whose inflated trading surpluses (born out of war shortages) were suspected by many working-class families to be the root cause of the increased cost of living.[82]

The Munitions Act was just the beginning of Lloyd George's turbulent relationship with Britain's labour movement. The weakness of the minister's position was soon exposed by a strike of 200,000 South Wales miners over a pay dispute in July 1915, just two weeks after the Act passed into law. The valleys of South Wales were described as the 'Wild West' of industrial relations. Its mining communities were strongly united in their defence of hard-won trade union rights.[83] Under the terms of the Act, the government had powers to arrest strikers rather than their leaders, yet the prospect of apprehending and trying 200,000 men was, as the government's legal adviser warned, 'impossible ... only a few can at first be dealt with and the length of time before there can be any real enforcement of the sentence will, I fear, only lead the men generally to regard the act as ineffective'.[84] It was an uncomfortable reality. If a strike had enough popular support, workers could challenge the law and win with impunity. The miners' demands were subsequently met in full and without penalty.[85] Other instances followed. In November 1916, following a strike at a Sheffield plant over the call-up of a skilled engineer, a 'trade card' scheme was negotiated with the ASE, giving the union the right to issue its own military exemption certificate, which was subsequently extended to cover 32 unions within the Engineering Unions Federation.[86] The move enraged other unions, particularly those representing unskilled workers, and was held responsible for the shortfall of 148,000 army recruits. The scheme was withdrawn in April 1917.[87] At the same time, the terms of the leaving certificate were modified under an amendment to the Munitions Act, following unrest amongst Clydeside workers.[88] Thus, rather than trying to put the trade union cat back in his sack, Lloyd George chose a strategy of compromise, conciliation and concession. Confrontation meant an unaffordable disruption in output.

The policy, however, was not enough to handle the deeper tensions simmering amongst the wider industrial workforce. Increases in rents and food costs were outstripping earnings; there was unhappiness at the curtailment of basic workplace rights and freedoms; the intense friction caused by successive government 'comb-outs' of skilled munitions men for the Army, and wartime profiteering amongst coalmining, shipbuilding, iron and engineering firms, all contributed to a growing climate of discontent.[89] From the beginning of the war, the government and military leaders had encouraged a belief in noble sacrifice for King and Country; now, it appeared, on the Home Front at least, that the scale of the worker's sacrifice was not being matched by that of the more prosperous classes. For the historian Bernard Waites such perceptions proved the existence of wartime 'moral economy', where general grievances, while not directly provoking industrial walkouts, greatly 'increased the propensity to strike'.[90] To the workforce, however, the complaints were real enough to trigger action. Following the first serious dispute, which erupted in Glasgow during February 1915 (when 5,000 engineers at the Weir firm in Cathcart walked out over the hiring of American workers at higher wage rates), three million days were subsequently lost through strike action in 1915 and 2.5 million in 1916.[91] The wave of strikes peaked in 1917, resulting in the loss of 5.5 million working days. Serious outbreaks of unrest took place in Coventry and Sheffield and other engineering centres across the Midlands during May, whilst disputes in 48 towns across other regions saw some 200,000 engineers and shipbuilders down tools over various local disputes.[92] The German spring offensive in March 1918 brought a temporary lull, before engineers in Leeds and Birmingham took strike action in April, whilst the reintroduction of leaving certificates brought renewed action in the Midlands during July. The disputes ended when strikers were threatened with conscription.[93]

The press rained down accusations of treachery and selfishness on the strikers, but the scale of the unrest meant that the strikes could not be ignored, especially as further investigation revealed that the discontent sprang from shop-floor workers who were neither ordered nor controlled by union hierarchies. In his study of workplace politics in 1922, the labour historian G.D.H. Cole identified the strikes as a 'workshop movement', initiated by local union activists, or 'shop stewards'. Drawing their power from the disillusionment of rank-and-file workers with national union leaders, shop stewards took the initiative in settling parochial disputes over piece-rates, implementing dilution and introducing new working practices. Cole described the movement as a 'spontaneous growth', organized within workplaces, led by men 'who shaped their own policy in accordance with local conditions'. When local disputes began to spread, it was not necessarily a reaction to an official call for strike action; it was usually because 'the same conditions produced in different areas the same response'.[94] As such, though the workshop movement had no identifiable national structure, it had two distinct strands, the 'shop stewards organizations' and the 'shop stewards movement'. For the most part, the shop stewards organizations were mostly comprized of moderates, motivated less by a political imperative than a need to provide important leadership for a workforce struggling to adapt to new working methods. The shop stewards movement, by contrast, presented a more radical front. This was most evident in Glasgow, where genuine grievances over working and living conditions had deeply radicalized the workforce. Local leaders even formed a soviet-style Clyde Workers Committee (CWC) in October 1915 which aimed 'to maintain the class struggle until the overthrow of the wages system, the freedom of the workers, and the establishment of industrial democracy have been obtained'. The CWC could not claim to represent the views of the entire Clydeside workforce, but its example proved contagious and encouraged small socialist groups to organize shop-floor movements in other areas.[95]

The revolutionary characteristic of the shop stewards movement has enticed some historians into claiming that Britain's workers were poised to unleash a major socialist upheaval, inspired perhaps by the outpourings of political propagandists who attached themselves to the engineering strikes of 1917. This idea has since become hugely contentious, with a number of historians arguing that such claims have been exaggerated.[96] Even so, with no end to the war in sight, and events in Russia stoking fears that a Bolshevik-style takeover was possible, some strikes were accompanied by a revolutionary narrative that government ministers took very seriously. The CWC was the first to feel the heat of official reaction. It caused the ministry so much trouble that it was eventually suppressed, and its leaders, among them the radical socialists William Gallacher, John Maclean and Arthur MacManus, were gaoled, and Glasgow's socialist weeklies, *Forward, Vanguard* and *The Worker*, were banned and their publishers arrested.[97] Ministers were thus acutely sensitive to the actions of shop stewards. They tried (with difficulty) to prise apart the strikes for industrial aims from strikes for political objectives, mostly through covert propaganda and by launching semi-official investigations into potential revolutionary activity led by Basil Thompson, an agent employed by Scotland Yard.[98] The documentary record that was produced by such activities can capture the historian's imagination and it is easy to be seduced into interpreting the words of a few as the attitude of many. But it should be noted that the rate of wartime strikes never approached the 41 million days lost in 1912, or the ten million in 1913 and 1914.[99] Moreover, workers' dissatisfaction with their conditions did not necessarily diminish their commitment to the war. Gerard DeGroot detects a 'populist moral code' against strikes as each day lost deprived fathers, sons, brothers and nephews of the means of winning the war. Concluding its report on unrest in Sheffield in 1917, the Ministry of Labour commented:

Many of the men seemed uncertain whether they really desired to strike or not ... . On the one hand [the men] were reluctant to hold up the war to the detriment of their relatives in the trenches. On the other hand, it seemed important to them, in their own interests, to keep their trade privileges intact. One has the impression, in short, of unrest paralysed by patriotism – or, it may be, of patriotism paralysed by unrest.[100]

The government made tentative moves towards accommodating the shop stewards organizations within a wider reform of workplace practices and management.[101] Yet it was still a measure of the government's ignorance of the industrial workers' condition that Lloyd George felt compelled to appoint a Commission of Enquiry into Industrial Unrest in 1917, co-ordinated by the Labour MP George Barnes. Three commissioners – an employer, a labour representative and a chairman – were assigned to investigate the causes of unrest in eight munitions areas. Their enquiries and reports were completed in just six weeks, giving rise to suspicions that their findings were little more than hearsay.[102] Nevertheless, out of the eight commissioners' reports returned, seven highlighted high prices and unequal distribution of food, state regulation and restriction of personal freedom in moving jobs, restrictions on drink, lack of confidence in the government, poor housing and a shortage of accommodation as the major sources of unrest.[103] Commissioners in Wales offered a telling indictment:

[T]he workers feel deeply discontent with their housing accommodation and with their unwholesome and unattractive environment generally. The towns and villages are ugly and overcrowded: houses are scarce, and rents are increasing, and the surroundings are insanitary and depressing. The scenery is disfigured by unsightly refuse tips, the atmosphere polluted by coal dust and smoke, and the rivers spoilt by liquid effuse from works and factories. Facilities for education and recreation are inadequate and opportunities for the wise use of leisure are few. The influence of the social factors on the creation of industrial unrest cannot be easily measured, but that their influence is great is undeniable.[104]

Conclusions

By the time of the Armistice, the Ministry of Munitions had managed to turn almost every corner of British industry over to war production and harness the usually passive activity of scientific research and technological innovation to the development of new weaponry. Therein, however, lay its limitations. The ministry's best efforts to equip the Army with devastating new firepower could do little to shorten the war: nobody solved the problem of turning an advance into a breakthrough. Furthermore, the ministry's historical reputation has been afflicted by its own contradictions. Doubtless many of the ministry's innovations had a lasting effect. As a body, it was always open to new ideas for organizing production and incorporating the latest techniques in technology, as well as in management and working practices, in those factories and companies that fell within the ministry's remit. Its experiences left a mark on the minds of politicians and officials that would be invaluable in the next world war. Nevertheless, the basis of the ministry's existence was strictly short term; intervention and innovation were shaped as a piecemeal response to immediate circumstances, not as a pointer to longer-term industrial development. Such was the way the ministry handled its workers. The labour movement's resistance to diluters was largely overcome by 1917, but only on the promise that they would be removed after the war. And yet, at the same time, the war greatly enhanced the industrial strength and political power of the working classes; its main representatives, the trade unions, became part of a 'corporate economy', given full recognition by employers and government, with a substantive say in industrial matters. The ministry did much to modernize the character and culture of Britain's industrial structure. But, in doing so, it uncovered deeper narratives of social reform and amelioration of economic inequity that required a more political response.

Notes

1 Quoted in Duncan Crow, *A Man of Push and Go: The Life of George Macauley Booth*, London: Hart-Davis, 1965, p. 71.

2 *History of the Great War: Military Operations, France and Belgium, 1914*, compiled by Brigadier-General J.E. Edmonds (hereafter '*Official History*'), London: Macmillan 1925, pp. 12–13; see also Hew Strachan, *The First World War*, vol. I, *To Arms*, Oxford: Oxford University Press, 2001, pp. 997, 1067.

3 Hew Strachan, *To Arms*, op. cit., p. 999; NA, WO, 32/5152, 'French to the Secretary of the Army Council, 31st December 1914'; see also NA, PRO 30/57/4, Sir John French to Kitchener, 25th December 1914.

4 History of the Ministry of Munitions (hereafter 'HMM'), vol. I, part I, ch. III; Clive Trebilcock, 'War and the Failure of Industrial Mobilisation: 1899–1914', in J.M. Winter, ed., *War and Economic Development: Essays in Memory of David Joslin*, Cambridge: Cambridge University Press, 1975, pp. 139–64; Hew Strachan, *To Arms*, op. cit., pp. 1066–67.

5 NA, CAB 19/33, 'Special Commissions to Enquire into the Operations of War in Mesopotamia and in the Dardenelles, 1st–89th day, 1916–17, QQ197990–91'; WO 79/84, 'The Supply of Munitions to the Army, Notes by Major-General Sir Stanley von Donop', 12th July 1919; CAB 19/52, 'Supplementary Statement on the Provision of Guns and Gun Ammunition by Major-General Sir Stanley von Donop', 15th February 1917; HMM, vol. II, part I, ch. II.

6 *Statistics of the Military Effort of the British Empire during the Great War*, HMSO: London, 1922, pp. 470–71.

7 George A.B. Dewar, *The Great Munition Feat 1914–1918*, London: Constable, 1921, p. 127.

8 Strachan, *To Arms*, op. cit., p. 1067; *Official History*, op. cit., pp. 13–14.

9 Chris Wrigley, 'The Ministry of Munitions: An Innovatory Department', in Kathleen Burk, *War and the State: The Transformation of British Government 1914–1919*, London: Unwin, 1982, p. 27; NA, Ministry of Munitions Papers (hereafter 'MUN'), 5/6/170/27, 'Negotiations for Shell Supplies with Certain Important Firms Prior to the Formation of the Ministry of Munitions', n.d.

10 HMM, vol. II, part II, op. cit., p. 37; NA, CAB 37/126/28, 'Output of Munitions of War' (R.McKenna) 25th March 1915; NA, T 181/50, 'Royal Commission on the Private Manufacture of, and Trading in, Arms', Appendix 5; David French, *British Economic and Strategic Planning 1905–1915*, London: Allen & Unwin, 1982, p. 154.

11 HMM, vol. I, part I, appendix III, pp. 146–49; NA, MUN 5/8/172/17, Memorandum on Munitions Supply 13 April–31 May 1915; Strachan, *To Arms*, op. cit., p. 1068; see also Peter Simkins, *Kitchener's Army: The Raising of the New Armies 1914–1916*, Barnsley: Pen and Sword, 2007, pp. 284–86.

12 David Lloyd George, *War Memoirs*, new edn, vol. I, London: Odhams, 1938, p. 160.

13 NA, CAB 42/1/39, 'Some Further Considerations on the Conduct of the War', 25th February 1915; also available in NA, MUN 5/6/170/23.

14 HMM, vol. I, part III, ch. II; David French, *British Economic and Strategic Planning 1905–1915*, op. cit., pp. 163–65; Strachan, *To Arms*, op. cit., pp. 1070, 1072–73. For a critique of Lloyd George's methods and motives in the munitions issue, see George H. Cassar, *Kitchener: Architect of Victory*, London: William Kimber, 1977, ch. 16; John Pollock, *Kitchener*, London: Constable, 1998.

15 HMM, vol. I, part I, p. 104.

16 HMM, vol. I, part III, pp. 24–25; NA, MUN 5/342/170/2/8, 'Work of Mr. G.M. Booth, Armaments Output Committee and Munitions of War Committee'; NA, MUN 5/342/170/2/10, 'Work of Mr G.M. Booth, Formation of Co-operative Groups'; Strachan, *To Arms*, op. cit., pp. 1074–75.

17 Hew Strachan, *To Arms*, op. cit., pp. 1074–75; see also NA, MUN 5/8/171/21, 'Notes from a Copy of Sir Percy Girouard's Scheme for Central Organisation for Labour Supply'; NA, MUN 5/342/170/2/11, 'Sir P. Girouard's Scheme for Co-ordinating A and B Areas Under a Central Department', 26th April 1915; Duncan Crow, op. cit., pp. 87–112; Fletcher H. Moulton, *The Life of Lord Moulton*, London: Nisbet, 1922, pp. 179–82, 271.

18 HMM, vol. II, part I, ch. II, pp. 17–20; R.J.Q. Adams, *Arms and the Wizard: Lloyd George and the Ministry of Munitions, 1915–1916*, London: Cassell, 1978, ch. 4; NA, MUN 5/342/170/2/14, 'Formation of the Ministry'; Chris Wrigley, 'The Ministry of Munitions: An Innovatory Department', op. cit., pp. 40–43; David Lloyd George, *War Memoirs*, op. cit., pp. 147–53.

19 HMM, vol. II, part I, ch.V; Strachan, *To Arms*, op. cit., p. 1079; R.J.Q. Adams, *Arms and the Wizard*, op. cit., ch. 5; NA, MUN 5/342/170/2/14, 'Formation of the Ministry'.

20 Chris Wrigley, 'The Ministry of Munitions: An Innovatory Department', op. cit., p. 42.

21 Winston Churchill, *The World Crisis* (1931), London: Penguin edn, 2007, pp. 721–22.

22 NA, T 170/73/6.10.15; Hew Strachan, *To Arms*, op. cit., p. 1077.

23 HMM, vol. VII, part II, ch. III; NA, MUN 5/146/1122/5, 'Lists of National Munitions Factories'; Hew Strachan, *To Arms*, op. cit., pp. 1079–80; Chris Wrigley, 'The Ministry of Munitions: An Innovatory Department', op. cit., pp. 45–50. See also Angela Woollacott, *On Her Their Lives Depend: Munitions Workers in the Great War*, London: University of California Press, 1994, pp. 28–30.

24 HMM, vol. I, part I, ch. II, p. 38.

25 HMM, vol. X, part I, pp. 6–27; R.J.Q. Adams, *Arms and the Wizard*, op. cit., pp. 164–72; Hew Strachan, *To Arms*, op. cit., pp. 1082–83.

26 George Dewar, *The Great Munition Feat*, op. cit., pp. 101–2.

27 NA, MUN 5/342/170/2/12, 'The National Shell Factory, Early History of Leeds Factory'.

28 HMM, vol. VII, part II, ch. III; NA, MUN 5/146/1122/5, 'Lists of National Munitions Factories'; Hew Strachan, *To Arms*, op. cit., pp. 1079–80; Chris Wrigley, 'The Ministry of Munitions: An Innovatory Department', op. cit., pp. 45–50.

29 HMM, vol. VIII, part II, chs. II–III; R.J.Q. Adams, *Arms and the Wizard*, op. cit., pp. 56–69; Hew Strachan, *To Arms*, op. cit., p. 1080; Chris Wrigley, 'The Ministry of Munitions', op. cit., pp. 47–51.

30 See NA, MUN 7/236, 'Reports by Dr Charles Weizmann in Production of Acetone'; Chaim Weizmann, *Trial and Error*, London: Hamish Hamilton, 1949; Jehuda Reinharz, 'Science in the Service of Politics: The Case of Chaim Weizmann During the First World War', *English Historical Review*, vol. 100, no. 396, 1985, pp. 572–603; HMM, vol. I, part I, pp. 32, 110–12; vol. III, part I, pp. 30–31; vol. X, part IV, pp. 4–76, 127–40; Guy Hartcup, *The War of Invention: Scientific Developments, 1914–18*, London: Brassey's, 1988, pp. 50–53; Hew Strachan, *To Arms*, op. cit., pp. 1083–84.

31 HMM, vol. VIII, part II, ch. II.

32 A term coined by Sir Arthur Conan Doyle, then a war correspondent, on a visit to the factory in 1916.

33 HMM, vol. VIII, part II, ch. II, pp. 58–61; see also Christopher Addison, *Four and a Half Years: A Personal Diary from June 1914 to January 1919*, vol. 1, London: Hutchinson, 1934, pp. 210–11; Gordon Routledge, *Miracles and Munitions*, Longtown, Cumbria: Arthuret, 2003, pp. 38–75.

34 Christopher Addison, *Politics from Within 1911–1918*, London: Herbert Jenkins, 1924, pp. 152–53.

35 Winston Churchill, *The World Crisis*, op. cit., p. 721.

36 R.J.Q. Adams, *Arms and the Wizard*, op. cit., p. 172. See also NA, MUN 5/123/1000/24, 'Tables of Proportionate Increases in Munition Output and Capacity from August 1914 to May 1916'; NA, MUN 5/177/1200/12, 'Statement Showing Proportionate Increase in Gun Output from June 1914'.

37 *Official History*, op. cit., pp. 13–14; Hew Strachan, *To Arms*, op. cit., p. 1085; Shelford Bidwell and Dominick Graham, *Fire-power: British Army Weapons and Theories of War 1904–1945*, Barnsley: Pen & Sword, 2004, pp. 98–99; Guy Hartcup, *The War of Invention*, op. cit., pp. 48–49; Hew Strachan, *To Arms*, op. cit., p. 1085.

38 Guy Hartcup, *The War of Invention*, op. cit., pp. 96–97.

39 See Guy Hartcup, *The War of Invention*, op. cit., pp. 181–84; Roy MacLeod and Kay MacLeod, 'War and Economic Development: Government and the Optical Industry in Britain, 1914–18', in J.M. Winter, ed., *War and Economic Development: Essays in Memory of David Joslin*, op. cit., 1975, pp. 165–203; George Dewar, *The Great Munition Feat*, op. cit., pp. 212–23; Stephen C. Sambrook, 'The Optical Munitions Industry in Great Britain 1888–1923', unpublished PhD thesis, University of Glasgow, 2005.

40 Stephen Sambrook, 'The Optical Munitions Industry in Great Britain 1888–1923', op. cit., pp. 123–25.

41 Roy Macleod and Kay Macleod, 'War and Economic Development: Government and the Optical Industry in Britain, 1914–18', op. cit., p.171.

42 Roy Macleod and Kay Macleod, 'War and Economic Development: Government and the Optical Industry in Britain, 1914–18', op. cit., p. 171. Macleod's figures differ from those of Hartcup, *The War of Invention*, op. cit., p. 182.

43 Stephen Sambrook, 'The Optical Munitions Industry in Great Britain 1888–1923', op. cit., pp. 212–13.

44 Roy MacLeod and Kay MacLeod, 'War and Economic Development: Government and the Optical Industry in Britain, 1914–18', op. cit., pp. 170–71.

45 Roy MacLeod and Kay MacLeod, 'War and Economic Development: Government and the Optical Industry in Britain, 1914–18', pp. 172–79, *passim;* Guy Hartcup, *The War of Invention*, op. cit., pp. 183–84.

46 Chris Wrigley, 'The Ministry of Munitions: An Innovatory Department', op. cit., pp. 47–48.

47 Michael Pattison, 'Scientists, Government and Invention', op. cit., p. 83.
48 See, for example, Lord Hankey, *The Supreme Command*, vol. I, London: Allen & Unwin, 1961, pp. 227–31.
49 NA, MUN 5/43/263.8/7, 'Copy Correspondence, etc., of 6 July to 26 November 1916 on Formation of Munitions Inventions Department and Transfer of Functions from the War Office'; *The Times*, 12th August 1915; *The Times*, 7th September 1915; Michael Pattison, 'Scientists, Government and Invention', op. cit., p. 83.
50 NA, MUN 5/118/700/27, 'Miscellaneous Collection of Papers re: Inventions'.
51 NA, MUN 7/305, 'Russell Clarke's Heat Ray', 8.12.1917; Michael Pattison, 'Scientists, Government and Invention: The Experience of the Inventions Board 1915–18', in Peter H. Liddle, ed., *Home Fires and Foreign Fields: British Social and Military Experience in the First World War*, Brasseys: London, 1985, pp. 83–100.
52 NA, MUN 5/117/700/1, 'Suggestions Sent to the Minister of Munitions, June–July, 1915: Specimens'; Michael Pattison, 'Scientists, Government and Invention', op. cit., pp. 87–88.
53 NA, MUN 5/117/700/1, op. cit.; Bernard Livermore, *Long 'Un; A Damn Bad Soldier*, Batley: Harry Hayes, 1974, p. 51.
54 Guy Hartcup, *The War of Invention*, op. cit., pp. 87–88, 189.
55 Guy Hartcup, *The War of Invention*, op. cit., pp. 76–79.
56 HMM, vol. IX, part II, ch. V, p. 62; HMM, vol. XII, part I, ch. I. See also Walter Raleigh and H.A. Jones, *The War in the Air*, vols. I–IV, Oxford: Oxford University Press, 1922–37; John Murrow, 'The War in the Air', in Hew Strachan, ed., *The Oxford Illustrated History of the First World War*, Oxford: Oxford University Press, 1998, pp. 265–77.
57 HMM, vol. IX, part II, ch. V; Christopher Addison, *Four and a Half Years*, op. cit., pp. 248–49; Winston Churchill, *The World Crisis*, op. cit., pp. 303–16; Guy Hartcup, *The War of Invention*, op. cit., pp. 83–90. See also David Fletcher, *Landships: British Tanks in the First World War*, London: HMSO, 1984; Charles Messenger, *Call to Arms: The British Army 1914–18*, London: Cassell, 2005, pp. 177–80; R.J.Q Adams, *Arms and the Wizard*, op. cit., pp. 154–63; Patrick Wright, *Tank: The Progress of a Monstrous War Machine*, London, Faber, 2000, ch. 1.
58 Christopher Addison, *Politics from Within 1911–1918*, op. cit., p. 113.
59 NA, WO 159/15, 'Major-General Sir S.B. von Donop, Correspondence with Officers of the BEF', Nov–Dec. 1914; Charles Messenger, *Call to Arms: The British Army 1914–18*, op. cit., pp. 181–82.
60 HMM, vol. XI, part I, pp. 92–94; NA, MUN 5/196/160/5, 'Outline History of Stokes Gun'; MUN 5 196/1611/6, 'Minute on Design of Stokes Guns and Shells, 1916'; MUN 5/196/1610/12, 'Extracts from Diary of Lieut. F.A. Sutton for Period June to October 1915 on Early History of Stokes Gun'; T 173/453, 'Sir Wilfred Stokes' Trench Mortar'; Sir W. Stokes, 'The Stokes Gun and Shell and Their Development', *Journal of the Institute of Engineers*, vol. XXVIII, part X, 1918. See also Charles Messenger, *Call to Arms: The British Army 1914–18*, op. cit., p. 182; Hew Strachan, *To Arms*, op. cit., pp. 1069–70; R.J.Q. Adams, *Arms and the Wizard*, op. cit., pp. 151–52.
61 NA, WO 33/1072, 'German Chemical Warfare Organisation and Policy, 1914–18: Development of Protective Devices'; Guy Hartcup, *The War of Invention*, op. cit., pp. 98–99.
62 Richard Holmes, *Tommy: The British Soldier on the Western Front 1914–1918*, London: Harper Collins, 2004, p. 421.
63 Richard Holmes, *Tommy*; op. cit., p. 421; NA, T 173/97, 'SJM Auld, Impregnating Solution for Phenate-hexamine Gas Helmets'; T 173/314, 'B. Lambert: Lime Permanganate for Respirators'; WO 142/267, 'Diary of Development of British Respirator'; WO 142/318, 'Protection Given by Box Respirators Against Various Substances, 1917'; Guy Hartcup, *The War of Invention*, op. cit., pp. 103–4.

64 HMM, vol. XI, part I, ch. V. pp. 100–102; NA, WO 79/84, 'Steel Helmets', 3rd October 1916; George Dewar, *The Great Munition Feat, 1914–1918*, op. cit., pp. 90–92; Michael J. Haselgrove and Branislav Radovic, *History of the Steel Helmet in the First World War*, vol. 2, Pennsylvania, USA: Shiffer, 2006; Michael J. Haselgrove and Branislav Radovic, *Helmets of the First World War*, Pennsylvania, USA: Shiffer, 2000. See also www.greatwarcollection.nl/html/brodie.html.

65 Chris Wrigley, 'The Impact of the First World War on the British Labour Movement', in Michael Dockrill and David French, eds, *Strategy and Intelligence: British Policy During the First World War*, London: Hambledon, 1996, pp. 141–42.

66 Chris Wrigley, 'The Impact of the First World War on the British Labour Movement', op. cit., p. 140.

67 See George Robb, *British Culture and the First World War*, Basingstoke: Palgrave, 2002, pp. 72–73.

68 See John Grigg, *Lloyd George: From Peace to War, 1912–1916*, op. cit., pp. 221–22; Martin Pugh, *Lloyd George*, Harlow: Longman, 1988, pp. 81–89.

69 HMM, vol. I, part II, ch. IV, pp. 89–90.

70 HMM, vol. I, part II, chs 1–3; Hew Strachan, *To Arms*, op. cit., p. 1071.

71 Hew Strachan, *To Arms*, op. cit., p. 1071; R.J.Q. Adams, *Arms and the Wizard*, op. cit., p. 72; George Dewar, *The Great Munition Feat*, op. cit., p. 48.

72 NA, MUN 5/10/180/43, 'Notes and Correspondence on the Issue of Badges to Munition Workers', April 1915; NA, MUN 5/62/322/8, 'Papers on Munitions Work Badges: Army and Navy Practice for Reserved Occupations', Dec. 1914–Apr. 1915; Humbert Wolfe, *Labour Supply and Regulation*, Oxford: Clarendon, 1923, p. 19; R.J.Q. Adams, *Arms and the Wizard*, op. cit., pp. 76–77.

73 The methods of dilution and substitution as they were applied to working practices are discussed further in Chapter 5.

74 See G.D.H. Cole, *Trade Unionism and Munitions*, Oxford: Clarendon, 1923, pp. 34–37, 82–114.

75 George Dewar, *The Great Munition Feat*, op. cit., pp. 81–83.

76 HMM, vol. II, part I, ch. II; p. 37; HMM, vol. VI, part IV, pp. 105–10; *The Times*, 27th December 1915; Hew Strachan, *To Arms*, op. cit., p. 1081.

77 See G.D.H. Cole, *Trade Unionism and Munitions*, pp. 52–54, 67–69; NA, MUN 5/10/180/29, 'Memorandum of Agreement Between Engineering Employers' Federation and Amalgamated Society of Engineers on Production of Shells and Fuses', March 1915; R.J.Q. Adams, *Arms and the Wizard*, op. cit., pp. 78–80.

78 HMM, vol. II, part I, ch. II, pp. 8–10.

79 NA, CAB 1/11/46, 'Fourth interim report of the committee on production of engineering and shipbuilding establishments engaged on government work', 5th March 1915; NA, CAB 22/1/17, 'Minutes of the War Council', 3rd March 1915; NA, MUN 5/6/170/22, 'Minutes of Conference of Ministers on the Supply of Munitions Held at 10 Downing St', 5th March 1915; *Hansard Parliamentary Debates*, Fifth series, vol. LXX, cols 1271–74, 9th March 1915, col. 1460, 10th March 1915; David French, *British Economic and Strategic Planning*, op. cit., pp. 161–62; Hew Strachan, *To Arms*, op. cit., pp. 1072–73.

80 HMM, vol. I, part II, ch. IV; NA, 5/10/180/17, 'Minutes of Conference Between Government and Trade Union Representatives on Mobilisation of War Industries', March 1915; MUN 5/10/180/42, 'Conference Agreement Between Government and Amalgamated Society of Engineers on Means of Increasing Output', March 1915; NA, MUN 5/342/170/2/8, 'Work of Mr. G.M. Booth, Armaments Output Committee and Munitions of War Committee'; R.J.Q. Adams, *Arms and the Wizard*, op. cit., pp. 80–81.

81 G.D.H. Cole, *Trade Unionism and Munitions*, op. cit., pp. 77–82; HMM, vol. IV, part IV; R.J.Q. Adams, *Arms and the Wizard*, op. cit., pp. 84–89.

82 NA, CAB 37/127/41, 'Taxation of War Profits, April 1915'; NA, MUN 5/20/ 211.1/35, 'Memoranda and Notes on Munitions of War Bill and Profits Limitation, June–July1915'.

83 Adrian Gregory, *The Last Great War: British Society and the First World War*, Cambridge: Cambridge University Press, 2008, pp. 186–87.

84 Gerard DeGroot, *Blighty: British Society in the Era of the Great War*, Harlow: Longman, 1996, p. 115.

85 NA, MUN 5/349/341/1, 'Welsh Coal Strike'.

86 NA, MUN 5/62/322/18–20, 'Minutes of Proceedings with Amalgamated Society of Engineers' Representatives on Trade Card Scheme, April 1916–May 1917'; Keith Grieves, *The Politics of Manpower, 1914–18*, Manchester: Manchester University Press, 1988, pp. 57–58.

87 NA, CAB 23/2, w.c. 108, 29th March 29th 1917; Keith Grieves, *The Politics of Manpower, 1914–18*, op. cit., p. 127.

88 G.D.H. Cole, *Trade Unions and Munitions*, op. cit., pp. 202–3; Chris Wrigley, 'The Impact of the First World War on the British Labour Movement', op. cit., p. 148.

89 Sylvia Pankhurst, *The Home Front: A Mirror to Life During the World War*, London: Cresset Press, 1932, 1987 edn, pp. 129–30; George Robb, *British Culture and the First World War*, op. cit., pp. 74–75; see also J. Boswell and B. Johns, 'Patriots or Profiteers? British Businessmen and the First World War', *Journal of European Economic History*, vol. 11, 1982, pp. 263–82.

90 Cited in Adrian Gregory, *The Last Great War*, op. cit., p. 198.

91 HMM, vol. IV, part II, ch. II; Iain McLean, *The Legend of Red Clydeside*, Edinburgh: Donald, 1983.

92 HMM, vol. VI, part I, ch. V; see also Gerard DeGroot, *Blighty*, op. cit., p. 118.

93 See Ian Beckett, *Home Front 1914–1918: How Britain Survived the Great War*, op. cit., pp. 48–49.

94 G.D.H. Cole, *Workshop Organization*, Oxford: Clarendon Press, 1923, p. xiv, pp. 26–37.

95 HMM, vol. VI, part IV, ch. VI; G.D.H. Cole, *Workshop Organization*, op. cit., pp. 32–33, 143–49; Wal Hannington, *Industrial History in Wartime*, London: Lawrence & Wishart, 1940, pp. 54–66; Keith Middlemas, *The Clydesiders: A Left-wing Struggle for Parliamentary Power*, London: Hutchinson, 1965, p. 61.

96 See James Hinton, *The First Shop Stewards' Movement*, London: Allen & Unwin, 1977, p. 14; James Hinton, *Labour and Socialism: A History of the British Labour Movement, 1867–1974*, p. 107; Gerard DeGroot, *Blighty*, op. cit., p. 109.

97 HMM, vol. IV, part IV, chs IV, VIII; George Robb, *British Culture and the First World War*, op. cit., p. 75.

98 Chris Wrigley, 'The First World War and the Labour Movement', op. cit., p. 149.

99 See Adrian Gregory, *The Last Great War*, op. cit., pp. 196–99.

100 NA, Ministry of Labour papers (hereafter 'LAB') 2/254/13, 'History of the ASE Strike, May 1917'; NA, LAB 2/254/ML 2189/8A/1917, 'Ministry of Labour: Concerning a Conference Between the Minister of Labour and Representatives of Government Departments in Relation to Labour Unrest, 1917'.

101 See NA, LAB 2/254/7, 'Ministry of Munitions: Labour Unrest, Memorandum on Workshop Committees 19:6:17'; G.D.H. Cole, *Workshop Organization*, op. cit., pp. 96–103, 115–23.

102 Peter Dewey, *War and Progress: Britain 1914–1945*, Harlow: Longman, 1997, pp. 40–41.

103 See Commission of Enquiry into Industrial Unrest, *Summary of the Reports of the Commission by the Right Honourable G.N. Barnes, MP*, Cmnd 8696, 1917.

104 Commission of Inquiry into Industrial Unrest, No. 7 Division, *Report of the Commissioners for Wales including Monmouthshire*, Cmnd 8668, 1917, pp. 23, 33.

4   The eclipse of party government

Like a boulder rolling down a mountainside, the political effects of the war gathered momentum as the conflict stretched out. The Liberals, senior partner in a Progressive Alliance with Labour and Irish Nationalist MPs, had managed to take the country into battle under a shaky banner of political unity, convinced that it was possible to wage war without betraying their libertarian sympathies. Yet they struggled to come to grips with the new realities of industrial warfare and, in May 1915, Prime Minister Asquith formed a new coalition government with Andrew Bonar Law's Conservatives. This itself was consumed 18 months later by a more fully fledged coalition led by Lloyd George, backed mainly by the Conservatives, but also with a group of his own Liberal supporters and a smattering of Labour MPs. Ever since the days of Walpole, Britons had seen their parliamentary political system develop as an essentially two-party contest, so coalition government of this type was relatively new to British politics. Pushing aside traditional party loyalties for the sake of defeating Germany persuaded some in Westminster that coalition was the future model of political governance. But, though coalition certainly strengthened wartime government at the expense of political allegiance, it only smothered party ties instead of burying them.

Origins of coalition

The idea of coalition was circulating amongst the political classes well before 1914.[1] Pre-war concerns over the slippages in Britain's economic supremacy and decline in national character were the main drivers behind the emergence of the National Efficiency movement, led by the former Liberal Prime Minister and Foreign Secretary Lord Rosebury and the Liberal Imperialist Lord Milner.[2] As a former imperial administrator in Egypt and South Africa, Milner had returned to Britain in 1905 expressing his disdain for the 'Rotten Assembly of Westminster', arguing that the country's maladies could only be tackled by a non-party government stuffed with scientists, 'experts' and businessmen.[3] The bottom could easily have fallen out of the coalition idea had it not been for Rosebury's and Milner's ability to attract acolytes. Milner cultivated a *kindergarten* of like-minded Oxford intellectuals including L.S. Amery and future *Times* editor Geoffrey Dawson.[4] Rosebury found listeners in the more radical and impatient sections of the Liberal Party, most notably Winston Churchill and Lloyd George. Churchill (whose interest in Rosebury's arguments stemmed from work on a biography of his father Lord Randolph) tried to put his ideas into practice whilst President of the Board of Trade in the first Asquith government. During the debates on the National Insurance Bill, Churchill's mind was bent towards the notion of benign government, designed to build bridges between the social classes and unify people from different backgrounds.[5]

Lloyd George felt much the same way. His sympathies for coalition government also grew during his time at the Board of Trade. But they became much bolder during the all-party conferences convened at Buckingham Palace to surmount the political stand-offs over Lords Reform and Irish Home Rule.[6] In the autumn of 1910, Lloyd George approached Balfour with the idea of establishing a Coalition Ministry that combined the 'first rate men' of both parties to begin a programme of 'national reorganization' along the lines of the proposals outlined in his famous Criccieth Memorandum dictated in the summer.[7] Much of this came to nothing. In the febrile atmosphere of Edwardian politics, those who advocated coalition government spoke in isolation. Besides, even if some party leaders were ready to talk about coalitions, their grass-roots supporters were not. Nevertheless, pre-war mutterings about coalition helped to nurture the idea amongst MPs and public alike that all-party government may be a necessary mechanism for action and a symbol of unity during a national emergency. 'Here in short', writes G.R. Searle, 'was a political expedient which stood waiting in the wings, ready to be summoned on to the stage when Destiny called.'[8]

Early in the war, then, coalition government existed more as an unspoken thought, but this did not mean that the impulse for political unity was absent.[9] An all-party truce was declared in the Commons on 28th August 1914. All contested wartime by-elections were suspended and a spirit of togetherness had unified the parties into organizing the recruitment campaign.[10] The truce benefited Asquith more than his adversaries. Parliament's role in monitoring the government's conduct of the war was effectively suppressed. Debates on war strategy and domestic policy were conducted mainly in the Lords. The Conservatives could only voice their criticism through the veil of 'patriotic opposition': their one moment of outrage was restricted to a staged walkout over the government's decision to delay implementation of the Irish Home Rule Act until after the war.[11] None of this bothered Asquith unduly. His ministers expected a short war with disruption to the country's economic and social infrastructure being kept to a minimum, while the Liberals' majority in the Commons was held in place by the Progressive Alliance. The government looked relatively secure. Yet, within nine months Asquith felt obliged to form a coalition with the Conservatives. What went wrong?

Initially, the war did little to disrupt Asquith's style of government. Policy control was left in the hands of the peacetime 20-man Cabinet, supported by the newly created Council of War (consisting mostly of army and naval chiefs and a select group of ministers, including Churchill, Asquith, Grey and Kitchener), and occasional meetings of the Committee of Imperial Defence. In November, Asquith decided that this system was too large and unwieldy to meet the immediacy of wartime decision making, so he eased the process by setting up a smaller War Council, made up of the service chiefs and a few senior ministers, which rapidly became a cabinet within the Cabinet. Yet, Asquith's inability to resist pleas from other Cabinet members to join the Council resulted in a ballooning of its membership from eight to 13 in less than four months, and its importance in policy making grew accordingly.[12]

Asquith's reluctance to take a grip on his government seriously undermined its management of the war. In the autumn months of 1914 this was hardly noticed. Asquith's appointment of Kitchener to the War Office was seen as a masterstroke, and the Prime Minister's relaxed, 'wait-and-see' approach was widely interpreted as a necessary calm in the face of the storm. Trouble spots were confined to the outbreak of spy mania, which caught the Home Secretary Reginald McKenna in a blaze of criticism from the Commons, and grumbles amongst munitions suppliers over the inefficiencies of the War Office in awarding arms contracts.[13] Still, those who cared to look behind the facade of quiet efficiency would have seen the cracks. Neither Asquith (nor anyone else in the Cabinet) had the slightest notion of how to enact the emergency contingencies of the War Book when hostilities were declared, compelling the Prime Minister to haul Hankey (then secretary to the Committee of Imperial Defence) from his Mayfair club to give an impromptu briefing on its implementation.[14] Furthermore, the government had become obsessively secretive. The press were banned from publishing weather reports and chess games for fear that they could convey secret enemy conspiracies. The public were not told of the BEF's despatch until the end of August, and news of the sinking of HMS *Audacious* in October 1914 was not released until November 1918.[15] Hankey later complained to Asquith that 'the secrecy which is so vital to naval and military operations has been carried to such lengths as to be positively injurious to the conduct of the war'.[16] More damning perhaps was that, thanks to press censorship, the public's view of the fighting was framed within a discourse of heroism and battlefield success, obscuring the truth that the government had no clear strategic policies. But the growing stalemate on the Western Front and the shelling of Scarborough, Whitby and Hartlepool by the German navy in December 1914 put to rest all the fallacies of a quick victory and British military superiority and brought some stinging press criticism upon Asquith's administration.[17] The future of one-party government in this war looked increasingly untenable.

The eventual demise of Asquith's government came with the convergence of two separate crises. The first was provoked by the resignation on 15th May

1915 of the First Sea Lord Admiral Jacky Fisher in protest over the ill-fated Dardenelles campaign. Inspired by Churchill, the aim was to launch a naval offensive on Germany's ally, Turkey, through the Dardenelles straits, in the hope of achieving a strategic breakthrough in Europe without the use of troops. But, when the Navy's assault failed in March 1915, the campaign grew into a military and maritime operation that, afflicted by poor intelligence, poor leadership and poor planning, turned a setback into a disaster.[18] Fisher had quarrelled constantly with Churchill over the operation from the start. But the political injury that his resignation inflicted on the government could have been contained were it not for the publication the day before of Charles Repington's famous despatch in *The Times* (and the accompanying editorial, 'Shells and the Great Battle') pinning the blame for shell shortages at the Western Front on government mismanagement. Some historians have argued that the article in *The Times* was the result of collaboration between Repington (a retired officer) and Sir John French (Commander-in-Chief of the BEF) to explain away the 1st Army's failure to break the German lines in an attack on Aubers Ridge on 8th May.[19] In Asquith's eyes, however, it appeared as a carefully laid trap. He had been constantly pilloried in the Northcliffe newspapers for the perceived failings in armaments supply, yet, just three weeks before, Sir John had informed Kitchener that the BEF had sufficient ammunition to carry it through the next offensive.[20] Buoyed by this assurance, Asquith proceeded to give a morale-boosting speech to armaments workers at Newcastle in May 1915, scotching the rumours of shortages as an exaggeration, only for the Repington despatch to explode under his feet. It appeared that Asquith had been deliberately misled.[21] All the same, the political damage to his administration was irreparable. On 17th May 1915, Asquith dismantled what turned out to be Britain's last Liberal government and entered into a new coalition with Bonar Law's Conservatives.

There was more to Asquith's decision than selfless expediency. Historians may argue over the finer details of the coalition's formation;[22] some have suggested that Asquith's judgement was impaired by the break-up of his close (and emotionally intense) friendship with the socialite Venetia Stanley.[23] Asquith maintained that both the shell scandal and Fisher's resignation were equally important factors in his deliberations, but the final decision was taken to keep the political truce intact, and to uphold national morale at a time when Italy was contemplating joining the *entente*.[24] Yet, while there was no doubt that Asquith was having a bad war, the Conservatives' position was less than favourable. As leader of this 'patriotic opposition', Bonar Law had been happy to support the truce, but it left his party in a political straightjacket. By voluntarily refraining from attacking the government, the Conservatives found that they had no influence on its decisions. Senior member Lord Curzon protested to his leader that the government had 'all the advantages while we have all the drawbacks ... . They tell us next to nothing of their plans, and yet they pretend our leaders share both their knowledge and their responsibility'.[25] Growing frustration with this state of affairs drove many backbenchers to nurse their grievances through the Unionist Business Committee (UBC). Constituted in January 1915, the UBC, which claimed the support of around 40 backbench MPs, practically became an unofficial opposition, with room to criticize the government without breaking the truce and sending out warning signals to the leadership that mainstream party support could not be taken for granted.[26] Hence, according to Martin Pugh, the Conservative front bench became torn between supporting the war effort, whilst not being seen as a government prop, and carefully aiming their criticisms of government policy lest they be seen as unpatriotic.[27]

The munitions crisis, however, changed everything. Sympathizing with the Army's complaints over armament shortages, the level of Tory backbench disquiet rose to a point where the UBC threatened to call a parliamentary debate on the issue, openly challenging the truce. Asquith, with a comfortable Commons majority, was not particularly anxious. Bonar Law, on the other hand, was now faced with the threat of a 'Tory Revolt' and a potential challenge to his leadership. On 15th May, in an attempt to meet his critics halfway, Bonar Law adopted a more critical stance to the government by drafting a letter to Asquith urging a more aggressive and systematic policy on munitions. But it took the intervention of another Liberal to rescue Bonar Law from his dilemmas.

As Asquith's principal adjutant in the government, Lloyd George was far from an innocent bystander in the unfolding crisis. His concern with Bonar Law's difficulties intertwined with the political possibilities that they offered.[28] Lloyd George's sympathies for coalition government were long felt and well known, and the May crisis threw up an opportunity to form an all-party administration that was hard to resist. But the Chancellor was anxious not to be seen as a conspirator. Indeed Lloyd George's motives for forming a new government sprang primarily from his desire to wrest control of munitions supply from his adversary Lord Kitchener, a cause that attracted considerable cross-party support. Not surprisingly, it was Lloyd George who suggested to Bonar Law, during their meeting at the Treasury on 15th May, that only a new coalition government could resolve the political crisis: an offer that Bonar Law, and subsequently Asquith, could not refuse. An agreement between the three men was sealed in less than 15 minutes during a meeting in Downing Street later that day. It could be said that the Asquith coalition was formed out of a sense of public duty or national concerns. In reality, Bonar Law, Lloyd George and Asquith came together out of mutual self-interest. Bonar Law hoped that a place in government would quell his agitated party and secure his leadership; Lloyd George would be given a chance to take control of munitions. Asquith, on the other hand, was more fearful of a general election which, under the terms of the 1911 Parliament Act, was due either at the end of 1915, or, at the latest, the following January. All three men baulked at the prospect of a wartime general election, but Asquith baulked the most; he was not confident of victory.[29] One historian noted that coalition government held two virtues for Asquith, 'it preserved national unity; and it preserved him'.[30]

Wobbling through: Asquith's coalition

Asquith's move perplexed his party. Grass-roots Liberals were entirely ignorant of the Downing Street agreement. Ministers knew nothing of the coalition until they were summoned to submit their resignations on 17th May 1915. Shocked and outraged, Liberal members compelled Asquith to explain his actions at 'an indignation meeting' on 19th May.[31] Coalition threatened the party with two dangers. One was the break-up of the so-called Progressive Alliance, which had effectively kept the Conservatives in opposition since 1910.[32] Another was a resurgent Labour Party. Having begun the war as a largely pacifist party, symbolized by the Union of Democratic Control, Labour had now turned to the *realpolitik* approach of Sidney Webb and Arthur Henderson, who saw that the party's anti-war stance was out of step with the evident patriotism of the working classes, alongside the need to defend Britain's parliamentary system, which offered the only realistic prospect of social reform. Labour members came together with the establishment of the War Emergency Workers' National Committee, formed to protect working-class living standards against the economic distress and social dislocation brought on by the war. This new outlook was recognized when Asquith invited Henderson to join the coalition as President of the Board of Education. Henderson's role was small, but its symbolic nature was immense. As mediator between government and the trade unions on domestic and industrial policy, he brought the voice of organized labour into the heart of government.[33]

For their part, the Conservatives entered the coalition believing that they commanded equal representation in the new ministry and could invigorate the government's domestic wartime strategy with the introduction of conscription and greater economic and industrial controls. But their high hopes were followed by low blows. Asquith aimed to minimize Conservative influence in policy making by keeping the reins of power firmly in Liberal hands. Not surprisingly, in Asquith's first coalition Cabinet, Liberals hung on to all the major government posts. McKenna took over at the Treasury following Lloyd George's move to Munitions; Grey was retained at the Foreign Office; Walter Runciman continued at the Board of Trade; Churchill was demoted to the Duchy of Lancaster as a stepping stone to his eventual resignation. Of the Conservatives, only the trusted Balfour was given any influence, replacing Churchill as First Lord of the Admiralty. Otherwise, Balfour's party colleagues were consigned to the administrative backwaters. Bonar Law was appointed to the Colonial Office; Austen Chamberlain went to the India Office. Other leading Conservatives (Curzon, Carson and Walter Long) were given minor government posts. Kitchener, however, remained as War Secretary. Public popularity made the Field Marshal almost impossible to replace and his presence sheltered Asquith from the opprobrium of the press and backbench MPs.[34]

Asquith's first and last concern was to keep the coalition intact, ostensibly for the sake of national unity, but also for his own political survival. The obstacles to achieving this were encapsulated in two contentious issues – war strategy and conscription. The debates over strategy were grounded in the trenches. Some ministers (including Lloyd George), who had long despaired of making any progress on the Western Front, began to argue for an indirect 'peripheral approach', opening a new offensive against Germany by attacking Austria in the Balkans with support from Serbia and other local allies. Though this argument had been partially undermined by the Dardenelles catastrophe, it failed to dent the enthusiasm of the 'Easterners' in the Cabinet. However, their views were challenged by the 'Westerners' (including many Conservatives, with support from Army High Command), who believed that the focal point of the war effort should remain on the Western Front, with France as the main theatre of operations. Asquith brought the two sides together when he replaced the ineffective War Council with a new Cabinet body, the Dardenelles Committee, in May 1915. Composed of nine senior ministers (although without serving officers), its brief was initially confined to diplomatic and war-related issues in the Eastern Mediterranean. Yet the Committee's effectiveness was quickly compromised by Asquith's old weakness in resisting the claims of ministers who yearned for the political kudos of membership – three ministers joined soon after its formation and three more were added before it was dismantled in October 1915. This move did little to defuse ministerial tensions (as witnessed in the disputes over terminating the Dardenelles campaign)[35] and, because its decisions could be challenged in Cabinet, the Committee lacked the authority of the old War Council.[36]

Asquith attempted to reconcile the two sides by some nimble committee management. The flow of military information to ministers was greatly eased with the appointment of a new Chief of Imperial General Staff (CIGS), Sir Archibald Murray, who, in contrast to Kitchener's obsessive secrecy, was much more open and forthright in his approach. Asquith then broadened the forum for strategic debate by replacing the clearly dysfunctional Dardenelles Committee on 5th October 1915 with a new War Committee, consisting initially of himself, Balfour, Lloyd George and McKenna.[37] The reforms promised improvement. The responsibilities of the committee and the Cabinet were more clearly demarcated; the committee's meetings were more frequent, with the military and admiralty chiefs in regular attendance. Moreover, Asquith attached the effortlessly efficient Maurice Hankey to the committee as its secretary, who subsequently ensured that all its meetings were noted and its conclusions freely distributed amongst the Cabinet and affected ministries.[38]

The War Committee was a sound move, but it was still disrupted by political meddling. Soon after its formation, Asquith expanded its membership to include McKenna and Bonar Law, who (with Lloyd George's complicity) then threatened to resign if Kitchener was not removed. Asquith responded in December 1915 by appointing Sir William Robertson as a new CIGS: a move that was part of a shake-up in Army High Command, when Douglas Haig replaced Sir John French as Commander-in-Chief of the BEF in France. Kitchener's influence on the committee (and the Cabinet) was certainly reduced, but its members were powerless to contest Robertson's obdurate view that the Western Front was the only war that mattered. His refusal to attend every session, or reveal full details of military operations, prevented the War Committee from having any influence on strategy or military decisions.[39] The committee's effectiveness was compromised further by Asquith's insistence that responsibility for war policy still resided with the Cabinet, allowing those excluded members freedom to challenge its decisions. This indeed is what occurred in December 1915, when the 'Westerners' on the War Committee secured an agreement to abandon the Dardenelles campaign, only for the Cabinet to overrule the decision in favour of delay, leaving the land army in Gallipoli to face winter conditions without adequate provisions. In despair, Hankey wrote in his diary, 'They put off decisions, squabble [and] have no plan of action or operation ... I see only one solution – to suspend the constitution and appoint a dictator.'[40]

It was conscription, however, that pushed the integrity of Asquith's coalition to its limits. The divisions within the Cabinet ran deep and Asquith knew full well that the question could break the government. As discussed earlier, the Army viewed conscription as vital for securing the troops needed to continue the war; the Conservatives saw conscription as essential for the management of resources, money and manpower (see Chapter 2 text box, Manpower); the Liberals viewed the issue as one of individual morality. Later, Charles Hobhouse, a minister in Asquith's first war ministry, recalled Runciman's picture of Cabinet dissension:

> Lansdowne, Curzon, Law, A. Chamberlain were for leaving the Cabinet if conscription were not proposed ... Balfour and Long would remain in whatever happened, to carry on the Govt. A.J.B. [Balfour] being against and Long for compulsory service. With them would go Churchill who was pining to get abroad to the Dardenelles, and Ll.G who saw no opening to a leadership, and was much afraid that he had muddled the Ministry of Munitions ... . The P.M. was still a convinced voluntarist, but equally determined on keeping the Govt. together, and was trying to find a hypothetical formula of a Bill falling due 3 months hence! McKenna who was the P.M.'s only confidant was determined to resign as was W.R. [Walter Runciman] ... Henderson had a violent altercation with Ll.G and told him and the Cabinet squarely that Labour would resist conscription by every means, in and out of Parliament.[41]

Asquith pondered resignation.[42] In his heart, he probably wanted to find a quiet corner and wish that the conscription issue would just go away, but in a

Figure 4.1 A troubled Prime Minister. Asquith leaving Downing Street, *c*. October 1915

valiant attempt to maintain unity he chose to percolate the issue through a network of *ad hoc* Cabinet Committees.

The conscription crisis broke over the government in two waves. The first came when the Conservatives forced the issue in Cabinet soon after the coalition had been formed. Asquith immediately referred the whole question to a rapidly assembled Cabinet Committee, which eventually recommended the National Registration Bill (which became law on 15th July) and a national manpower census scheduled for 15th August. This did little to quell the debate. Focusing on manpower, Asquith then established a War Policy Committee during the late summer of 1915, chaired by Lord Crewe, which attempted to assess the Army's demands in relation to the evidence produced by national registration. But the committee quickly became ensnared between the pro- and anti-conscriptionist camps, and Crewe was forced to report in September 1915 that the evidence was too contradictory to make a full recommendation for conscription, with all but two of its members (himself and Henderson) voicing their support for the measure.[43]

Faced with trying to extract a decision through indecision, the Cabinet then compelled Asquith to dismantle the War Policy Committee and integrate it (along with the Dardenelles Committee) into the new War Committee, with a carefully balanced membership between the two camps. The move backfired when the conscriptionists decided to simplify matters by attempting to force the Cabinet to make up its mind. Asquith reacted by announcing the Derby Scheme at the War Committee's meeting on 15th October, before falling seriously ill. On his return to work in November, the Derby scheme was still being opposed by senior Conservatives and Lloyd George, who all threatened resignation until Asquith compromised with his 'married men' pledge. Following the failure of the Derby scheme and the subsequent passing of the conscription act in Parliament, Asquith then moved, in January 1916, to establish a Military Finance Committee, embracing himself, Austen Chamberlain and Reginald McKenna, to settle upon an acceptable size for the Army.[44] When the Military Finance Committee reported for the second time in April 1916, after experiencing profound difficulties in balancing the claims of government departments and the military, Conservative backbenchers provoked a second conscription crisis by using the grievances of attested married men (see Chapter 2) as grounds for introducing general conscription.[45] Though the committee's report had deduced that this would not resolve the manpower problem, Lloyd George insisted that the matter be referred to the Army Council, who promptly demanded an expansion of the Army to 70 divisions or more. Unable to reconcile High Command's stipulations with the wider questions of industrial manpower, Asquith then convened a Committee on the Size of the Army, set up to liaise with the Military Finance Committee, which met for one day on 18th April 1916. The resulting compromise report drew heavily from Lloyd George's suggestion of expanding weekly recruiting targets with the proviso that general conscription would be introduced if the new objectives were not met, but this only provoked further Cabinet arguments.[46] When Asquith stated in the Commons that his ministers could not agree on extending compulsion, MPs erupted in anger. On 20th April the Cabinet finally endorsed a measure very close to Lloyd George's suggestion and a concord on introducing general conscription was uneasily reached by 29th April.[47] Lloyd George's compromise formula had practically saved the government. But where did this leave Asquith?

Without doubt, Asquith's committee culture helped to keep his government together, but the constant infighting over conscription weakened the Cabinet's authority and distracted attention from pressing issues. Reginald McKenna's pronouncements to the Military Finance Committee that the war was costing almost £5 million a day and the country's deficit would mount to £600 million by March 1916, and £2,000 million a year later, highlighted the alarming gaps in Britain's finances, but the question was never fully addressed.[48] (See Chapter 4 text box, Budgets.) Another intrusion was Ireland. The eruption of violence in Dublin during the Easter weekend of 1916, and the attempt by members of the Irish Republican Brotherhood to proclaim an Irish Free State from the General Post Office, were quickly suppressed by the Army. But the delays in replacing the government's Chief Secretary in Ireland (Augustine Birrell), by another civilian governor, left an administrative vacuum in which the Army was allowed free rein to execute 12 captured rebels and one innocent journalist without trial. Asquith took temporary charge in May, leaving Lloyd George to negotiate a settlement that involved an immediate implementation of Home Rule, but keeping the six counties of Ulster within the United Kingdom. Yet Lloyd George's plan was contested by Lansdowne and Long in the Cabinet, and a Unionist backbenchers' revolt in the Commons put paid to Lloyd George's solution until after the war. 'Ireland', in John Turner's words, 'was a mess'. It had reverted to direct rule from Westminster, while the Army's perfunctory treatment of the rebels turned many Irish people against Britain's authority in their country.[49]

Other questions lay unresolved. The control of military aviation was a constant source of friction between the Admiralty and the War Office; the Admiralty's failure to combat the growing U-boat threat to Britain's imports was almost unforgivable given a poor harvest. The attempts of the Agriculture Secretary Lord Selborne to warn the Cabinet of an impending crisis in domestic food supplies were ignored. Public and parliamentary anger was roused by the Royal Navy's losses in the battle of Jutland on 31st May, exposing as it did evidence of inadequate training, shortcomings in communications, mediocre leadership and technical deficiency. The coalition also bore the brunt of public anger (somewhat unfairly) for the military failures at Loos and the collapse of British strategy in the Eastern Mediterranean, culminating in General Townshend's surrender to the Turks at Kut-el-Amara on 29th April 1916. Some of the blame for the coalition's weakness must rest with Asquith. His languid leadership style, with a readiness to allow ministers to perform their jobs without Cabinet accountability and almost in isolation from the rest of the government, proved unworkable in wartime, as individual departments built their own small administrative hinterlands and fought private battles for resources. Perhaps Asquith's greatest mistake was to cede political control of military matters to the generals, leaving Sir William Robertson (the CIGS) as the sole channel of military advice and information to the government, and impervious to ministerial questioning. Thus, at a critical period in the war, Army High Command lay outside government control and accountability, leaving the Cabinet to approve new campaigns half-blind, including the 1916 Somme offensive. Such errors were exacerbated by

Asquith's reluctance to let go of the old system of Cabinet government. Sprawling cabinets of 22 conflicting temperaments and attitudes were not conducive to making quick decisions and formulating decisive policies. In his memoirs, Hankey cited Curzon's account of Asquith's governing style:

> There was no agenda; there was no order of business. Any Minister requiring to bring up a matter either of departmental or of public importance had to seek the permission of the Prime Minister at No. 10. No one else, broadly speaking, was warned in advance. It was difficult for any Minister to secure an interstice in the discussion in which he could place his own case. No record whatever was kept of our proceedings, except the private and personal letter written by the Prime Minister to the Sovereign, the contents of which, of course, are never seen by anyone else. The cabinet often had the very haziest notion as to what its decisions were … cases frequently arose when the matter was left so much in doubt that a Minister went away and acted upon what he thought was a decision which subsequently turned out to be no decision [at] all, or was repudiated by his colleagues. No one will deny that a system [that] was destined immediately it came into contact with the hard realities of war, to crumble into dust at once … .[50]

A new government

It could be said that Asquith's coalition was a catastrophe waiting to happen. Yet, without a credible rival in the Cabinet, or an issue around which his bickering ministers could unite against him, Asquith's premiership remained secure. Even so, by November 1916 the political ground at Westminster was beginning to move. Now ensconced at the War Office following Kitchener's death in June, Lloyd George had become increasingly restless at the coalition's rudderless character. Following the Inter-Allied Conference in Paris, he discussed with Hankey the possibility of forming a new four-member War Committee (or a civilian General Staff), headed by himself, with the authority to impose decisions on government departments, while Asquith would continue in a nominal role as Prime Minister.[51] It was a viable proposition, but Lloyd George needed support. It came first in the unlikely guise of Edward Carson, the former rabble-rousing leader of Ulster Protestantism, who had resigned from the government a year earlier and had subsequently led 64 Conservatives to vote against the coalition during an innocuous Commons debate over the sale of confiscated enemy property in Nigeria. Carson's actions pulled in Bonar Law. Suspicious of Lloyd George's ambition, and still reluctant to work against Asquith, the Tory leader could not ignore the threat that Carson posed to party unity (and the truce) and thus felt the need to support Lloyd George's plan following a series of meetings and dinner dates arranged by Sir Max Aitken (proprietor of the *London Evening Standard* and the *Daily Express*, who was ennobled as Lord Beaverbrook in 1917).[52] This triumvirate – Carson, Bonar Law and Lloyd George – resolved to confront Asquith with the new proposals.[53]

Bonar Law's first approach to Asquith on 25th November 1916 was rejected, however.[54] And the rebuttal exposed Bonar Law's own shaky position, when he faced criticism from leading Conservatives resentful of a plan to reform the government to the advantage of two untrustworthy individuals, Lloyd George and Carson. Lloyd George then reshaped the plan, proposing to form a three-man War Committee with himself as chairman, whilst Asquith retained the premiership, but without any influence on the committee. Asquith again repudiated the move, insisting that 'whatever changes are made in the composition or function of the War Committee, the Prime Minister must be its chairman'.[55] Proceedings then stalled momentarily. The triumvirate agreed that, although Asquith's methods were intolerable, his value as a political figurehead was inestimable. As premier, Asquith alone remained capable of introducing controversial measures without dividing politicians and the public.[56] Nevertheless, the pressure for change had to be maintained. On 2nd December, Lloyd George decided to push matters further by drafting a letter of resignation, fully aware that Bonar Law had called an impromptu meeting of Conservative ministers for the next day with a view to presenting Asquith with an ultimatum: submit the resignation of his entire Cabinet immediately, or the Conservatives would withdraw from the coalition.[57] Faced with the impending collapse of his government, Asquith, on the afternoon of 3rd December, accepted Lloyd George's proposition.

But Asquith then turned. On 4th December all his Cabinet Liberals, along with three Conservative ministers – Curzon, Cecil and Chamberlain – voiced their opposition to the prospect of joining a new *de facto* Lloyd George government, hoping to goad Asquith into taking a stronger hold on the coalition's conduct of the war. This unexpected show of support was enough to persuade Asquith that his government could withstand a Lloyd George resignation and, using the cover of a notorious article in *The Times* denigrating him, the Prime Minister repudiated the agreement he had made the previous day.[58] The following morning Lloyd George resigned, along with Bonar Law.[59] Unnerved at the prospect of serving in an Asquith regime without the presence of either Lloyd George or their leader, the three Conservative ministers then decided to leave the government. Asquith had little choice but to resign that evening.[60]

Asquith's coalition had gone; but uncertainty surrounded its successor. In constitutional terms the King was obliged to ask Bonar Law, as leader of the second largest party in the Commons, if he would form a new government. The King refuted Bonar Law's initial response to dissolve Parliament. Negotiations then settled on establishing a new coalition, retaining the two Liberal leaders with Bonar Law acting as a 'neutral' prime minister. Lloyd George was prepared to accept. Asquith, however, regarding Bonar Law as a conspirator who had destroyed his government, was not. The following day the four men reconvened at Buckingham Palace. Asquith, convinced that neither

Bonar Law, Lloyd George nor Balfour could form a government, refused to negotiate. At 7 p.m. on 6th December, Bonar Law and Lloyd George appeared together at the Palace, informing the King that the Conservative leader's failure to form a government left Lloyd George as the only man left who could realistically put together a new administration.[61] After consulting with the Labour Party, sounding out his support from Liberal backbenchers and complex negotiations over the distribution of offices amongst Bonar Law's Conservatives, Lloyd George was convinced that he had enough backers in the Commons to form a new government, and he was appointed Prime Minister the next day. Writing in her diary, Frances Stevenson recorded that it was touch and go for her 'little Welsh attorney'. But by the afternoon she found 'D' in high spirits. 'I think I shall be Prime Minister before 7 o'clock', he said to me. And he was.'[62]

The Lloyd George coalition took the known systems of party *and* government into unfamiliar terrain, highlighting Michael Fry's assertion that the debates over critical war issues had become so intense that they could no longer be contained within the old political structures.[63] In a sense, Lloyd George's stature in the new government was almost presidential. He had become Prime Minister when the British public were set for more resolute leadership, and realistically Lloyd George was the only man who possessed the attitude and determination to guide the country through future hardships and dangers. Lloyd George alone was intellectually and politically equipped to meet the challenges of industrial labour and capable of drawing support across the social and political divides.[64] His voluble arguments in the Asquith Cabinet and his achievements at the Munitions Ministry sustained the new Prime Minister's policy of deploying state power to organize Britain's people and her material resources to win the war. Above all, in the aftermath of military failure following the tragic debacle of the Somme campaign, Lloyd George voiced (and perhaps reflected) a national determination to see the war through to a 'decisive finish'. In an unauthorized interview with an American journalist in September 1916, Lloyd George announced that, 'Peace now or at any time before the final and complete elimination of this [German] menace is unthinkable. No man or no nation with the slightest understanding of the temper of the citizen army of Britons, which took its terrible hammering without a whine or a grumble, will attempt to call a halt now.'[65] While not quite matching the high emotions later called forth by Churchill's rhetoric of 1940, in the circumstances it was enough.

But Lloyd George's ascendancy came at a price, part of which was paid by the Liberal Party. In taking 120 'Lloyd George Liberals' with him to the government benches, Lloyd George delivered a body blow to the party from which it would never recover. Few senior and high-status Liberals were willing to serve and support him. Indeed, the new arrangements left the House of Commons contemplating the spectacle of two Liberal parties. Asquith retained his Chief Whip, managed the party organization, controlled its headquarters and administered its funds and officials with the support of the

National Liberal Federation. Lloyd George remained a member of the party (in theory still under Asquith's authority), but appointed his own 'coalition' Chief Whip, and even purchased the *Daily Chronicle* to counter the pro-Asquith Liberal press.[66] Furthermore, as Lloyd George had used the support of his opponents to gain power, so they used him. Labour sided with him for their own gain, levering Lloyd George into promising to nationalize the mining industry and give the party political control of vital domestic ministries.[67] And Lloyd George's methods appeared to chime with the ideas of the 'mechanical reformists', such as Sidney and Beatrice Webb, who saw in the use of state power a model for future reform.[68] But it was the Conservatives who were the true beneficiaries of the new political settlement. They were the largest party in the Commons and had used Lloyd George to lever themselves into government. He was the leader whom many of their MPs wished they had. Lloyd George had thus secured the Conservatives' parliamentary supremacy; he was the Prime Minister of an essentially Conservative regime, and their support kept him in office.

For the time being, the 'new' politics begat a 'new' governance. Lloyd George's administration was formally structured in three tiers. Policy and decision making was centred within a new five-man Cabinet. Lloyd George as Prime Minister was joined by Bonar Law, who combined his appointment as Chancellor with taking the position of Leader of the Commons (two senior positions that reflected the Conservative dominance of the new government). Other Cabinet members sat without portfolio. Lord Curzon was included, partly because of his capacity for hard work, partly to stifle his opposition to Law: his scope for mischief making was thus much reduced. The same reasons applied to Lord Milner's surprising inclusion, although this was a signal to the Tory right of Lloyd George's resolve to win the war at all costs. Arthur Henderson was added in recognition of the labour movement's centrality to the war effort, despite Lloyd George's misgivings over his ministerial capabilities.[69] Occupying a second tier of government was an extensive apparatus of new and older ministries staffed by men who were in tune with Lloyd George's political and personal inclinations, as well as his patronage. With experienced Liberals thin on the ground, Lloyd George turned to some trusted businessmen and industrialists to fill major government posts. Albert Stanley (a railway company director) was appointed to the Board of Trade; shipping-magnate Joseph Maclay became Minister for Shipping; Eric Geddes was appointed to the Admiralty; the historian and don H.A.L. Fisher became Secretary for Education; the grocer Lord Devonport became responsible for food.[70]

Otherwise, Christopher Addison (a devout Lloyd George Liberal) was placed in charge of the Munitions Ministry, while Lord Rhondda took over the department for local government. Two Labour MPs were also included, George Barnes at the new Pensions Ministry and John Hodge at the Ministry of Labour. These structures were serviced, on the one hand, by a new Cabinet Secretariat, led by Maurice Hankey, which formalized the operations of the

War Cabinet with preparation of agendas, recording of minutes of Cabinet meetings, circulation of its decisions amongst government departments and arrangement for individual ministers and advisers to attend War Cabinet meetings[71] and, on the other, by the formation of a new personal secretariat for Lloyd George, which furnished him with information and advice outside the normal civil service channels. Housed in wooden huts in the Downing Street garden, it became known irreverently as the 'Garden Suburb' and contained a number of Milnerites and admirers, including Waldorf Astor, Joseph Davies, Philip Kerr and Professor W.S.G. Adams.[72] Hankey later called this system a 'dictatorship in commission'. Ministers were only invited to meetings to report and receive instructions for their own departments, while only Bonar Law, as Chancellor, and Balfour, as Foreign Secretary, regularly attended Cabinet meetings. But, in practice, the Lloyd George revolution only went so far.[73] Difficult questions were delegated to individual War Cabinet members and then passed on to a growing web of smaller *ad hoc* committees staffed by officials and departmental ministers for further consideration. This diffusion of authority was taken to another level by a series of Standing Committees, chaired by War Cabinet members, whose job was to co-ordinate policy between departments with overlapping responsibilities. Much to Hankey's frustration, instead of handling matters of the utmost priority, the Cabinet became bogged down in Asquithian methods and preoccupied with pettifogging details and procedures.[74] Some committees, though, were effective. The War Priorities Committee strengthened the Cabinet's influence over both military and civilian departments by separating the formulation of strategic policy from everyday administration, enabling Lloyd George to govern unhindered by internal opposition. Whether the new Prime Minister ever fulfilled his ambition to overhaul the system of government in the manner of his achievements at Munitions is a matter for debate.

Of course, the coalition's primary function was to win the war and, in this respect, its ministers had much work to do. One immediately pressing issue was Germany's unrestricted submarine campaign, declared against Britain's merchant marine in February 1917. Between January and April shipping losses rose alarmingly from 153,666 gross tons in January 1917 to 545,282 by April. In the 'black fortnight' of 17th to 30th April nearly 400,000 tons of British shipping was sunk.[75] The country's fighting capacity depended heavily on obtaining vital overseas supplies of iron ore, paper, timber and food (especially North American wheat), yet this was where government policy was weakest. Addressing the threat involved a dual strategy: increasing the construction of new ships – a policy met by Maclay's introduction of standardization at shipyards – and reducing unloading times in port, as well as arming merchant vessels.[76] Most effective was increasing protection for ocean-going vessels. Hankey, who had first highlighted the problem in a memorandum to Jacky Fisher in 1915, urged the adoption of a convoy system (a tactic first used successfully during the Napoleonic wars), which involved grouping merchant ships together in formation, protected by an escort of warships.[77]

Admiralty conservatism, however, proved difficult to surmount. Navy commanders, still wedded to the notion of sea-going warfare as a series of set-piece battles, initially refused to take the U-boat menace very seriously. Moreover, Admiralty staff insisted that it was unable to discipline merchant vessels to sail at a uniform speed and that such a concentration of ships would lead to collisions and present enemy submarines with an easy target. Besides, the Navy could not spare enough escort vessels, whilst unloading convoy ships *en masse* would overwhelm the ports.[78]

The 'black fortnight' forced a rethink. Opinions began to turn when the Admiralty realized that its figures were wrong. Commander Reginald Henderson discovered that previous Admiralty assumptions of 300 ships entering and leaving British ports daily were wildly inaccurate. Using navy statistics, he calculated that the numbers were closer to 20. At the same time, the Admiralty discovered that ocean-going vessels, which were less than 10 per cent of total shipping, were the most vulnerable to U-boat attack. Together with the realization that troopships had been escorted throughout the war without loss, the principle of convoy suddenly became feasible. Indeed, with entry of the United States of America into the war, the supply of naval warships available as escorts increased, forcing Jellicoe, the First Sea Lord, to recognize that convoys at least offered an alternative to previous policy. By the time the crisis reached the War Cabinet, the shipping problem was halfway to being resolved. Lloyd George, after much cajoling from Hankey, held one of his breakfast meetings with Admiralty officials on 30th April and learned that the Navy had already conducted a successful experiment in escorting a cross-Channel shipment of coal and had decided to run another experimental convoy from Gibraltar on 10th May. Even so, it was not until mid-August that the convoy system was in general use. Cautious Admiralty deployment ensured that the first convoys were (unnecessarily) small, yet they moved rapidly with numerous escorts. The results were spectacular. Of the 5,090 merchant ships convoyed during 917, only 63 were lost. By October, shipping losses fell to about 270,000 tons and in December it was only a little over 170,000 tons. The convoy initiative was one of the few success stories in 1917 and was the result of quick and flexible thinking, mainly by officials, in the face of an emergency. Yet it was Lloyd George who took the credit.[79]

The easing of the shipping problem allowed greater attention to be given to other equally vital issues, though success was more elusive. A combination of bad harvests and submarine warfare compelled the government to safeguard food supplies by appointing a succession of food ministers and introducing subsidies, price controls and, eventually, rationing.[80] Labour relations presented further concerns. Caught out by the rise of unrest across the engineering industries in the spring of 1917, the government instinctively believed that the strikes were influenced by events in Russia, without fully realizing that the disturbances had exposed weaknesses in government policy. In one respect, the strikes revealed how far the government's difficulty with the workforce was a consequence of insensitive army demands. It was military pressure for a

Figure 4.2 Prime Minister at work. Lloyd George at home studying papers, March 1917

new 'comb out' of skilled workers at the beginning of 1917 that compelled Christopher Addison to step up dilution rates in vital industries, firstly by tearing up the trade card scheme, which protected men in the engineering unions from the call-up, and replacing it with a new Schedule of Protected Occupations, which was much more selective in its operation. The move caused great resentment amongst the workforce in spite of its endorsement by the ASE leadership and Lloyd George. Addison's troubles arose from his botched attempt to imprison the strike leaders and subsequent leaking to the press, without official authorization, of the new agreements, leaving the minister alone to defend himself against accusations of incompetence from Conservative MPs.[81] Moreover, the strikes provided clear evidence that, in negotiating settlements with union leaders, ministers had failed to acknowledge the groundswell of rank-and-file opinion as voiced by the shop stewards. As the subsequent Industrial Unrest Commissions revealed, the strikes were less about the introduction of the new schedules than genuine grievances over rising prices, wages and social conditions[82] (see Chapter 3). The government could not now ignore the effect the war was having on the country's social and political fabric, and the commissioners' reports gave Lloyd George an opportunity to move his troubled Munitions minister, who was now assigned to the task of responding to working-class grievances by formulating a package of social reforms in a reorganized Ministry of Reconstruction.

War Cabinet member Arthur Henderson had also been struck by the Russian upheavals, but became caught between conflicting priorities. His enforced resignation in August 1917 arose from his proposal for a peace conference in Stockholm after Lloyd George, fearing that Russia would pull out of the war, had dispatched him to Moscow for meetings with the new Provisional Government. Convinced that the Provisional Government could not counter the pressure of the extreme left, Henderson argued that peace was essential for the new regime's survival. But the War Cabinet feared that talk of peace could bring on the collapse of the Eastern Front and instructed Henderson to make this point to the Labour Party conference. Henderson refused and was replaced by the more compliant George Barnes. In the short run, Henderson's departure was of little consequence to Lloyd George. But Henderson would return to haunt the Prime Minister. He played a significant part in reunifying the pacifist and patriotic elements within the Labour Party, allowing it eventually to break with the Liberals and concentrate its efforts on becoming a party of government.[83]

Ultimately, the integrity of the Lloyd George coalition hinged upon battlefield success. Asquith's governments had been broken by military failure, and Lloyd George was determined to avoid previous errors. His lack of confidence in the Army High Command was well known, but he could do little to wrest control of military policy from the generals without destabilizing his government. In Sir William Robertson as CIGS and Sir Douglas Haig, commander of the BEF in France (both convinced 'Westerners' who enjoyed wholesale Conservative support), Lloyd George faced an immovable object when formulating new strategic initiatives. Early attempts to circumvent their power floundered. The appointment of Lord Derby as War Secretary in 1917, as an alternative voice to Robertson's, was thwarted by his tendency to support Army High Command. Lloyd George's efforts to breathe life into an 'Eastern strategy' by advocating the transfer of British troops to Salonika, offering greater support for the Russians and bolstering the Italian front met with the unified hostility of the War Cabinet, alongside threats from the Conservative press to destroy the government through a campaign of unrelenting criticism. His move to subordinate Haig by placing him within a combined Allied Command Structure during the failed Nivelle Offensive in April 1917 aroused similar hostility.[84]

By the summer of 1917, Lloyd George's luck turned. In June, he successfully established a new Cabinet War Policy Committee, comprising himself, Curzon and Milner, with alternative military advice provided by the inclusion of General Jan Smuts, a veteran of the South African war. Smuts's approval of Haig's Passchendaele offensive dented the Committee's initial impact, yet Haig's failures pushed Lloyd George into seeking alternative military advice through General Sir Henry Wilson, Director of Military Operations. Wilson, who was more strategically flexible, agreed with Lloyd George that the experiences of Passchendaele (and the rout of the Italian Army at Caporetto in October 1917) highlighted the need for proper co-ordination of the Allied war effort, and in November 1917 a Supreme War Council was established at Versailles. Robertson was now effectively sidelined. His demise came following the formation of an Inter-Allied Reserve in France during February 1918 under the command of a special executive. Robertson's insistence on being the British representative on that body was rebuffed when Lloyd George pointed out that it was impossible for him to offer military advice in London as well as France, and Robertson's rejection of both was accepted as a resignation. Wilson was appointed CIGS. Haig, surprisingly, survived the overhaul, mainly through Smuts's support, but he, too, was subordinated (on Milner's initiative) to the French General Foch, who became Commander-in-Chief of the Allied Armies in France following the initial successes of the German spring offensive in 1918. Lloyd George then assumed strategic control of the fighting in France by forming a new 'X' committee, consisting of himself, Milner, Wilson and Hankey, which met before each War Cabinet to discuss the progress of events in France. The committee often took essential decisions on manpower and domestic policy, whilst continuing to supervise strategy right through to the Armistice, and without referral to the War Cabinet.[85]

Meanwhile, the military retaliated. In May 1917, General F.D. Maurice, a close associate of Robertson and former Director of Military Operations, published a letter in *The Times* (and other leading newspapers) accusing the Prime Minister of misleading the Commons about the numerical strength of the British Army in France and 'impairing the morale of our troops'.[86] Lloyd George's figures did leave room for doubt. His assertions damaged relations with other Cabinet members and there were rumours that the Prime Minister had set out to undermine Haig's authority by deliberately withholding troops for France. Yet it was clear that Maurice's underlying aim was to destabilize the Prime Minister by accusing him of lying to Parliament and leaving the BEF vulnerable to German attack in March. In the Commons, Asquith demanded the setting up of a select committee to investigate Maurice's accusations, thus drawing Lloyd George into a major debate with the Liberal opposition. The Prime Minister regarded this as nothing less than a vote of confidence in his administration. The subsequent debate failed to shake Lloyd George. Helped by many Liberal abstentions, the government easily won the division by 298 votes to 106. Even though many Liberals still shrank from openly criticizing Lloyd George's conduct (albeit that Asquith broke ranks and voted against the government), there was now a clear division of opinion within the party over two alternative notions of war leadership and war policy. Lloyd George had proved to be an effective war leader; but now the realities of party politics were about to touch him once more.[87]

The Maurice debate affirmed Lloyd George's political dominance and, once the war had begun to turn in the Allies' favour after July 1918, it became increasingly clear that the Prime Minister's arm of the Liberal Party was well placed to profit from the public acclaim brought on by impending victory. But in government Lloyd George remained politically isolated and vulnerable. In 1917 he moved to strengthen his position by bringing some of his erstwhile Liberal colleagues into the government, notably Edwin Montagu, a disillusioned Asquith supporter who was appointed to the India Office, and, more controversially, Churchill, who took over as Minister of Munitions. Even so, this still left Lloyd George politically homeless. He briefly flirted with the idea of establishing a 'national party' or a new 'Coalition Party of Patriots', based on the wartime coalition. Some of his supporters had been canvassing Liberal MPs since 1917 about the prospect of setting up a 'Lloyd George Liberal' organization in opposition to Asquith. Lloyd George tried to take matters a step further by attempting to create a party fund of his own, financed by the selling of public honours.[88] In the event, two factors persuaded Lloyd George of the need to continue the coalition. First, without an election since 1910, the House of Commons as a representative assembly was now outdated.[89] The huge shifts in Britain's electoral topography heralded by the Representation of the People Act, which had enfranchised all men over the age of 21, women aged 30 or over (ratepayers and in possession of a local government qualification) and 19-year-old men who had been on active service, had created a new mass electorate of some 21 million people (see also Chapter 10).[90] This was a cause for celebration, no doubt. But it only brought on further concerns over the rise of Labour. In many respects, the struggle with Germany since 1914 had become a 'people's war'. In spite of all the privations, the war had stimulated working-class communities; the standard of living for many working-class families had risen; and, with trade union membership accelerating to over 6.5 million, the political presence of organized industrial labour could not be ignored. Many trade unions, now legally permitted to set up political funds out of members' contributions under the immunities granted by the Osborne Judgement of 1913, furnished the Labour Party with the necessary funding to extend its local organizational network and place a candidate in every constituency by 1917.[91] By 1918, 388 Labour candidates were ready to fight in a general election, independent of the Liberals, stoking Conservative fears of a 'socialist' government. Few could predict how the new electorate would behave; fewer still could pretend that Labour had no chance of winning. The prospect of demobilized soldiers coming home to face poverty and unemployment, and the dangerous messages of revolution that now emanated across Europe from Russia, were enough to send many Conservatives and Liberals running for the shelter that continuing the coalition would bring. At least it offered the prospect of a stable government for the rest of the war and an opportunity to secure a relatively smooth transition to peace.[92]

This meant, however, that Lloyd George had to arrive at a political settlement with the Conservatives. With an election being seriously considered in the summer of 1918, detailed negotiations began between Freddy Guest (Lloyd George's Chief Whip) and Sir George Younger, chairman of the Conservative Party, to apportion the constituencies among Tory, Lloyd George Liberal and National Democratic Party (NDP, a pro-coalition group that had broken away from the British Socialist Party) candidates. Though the smaller party in the grouping, the Liberals gained Conservative approval to allow 159 of their number to stand unopposed as coalition candidates, saving Lloyd George many seats in an election that he feared would produce a landslide Conservative victory. They were joined by 373 Conservatives, 75 independent Conservatives and 18 NDP representatives. For their troubles, each candidate carried a letter of endorsement signed by Lloyd George and Bonar Law, a scrap of paper later derided by Asquith as 'the coupon'.[93]

What did the Conservatives gain from the electoral pact? In one respect, the war had been very good for their interests. The curtailment of German imports had opened up the domestic market, and the dwindling of the enemy's foreign trade had presented new opportunities for British companies anxious to expand into areas previously closed to them. At the same time, more established companies had benefited hugely from the partnership with the wartime state, with many firms winning large contracts, enjoying huge profits and occupying virtual monopoly status within certain markets. Maintaining these advantages, together with possible reductions in taxation and protection from foreign competition, all under the umbrella of Lloyd George's undoubted popular support in the country, was very compelling. Then again, whatever their influence and numerical superiority within the coalition, the Conservatives lacked a leader who could match the charisma and energy of the so-called Welsh Wizard, and few had his experience of dealing with a self-confident and possibly dangerous Labour movement. In a letter to Lord Derby in July 1918, Walter Long spelled out the options. 'George Curzon', he wrote, 'has been taking active steps towards offering some guidance to the Party, but won't go down with our people'; Bonar Law, 'though he has done his work most admirably in the House of Commons ... would not receive anything like widespread support'. On the whole, Long felt that 'we must face the fact that ... I can see nobody else who is likely to command the support of the country'.[94] It was a cynical move by the Conservatives. They could campaign for government without trumpeting the comparatively listless Bonar Law as a potential prime minister. Offering to continue in government under a Lloyd George premiership was the Conservatives' most realistic option. At the very least, he was the devil they knew.[95]

Given his dominance of wartime British politics, especially after 1916, it has been tempting to rename this chapter 'Lloyd George's War'. His early realization of the scale of the conflict conditioned his mind as to how it should be fought and his unyielding self-confidence in using the state to mobilize resources and direct operations on the Home Front in the pursuit of survival and victory perhaps substantiates Lloyd George's historical reputation as 'The Man who won the War'.

There are question marks, however, as to whether this is wholly deserved. In spite of his quarrels with the generals and their policies, Lloyd George displayed no great talent as a military strategist. He could not claim that his ideas of defeating Germany were any better than those of Army High Command; and historians have noted that, in view of his pre-war career, there were no great advancements in domestic reform during his wartime premiership other than the Representation of the People Act and invigorating the Reconstruction Ministry, both of which were policy initiatives already underway before he became Prime Minister. Yet, in a political context, Lloyd George was significant as Britain's first fully fledged coalition politician, a man who restated the British 'centrist' tradition by pitching a tent in all parties, but having a home in none. His disrespect for orthodox party politics, which had been growing since 1910, led Lloyd George to smother his political weakness by adopting a dictatorial-cum-presidential style of government (one biographer called it 'incipient Caesarism')[96] that was quite alien to British politics, but was nonetheless accommodated for the sake of the war. Even then, Lloyd George's actions were constrained by his Conservative partners, a fiercely independent military and the reluctance of powerful interest groups, from trade unions to shopkeepers, to accept his recipe for wholesale state intervention. When Lloyd George managed to garner enough support to offer the wartime coalition as a viable peacetime regime in the election of 1918, he only dimly recognized that his premiership was tolerated because the Conservatives needed an electable leader, whilst he needed a power base.

All the same, despite the flaws in Asquith's experiment of 1915, the experience of wartime coalition government had taught both politicians and the public the value of tying the parties together to see out a national emergency. The precedents set between 1915 and 1918 allowed this apparatus of government to remain in place until 1922, being revived during the 1931 economic crisis, as well as the new war of 1939. Moreover, the coalition's more productive use of the state to maintain economic and social stability led some of its more liberal-minded members to talk of a shared interest between employers and workers (or capital and labour) to utilize the principle of state intervention for the common good. This view, however, departed from more orthodox political thinking within the parties. If anything, the continuing underlying attitude that all-party government was only a temporary construction was probably the reason why coalition government failed to break the British political system. While the Conservatives insisted that the war justified a more skilful and ruthless use of state power, in the peacetime coalition they would force Lloyd George to accept the hasty abandonment of both wartime controls and the application of state mechanisms to post-war social reforms. Such attitudes surprisingly found favour within organized labour, both inside and outside Parliament. It had always been suspicious of state meddling in industrial affairs even though the movement had been quite ready to accept the benefits of state intervention in welfare issues and the reduction of inequality between the social classes. The dilemma struck deepest, however, within the Liberal Party, some of whom were quite ready to accept the growth of government, but now found that the war had smashed their leadership and grabbed their constituency. Their reliance before 1914 on the support of a progressive middle class and an elitist sect within the working class was no longer tenable. The voting reforms of 1918 had created a new working-class electorate that had no tradition of voting Liberal or Conservative, but who could find a home in the rapidly rising Labour Party. Be that as it may, in 1918 the Labour Party still had to travel a considerable distance before it could call itself a party of government. Many unions remained sceptical over whether electoral politics could secure social progress and improvements in working conditions; there were many areas in the country where party organization was weak or absent, and the ideological and sectional divisions within the movement still persisted. And yet, if the war had seen the fruition of pre-1914 cries for coalition government, it also reinforced the structures of democratic politics. The party system in Britain survived, with its substance, if not necessarily its former shape, intact.

Budgets

The First World War was not good for the national wallet. In September 1915, the Chancellor of the Exchequer Reginald McKenna estimated that the war was costing Britain £4.5 million a day, a figure that he expected to rise to £5 million in 1916. By 1917, the figure had grown to £7 million. A measure of the government's wartime spending could be seen through the ever-larger bites it was taking out of the National Income. Government spending as a percentage of the country's gross national product (GNP) rose from 13.5% in 1914, to 58.9 % in 1917 and 59.3% by 1918. Indeed, if the total cost of the conflict for all participants was estimated at US $208,500,000,000, then Britain's total expenditure grew from £514 million in 1914 to £2,160 million in 1916, to £2,669 million in 1917, totalling £9,156 million for the entire conflict.

The challenge that this presented to successive wartime chancellors was without precedent. Lloyd George, the first wartime Chancellor, was fully aware that defence expenditure needed deep pockets, and he reached for two levers of taxation, increasing the levels of 'direct' taxes on personal incomes and levying higher 'indirect' taxes on individual spending. In his only wartime budget in November 1914, Lloyd George established lasting precedents when he doubled lower-bracket income tax rates to 2s 8d (approximately 13p) in the pound, whilst raising levels of 'super tax' on those whose yearly earnings exceeded £3,000, from 5d to 10d (4p) in the pound, and to nearly three shillings (15p) on incomes in excess of £11,000 – money that was to help fund the two 'credits' of £1 million and £2.5 million voted in by Parliament during the autumn of 1914. Lloyd George's proposals were deepened and widened by McKenna's infamous budget less than a year later. Forty per cent increases were imposed on existing income tax rates; the thresholds for exemption from tax were lowered from £160 to £130 per annum. Super tax rates were raised to 2s 8d for incomes of £8–9,000 a year; to 3s 2d for those who earned £9–£10,000; and to 3s 6d (approximately 18p) for higher earners. McKenna's *coup de grâce* was the introduction of an Excess Profits Duty (defined as a 50 per cent levy on company profits exceeding peacetime levels, a rate that rose to 80 per cent in three years), which became the government's main revenue source for the rest of the war. Overall, standard rates of income tax would rise from 5.8 per cent (1s 2d; 6p) to 30 per cent (6s; 30p). By 1918, as taxation itself became much more progressive, higher earners found themselves shouldering more of the burden than poorer workers: a position made worse by the additional taxes that were being levied on so-called unearned or investment income. As it was, some two million wage earners were brought within the income tax thresholds between 1916 and 1918, of which some 70 per cent were classed as manual labourers, contributing by 1919 approximately £8 million a year to the Treasury, about 4 per cent of total revenues.

The sting in McKenna's budget was his infamous duties. In order to supplement his direct tax 'take', McKenna broadened the base of indirect taxation, alongside steep rises in import duties. Levies on tobacco, spirits and beer had long been a lucrative source of Exchequer income. Lloyd George provoked a public storm with his zealous increases in beer duties from 7s 9d (39p) to 25 shillings (£1.25) a barrel in his November budget. McKenna applied the principle even harder. Customs' rates on sugar imports rose from 1s 10d (approximately 9p) to 9s 4d (47p) a hundredweight; duties on imports of tobacco, tea, cocoa, coffee, chicory and dried fruits were increased by 50 per cent. A pound of tea, which paid 8d duty before the war, now returned 1 shilling; coffee duties rose from 2d to 3d a pound; dried fruits from 7s to 10s 6d (35p to 53p, approximately) a hundredweight. Excise duties on 'motor spirit' (petrol) and 'patent medicines' were raised by 100 per cent. McKenna also introduced a new 'ad valorum' duty of 33.3 per cent on all imports of motor cars and motor cycles; admission tickets to cinemas, theatres, exhibitions, amusements and sporting events (the 'entertainments tax'); and watches, musical instruments and hats. Postal rates were increased, the halfpenny post and sixpenny telegram were abolished; telephone charges were raised; and new taxes were imposed on railway travel. McKenna added to the list of taxable items a year later when new charges were levied on mineral waters and matches. Across the war years Exchequer yields from direct and indirect taxation rose considerably, totalling £2,733 million.

But this still only accounted for 28 per cent of total government expenditure, which by 1919 had reached £9,647 million, a deficit of £6,914 million. This yawning gap in the national finances pushed the Treasury into borrowing first from the British public, and second from friends and allies overseas. Initially, appeals were made to the patriotism of domestic investors by selling government bonds. In November 1914, Lloyd George launched the government's first War Loan, carrying an interest rate of 3.5 per cent (yielding £350 million), which was oversubscribed. On 21st June the following year McKenna issued the second War Loan, bearing 4.5 per cent interest and accruing about £570 million, supplemented by Bonar Law's third War Loan in January 1917, producing £2,000 million, with a hefty interest rate of 5 per cent, offering investors the best deal of the war. Seeking finance from overseas markets, however, was risky. While £113 million was raised from Allied countries (a figure offset by the £1,568 million that Britain had lent them), the most important arena for raising money and acquiring materials was the United States of America. Between 1913 and 1915, British imports from America rose by almost 68 per cent; by October 1916 almost 40 per cent of the British government's purchases, for itself and her allies, were being made in North America. This created a two-headed problem for the Treasury as the conflict wore on. The first was to maintain the country's creditworthiness. Finding the dollars to afford American goods in peacetime was usually met by the export trades. But, with the collapse of overseas markets and the redirecting of industrial production to munitions, Britain was forced to rely more heavily on attracting money from foreign investors by keeping domestic interest rates abnormally high. Bonar Law, in his budget statement of 1917, admitted that high rates were necessary 'for keeping up the exchange': an admission that Britain was now reliant on its international currency value to maintain its dollar reserves and prevent a flight of investors from its shores. Moreover, any drop in sterling's convertibility value to other currencies (set at £1 = US $4.86 in 1914) added millions to her import bill. The precarious nature of this practice was revealed twice: once in August 1915, when a run on the pound in New York saw the pound's dollar value slide to $4.70, leaving the Treasury with only $4 million to pay for bills of $17 million that had to be met within seven days, and once more in December 1916, when the Federal Reserve warned American investors against the wisdom of buying British war bonds after her financial integrity had been undermined by failures at the Battle of the Somme, and the government's mishandling of the Dublin uprising. This meant that the Treasury had to find another $200 million a month just to finance supplies for the munitions drive.

It also ensured that Britain had to dip into her shrinking pool of American securities to offer collateral for two important loans of $250 million and $300 million in the autumn of 1916. Such a disposal of the country's assets came at the expense of long-term investment, which some historians argue inflicted long-term damage on the economy. Yet this avenue of support had been more or less exhausted by the end of 1916, leaving the government with enough gold and securities to finance just three weeks of goods by the time America entered the war in April 1917. Only short-term loans from Morgan's Bank kept the Treasury from reneging on its US obligations.

On balance, the government's wartime financial policies were successful. The First World War did not impoverish Britain, and the country's monetary system remained intact. But Britain was undoubtedly a diminished financial nation in 1918. Significant proportions of her wealth had been sold; some of her lucrative export markets had either disappeared or were lost to the Americans; and the City of London's place as the centrepiece of world capitalism had effectively been ceded to Wall Street. But the country's most immediate problem was the size of her debt: £840 million was owed to the United States of America; £92 million to Canada; and £113 million to her

Allies. Domestic state borrowing had driven up retail price inflation during the war years and, as the size of the National Debt ballooned from £650 million to £6,142 million between 1914 and 1919 (at a time of high bank rates), successive Chancellors would have to service a debt, the cost of which would remain stubbornly high throughout the 1920s and 1930s. In effect post-war taxpayers were obliged to pay the bill as a financial 'thank you' for the sacrifices of their wartime parents.

References

Primary sources

Hansard Parliamentary Debates, 5th series, vol. LXXIV, 15th September 1915, cols 350–66.

Hansard Parliamentary Debates, 5th series, vol. LXXXI, 4th April 1916, cols 1050–58.

Hansard Parliamentary Debates, 5th series, vol. XCIII, 2nd May 1917, cols 371–94.

NA, CAB 37/134/13, 'Financial Prospects for the Financial Year', J.M. Keynes, 9th September 1915.

NA, CAB, 37/134/14, 'War Taxation', R. McKenna, 10th September 1915.

NA, CAB 37/134/18, Asquith to the King, 10th September 1915.

NA, CAB 37/134/17, untitled, R.McKenna, 13th September 1915.

NA, CAB 24/1, 'Mr Bonar Law's Statement on Finance on the Seventh Meeting of the Imperial War Cabinet Held at 10 Downing Street, 3rd April 1917'.

The Scotsman, 13th October 1915, cited in Gerard DeGroot, *Blighty: British Society in the Era of the Great War*, Harlow: Longman, 1995, p.108.

The Times, 22nd September 1915.

Secondary sources

T. Balderston, 'War Finance and Inflation in Britain and Germany, 1914–18', *Economic History Review*, 2nd series, vol. xlii, no. 2, 1989, pp. 222–44.

Kathleen Burk, *Britain, America and the Sinews of War 1914–18*, London: Allen & Unwin, 1985, ch. 5.

Kathleen Burk, 'The Treasury: From Impotence to Power', in Kathleen Burk, ed., *War and the State: The Transformation of British Government 1914–19*, London: Allen & Unwin, 1982, pp. 84–107.

Stephen Constantine, *Lloyd George*, London: Routledge, 1992, p. 48.

Peter Dewey, *War and Progress: Britain 1914–45*, Harlow: Longman, 1997, pp. 28–31.

Peter Dewey, 'The New Warfare and Economic Mobilization', in John Turner, ed., *Britain and the First World War*, London: Unwin Hyman, 1988, pp. 70–84.

F.W. Hirst and John E. Allen, *British War Budgets*, Oxford: Oxford University Press, 1926.

David Lloyd George, *War Memoirs*, vol. I, London: Odhams, 1938, pp. 71–74.

Alan S. Milward, *The Economic Effects of the Two World Wars on Britain*, Basingstoke: Macmillan, 1970, pp. 12–14, 38.

B.R. Mitchell, *British Historical Statistics*, Cambridge: Cambridge University Press, 1988, pp. 590–613.

Robert Pearce, *Society, Economy and Industrial Relations 1900–939*, London: Hodder & Stoughton, 2nd edn, 2002, pp. 35–36.

David Stevenson, *1914–1918: The History of the First World War*, London: Allen Lane, 2004, pp. 219–28.

R.C. Whiting, 'Taxation and the Working Class, 1915–24', *Historical Journal*, vol. 33, no. 4, 1990, pp. 895–916.

Notes

1 See G.R. Searle, *Country Before Party: Coalition and the Idea of 'National Government' in Modern Britain 1885–1987*, Harlow: Longman: 1995, pp. 13–52.

2 Alfred Stead, *Great Japan: A Study in National Efficiency* (1905), quoted in G.R. Searle, *Country Before Party*, op. cit., p. 61.

3 G.R. Searle, *Country Before Party*, op. cit., p. 64. See also A.M Gollin, *Proconsul in Politics: A Study of Lord Milner in Opposition and in Power*, London: Blond, 1964, pp. 80–81.

4 G.R. Searle, *Country Before Party*, op. cit., p. 65.

5 Paul Addison, *Churchill on the Home Front*, London: Jonathan Cape, 1992, pp. 80–82.

6 Lloyd George, speech at the Law Society Hall, 29th January 1909, cited in Robert J. Scally, *The Origins of the Lloyd George Coalition: The Politics of Social-imperialism, 1900–1918*, Princeton: Princeton University Press, 1975, p. 144.

7 Parliamentary Archives, House of Lords (hereafter 'HL'), Lloyd George Papers, 'Mr Lloyd George's Memorandum on the Formation of a Coalition: Criccieth Memorandum', C/6/5/1, 17th August 1910. See also Kenneth O. Morgan, *The Age of Lloyd George: The Liberal Party and British Politics, 1890–1929*, London: Allen & Unwin, 1971, pp. 150–55.

8 G.R. Searle, *Country Before Party*, op. cit., p. 84.

9 Martin Pugh, *The Making of Modern British Politics 1867–1945*, 3rd edn, Oxford: Blackwell, 2002, pp. 149–52; G.R. Searle, *The Liberal Party: Triumph and Disintegration, 1886–1929*, 2nd edn, Basingstoke: Palgrave, 2001, pp. 124–31; Paul Adelman, *The Decline of the Liberal Party 1910–1931*, 2nd edn, Harlow: Longman, 1995, pp. 12–13.

10 Cameron Hazlehurst, *Politicians at War July 1914 to May 1915: A Prologue to the Triumph of Lloyd George*, London: Jonathan Cape, 1971, pp. 135–42; John Ramsden, *The Age of Balfour and Baldwin 1902–40*, Harlow: Longman, 1978, p. 111.

11 Stephen Koss, *Asquith*, London: Allen Lane, 1976, p. 162; Cameron Hazlehurst, *Politicians at War*, op. cit., pp. 138–39; R.J.Q. Adams, *Bonar Law*, London: John Murray, 1999, pp. 173–74. See also Michael and Eleanor Brock, eds, *H.H. Asquith: Letters to Venetia Stanley*, Oxford: Oxford University Press, 1982, p. 239.

12 John Turner, 'Cabinets, Committees and Secretariats: The Higher Direction of War', in Kathleen Burk, ed., *War and the State: The Transformation of British Government 1914–1919*, London: Allen & Unwin, 1982, pp. 57–58; George Cassar, *Asquith as War Leader*, London: Hambledon Press, 1994, p. 40; Edward David, ed., *Inside Asquith's Cabinet: From the Diaries of Charles Hobhouse*, London: John

Murray, 1977, pp. 180–84; Roy Jenkins, *Asquith*, London: Collins, 1964, p. 344; Lord Hankey, *The Supreme Command, 1914–1918*, vol. I, London: Allen & Unwin, 1961, pp. 175, 238.

13 David French, 'Spy Fever in Britain, 1900–915', *Historical Journal*, vol. 21, no. 2, 1978, pp. 335–70; John Turner, *British Politics and the Great War: Coalition and Conflict 1915–1918*, London: Yale University Press, 1992, pp. 56–57.

14 Asquith later remarked rather complacently that he found the episode all 'rather interesting because it enables one to realise what are the first steps in an actual war'; see Michael and Eleanor Brock, eds, *H.H. Asquith: Letters to Venetia Stanley*, op. cit., p. 133.

15 A.J.P. Taylor, *English History 1914–1945*, London, Penguin, 1970, p. 39.

16 Lord Hankey, *The Supreme Command*, op. cit., p. 326.

17 Michael Bentley, *The Liberal Mind 1914–29*, Cambridge: Cambridge University Press, 1977, p. 21.

18 The best account of the origins of the Dardanelles expedition remains Robert Rhodes James, *Gallipoli*, London: Papermac, 1989, chs 1–3. See also Robert Rhodes James, *Churchill: A Study in Failure 1900–1939*, London, Weidenfeld & Nicolson, 1970, pp. 63–72; Roy Jenkins, *Churchill*, Basingstoke: Pan, 2001, pp. 255–71; Winston Churchill, *The World Crisis 1911–1918*, abridged and revised edn, London: Penguin, 2007, chs XXII, XXIII; Lord Hankey, *The Supreme Command*, vol. I, op. cit., chs XXIII–XXVII; David French, 'The Origins of the Dardanelles Campaign Reconsidered', *History*, vol. 68, 1983.

19 See Richard Holmes, *The Western Front*, London: BBC, 1999, p. 63.

20 *The Times*, 14th May 1915; Cassar, *Asquith as War Leader*, op. cit., pp. 90–95.

21 Cassar, *Asquith as War Leader*, op. cit., pp. 93, 103.

22 See Trevor Wilson, *The Downfall of the Liberal Party 1914–1935*, London: Fontana, 1968, pp. 53–64; Stephen Koss, 'The Destruction of Britain's Last Liberal Government', *Journal of Modern History*, vol. 40, no. 2, 1968, pp. 255–77; Stephen Koss, *Asquith*, op. cit., pp. 182–83; George Cassar, *Asquith as War Leader*, op. cit., pp. 91–100; see also B.B. Gilbert, *David Lloyd George: The Organizer of Victory, 1912–16*, London: Batsford, 1992; A.J.P. Taylor, 'Politics in the First World War', in A.J.P. Taylor, *Essays in English History*, Harmondsworth: Penguin, 1976, pp. 218–54; Lord Beaverbrook, *Politicians and the War 1914–16*, two vols, London: Butterworth, 1928; Cameron Hazlehurst, *Politicians at War*, op. cit., pp. 232–69.

23 Roy Jenkins, *Asquith*, op. cit., pp. 322–23.

24 See Koss, *Asquith*, op. cit., p. 183; Cassar, *Asquith as War Leader*, op. cit., p. 98.

25 R.J.Q. Adams, *Bonar Law*, op. cit., pp. 177.

26 R.J.Q. Adams, *Bonar Law*, op. cit., p. 176; John Ramsden, *The Age of Balfour and Baldwin*, op. cit., p. 112.

27 Martin Pugh, 'Asquith, Bonar Law and the First Coalition', *Historical Journal*, vol. 17, no. 4, 1974, pp. 813–36.

28 George Riddell, *Lord Riddell's War Diary*, London: Nicholson, 1933, entry for 20th December 1914. See also B.B. Gilbert, *David Lloyd George: The Organizer of Victory, 1912–1916*, op. cit., p. 181; G.R. Searle, *Country Before Party*, op. cit., pp. 87–88; Lloyd George, *War Memoirs*, vol. I, London: Odhams, 1938, p. 136; Kenneth O. Morgan, 'George, David Lloyd, the First Earl Lloyd George of Dwyfor (1863–1945)', *Oxford Dictionary of National Biography*, Oxford: Oxford University Press, 2004.

29 Martin Pugh, 'Asquith, Bonar Law and the First Coalition', op. cit.

30 Cameron Hazlehurst, *Politicians at War*, op. cit., p. 263.

31 Edward David, ed., *Inside Asquith's Cabinet*, op. cit., p. 245.

32 Martin Pugh, *The Making of Modern British Politics*, op. cit., pp. 151–53.

33 See Jay Winter, *Socialism and the Challenge of War: Ideas and Politics in Britain 1912–18*, London: Routledge, 1974, pp. 150–65; Andrew Thorpe, *A History of the*

British Labour Party, 2nd edn, Basingstoke: Palgrave, 2001, pp. 28–29; Chris Wrigley, *Arthur Henderson*, Manchester: Manchester University Press, 1990, pp. 70–93.

34 George Cassar, *Asquith as War Leader*, op. cit., pp. 108–9; John Turner, *British Politics and the Great War*, op. cit., pp. 61–62; R.J.Q. Adams, *Bonar Law*, op. cit., pp. 187–92; Stephen Koss, *Asquith*, op. cit., pp. 189–97.

35 See Stephen Roskill, *Hankey: Man of Secrets*, vol. I, 1877–1918, London: Collins, p. 231.

36 John Turner, 'Cabinets, Committees and Secretariats', op. cit., pp. 59–60; Lord Hankey, *The Supreme Command*, vol. I, op. cit., pp. 333–37.

37 John Turner, 'Cabinets, Committees and Secretariats', op. cit., p. 60. Also NA, CAB 41/36/45, 'Proposal to Deal with (1) the Conduct of the War, and (2) the Financial Outlook', September 1915; Roy Jenkins, *Asquith*, op. cit., pp. 420–21.

38 Roskill, *Hankey: Man of Secrets*, op. cit., pp. 232–33.

39 John Turner, 'Cabinets, Committees and Secretariats', op. cit., pp. 60–61; John Turner, *British Politics and the Great War*, p. 72; NA, CAB 42/6/14, 'Minutes of the War Committee', 28th December 1915.

40 Stephen Roskill, *Hankey, Man of Secrets*, op. cit., p. 237. See also A.J.P. Taylor, ed., *Lloyd George: A Diary by Frances Stevenson*, London: Hutchinson, 1971, p. 85: 'Everyone has decided in favour of evacuation, but no one has the courage to carry the move out.'

41 Edward David, ed., *Inside Asquith's Cabinet*, op. cit., pp. 255–56.

42 A.J.P. Taylor, ed., *Lloyd George: A Diary by Frances Stevenson*, op. cit., p. 67.

43 NA, CAB 37/134/3, 'Supplementary Memorandum to the Report of the War Policy Committee', 3rd September 1915; John Turner, *British Politics and the Great War*, op. cit., p. 65.

44 John Turner, 'Cabinets, Committees and Secretariats', op. cit., pp. 61–62.

45 NA, CAB 27/4, 'Second Report on the Co-ordination of Military and Financial Effort', 13th April 1916.

46 NA, CAB 27/3, 'Report of the Committee on the Size of the Army', 18th April 1916.

47 Lord Hankey, *The Supreme Command*, vol. 2, London: Allen & Unwin, 1961, pp. 472–77; Stephen Roskill, *Hankey: Man of Secrets*, op. cit., pp. 263–67. See also *Hansard Parliamentary Debates*, 5th series, vol. LXXXI, cols 2611–79; A.J.P. Taylor, ed., *Lloyd George: A Diary by Frances Stevenson*, op. cit., pp. 105–6; John Turner, 'Cabinets, Committees and Secretariats', op. cit., p. 62.

48 John Turner, *British Politics and the Great War*, op. cit., p. 84.

49 John Turner, *British Politics and the Great War*, op. cit., pp. 91–94, 111.

50 Lord Hankey, *The Supreme Command*, vol. I, pp. 176–77.

51 Stephen Roskill, *Hankey: Man of Secrets*, op. cit., pp. 320–21; Martin Pugh, *Lloyd George*, Harlow: Longman, 1988, pp. 94–95; John Grigg, *Lloyd George: From Peace to War 1912–1916*, London: Methuen, 1985, pp. 444–45; John Turner, *British Politics and the Great War*, op. cit., pp. 124–25; Lord Hankey, *The Supreme Command*, vol. II, op. cit., pp. 562–63. For a fuller discussion of the issues that motivated Lloyd George, see Michael Fry, 'Political Change in Britain, August 1914 to December 1916: Lloyd George Replaces Asquith: The Issues Underlying the Drama', *Historical Journal*, vol. 31, no. 3, September 1988, pp. 609–27.

52 Martin Pugh, *Lloyd George*, op. cit., p. 94; R.J.Q. Adams, *Bonar Law*, op. cit., pp. 222–24; John Turner, *British Politics in the Great War*, op. cit., pp. 115–16, and his comments in pp. 127–28. See also Lord Beaverbrook, *Politicians and the War*, vol. II, op. cit., pp. 109–10; Robert J. Scally, *The Origins of the Lloyd George Coalition*, op. cit., pp. 318–23.

53 See, for example, John Grigg, *Lloyd George: From Peace to War 1912–1916*, op. cit., ch. 17; John Turner, *British Politics and the Great War*, op. cit., ch. 3; Martin

Pugh, *Lloyd George*, op. cit., pp. 94–99; Martin Pugh, *The Making of Modern British Politics*, op. cit., pp. 153–56; Stephen Koss, *Asquith*, op. cit., pp. 216–21.

54 R.J.Q. Adams, *Bonar Law*, op. cit., pp. 227–28.

55 H.H. Asquith to Lloyd George, 1st December 1916, in Kenneth O. Morgan, *The Age of Lloyd George*, op. cit., pp. 169–70; see also Lloyd George, *War Memoirs*, vol. I, op. cit., p. 588.

56 Martin Pugh, *Lloyd George*, op. cit., p. 95.

57 Edwin Montagu to H.H. Asquith, 2nd December 1916, in S.D. Waley, *Edwin Montagu*, London: Asia, 1964, pp. 104–06; John Grigg, *Lloyd George: From Peace to War 1912–1916*, op. cit., p. 452. See also H.A. Taylor, *Robert Donald*, London: Stanley Paul, 1934, p. 116; R.J.Q. Adams, *Bonar Law*, op. cit., pp. 231–33; George Cassar, *Asquith as War Leader*, op. cit., p. 218; The Marquis of Crewe, 'The Break-up of the First Coalition', in H.H. Asquith, *Memories and Reflections*, vol. II, London: Cassel, 1928, pp. 128–38.

58 Asquith to Lloyd George, 4th December 1916, in Lloyd George, *War Memoirs*, vol. I, op. cit., pp. 590–91; R.J.Q. Adams, *Bonar Law*, op. cit., pp. 234–35.

59 Lloyd George, *War Memoirs*, vol. I, op. cit., pp. 593–94; A.J.P. Taylor, ed., *Lloyd George: A Diary by Frances Stevenson*, op. cit., pp. 132–33.

60 Asquith to Lloyd George, 4th December 1916, in J.A. Spender and Cyril Asquith, *The Life of Lord Oxford and Asquith*, vol. II, London: Hutchinson, p. 266; Martin Pugh, *Lloyd George*, op. cit., pp. 96–97.

61 R.J.Q. Adams, *Bonar Law*, op. cit., pp. 237–40; Stephen Koss, *Asquith*, op. cit., pp. 222–23; John Turner, *British Politics and the Great War*, op. cit., pp. 138–41. See also H.A. Taylor, *Robert Donald*, op. cit., pp. 118–23; A.J.P. Taylor, ed., *Lloyd George: A Diary by Frances Stevenson*, op. cit., p. 133.

62 Christopher Addison, *Politics from Within*, vol. I, pp. 270–72; A.J.P. Taylor, ed., *Lloyd George: A Diary by Frances Stevenson*, op. cit., p. 134; Paul Adelman, *The Decline of the Liberal Party 1910–1931*, 2nd edn, Harlow, Longman, 1995, pp. 21–22.

63 See Michael Fry, 'Political Change in Britain, August 1914 to December 1916: Lloyd George Replaces Asquith: The Issues Underlying the Drama', op. cit., pp. 609–27.

64 See John Turner, *British Politics and the Great War*, op. cit., pp. 128–32.

65 *The Times*, 29th September 1916.

66 Paul Adelman, *The Decline of the Liberal Party 1910–1931*, op. cit., p. 23.

67 *The Times*, 7th December 1916; *Report of the Annual Conference of the Labour Party 1917*, p. 43; Chris Wrigley, *Arthur Henderson*, op. cit., pp. 108–9.

68 Peter Clarke, *Liberals and Social Democrats*, op. cit., pp. 88–89.

69 See Martin Pugh, *Lloyd George*, op. cit., pp. 100–101; John Grigg, *Lloyd George: From Peace to War 1912–1916*, op. cit., pp. 482–83.

70 Martin Pugh, *Lloyd George*, op. cit., pp. 104–05.

71 Lord Hankey, *The Supreme Command*, vol. II, ch. 57; John Turner, 'Cabinets, Committees and Secretariats', op. cit., pp. 69–71; John F. Naylor, 'The Establishment of the Cabinet Secretariat', *Historical Journal*, vol. xiv, no. 4, 1971, pp. 783–803.

72 John Turner, 'Cabinets, Committees and Secretariats', op. cit., p. 72; John Grigg, *Lloyd George: From Peace to War 1912–1916*, op. cit., pp. 500–02; John Turner, *Lloyd George's Secretariat*, Cambridge: Cambridge University Press, 1980. See also Kenneth O. Morgan, 'Lloyd George's Premiership: A Study in "Prime Ministerial Government"', *Historical Journal*, vol. 13, no. 1, 1970, pp. 130–57.

73 See Lord Hankey, *The Supreme Command*, vol. II, op. cit., pp. 573–80.

74 Hankey Diary, 18th March 1917, in Stephen Roskill, *Hankey, Man of Secrets*, op. cit., pp. 370–71; John Turner, 'Cabinets, Committees and Secretariats', op. cit., pp. 67–69; Ian Packer, *Lloyd George*, Basingstoke: Macmillan, 1998, pp. 56–57.

75 David Stevenson, *1914–1918, The History of the First World War*, London: Allen Lane, 2004, pp. 321–22.
76 Martin Pugh, *Lloyd George*, op. cit., p. 106.
77 David Stevenson, *1914–1918*, op. cit., p. 322.
78 Lord Hankey, *The Supreme Command*, vol. II, op. cit., p. 648, also pp. 641–49.
79 David Stevenson, *1914–1918*, op. cit., pp. 322–24; Lord Hankey, *The Supreme Command*, vol. II, op. cit., pp. 649–51; John Grigg, *Lloyd George: War Leader 1916–1918*, London: Penguin, pp. 50–54; Lloyd George, *War Memoirs*, vol. I, op. cit., pp. 667–95.
80 See Chapter 7.
81 John Grigg, *Lloyd George: War Leader 1916–1918*, op. cit., pp. 110–13.
82 Christopher Addison, *Four and a Half Years*, op. cit., p. 256; NA, MUN 5/57/320/16, 'Papers on Ministry Negotiations with Engineers, 1916'; John Turner, *British Politics and the Great War*, op. cit., pp. 167–68, 191–92; Chris Wrigley, *David Lloyd George and the British Labour Movement*, Hassocks: Harvester, 1976, pp. 191–97; Alistair Reid, 'Dilution, Trade Unionism and the State in Britain During the First World War', in S. Tolliday and J. Zeitlin, eds, *Shop Floor Bargaining and the State*, Cambridge: Cambridge University Press, 1985, pp. 46–74.
83 Chris Wrigley, *Arthur Henderson*, op. cit., pp. 112–43; John Turner, *British Politics and the Great War*, op. cit., pp. 205–09.
84 Martin Pugh, *Lloyd George*, op. cit., pp. 110–12.
85 John Grigg, *Lloyd George, War Leader*, op. cit., pp. 526, 411–18; John Turner, 'Cabinets, Committees and Secretariats', op. cit., pp. 66–67.
86 *The Times*, 7th May 1918. See also John Turner, *British Politics and the Great War*, op. cit., pp. 297–99.
87 Ian Packer, *Lloyd George*, op. cit., p. 61; Martin Pugh, *Lloyd George*, op. cit., pp. 116–17; John Grigg, *Lloyd George: War Leader*, pp. 489–511; Roskill, *Hankey: Man of Secrets*, op. cit., pp. 539–44.
88 G.R.Searle, *Country Before Party*, op. cit., p. 109; Kenneth O. Morgan, 'Lloyd George's Premiership: A Study in "Prime Ministerial Government"', *Historical Journal*, op. cit.
89 See Arthur Henderson's Cabinet memorandum, NA, CAB 37/147/31, 'Necessary Electoral Changes', 12th May 1916.
90 See Martin Pugh, *The Making of Modern British Politics*, op. cit., pp. 156–57; Martin Pugh, *Lloyd George*, op. cit., pp. 119–20.
91 See Andrew Thorpe, *A History of the British Labour Party*, op. cit., pp. 18–19, 20–21.
92 Andrew Thorpe, *A History of the British Labour Party*, op. cit., pp. 33–42.
93 Parliamentary Archives, HL, Lloyd George Papers, F/21/2/28, 'Captain Guest to Lloyd George, 20 July 1918'; Roy Douglas, 'The Background to the "Coupon" Election Agreements', *English Historical Review*, vol. 86, no. 339, 1971, pp. 318–36; John Turner, *British Politics and the Great War*, op. cit., pp. 308–12; Martin Pugh, *Lloyd George*, op. cit., pp. 123–25.
94 John Turner, *British Politics and the Great War*, p. 304.
95 Martin Pugh, *The Making of Modern British Politics*, op. cit., pp. 157–60.
96 Thomas Jones, *Lloyd George*, Oxford: Oxford University Press, 1951, p. 281.

5   Workplace women

One of the better-known features of Britain's First World War is, perhaps, its effect on women's employment. Until 1914, the female working population consisted mainly of working-class women employed in unskilled jobs across the textiles, engineering and mining industries, as well as in domestic service, earning on average about a third of men's weekly wage. Some women from the more prosperous classes had managed to claw their way into the professions, clerical work and teaching, but their 'careers' were always conditional on accommodating themselves to masculine attitudes and cultures. After a slow start, the war increasingly drew women from all social classes into new areas of work, with significant numbers entering armaments production and other trades in transport, services and offices. Patriotism, money and survival drove thousands to answer the government's call to 'do their bit', and the sight of women working on shells and guns, driving trams, shovelling coal, cleaning windows and delivering the post, captured the attention of a masculine society unaccustomed to such sights, inevitably drawing out some raw and mixed reactions. Some women hoped that their efforts would bring recognition and reward. The suffragist Millicent Fawcett declared in 1919 that 'the war revolutionised the industrial position of women. It found them serfs and left them free ... it revolutionised men's minds ... '.[1] A triumph of hope over experience, perhaps.

The problem of womanpower

The issue of working women between 1914 and 1918 presents the historian with a number of uncertainties. For example, it is never precisely clear as to how many women entered the national wartime workforce. In 1918 the Board of Trade calculated that the female workforce grew from 3,276,000 in July 1914 to 4,935,000 four years later.[2] This was more or less verified in 1921 in an independent analysis conducted by A.W. Kirkaldy, who suggested a slight revision in the government's figures from 3,277,000 women working in 1914 to 4,940,000 in 1918, with the proportion of women in the total workforce increasing from 24 to 37 per cent respectively.[3] Deborah Thom, however, argues that the government's figures cannot be trusted, as they do not represent an analysis of the labour market *per se*, but were part of a general monitoring of the production processes. The government used only the figures submitted by larger firms to construct its survey and, by representing trends rather than totals, these data were manipulated to emphasize the success of government dilution policies.[4] This picture was distorted further by the government's failure to take account of the most important women's occupation of the period, domestic service. Here again, figures are disputed. Angela Woollacott estimates that domestic service employed a total of 1,734,000 women in 1914.[5] Martin Pugh, however, argues that the number of female domestics stood at 1,658,000 in 1914, declining to 1,258,000 during the war, placing the female workforce at 4.93 million before the war, increasing to 6.19 million by 1918, a rise of 23.7 per cent.[6] Gerard DeGroot's calculations reveal similar figures.[7] Ian Beckett went a step further by suggesting that the data overlooked not just those women working in domestic service but also self-employed women, those employed by their husbands and the numbers involved in small-scale clothing manufacture. In his view, the numbers of women in paid employment rose from 5.9 million to 7.3 million, an increase of 1.4 million.[8]

So much for statistics. Yet the quantitative confusion does underline the fact that, for the most part, women were the hidden workforce of Edwardian Britain, their presence only partially highlighted by an array of social investigations which threw light on the misery and exploitation of women's work in the 'sweated' trades of textiles and clothing manufacture.[9] In truth, women were employed in an assortment of pre-war industries as full-time, part-time or seasonal workers. By 1914 approximately 834,000 women worked in textiles; 612,000 were employed in the clothing trades; 505,000 were employed in banking and commerce; 50,500 worked in the professions; the hotel and catering industry employed 181,000; 196,200 worked in education and local government; 170,500 toiled in the metal industries; whilst 80,000 did likewise in agriculture.[10] For the government then, women constituted an experienced and vital labour source that could be utilized, expanded and exploited. For many women, war work represented a chance for regular and better-paid employment.

Fall and rise

The demand for women's labour in the first months of the war was far from immediate and far from certain. The trade slump affected women's employment rates across a range of industries as the numbers of female workers in the workforce shrank from 190,000 in September 1914 to 139,000 in October, 75,000 in December, and as low as 35,000 in February 1915. One contemporary estimated that 44.4 per cent of all women workers were registered as unemployed in September 1914 (compared with 27.4 per cent of men) and that more than 110,000 women and girls were jobless as late as April 1915, with just under 50,000 vacancies being notified by employers.[11] The rise of unemployed, predominantly working-class, women kindled a spontaneous blossoming of philanthropic activity as innumerable organizations emerged across the country with the aim of generating alms for struggling families. Groups such as the Red Cross Society, the Belgian Refugees Fund, Queen Mary's Needlework Guild and the Soldiers' Parcel Fund, along with a multitude of local benevolent funds, sewing guilds and funds for the relief of soldiers' and sailors' dependants provided employment for jobless women in making clothes and 'comforts' for troops. Following Clementine Black's critical report of such activities in *Women's Industrial News* in September 1914, Lady Crewe and the leading trade union activist Mary Macarthur initiated the establishment of the Queen Mary's Work for Women Fund. Helped by sizeable donations (the scheme raised £20,000 in just one day), the organization ran workshops and retraining schemes for unemployed women to learn 'domestic skills', manufacturing toys and artificial flowers, and even making baby cots from orange crates and making baby clothes from old shirts.[12] Prohibited from competing with commercial firms, the Fund persuaded the War Office to spread its contracts amongst struggling small firms to help them retool for garment making and, once it secured larger government orders, the Fund distributed the work amongst them.[13] Similar schemes for middle-class workers were run by the Society for Promoting the Employment of Women, which sponsored a parallel Educated Woman's War Emergency Training Fund, retraining unemployed governesses and journalists for clerical work, while organizing hostels for those women who were made homeless upon losing their job. The National Guild of Housecraft endeavoured to teach home-making skills to women artists, actresses, clerks and secretaries, so that they 'might become good wives for the men who would return from the Front'.[14] Wages, however, were a vexed question. The socialist campaigner Sylvia Pankhurst criticized the wages scheme of the Queen Mary's Work for Women Fund, as, with hourly rates set at 3d (approximately 1.3p), average remuneration for women in the sewing workshops was around 6s (30p) a week, well below the government's recommendations, prompting her to call them 'Queen Mary's sweatshops'. G.D.H. Cole agreed that such rates were 'scandalously low', but at the same time noted that some 9,000 women had been employed in these workshops by January 1915.[15]

Much of this was very worthy, and well received, but ultimately failed to move the boundaries of women's work beyond the traditional role of wife, mother and homemaker. Employers seeking staff were still inclined to recruit from the swollen ranks of unemployed men (480,000 at the beginning of the war), often supplementing the core workforce with the retired, juveniles and, latterly, Belgian refugees. Women were regarded as problematic. They lacked the right skills and physical strength for industrial work; they required special training; discipline was difficult to enforce in workshops where women and men worked together; women required expensive special facilities in the factory workplace (such as toilets); and family commitments prevented them from moving to localities where their services were in demand.[16] Nonetheless, signs of a recovery in women's employment rates emerged towards the end of 1914, principally in enterprises where women had traditionally formed the bulk of the workforce – manufacturers of textiles and clothing; leather, boots and shoes; kit bags and haversacks; and tin boxes, jam and medical dressings all began to pick up War Office contracts. Contemporary analyst Irene Andrews estimated that 100,000 women found work in these trades as 1915 beckoned, making but a small dent in the female unemployment levels.[17]

In its own way, the government brought a new urgency into women's employment. In March 1915, the Women's War Register was launched to encourage unemployed women, whatever their status or experience, to enrol for war work, with some 33,000 women registering within the first two weeks and 87,000 overall.[18] Women's organizations gave two cheers for the initiative, but still suspected that more could be done. Hence, during the late spring, Lloyd George, after some very hard lobbying by Emmeline Pankhurst, gave his tacit support for a 'right to work' march, organized by the WSPU, which eventually took place in July 1915, attended by 30,000 people and sponsored by a £2,000 grant from the government to help with costumes and publicity.[19] Other initiatives followed. The government itself embarked on a well-organised advertising campaign, complete with pamphlets and large illustrated booklets such as 'Notes on the Employment of Women on Munitions of War', containing descriptions of processes on which women were then employed, illustrated by carefully posed photographs of women workers, with an emphasis on flexibility and the unusual. Images highlighted the 'novelty' of women in an industrial environment as coal heavers, munitions workers, lathe turners, navvies, pottery-makers, mechanics and clock-makers, in an attempt to persuade employers to recruit women workers.[20] All the same, these initiatives were augmented by the setting up in November 1915 of an interdepartmental committee of the Home Office and Board of Trade, which aimed to sustain a supply of women workers in their 'normal' occupations, as well as securing diluters for men's work through a hive of local committees across 37 towns staffed by organizations such as the Young Women's Christian Association and the Women's Co-operative Guild.[21]

The crucial spark for the expansion of women's employment came through a combination of two factors. One was the Treasury Agreement signed by Lloyd George and the trade unions in March 1915. Having codified it as the Munitions of War Act in July 1915, the government was now at liberty to reorganize wartime industrial production around the dilution and substitution of skilled labour, with employers cajoled into employing women in greater numbers by simplifying complex work processes and deploying a greater use of automation. The other was the more evident fact that the war was boosting British industrial activity, by generating a huge demand for army supplies and increasing the availability of women's work as more men were called into the military. By the summer of 1915 the terms of industrial employment had turned in women's favour. Opportunities had expanded, not only within traditional women's trades in clerical and commercial occupations, but also

through the revival of pre-war industries, particularly textiles, as they diversified into manufacturing military goods. A contemporary observer noted that
this was a time when 'industrial women found their outlet ... at the sewing
machine, knitting machine, weaving loom, boot-upper stitching machine,
tin-cutting power press, soldering bench, at tinning of meat, fruit and vegetable preserves for rations'.[22] Within 12 months another major avenue of
work had opened as the chemical, ordnance and military equipment industries geared up to full production, expanding the number of women employees considerably, with a growing concentration of women in commercial
engineering firms employed on government contracts, often working on
the heavier labouring tasks and in more skilled occupations traditionally
regarded as 'men's work'. By now women constituted almost half the total
workforce.[23]

On the surface the rise in female employment represented a sizeable impact
on the character of the wartime workforce. Yet, while the increase in female
workers was significant, at a rise of 25.5 per cent, the expansion rate was
relatively modest. Only 22 per cent could be classed as 'new workers', either
school leavers or the 'previously unoccupied'.[24] Several studies have attempted to explain this by suggesting that a large number of women who entered
wartime industrial occupations were either married or previously employed in
similar trades. On average, married women made up 40 per cent of the
national workforce. In Leeds, 44 per cent of women in the four main engineering firms were married and, even then, there were very few who were
without any work experience.[25] By the same token, the increase in the number
of women munitions workers could be largely attributed to those who had
transferred from trades that were in recession.[26] In a survey of 440,000
women workers in December 1917, the Board of Trade's *Labour Gazette*
concluded that 70 per cent had changed their trade during the war, some of
whom had moved from one factory job to another, whilst others had come
over from domestic service or other non-industrial work. In her study of the
engineering trades, Barbara Drake noted that what was once 'men's work'
tended to be taken by older women workers who had moved from the textile
industry. This was borne out by *ad hoc* surveys conducted by the press. The
Yorkshire Observer, for example, discovered that women undertaking munitions training in Bradford came from domestic service, dressmaking, other
factories, laundries and nursing, whilst even the wives of engineers signed up.
In 1915 the *Daily Chronicle* reported that large numbers of Nottingham
lacemakers were turning to munitions work, much to the chagrin of their
former employers.[27] Out of the 'new' women workers only a small proportion
could be classified as middle and upper class. Of these, only approximately
9 per cent took on armaments work and then mainly as War Volunteers or
week-end munition relief workers (WMRW): a motley group of dukes'
daughters, generals' wives, artists, authors, university students, teachers and
ministers' and lawyers' spouses, who worked to give the regular staff a rest
day. Otherwise, many of these women were drawn to clerical or white-collar

trades as supervisors, civil servants, local authority workers, secretaries and bank clerks.[28]

Perceptual errors also exist over the range of occupations women entered during the war. Despite its reputation as the 'glamour' trade of the period (a belief created partly by the attention it received from the government, the press and contemporary commentators), the ordnance industry was not the largest employer of women. Only 3,600 women out of the 25,000 who registered for war work in March 1915 opted for munitions work, and they were outnumbered by those attracted to banking, finance and commerce.[29] The numbers of female workers in these sectors grew from 506,000 to 955,000 between 1914 and 1918, according to the Board of Trade.[30] Large numbers of women were similarly drawn into the transport industry, with numbers increasing from 18,600 to 115,000, and with the number of women railway workers rising from 12,000 to 66,000 between 1915 and 1918. National and local government had 228,000 women in paid employment by the end of the war; in contrast, the number of women working in industrial trades experienced comparatively modest advances, from 2,178,600 in 1914 to 2,970,000 by July 1918, while the number of women working in government munitions' factories stood at 247,000.[31]

What drove women into work? Some women undoubtedly succumbed to the unofficial recruitment drives seen in the newspapers and magazines, whilst government officials constantly banged the drum for munitions work,

Figure 5.1 A coy-looking Winston Churchill at HM Factory Gretna, *c.* 1918

especially during times of labour shortages, with press notices and propaganda posters emphasizing work as a patriotic duty. Some were clearly compelled by the need to 'do their bit'.[32] 'It became almost a disgrace to be found at home; it required some justifying explanation', noted Caroline Playne, 'it was up to you to show that you were a patriotic worker all the time'.[33] L.K. Yates found in her investigations of a munitions factory some 'typical views': a woman toolsetter working for the war effort; a mother of seven sons in the Army who took pride in doing her own kind of work for the war; and a stewardess from a torpedoed ship working out of hatred for the Germans.[34] For women from poorer backgrounds, war work offered an escape from the dull routines of home and the oppression of low-paid domestic work. One woman spoke in her diary of 'the desire for change and new interest', while others spoke of the experience of war work as 'like being let out of a cage'.[35] *The Times* commented that, amongst women of the 'comfortable classes', there was a growing inclination 'to find in work that fullness and satisfaction of life which are never the fruits of idleness and dependence'.[36] In this sense munitions work was ideal. It offered fascination, novelty and adventure. A.K. Foxwell in *Munition Lasses* talked of her joy in taking part in 'real' war work, 'shorn of comfort, luxury or indulgence.'[37] Naomi Loughlan assured her readers that 'though we munition workers sacrifice our ease we gain a life worth living. Our long days are filled with interest, and with the zest of doing work for our country in the grand cause of freedom.'[38] In other quarters some types of war work became fashionable. Secretarial work became the aspiration of many younger women when Lloyd George appointed Frances Stevenson as his secretary on becoming Prime Minister in 1916. It now became the vogue for a shorthand typist to aim for the kudos of being a 'lady secretary'.[39]

Otherwise, for many women the reason for taking on war work was money. To the women who previously worked in the 'sweated' trades of dressmaking or domestic service, the higher wages (over double the rates in some cases) paid in factory work proved irresistible. Women engaged on lathe-turning could increase their take-home pay considerably by working the overtime and bonus systems to their advantage.[40] Women munitions workers in Leeds could earn on average £3 a week. With bonuses, it was not unknown for women to take home between £10 and £12.[41] A worker on the Ministry of Munitions rolling mill in Southampton remembered '£3 a week and ... we thought we were the richest people in Southampton'. With overtime, she earned £4. 'Course that was joy. We could go out on the town on that.'[42]

The workplace experience

When attempting to recapture life for women at the wartime workplace historians have to exercise caution. The multifarious range of occupations women entered during the war makes it difficult to extrapolate a common experience, and it hardly needs stating that everyday secretarial tasks differed hugely from work encountered in the transport industries and armaments factories. Historical eyes are invariably drawn to munitions, as it is here that the archival record is at its thickest. The government's interest in the manufacture of ordnance and military hardware undoubtedly injected a new dynamic into the industrial workplace. At one level, the recruitment of women in large numbers into munitions factories compelled the government to put workplace management in the hands of the state, with a small army of production managers, social investigators and medical experts called in to monitor the work and welfare of women on an unprecedented scale.[43] Furthermore, the ambit of munitions production had no discernible circumference. Writing in 1915, labour leader Susan Lawrence explained:

> Tents are munitions; boots are munitions; biscuits and jam are munitions; sacks and ropes are munitions; drugs and bandages are munitions; socks and shirts and uniforms are munitions; all the miscellaneous list of contracts which fill up three pages of the Board of Trade Gazette, all, all are munitions.[44]

Behind all this activity lay a new style of interventionist state: innovator of output-efficient work practices; deviser of fresh solutions to industrial hazards; and employer of a tier of educated technocrats whose accumulated outpourings produced an intensive and voluminous historical record that

Table 5.1 Numbers of women employed in non-industrial sectors, 1914–1918

Occupations	Number of women employed, July 1914	Number of women employed, November 1918	Percentage of women in total workforce, July 1914	Percentage of women in total workforce, November 1918
Banking & Finance	9,500	75,000	5	43
Commerce	496,000	880,000	29	54
Post Office	61,000	121,000	24	53
Civil Service	5,000	107,000	8	59
Hotels, Public Houses, Cinemas & Theatres	181,000	222,000	48	66
Hospitals (Civil and Military)	33,000	80,000	–	–
Teachers (under Local Authority)	142,000	154,000	73	82
Professions (Clerks, Accountants, Solicitors)	18,000	40,000	12	37
Miscellaneous Municipal Services	54,000	75,000	14	26
Total	999,500	1,754,000	24	47

Source: A.W. Kirkaldy, *British Labour: Replacement and Conciliation 1914–1921*, London: Pitman, 1921

Table 5.2 Numbers of women employed in metal and chemical trades and government establishments, 1914–1918

Trade	Number of women employed, July 1914	Number of women employed, November 1918	Percentage of women in total workforce, July 1914	Percentage of women in total workforce, November 1918
Iron & Steel*	3,400	39,000	1	11
Hardware & Hollow Ware	29,000	42,000	27	43
Engineering	12,000	101,000	3	21
Electrical Engineering	16,000	56,000	17	39
Marine Engineering & Shipbuilding	2,300	31,000	1	7
Cycles, Motors, Aircraft & Other Vehicles	13,000	99,000	6	29
Cutlery & Other Edged Tools	6,200	9,000	17	26
Non-ferrous Metals	17,000	30,000	17	28
Precious Metals	20,000	25,000	36	53
All Other Metal Trades (under Private Ownership)	51,000	165,000	25	41
Chemical Trades (under Private Ownership)	40,000	103,000	20	39
Admiralty Dockyards	400	17,000	1	39
Ministry of Munitions Establishments	300	216,000	2	14
War Office Establishments	1,500	14,000	27	57
Total	212,100	947,000	1	32

* includes Blast Furnaces, Steel Manufacture, Iron & Steel Founding, Forging and Rolling
Source: A.W. Kirkaldy, *British Labour: Replacement and Conciliation 1914–1921*, London: Pitman, 1921

draws in historians like moths around a flame. Women who entered armaments occupations at the time found themselves confronted with work that was markedly different from peacetime activities, requiring training, a refinement of skills and adaptation to unfamiliar work patterns and different rhythms of work, within new and alien environments. All this overlay women's war work with a sense of novelty and uniqueness, which was emphasized by the government's publicity campaigns. 'Munitions' thus became a magnet for journalists, social commentators and intellectuals keen to relate women's wartime working experiences as if 'women's work' was a purely wartime phenomenon.[45]

Central to most wartime work experiences for women were the practices of dilution and substitution. The difference between the two is indistinct and the subject of some controversy. In 1916, *The Times* defined substitution as 'the direct replacement of men in processes where women were previously unknown; [and] the indirect substitution of boys by women'.[46] G.D.H. Cole defined 'dilution' as:

> the introduction of less skilled workers to undertake the whole, or a part of the work previously done by workers of greater skill or experience, often but not always, accompanied by simplification of machinery, or the breaking up of a job into a number of simpler operations.[47]

Deborah Thom agrees.[48] Gail Braybon outlined a more nuanced approach, however, arguing that dilution entailed placing skilled men on skilled work, while women worked on easier or preparatory stages of the job. By contrast, substitution operated on different levels. One was complete, or direct substitution, where one woman replaced one man, taking on all his work; the second was 'indirect' substitution, in which women replaced unskilled or semi-skilled men who were moved on to more intricate or more arduous work; thirdly, Braybon identified 'group' substitution, where several women replaced fewer numbers of men; and finally, there was 'rearrangement' substitution, whereby working tasks were reorganized to allow women to replace men with the aid of improved or new machinery. Though the difference between a substitute and a diluter was never distinct, the essential outcomes were the same: the pre-war complexities of industrial work tasks were broken down and simplified or, in the modern parlance, 'deskilled'.[49]

Thus, women's war work has to be understood as a process in which government, employers and trade unions viewed dilution and substitution as a means of spreading scarce skills more thinly, but more efficiently, in order to sustain supplies of men to the armed forces. This was not the result of changes in workplace technology, but more a reorganization of work tasks to accommodate large groups of women. Production techniques were adjusted to enable more unskilled and semi-skilled operators to be engaged in workshops on jobs formerly performed by highly trained workers, producing the same outputs, but at a slower pace. For women this meant entering an industrial world that had been redesigned to accommodate their inexperience, with tasks reduced to simple and repetitive chores and wages related to systems devised to maintain rising outputs. If some women were trained to do 'men's jobs', others were taught just one aspect of a skilled task or were trained to operate new and simply activated machinery.[50]

Accordingly, women's work meant repetitive and low-status jobs. G.D.H. Cole reported that in City banks the job of clerk was undergoing 'a process of regrading', with some of the more straightforward and mechanical work detached from the main tasks and entrusted to women who were 'paid at a lower rate than the old bank clerk, whose duties thus [became] more specialised'.[51] In the great department stores, such as Whiteley's and Harrods, women were taken on as doorkeepers and lift attendants. Female bus conductresses, 'clippies', were more common than female bus drivers. Indeed, the sight of women driving post office vans and London taxis raised eyebrows in the press.[52] Gareth Griffiths described how women in the heavy chemical industries were employed mainly as labourers – packing, loading, unloading, trucking, wheeling and otherwise moving materials – and in general yard work. For women engaged in shell filling, their days were spent in what one former worker described as 'boring and laborious' tasks: 'stemming' the shells, filling each case with a measured dose of explosive powder, pushed in using a stem and wooden mallet.[53] One factory inspector described a woman's task in the leather trades thus:

> There was a huge vat filled with a boiling starchy liquid into which the bags of dried skins were emptied and allowed to pregnate for a period of time, they were then removed and drained on a huge slimey table from which they were weighed out. The girl would take the portion of the slimey mess to her table on which was placed an iron frame, similar to a picture frame, measuring about 24 inches by 18. There she would pick out the larger skins, none of them more than four to five inches and stretch them on to the frame which stood on a hessian base. She would then proceed to fill in the centre of the frame with the pulpy mass left over, when this operation had been done she would take up the mallet and hammer the horrible mess until it was level and smooth, no holes left. Then she would turn in the edges of the layer on the bottom, the ends having been left over the rim of the frame in order to make a seal. This done she would proceed to place the skins left over on to the top of the layer of hammered pulp, this must be a neat operation otherwise the work was spoiled. Then she would dash to the press which stood on the other side of the room and take up a square flat tin the same size as the sheet of work she had made, return to her table and transfer the whole thing on to the tray, place her number on the work, rush over to the overlooker who could, if she so decided, tear up the whole construction, or send you back to your table to patch it up.[54]

Demanding work was matched by demanding working hours. In its haste to increase armaments production at the outset of war, the government suspended the pre-war regulations governing hours and conditions of factory work. Longer hours, obligatory overtime, Sunday work and shorter breaks became almost the norm for all employees, although experiences varied across the country. The standards set by the government's shell-filling factory at Georgetown, in Renfrewshire, Scotland, where women worked on average a 48-hour week in shifts of either five and a half days or five nights, were widely exceeded. Women employed in engineering shops in Manchester, for example, worked a 'typical' week of 53 hours, some working longer with overtime. Twelve-hour shifts day and night were the norm at Woolwich Arsenal, while one woman at the Fairey Aviation Company in Southampton worked for 74.5

hours, with 18 women working continuously on shifts of 23 to 24 hours. Excessive working hours peaked between 1914 and 1915 as factories raced to fulfil urgent government munitions contracts and would peak again at the onset of a major offensive on the Western Front.[55] However, by 1917 employers (and the government) began to grasp the fact that long hours, high output and worker efficiency did not always correlate. Widespread reports that armaments production was being affected by fatigue and exhaustion amongst women in the factories prompted an intensive investigation by the Ministry of Munitions' Health of Munitions Workers Committee, where it was discovered that women's average output in a factory turning aluminium fuse bodies on capstan lathes increased when the working week was reduced from 75 to 55 hours.[56] This formed the basis of the committee's recommendation for shortening the working week. Employers were slow to respond. By 1917 the Sheffield engineering firm Hadfields reported a 'slight increase' in output when its working week for women was reduced from 57 hours to 52. Pilkingtons, the Lancashire glass manufacturer, found that, when altering its shift system from two 12-hour shifts to three eight-hour shifts, the hourly output per person was increased by 16 per cent. This trend continued through the rest of the war. By 1918 the average working day for women had been trimmed to eight hours, with workshops operating on a daily three-shift basis over 24 hours, instead of two shifts of 12 hours. Sunday working for full-time employees was abolished.[57]

Long hours did not result in remuneration rates becoming level with men's. Women had long been victims of wage discrimination in the workplace, and the war merely accentuated existing patterns. Paid by the hour, rather than on the more lucrative 'piece-rates' which paid by output, money was often deducted in the event of stoppages resulting from machinery breakdown or air raids, sanctions that did not apply to men. Given its desperate need for female labour, the government found itself obliged to confront the problem, and, in October 1915, issued Circular L2, which advised employers that women employed at 'men's work' should be paid a minimum of one pound for a normal working week and those undertaking skilled 'men's work' or piecework were to receive the men's rate.[58] But employers could easily evade the regulations simply by treating the minimum as a standard wage and keeping women away from piecework. Hence, by April 1918 women in shell factories earned a national weekly average of £2 2s 4d compared with men's £4 6s 6d; £2 16s 8d was earned by women in projectile factories, as against the male rate of £4 14s 8d. Women working in the banking trades were paid 40 to 50 shillings a week, just under half of men's salaries.[59] Women's activists Mary Macarthur and Sylvia Pankhurst tried to force Lloyd George into committing the government to enforce a women's minimum wage, but were told that, because many were unskilled and untrained, they could not turn out as much work as men 'who have been at it a long time'. This left employers free to hire women on lower pay scales without official hindrance, which Lloyd George felt was necessary if this vital source of labour was to be used effectively. Besides, greater automation and adaptation of the existing machinery to break skilled jobs into simpler tasks gave many the excuse to claim that women were not entitled to parity with skilled men. It was a way of keeping both employers and unions quiet on an issue that never registered highly amongst the government's priorities, while it kept the equal pay question ringed with the tag of 'a social revolution', but one that was 'undesirable to attempt during war time'.[60]

At any rate, the expansion in the numbers of working women spilt over into rises in their trade union membership. Some women took the opportunity to join the National Federation of Women Workers, founded in 1906 mainly for workers in the 'sweated' trades, whose membership reached 80,000 by 1918. Otherwise women had to run the gauntlet of male prejudice when seeking some kind of union representation. Craft-based and skilled workers' unions such as the ASE and the Union of Carpenters and Joiners simply refused to accept women into their ranks, either because they lacked a presence in the industries they covered, or because women worked on different processes from men. However, 'general unions', including the National Union of Railways and the unions of Silk Workers, Electrical Trades and Bakers, embraced women, alongside the General Union of Municipal Workers and the Workers' Union, which gained many women members who were prevented from joining other unions.[61] As a result, female union membership expanded significantly during the war, from 437,000 in 1914 to a peak in 1920 at 1,342,000.[62] Unions were an important defence against discrimination and unfair practices, as well as being advocates for reform and equal pay rates, but invariably they were subject to the vagaries of women's employment rates and would suffer some decline when women's unemployment began to climb towards the end of the war.

On the positive side, the growing numbers of women in the workforce threw more light on working conditions. Munitions factories at the beginning of the war could be oppressive and grimy places that would not have looked out of place in a Dickens novel. Monica Cosens, in her account of her life as a 'munitionette', described her workshop as:

> long lines of black machinery on either side with its tiny wheels spinning round so quickly that they look as though they are trying to outdo in speed the bigger ones that revolve with dignity beneath them … . In front of each machine is a wooden platform on which we stand while we work. Sometimes there comes a moment when I can turn my back on my lathe and look away to the far corners of this large square factory. Above the lines and lines of machines that stretch in front of me there rises a thin haze – the steam from the hot shells as their oil-bespotted covering comes into contact with the tool. Here and there out of this haze when the twilight is falling there peeps an electric light, softened by the mist about it, or a gaily-coloured handkerchief lightly swathed round the head of the worker … .[63]

In smaller factories located in remote parts of the country even worse conditions prevailed. Gabrielle West, a factory inspector, and later a member of the Women's Police Service, commented on one factory at Pembrey, South Wales, as being:

> very badly equipped as regards the welfare of the girls. The change rooms are fearfully crowded. Long troughs are provided instead of wash basins, & there is always a scarcity of soap & towels. The girls' danger clothes are often horribly dirty & in rags ... . Although the fumes often mean 16 or 18 'casualties' a night, there are only 4 beds in the surgery for men & women & they are all in the same room ... . There are no drains owing to the ground being below sea level ... . The result is horrible & smelly swamps. There were until recently no lights in the lavatories, & as these same lavatories are generally full of rats & often very dirty the girls are afraid to go in.[64]

Fatigue was a constant problem. A combination of long hours and poor housing, which was always filled with outside street sounds and lack of privacy, impeded sleep, with night shift workers particularly affected.[65] 'I wondered how these girls would stand it', Monica Cosens wrote, 'for more than half of them were sitting round these tables, their heads buried in their hands, trying to snatch a few last winks of sleep before the shift began'.[66] Another 'munitions girl' recollected, 'I was always tired, especially about mid-night. I would find I could not keep awake and would suddenly come to life with a start with the foreman shaking me and my head was almost a hair's breadth from the spinning fly wheel.'[67] As for the provision of food, quality of diet varied considerably. Some women had to survive on main meals of bread and margarine. Others plucked themselves up to experience the daily delights of pie and mash (occasionally served with gravy). Woolwich Arsenal workers, on the other hand, benefited from full canteen facilities with a range of nutritious dishes and generous helpings of fresh fruit.[68]

All the same, it was the nature of wartime factory work, especially in munitions, that regularly heightened the threat to life and limb. The dangers came in two forms: accidents and longer-term risks to health. Machine operators were constantly afflicted by eye injuries, which frequently occurred through the absence of bodily safeguards. Others, too, who disregarded the regulatory safety requirements were vulnerable to having their hair and hands ensnared in machinery, with some victims losing part or all of their scalps. Adelaide Anderson remembered that some women drivers of overhead cranes 'met with fatal accidents', while others told tales of broken limbs, severed arms, scalpings and crushed hands.[69] And then there was the threat of explosions. Catastrophes were, more often than not, caused by careless usage of dangerous and unstable substances by workers unaware of their potentially lethal properties. Fear of undermining public and workforce morale meant that such factory disasters went under-reported by the government and the press. Official statistics on the numbers of explosions and casualties during the war were never published. Yet explosions in ordnance factories occurred with far more frequency and with far worse consequences than the public ever knew. The first notable accident occurred on 5th December 1916 at a National Filling Factory in Barnbow near Leeds, when a shell packed with high explosive spontaneously detonated while being fused, killing 35 women workers.[70] Another disaster at a chemical works at Pitsea in Essex was caused by a scientist inadvertently knocking over a jar of nitroglycerine. Investigations into an explosion at the National Filling Factory at Cardonald found traces of bread crumbs and jam on the workbenches alongside jars of explosive chemicals.[71] The most devastating event occurred at Mond & Co.'s munitions factory at Silvertown in East London on 19th January 1917 when a large explosion killed 69 people and injured over 1,000, many of them women workers, while damaging 70,000 houses in the surrounding neighbourhood. It was reported that the blast was heard in Cambridge.[72]

If accidents were the more visible aspects of poor working practices, then poisoning from toxic substances was no less lethal and, if anything, was more insidious. Operatives on the manufacturing process of TNT (the demand for which varied greatly during the war) were exposed to toxic infection through contact with some of its ingredients (notably amatol), either in liquid form or through handling congealed lumps left on shells, trucks and floors, or by inhaling infected dust and fumes.[73] Other substances such as lead were major sources of gynaecological illness and miscarriage; 'CE' (compound explosive), a powder used in shells, caused sickness, discolouration and swelling of the skin (dermatitis); lyddite caused jaundice, and cordite, which some workers took to chewing because of its sweet taste, produced toxic fumes and generated sickness and heart trouble if consumed. Finally, there was 'dope', a highly poisonous substance used in varnishing aircraft wings (a job performed largely by women), that precipitated fainting, nausea, unconsciousness and occasionally death if inhaled.[74] Symptoms of poisoning took many forms, including drowsiness and frontal headache, eczema, dermatitis, loss of appetite, bloated stomach, anaemia, constipation, shortness of breath, a staggering gait, palpitations, depression and a metallic taste in the mouth; symptoms surfaced either gradually after several days' or weeks' work, or occasionally quite suddenly after a few hours' work on a hot day.[75]

The most visible signs of infection occurred on the faces and hands of TNT workers, whose direct daily contact with the substance turned their skin bright yellow (or tawny orange), and who were publicly ridiculed as 'canaries'.[76] TNT workers at Woolwich Arsenal were isolated in their own canteen as, one worker recalled, 'everything they touched went yellow, chairs, tables everything'. Another, who worked with tetryl, remembered how her skin was yellow yet her black hair went 'practically green ... you'd wash and wash and it didn't make no difference. It didn't come off. Your whole body was yellow.'[77] TNT-poisoning thus created a new visual language for women's war work, yet the government was slow to recognize the dangers. 'Expert' opinion before the war regarded TNT as harmless 'in ordinary use'.[78] By January 1916, however, the first fatality had been recorded and in March three deaths were reported from Woolwich Arsenal and HM Factory Slade's Green. By July, 29 cases of toxic infection with ten deaths had occurred, seven of whom were workers in National Filling Factories. Moreover, rumours of the effects of working in ordnance factories were affecting women's recruitment rates, while some existing employees were becoming 'disorganized through fear of contact', and absenteeism was growing.[79] By 1917, the HM Inspector of Factories estimated that over 50,000 workers had become exposed to TNT with the 'wastage of labour' (ministry-speak for those who were taken off munitions work through illness) ranging from 60 per cent to 100 per cent annually by 1917, the most vulnerable being those employees with under six months' service.[80]

The government's initial reaction was to censor news of the TNT hazard in newspapers and the medical press. But the urgencies of war, the all too evident effects of working in munitions and the predominance of women in the industrial workforce created new imperatives. Welfare was an unfamiliar concept in factory work, although protecting workers through workshop regulations was not. Parliament had a long tradition of endeavouring to improve conditions in industrial workplaces by laying down minimum standards for ventilation and sanitary facilities, monitored and enforced by a well-organized network of factory inspectors. Yet the scale of need after 1914 was unprecedented. As such, the government's approach to workforce welfare was bounded by three factors. First was the assumption that women were physiologically weaker than men. Women who performed heavy-duty tasks in masculine industrial environments may have dented this notion to an extent, but those who retained a more traditional view of women's social role were supported by a series of investigations undertaken for the Ministry of Munitions in 1916 that appeared to confirm the masculine belief in women's innate biological inferiority.[81] This helped to sustain the prevailing opinion that women workers needed welfare support if they were to continue working whilst fully exercising the 'privilege' of being the fulcrum of family life, as well as acting as a counterweight to men's more primitive instincts. Women workers had, as *The Times* put it, 'the double burthen [*sic*] of family life and industry to carry'; in their hands they carried the future of the race.[82]

Second, female employees were never regarded as anything other than temporary. Mary Macarthur had always claimed that women were 'meantime workers': in the pre-war labour force they worked between school and marriage; in war they became 'meantime' workers for its duration.[83] Thus, women workers were seen as industrial soldiers, dressed in specialized uniforms, performing specific roles in rigid and highly disciplined environments, answering a call of duty (being described as 'war workers' smothered all the differences of class, nationality and region). Like soldiers, they would be demobbed after the war. Third, and above all, the health of the female worker was considered to be essential in the interests of efficiency and output.

A welfare supervisor at the government's factory in Gretna poignantly summarized this view by commenting that 'the welfare of the women operatives was considered by the ministry and factory management as second only to the production of cordite'.[84] Ministry of Munitions officials talked of welfare only in such terms. Factory doctors were seen in the same class as production managers. The precautions developed for workers' safety were implemented as a systematic, theorized and strictly regulated process geared almost exclusively to productivity. TNT-poisoning, cordite chewing, the dangers inherent in machine operating, were treated as problems of production, affecting output, rather than industrial hazards in themselves.[85]

The government's first moves towards protecting female employees from the terrors of the industrial workplace were more *ad hoc* than methodical. Safeguards against explosions were given priority. Workshops were divided into clean and dirty areas; women donned overalls, overshoes and caps when working on machinery; workers in filling and explosives factories were subjected to body searches to prevent forbidden matches, lighters or cigarettes entering the factory; women had to remove all their hair ornaments, jewellery and metal buttons (as a prevention against explosions), identifying and isolating ordnance workshops from the everyday routines of factory life.[86] A more systematic approach was promised by the establishment of a Welfare Department in the Ministry of Munitions, led by the social reformer Seebohm Rowntree. Typically, Rowntree aimed to 'raise the well being' of women and child munitions workers by attaching numerous specialists to the department, most notably H.M. Vernon (a physiology specialist from Oxford University and an advocate of the American doctrines of 'scientific management'), to advise on working hours and output; and Captain M. Greenwood, reader in medical statistics at London University, to examine workers' nutrition and diet.[87] These early moves were harnessed in September 1915 by Rowntree's appointment of a Health of Munitions Workers Committee chaired by Sir George Newman, to consider and advise on questions of industrial fatigue, hours of labour and other matters affecting the personal health and physical efficiency of women workers in munitions factories and workshops.[88] After a series of intensive inquiries, the committee not only produced a substantive and highly detailed report covering all aspects of welfare in industry, but also spawned the publication of a string of memoranda on fatigue, hours of work and other health matters, together with a host of studies from bodies in other departments, such as the ministry's Medical Research Committee and Home Office's Industrial Fatigue Board, enforced by a beehive of welfare officers who visited factories to help deploy new measures and recommendations. And so a new state-sponsored bureaucratic management of the wartime workplace came into being. Factory welfare incorporated a small army of production managers, medical researchers, welfare workers and doctors and their nursing assistants, who were regarded in the same manner as army medics. Factories thus became a new frontier in state policy during the war: but a frontier with a singular purpose that could be easily dismantled.[89]

The primary impulse of welfare was the general improvement of workplace conditions. As noted, working hours were shortened; heavy and demanding physical tasks were restricted to the young and physically fit and those without 'arduous home duties to perform'. Proposals were made for improvements in daily meals and the building of canteens; incorporation of rest breaks within the working day; the provision of rest seats in workshops; cloakrooms; improved washing, bathing and sanitary facilities; and the setting up of recreational activities and educational services.[90] Numerous factories constructed a culture around sports and leisure activities, sometimes organized by the workers themselves, intended to break the 'all bed and work' routine of working life. Mealtime concerts, film shows and lectures were popular. Several factories spawned social clubs, theatrical and operatic societies and arranged dances and social evenings, picnics and outings. Classes in particular skills and crafts, such as sewing and typing, were also given.[91] In other places women workers attempted to generate a shop-floor culture through the production of magazines that parodied the national press and the ministry's literary outpourings in a manner and style that mirrored the more famous trench journals on the Western Front. Magazines such as the *Cardonald News* from the filling factory in Glasgow, *Bombshell*, *Shell Clippings* and *Carry On* (published by workers in the Armstrong Works in the North East) gave workers a forum to vent grievances through humour and satire.[92]

Equally significant were the welfare measures formulated directly for specific sets of workers. Wartime concerns about the wastage of men at the front and a declining birthrate led to unprecedented efforts to help pregnant workers and working mothers with crèches and nurseries in factories. By contrast, civil servants and factory officials treated the safety of TNT workers more clinically as a question of bodily management. Women engaged on shell filling were instructed to wash frequently and habitually change their underwear. Ministry of Munitions' instructions for the prevention of TNT-poisoning, issued in February 1917, argued that the absorption of toxic substances through the skin could be prevented by the twice-weekly washing of work 'costumes'. In addition, a daily ration of a free pint of milk for each worker was issued as a prophylactic against poisoning. TNT workers were also required to undergo weekly medical examinations, with any workers infected summarily removed from the workplace. An advisory government committee on TNT-poisoning advocated mechanizing shell filling, greater use of respirators and protective clothing, proper workshop ventilation and alternating periods spent on TNT work with so-called clean tasks.[93]

Welfare also extended beyond the factory gates. Housing supply for workers was in constant crisis. The enormous influx of new employees into munitions areas placed intense strain on local housing resources, pushing up rents and creating severe shortages of billeting accommodation and overcrowding. Building projects sponsored by the Ministry of Munitions had produced some 494 hostels in 206 different locations in Britain in 1917, accommodating some

24,000 women workers, rising to 524 hostels by January 1918. Hostels, how-ever, were of variable quality and not always popular. On a tour of the 'wooden bungalow huts' on a Midlands site in 1916, one journalist conveyed his approval of their comfort and cleanliness. Each room had an electric light, the bathrooms had a constant supply of hot water, rooms were well furnished, with comfortable bedding, lockers, washstands and vanity mirrors. By con-trast, the Ministry of Munitions hostel at Gloucester had just two baths for 38 tenants, and at Lancaster one bath for 21 tenants.[94] Hostels lacked privacy, were not homelike and subjected their inhabitants to strict regulations. The government responded by passing the Billeting of Civilians Act of 1917, creating a Central Billeting Board, which enforced the compulsory billeting of workers in local households, operating through local authority-administered committees that regulated standards of lodging accommodation and fixing rents.[95]

Ultimately, the purpose and process of welfare administration was perso-nified in the shape of the welfare supervisor, a role directly aimed at managing the welfare of women and child workers. Applicants for the job needed to have 'recognized status', a stipulation that almost ensured the interest mainly of educated middle-class women anxious to pursue what was a new area of professional employment, but often meant that women were brought to the job with little or no direct experience of handling a young working-class female workforce.[96] The job of the welfare supervisor was as broad as it was long.[97] They were workplace managers, dealing with employee complaints, checking wages, monitoring timekeeping and absenteeism, collecting doctors' certificates and enforcing discipline. Supervisors often oversaw experiments with new facilities and investigated accidents, while recommending improve-ments to machinery and work practices. They also undertook personnel mat-ters. Decisions on recruitment and assigning workers to areas of work usually fell within the supervisor's realm of responsibility, as did the job of matron – administering ambulance rooms, first-aid facilities, rudimentary dental care and regular health checks, and monitoring washing and bathing, cloakrooms, lockers, lavatories and changing areas.

In another flick of the wrist, a supervisor took on the role of social worker and 'moral guardian'. The welfare supervisor at the Vickers' works in Barrow thought the aim of her job was the moral and physical welfare of her young female workers, supplying them with 'home care and comforts' as part of a 'big family'.[98] This frequently meant visiting sick workers in hospital; home visits to check on an employee's living circumstances, especially if they were the source of lateness or absenteeism; encouraging healthy habits such as proper eating amongst workers; monitoring the child-care arrangements of working mothers; and weeding out 'undesirables', those women who were caught pilfering, even to the extent of giving testimony to the police or a court in the case of prosecution. By 1917 approximately 600 welfare super-visors had been appointed throughout the country; by the end of the war there were as many as 1,000. The ratio of welfare supervisors to women workers varied greatly, but averaged about one to 300 employees, although at Woolwich Arsenal the ratio was one to 20.[99] Supervisors attracted a mixed press. Invariably female, they were often caricatured as large-framed ladies with stentorian voices, and were loved and loathed in equal measure. One of the most prominent, Lilian Barker, Chief Welfare Superintendent at Woolwich Arsenal, appeared to encapsulate all that was good and bad in the role. With a formidable physical presence and a 'no-nonsense' reputation, some journalists were convinced Barker was a man in disguise. She would berate women who reported for work wearing make-up and single-handedly resolve workplace disputes. Yet at the same time Barker could be remarkably supportive of the women under her charge, providing help with errands for sick or injured workers and even organizing financial aid for women who were unable to work. Lilian Barker was later honoured by becoming a Dame of the British Empire, but her protective authoritarianism provides us with an image of wartime welfare that has proved difficult to dislodge.[100]

Women as society

For many women, the workplace experience was a mixed bag. Despite trade union scepticism of the government's welfare schemes, cash support for mothers and the setting-up of nurseries was well received.[101] Then again, while the measures were adopted in the National Factories, provision was less than complete. In 1916 the Ministry of Munitions admitted that 69 per cent of its 'controlled establishments' contained 'a partial or complete lack of food ... inadequate or non-existent cloakrooms and washing appliances, lack of seats, lack of first-aid facilities and rest rooms, supervision of numerous young girls by men only, and other defects in factories mostly working twelve-hour shifts'. In some establishments crèches were planned, but construction was thwarted through labour shortages and petty negotiations. The *Women's Industrial News* reported in April 1916 that improvements in cloakrooms and canteens were 'rare', and by 1917 the Health of Munitions Workers Committee stated that canteen accommodation had been provided for just 45 per cent of all munitions workers.[102]

Not that the wartime workplace was one of sisterly concord. L.K. Yates spoke fancifully of 'Social status, so stiff a barrier ... in pre-war days, was forgotten in the factory ... they were all working together as happily as the members of a united family.'[103] Certainly, the expansion of wartime employment drew in a significant minority of middle- and upper-class women for whom, like Cynthia Asquith, paid work was a new experience.[104] Indeed, this class of female employee arrived in the factory expecting high standards of health and comfort and, free of the fear of sanction or dismissal, were more likely to demand, and receive, improvements in sanitary facilities and rest places that ultimately benefited all workers.[105] Yet the sight of upper-class 'gals' on the factory floor was usually an occasion for displays of unconcealed dislike and suspicion from their more 'ordinary' colleagues. In some ways this was hardly surprising. At Woolwich Arsenal a special hostel was built for 'lady' munitions workers, emphasizing the cultural gap between the classes, a divide that was unconsciously reinforced by attitudes expressed by Naomi Loughnan, who infamously wrote that the ordinary factory hand lacked interest in their work 'because of the undeveloped state of their imaginations'.[106] On her first day, Monica Cosens regarded her new colleagues as 'rough, loud-voiced, and … ill-natured' and nothing but 'vulgar little hussies', before she grew to appreciate and eventually 'love them'. The antagonism was mutual. The clipped accents of the 'lady volunteers' in Cosens's factory encouraged the full-time workers to ridicule them as 'meows'. Cosens further warned:

> There is no denying immediately a new Volunteer comes into a street there is defiance in the air. She is not gently treated. … One girl will put out her tongue at the unconscious worker's back, another will deride her with an admiring crowd about her, while a third will do everything she can to worry the novice, by borrowing her crowbar and not bothering to return it, and when it is claimed with diffidence, will treat the inquirer with scornful silence and a look of contempt which sets the others giggling.[107]

In ordnance factories the rank-structured workforce was a further source of class enmities. Shop-floor workers were subject to the orders of chargehands, overlookers, foremen or forewomen, welfare supervisors, women police and other security personnel and numerous managers. The jobs of chargehand (responsible for a small gang of workers, monitoring attendance and sickness and applying factory rules), overlooker (responsible for the supervision of a whole 'shop', that is, a building or area of workers) and foreman were usually given to women of superior education, or responsible workers promoted from the ranks.[108] Positions of authority were usually accompanied by paternalistic attitudes and resentment from workers at assumptions of moral authority. Women living in hostels became subject to strict controls. Gates were locked and lights put out between 10.00 and 10.30 p.m.; neither alcohol nor male visitors were allowed inside. Workers resented criticism of their dress and domestic behaviour. 'If you go to the picture-house three times a week, you hear about it from her', complained one girl at Woolwich Arsenal, and welfare supervisors were caricatured as 'interfering cats' or 'green-eyed frumps', while one supervisor who questioned her charges' capability of setting up a club met with a mixture of anger, indignation and a shower of half-eaten lunches.[109]

Still, in a patriarchal world dominated by rigid assumptions about women's societal role and their mental and physical limitations, the achievements of female workers surpassed expectations. Women excelled at difficult and delicate operations. They proved surprisingly adept at aircraft work, machine lathe turning, oxyacetylene welding and the making of scientific instruments.

However, Barbara Drake's rapturous comment that 'the masculine monopoly of muscles itself is threatened by a feminine Sandow' borders on hyperbole.[110] Nevertheless, men were scared. Women were traditionally associated with low wages, and their use as cheap labour on skilled tasks threatened masculine workplace status and wider social identity, especially as underpaid women were more likely to retain their low-grade positions after the war.[111] Men's hidden fears were invariably expressed as open resistance to women workers. Much anger was aroused by exaggerated press reports about women's capabilities, and the archives contain many personal reminiscences of both petty and more serious hostile attitudes from men towards their female colleagues. The sharpest antagonism was felt across the transport, textiles and engineering industries, where the lax application of government controls ensured that the use of women on skilled work provoked the worst behaviour. Reports of men spitting tobacco juice into the pockets of female employees in aircraft factories came accompanied with tales of Hull transport workers threatening strike action if women were employed as conductresses. James Billington, secretary of the Preston Operative Spinners Association, exclaimed in a notorious outburst in 1917 that, 'if the spinners of Preston think fit at any time to work with females that is their business .... For my own part ... I would sooner see my daughter dead than do such work.'[112]

Employers, for their part, were undecided. Of course, a premier interest in employing women was embedded in the advantages of acquiring a cut-price workforce. Constantly bombarded by ministry booklets, travelling exhibitions and visits from factory inspectors in an effort to persuade them to accept women workers as part of the government's dilution policy, companies still recruited women as much on the basis of personal attitude as clear-eyed business judgement. 'Those who take their work seriously', commented one City of London bank manager, 'do excellently [but] too many only regard their earnings as so much pocket-money and throw up their work on the slightest pretext.'[113] One witness of wartime factories remarked:

> There is a traditional mistrust of women in the business world: men fear they cannot keep their tongues or their fingers from interfering with other people's work. A manager pictures to himself an irresponsible woman let loose in his factory among his tried and trusted foremen who, over-worked and on the edge of worries of wartime, are only too likely to be irritated by trifles.[114]

Generally, however, women were regarded as docile workers, tolerant of boredom, and their lack of union organization allowed some of the more unscrupulous workplace managers to evade local agreements on pay and conditions. But the hidden costs of employing female labour could not be sidestepped. Women required their own lavatories, catering, washing and first-aid facilities. And the complaints from some employers of bad timekeeping,

Figure 5.2 Bus conductress being inspected, *c.* 1917

dishonesty and absenteeism were made without fully comprehending the need of women to work whilst trying to maintain home and family. For the most part, unskilled and semi-skilled women were of little threat to the apprenticed skilled factory worker, and many employers would continue to use them after the war. It was in those industries where men and women were engaged on similar tasks that the tensions were most visible.

Moreover, women's greater social prominence in wartime only resulted in greater social ambivalence. The sight of a young working-class female munitions worker, brash, self-confident and economically independent, raised eyebrows amongst the moral guardians of the middle and upper classes. At first sight, it would seem that working women challenged existing preconceptions of their role and character but, more usually, they often reinforced traditional attitudes. Newspapers talked of the nation's gratitude to women, without fully recognizing that women *were* part of the nation. Journalists excelled in relating stories about the success of working women, yet serious talk of pay and prospects, hours and the nature of work, was usually subsumed by comments on women's physical appearance. Thus, typically perhaps, the *Daily Mail* could write of women engineers at Notting Hill in London during 1916 as 'Overalled, leather-aproned, capped and goggled – displaying nevertheless women's genius for making herself attractive in whatsoever working guise'.[115] Another journalist, in all seriousness, wrote, 'I could not help contrasting the dainty little khaki-class miss, curls peeping from underneath her spongehat, with the setting. She might have stepped out of a West End Revue. Actually she was a checker, fulfilling her important and appointed task amidst the scream and noise and steam, the clanging of a thousand hammers.'[116]

Nonetheless, women workers stretched social tolerances and drew out older prejudices. 'Are women capable of driving at night?' enquired the *Daily Telegraph* in 1917.[117] Pretty munitions workers 'doing their bit' could just as easily be feckless and flighty girls who were overpaid and underworked. Women working in the clerical trades, particularly in London, came in for carping criticism. 'Women in Whitehall: do they make tea, smoke and endlessly chatter?' asked the *Daily Sketch* in 1917. The *Evening News* parodied the 'government office girls'' daily routine: 'Arrival about 10 a.m.; half-an-hour powdering the nose; a little work, if it is pointed out; tea; another powder.'[118] Myths circulated of women workers spending their earnings on fur coats, excessive drinking, elaborate jewellery and gramophones. These mingled with equally powerful rumours of child neglect, sexual profligacy, high illegitimacy rates and drunkenness, all of which signified the modern woman's abandonment of her traditional role. In this vein, munitions workers were an easy target. In public they could be noisy, boisterous and instantly recognizable, raising fears about uncontrolled sexuality and of 'profiting' from the sacrifices of the war.[119] Madeline Ida Bedford, in an oft-quoted poem, parodied the munitions workers' high living:

> Afraid! Are you kidding?
> With Money to spend
> Years back I wore tatters
> Now – silk stockings, mi friend![120]

These tangled feelings towards women workers raise questions over how far women 'progressed' during the war. On the surface they had made huge strides. Many women proved that they could survive and prosper in a man's world, their intelligence and abilities had taken them far beyond their traditional domains of hearth and home, and their invaluable contribution to the war effort was rewarded with the vote under the franchise reforms of 1918. Revelling in the new wartime opportunities to enter paid work for the first time, many middle- and upper-class women spoke loudly of experiencing an independence in their personal lives that was largely unknown before 1914, leading them to regard this freedom as a sign of their growing emancipation. Yet these overtures of social advancement are not matched by the evidence. Assumptions about the 'temporary' nature of women's work were being realized a year before the Armistice with the first reports of lay-offs in the munitions industries as armaments orders were cancelled following Russia's exit from the war. The enforcement of the Restoration of Pre-War Practices Act (1919) strengthened the trend as some trade unions used its terms to force women out of the workplace. By April 1919 there were some 486,945 women and 31,070 girls who were in receipt of out-of-work benefits, sparking demonstrations and angry deputations of women's groups to the government.[121] Conversely, those who remained in work had to contend with press accusations of selfishly keeping jobs meant for returning soldiers, and there were still huge discrepancies between women's and men's pay rates. Moreover, Parliament's nervousness about the unpredictable nature of a politicized female working class ensured that only middle-class, propertied women over the age of 30 received full voting rights. Traditional masculine attitudes may have been disrupted by the war, but the conflict failed to dislodge deeper social orthodoxies. Angela Woollacott has argued that the First World War acted as a catalyst for change – a 'raising of consciousness' that would bring women's economic, social and political status much closer to men's.[122] In the immediate post-war period this 'emancipation' culture, epitomized by rising hemlines, public drinking and smoking and openly advancing new 'feminine' social attitudes, was the prerogative of a fortunate few. Many more women retreated to hearth, home and motherhood, having worked because of financial necessity, whilst still being regarded as exploited and exploitable, in economic, social and cultural terms. So much had changed; but so much remained the same.

Land Army

'Breeched, booted and cropped', exclaimed Lloyd George of the typical Land Army girl. 'She was certainly the most picturesque figure, and perhaps in some ways the most valuable.' Such reverence of the 'bronzed and freckled ... splendidly healthy' land girl is perhaps illustrative of how history can occasionally magnify the significance of some events out of all proportion to their factual reality. The emergence of the Women's Land Army (WLA) in 1917 grew out of a need to provide a skilled, permanent and essentially mobile female labour force to fill the manpower shortages on British farms during the last two years of the war. Following the appointment of Miss Meriel Talbot of the Women's Branch of the Board of Agriculture as head of the WLA in January 1917, its progress was prone to mythologizing. In the first instance, the WLA was not that large. The initial call for recruits in July attracted (according to Lord Ernle) around 45,000 applications, of whom just 5,000 were accepted. By November, recruitment figures grew to 6,672; by March 1918, 7,665 women had been accepted; and during the harvest period of September 1918 the WLA's working strength had increased to 16,000. Even so, the number of WLA workers on British farms was far outweighed by the numbers of 'village women' employed. During 1918, for example, just 143 land girls were employed in Cambridgeshire, against 2,533 village women working full- and part-time; in Devon the numbers were, respectively, 127 and 3,801; and in the East Riding of Yorkshire, 64 against 1,358. Moreover, WLA recruitment came in waves. The initial rush in 1917 was followed by two quiet periods during the following autumn and winter. Numbers grew strongly after a major recruitment drive in April 1918, and peaked in the summer and autumn. Nevertheless, when viewed in numerical terms, the WLA was only a minor agricultural labour source. In the second instance, although the character of the WLA was dominated by educated, middle-class recruits, its primary task was to encourage village women to sign up for farm work during times when labour shortages threatened national agricultural output.

Yet, in its day, the WLA created much interest because of its all-female staff. The ministerial administration was staffed by women and responsibility for selection and recruitment fell to local Women's War Agricultural Committees. Women were selected primarily on the grounds of physical fitness and moral character, since many would be working alone on farmsteads in isolated areas. Hence, recruitment committees tended to accept far fewer applicants than were rejected and inclined to favour educated, middle-class women, who were seen as able to apply the high moral standards expected and uphold the WLA's reputation.

However, those women who were given to the sylvan fantasies of rural work in the WLA had a very rude awakening. The WLA was marked out by its quasi-military uniform of overalls, hat, boots, leggings, a single jersey, clogs and mackintosh, with strict instructions that breeches (essential for working on wet crops or heavy ploughland) should not be worn in public unless covered by an overall. What is more, Agricultural Board President Rowland Prothero warned that there would be no occasion for 'lilac sunbonnets'. Women who survived the training schemes, tolerated the low remuneration (weekly wages were set initially at 18s (90p), rising to 20s (£1) in March 1918) and faced down the prejudice of farmers and the loneliness of being ostracized from local communities could look forward to a life of hoeing crops; planting and harvesting potatoes; tending to livestock; ploughing; milking; egg collecting; making hay; and harrowing, in all weathers, and often at a moment's notice. In some areas land girls were seen as a substitute for domestic servants.

The WLA has become one of the great symbols of women's war work. Its exaggerated historical presence probably owes much to the developed intelligence of the participants, whose education, motivation and opportunity to put their memories into print were far greater than that available to their more humble lower-class compatriots. Indeed, when set against the contribution of ordinary villagers, who shouldered a sizeable burden of the agricultural war effort, the WLA's contribution can only be regarded as peripheral. All the same, along with other middle-class organizations undertaking rural work, the WLA did highlight the status and importance of women land workers and established important precedents for British farming in the Second World War. The WLA never completely lived down the image of nice girls on the farm, but at least it contributed what Pamela Horn noted as 'a softening of hostility'.

References

Alan Armstrong, *Farmworkers; A Social and Economic History 1770–1980*, London: Batsford, 1988, p. 164.

Peter Dewey, *British Agriculture in the First World War*, London: Routledge, 1989, pp. 130–36.

Pamela Horn, *Rural Life in England in the First World War*, Dublin: Gill & Macmillan, 1984, pp. 124–36.

Alun Howkins, *Reshaping Rural England: A Social History 1850–1925*, London: Routledge, 1991, pp. 264–65.

Imperial War Museum, Women's Work Collection, Women's Land Army, 'Reports and Correspondence' LAND 1–7.

NA, MAF 42/8, 'Report for the Year 1918'; NATS 1/1275, 'Women's Agricultural Section, Report of Work and Organisation; Scottish Women's Land Army Scheme', 1918.

'The Story of the Land Girls', in E. Royston Pike, *Human Documents of the Lloyd George Era*, London: Allen & Unwin, 1972, pp. 182–83.

Notes

1 M.G. Fawcett, *The Women's Victory and After – Personal Reminiscences 1911–1918*, London: Sidgwick & Jackson, 1920, p. 106.

2 Imperial War Museum (hereafter, 'IWM'), Women's Work Collection, EMP 25/10, Board of Trade, *The Increase in Employment of Women During the War: Individual Industries*, 1917; Board of Trade, *Report on the State of Employment in all Occupations in the United Kingdom in July 1918*, 1919.

3 A.W. Kirkaldy, ed., *British Labour: Replacement and Conciliation 1914–21*, London: Pitman, 1921, p. 2.

4 Deborah Thom, *Nice Girls and Rude Girls: Women Workers in World War I*, London: I.B. Tauris, 2000, p. 32.

5 Angela Woollacott, *On Her Their Lives Depend: Munitions Workers in the Great War*, London: University of California Press, 1994, p. 20.

6 Martin Pugh, *Women and the Women's Movement in Great Britain, 1914–1959*, Basingstoke: Macmillan, 1992, pp. 20–21.

7 Gerard DeGroot, *Blighty: British Society in the Era of the Great War*, Harlow: Longman, 1996, p. 128.

8 Ian Beckett, *Home Front 1914–1918: How Britain Survived the Great War*, London: National Archives, 2006, p. 81.

9 See, for example, Clementine Black, ed., *Married Women's Work, Being the Report of an Inquiry Undertaken by the Women's Industrial Council*, London: Bell, 1915; C. Black, ed., *Sweated Industry and the Minimum Wage*, London: Duckworth, 1907.

10 IWM, EMP 25/10, Board of Trade, *The Increase in Employment of Women During the War: Individual Industries*, op. cit.; Barbara Drake, *Women in the Engineering Trades*, London: Allen & Unwin, 1917, pp. 8–9.

11 G.D.H. Cole, *Labour in War Time*, op. cit., p. 229; Angela Woollacott, *On Her Their Lives Depend*, op. cit., pp. 22–23; Irene Andrews, *Economic Effects of the War upon Women and Children in Great Britain*, op. cit., p. 23; Gerard DeGroot, *Blighty*, op. cit., pp. 126–27; Sylvia Pankhurst, *The Home Front: A Mirror to Life in England During the First World War*, London: Cresset Library, 1932, p. 60.

These figures are suspect, as they exclude those women employed in the clothing and textile industries, luxury trades and food manufacture, who were either made redundant or put on short-time working.

12 Martin Pugh, *Women and the Women's Movement in Great Britain, 1914–1959*, op. cit., pp. 18–19; Deborah Thom, *Nice Girls and Rude Girls*, op. cit., pp. 30, 86; *The Times*, 5th September 1914.

13 *The Times*, 12th October 1914.

14 Gerard DeGroot, *Blighty*, op. cit., p. 127; Martin Pugh, *Women and the Women's Movement in Britain*, op. cit., p. 19; Deborah Thom, *Nice Girls and Rude Girls*, op. cit., p. 32.

15 See E. Sylvia Pankhurst, *The Home Front: A Mirror to Life in England During the First World War*, op. cit., pp. 53–55; G.D.H. Cole, *Labour in War Time*, op. cit., pp. 233–35; Ian Beckett, *Home Front*, op. cit., p. 66; Keith Laybourn, *Unemployment and Employment Policies Concerning Women in Britain, 1900–1951*, Lampeter: Edwin Mellen, 2002, pp. 38–40.

16 A.W. Kirkaldy, *British Labour: Replacement and Conciliation*, op. cit., pp. 13–14; Irene Andrews, *Economic Effects of the War upon Women and Children in Great Britain*, op. cit., p. 31.

17 Irene Andrews, *Economic Effects of the War upon Women and Children in Great Britain*, op. cit., p. 31; G.D.H. Cole, *Labour in War Time*, op. cit., p. 236.

18 *The Times*, 18th March 1915; G.D.H. Cole, *Labour in War Time*, op. cit., pp. 236–237.

19 David Lloyd George, *War Memoirs*, vol. I, London: Odhams, 1938, pp. 174–75; E. Sylvia Pankhurst, *The Suffragette Movement: An Intimate Account of Persons and Ideals*, London: Longmans, 1932, pp. 593–97; NA, MUN 5/70/324/26, 'Copy Correspondence of 11 and 28 August 1915 on Expenses incurred by Women's Social and Political Union for Organised Procession to Secure More Women Munition Workers'.

20 See, for example, NA, MUN 5/70/324/16–28, 'Catalogue: Exhibition of Sample of Women's Work and Official Photographs, 1918'; Irene Andrews, *Economic Effects of the War upon Women and Children in Great Britain*, op. cit., pp. 52–54; see also Deborah Thom, *Nice Girls and Rude Girls*, op. cit., ch. 4.

21 Irene Andrews, *Economic Effects of the War upon Women and Children in Great Britain*, op. cit., pp. 58–59.

22 Adelaide Mary Anderson, *Women in the Factory: An Administrative Adventure 1893 to 1921*, London: John Murray, 1922, p. 228.

23 Gareth Griffiths, *Women's Factory Work in World War I*, Stroud: Alan Sutton, 1991, p. 15.

24 Irene Andrews, *Economic Effects of the War upon Women and Children in Great Britain*, op. cit., ch. 4; Gail Braybon, *Women Workers in the First World War*, London: Routledge, 1989, p. 48; Deborah Thom, *Nice Girls and Rude Girls*, op. cit., p. 34.

25 Gail Braybon, *Women Workers in the First World War*, op. cit., pp. 49–50.

26 Irene Andrews, *Economic Effects of the War upon Women and Children in Great Britain*, op. cit., pp. 70–71.

27 Gail Braybon, *Women Workers in the First World War*, op. cit., pp. 49–50; Irene Andrews, *Economic Effects of the War upon Women and Children in Great Britain*, op. cit., pp. 70–71.

28 Gerard DeGroot, *Blighty*, op. cit., pp. 128–29; Henriette R. Walter, *Munition Workers in England and France: A Summary of Reports Issued by the British Ministry of Munitions*, New York: Russell Sage Foundation, 1917, p. 138; Irene Andrews, *Economic Effects of the War upon Women and Children in Great Britain*, op. cit., p. 70.

29 *The Times*, 30th March 1915.

30 *The Times*, 8th February 1915; Board of Trade, *Labour Gazette*, January 1917, Appendix 'C'.

31 *The Times*, 8th February 1915; Board of Trade, Labour Gazette, op. cit.; see also A.W. Kirkaldy, ed., *British Labour: Replacement and Conciliation 1914–21*, op. cit., pp. 2, 73–76, 77–84; *Report of the War Cabinet Committee on Women in Industry*, Cmnd 135, London: HMSO, 1919, pp. 80–96.

32 Gail Braybon and Penny Summerfield, *Out of the Cage: Women's Experiences in Two World Wars*, London: Pandora, 1987, p. 58.

33 Carolyne E. Playne, *Society at War 1914–1916*, London: Allen & Unwin, 1931, p. 137.

34 L.K. Yates, *The Woman's Part; A Record of Munitions Work*: London: Hodder & Stoughton, 1918, pp. 10–11.

35 IWM, Documents Collection, 97/3/1, Diary, Mrs A. Purbrook, part III, August 1914, p. 5; Miss Lillian Miles, quoted in Gail Braybon and Penny Summerfield, *Out of the Cage: Women's Experiences in Two World Wars*, op. cit., p. 58.

36 *The Times*, 3rd October 1916.

37 A.K. Foxwell, *Munition Lasses: Six Months as Principal Overlooker in Danger Buildings*, London: Hodder & Stoughton, 1917, p. 5.

38 Cited in Gail Braybon and Penny Summerfield, *Out of the Cage: Women's Experiences in Two World Wars*, op. cit., p. 62.

39 Martin Pugh, *Women and the Women's Movement in Great Britain, 1914–1959*, op. cit., pp. 22–23.

40 See Monica Cosens, *Lloyd George's Munitions Girls*, London: Hutchinson, 1916, pp. 38–40.

41 See Leeds Library and Information Services, 'Barnbow Lasses – Munitions Workers at Barnbow, Leeds during the First World War', in www.historic-uk.com/England-History/BarnbowLasses.htm.

42 Gail Braybon and Penny Summerfield, *Out of the Cage: Women's Experiences in Two World Wars*, op. cit., p. 58.

43 See Deborah Thom, *Nice Girls and Rude Girls*, op. cit., pp. 54–55.

44 A. Susan Lawrence, 'Women on War Work', *Labour Woman*, no. 3, August 1915, cited in Angela Woollacott, *On Her Their Lives Depend*, op. cit., pp. 24–25.

45 See Deborah Thom, *Nice Girls and Rude Girls*, op. cit., ch. 4.

46 *The Times*, 3rd October 1916.

47 G.D.H. Cole, *Workshop Organisation*, Oxford: Clarendon Press, 1923, p. 48.

48 See Deborah Thom, *Nice Girls and Rude Girls*, op. cit., pp. 5, 55–56.

49 Gail Braybon, *Women Workers in the First World War*, op. cit., pp. 61–62; Irene Andrews, *Economic Effects of the War upon Women and Children in Great Britain*, op. cit., pp. 49–63.

50 See Deborah Thom, *Nice Girls and Rude Girls*, op. cit., pp. 5, 55–56.

51 G.D.H. Cole, *Labour in War Time*, op. cit., p. 241.

52 *Daily Sketch*, 18th January 1917; National Union of Women's Suffrage Societies, *Bulletin*, 6th March 1917.

53 Gareth Griffiths, *Women's Factory Work in World War I*, op. cit., p. 56.

54 Gareth Griffiths, *Women's Factory Work in World War I*, op. cit., pp. 112–13.

55 NA, MUN 2/28, 'Labour', see report of 9th June 1917; Angela Woollacott, *On Her Their Lives Depend*, op. cit., pp. 65–68.

56 NA, LAB 15/96, 'Memorandum on the Hours of Employment of Women and Young Persons in Factories During the War', November 1917; Adelaide Anderson, *Women in the Factory*, op. cit., p. 240; H.M. Vernon, *The Health and Efficiency of Munition Workers*, Oxford: Oxford University Press, 1940, pp. 17–18.

57 NA, LAB 15/96, 'Memorandum on the Hours of Employment of Women and Young Persons in Factories During the War', November 1917; NA, MUN 5/70/324/12, 'Ministry of Munitions: Central Munitions Labour Supply Committee, Memo 44', n.d. See also Ministry of Munitions, *Health of Munitions Workers*

Committee, *Final Report*, Cmnd 9065, London: HMSO, 1918, pp. 25–26, 40–41; *Report of the War Cabinet Committee on Women in Industry*, Cmnd 135, London: HMSO, 1919, pp. 237–40; Angela Woollacott, *On Her Their Lives Depend*, op. cit., p. 67,

58 See *History of the Ministry of Munitions*, vol. IV, part I, Appendix IV, pp. 103–4.
59 IWM, Women's Work Collection, EMP 48/2.
60 Paragraph distilled from Martin Pugh, *Women and the Women's Movement in Great Britain, 1914–1959*, op. cit., pp. 27–28; Angela Woollacott, *On Her Their Lives Depend*, op. cit., pp. 113–17; Deborah Thom, *Nice Girls and Rude Girls*, op. cit., pp. 33, 60–61; *Report of the War Cabinet Committee on Women in Industry*, op. cit., pp. 109–33. See also Harold Smith, 'The Issue of "Equal Pay for Equal Work" in Great Britain, 1914–19', *Societas*, vol. VIII, 1978.
61 Gail Braybon, *Women Workers in the First World War*, op. cit., p. 68.
62 See Gerard DeGroot, *Blighty*, p. 136; Deborah Thom, *Nice Girls and Rude Girls*, op. cit., ch. 5; *Report of the War Cabinet Committee on Women in Industry*, op. cit., p. 94; Martin Pugh, *Women and the Women's Movement in Great Britain, 1914–1959*, op. cit., pp. 26–27; Angela Woollacott, *On Her Their Lives Depend*, op. cit., pp. 101–5; Barbara Drake, *Women in Trade Unions*, London: Allen & Unwin, 1920.
63 Monica Cosens, *Lloyd George's Munitions Girls*, op. cit., pp. 127–28.
64 IWM, Documents, Catalogue No. 7142, box 77/156/1, Diary of Miss G.M. West.
65 *Daily News*, 14th December 1915, 'Middle-Class Women in Factories'.
66 Monica Cosens, *Lloyd George's Munitions Girls*, op. cit., pp. 73–74.
67 IWM, Documents, Private Papers, Catalogue No. 4538, box 81/9/1, Miss E. Airey.
68 IWM, Documents, Private Papers, Catalogue No. 4181, box 83/17/1, Miss O.M. Taylor; A.K. Foxwell, *Munition Lasses: Six Months as Principal Overlooker in Danger Buildings*, op. cit., p. 120.
69 Adelaide Anderson, *Women in the Factory*, op. cit., p. 234; Deborah Thom, *Nice Girls and Rude Girls*, op. cit., p. 136.
70 Leeds Library and Information Services, 'Barnbow Lasses – Munitions Workers at Barnbow, Leeds During the First World War', op. cit.
71 See NA, HO 45/10484/104216, 'Explosion at Picric Munitions Works, Bradford, 1916'; EF 2/3, 'Records of the Home Office: Explosives Inspectorate', 1917.
72 *The Times*, 20th January 1917; Graham Hill and Howard Bloch, *The Silvertown Explosion, London 1917*, London: History Press, 2003; Angela Woollacott, *On Her Their Lives Depend*, op. cit., pp. 84–88; Ian Beckett, *The Home Front*, op. cit., p. 88.
73 *History of the Ministry of Munitions*, vol. V, part III, p. 70.
74 Deborah Thom, *Nice Girls and Rude Girls*, op. cit., pp. 133–34; Angela Woollacott, *On Her Their Lives Depend*, op. cit., p. 81.
75 NA, MUN 5/94/346/5, 'Poisoning by Nitro-derivatives of Benzene'; Deborah Thom, *Nice Girls and Rude Girls*, op. cit., p. 125.
76 *History of the Ministry of Munitions*, vol. V, part III, p. 70.
77 IWM, Sound Recordings, Catalogue No. 566, Caroline Rennles; Gareth Griffiths, *Women's Factory Work in World War I*, op. cit., p. 56; Deborah Thom, *Nice Girls and Rude Girls*, op. cit., p. 135.
78 *History of the Ministry of Munitions*, vol. V, part III, p. 69.
79 *The Star*, 7th December 1916; Deborah Thom, *Nice Girls and Rude Girls*, op. cit., pp. 124–25.
80 *History of the Ministry of Munitions*, vol. V, part III, pp. 70–71.
81 Health of Munitions Workers Committee, *Final Report, 'Industrial Health and Efficiency'*, Cmnd 9065, London: HMSO, 1918, pp. 21–22.
82 *The Times*, 4th October 1916.
83 Deborah Thom, *Nice Girls and Rude Girls*, op. cit., p. 57.

84 IWM, Women's Work Collection, MUN 14/8/3, 'Women and Their Work During the War at H.M. Factory Gretna', 1919.

85 Deborah Thom, *Nice Girls and Rude Girls*, op. cit., pp. 124–33.

86 See NA, MUN 5/94/346/5, 'The Toxic Effects of TNT and the Means for their Prevention', 1917; Health of Munitions Workers Committee, Memorandum No. 4, *The Employment of Women*, Cmnd 8185, London: HMSO, 1916, p. xxiii; NA, MUN 5/94/346/39, 'Papers of Dr. E.L. Collis, Director of Welfare and Health Section, on Welfare Matters'; NA, MUN 5/92/346/31, 'Reports on Welfare and Health Research Work … from 1917 to 1918'; Deborah Thom, *Nice Girls and Rude Girls*, op. cit., pp. 130–31.

87 Irene Andrews, *Economic Effects of the War upon Women and Children in Great Britain*, op. cit., p. 131.

88 NA, MUN 5/94/346/39, 'Report of the Welfare and Health Section for the Year Ending 1917'; *History of the Ministry of Munitions*, vol. V, part III, ch. 1, pp. 4–9.

89 See *History of the Ministry of Munitions*, vol. V, part III, ch. 1, pp. 7–9.

90 Health of Munitions Workers Committee, *Final Report, 'Industrial Health and Efficiency'*, Cmnd 9065, London: HMSO, 1918; Gail Braybon, *Women Workers in the First World War*, op. cit., p. 141.

91 See Angela Woollacott, *On Her Their Lives Depend*, op. cit., pp. 136–38.

92 IWM, Women's Work Collection, MUN, 7/13. See also Deborah Thom, *Nice Girls and Rude Girls*, pp. 154–55.

93 Irene Andrews, *Economic Effects of the War upon Women and Children in Great Britain*, op. cit., pp. 133–34; IWM, Woman's Work Collection, MUN 18.9/17, 'A Report of Work Done for Expectant Mothers'; NA, MUN 2/28, 'Welfare'; NA, MUN 5/94/346/5, 'The Toxic Effects of TNT and the Means for their Prevention', 1917; *History of the Ministry of Munitions*, vol. V, part III, pp. 24–31; Deborah Thom, *Nice Girls and Rude Girls*, op. cit., pp. 124–25.

94 Irene Andrews, *Economic Effects of the War upon Women and Children in Great Britain*, op. cit., p. 143.

95 *History of the Ministry of Munitions*, vol. V, part V, chs 3 and 4.

96 Health of Munitions Workers Committee, *Final Report, 'Industrial Health and Efficiency'*, Cmnd 9065, London: HMSO, 1918, pp. 27–29; Angela Woollacott, *On Her Their Lives Depend*, op. cit., pp. 72–75. See also NA, MUN 5/92/346/33, Report by Miss Lilian Barker, 'Welfare Work at Woolwich Arsenal, Dec. 1915–Nov. 1918'.

97 See *History of the Ministry of Munitions*, vol. V, part III, ch. 2, pp. 31–37.

98 Angela Woollacott, 'Maternalism, Professionalism and Industrial Welfare Supervisors in World War I Britain', *Women's History Review*, vol. 2, no. 1, 1994, pp. 29–56.

99 *History of the Ministry of Munitions*, vol. V, part III, ch. 2, pp. 31–37.

100 See Angela Woollacott, *On Her Their Lives Depend*, op. cit., pp. 168–69; Deborah Thom, *Nice Girls and Rude Girls*, op. cit., pp. 156–57; Elizabeth Gore, *The Better Fight: The Story of Dame Lillian Barker*, London: Geoffrey Bles, 1965.

101 Deborah Thom, *Nice Girls and Rude Girls*, op. cit., pp. 116, 181–82; Angela Woollacott, 'Maternalism, Professionalism and Industrial Welfare Supervisors in World War I Britain', op. cit., pp. 29–56.

102 Irene Andrews, *Economic Effects of the War upon Women and Children in Great Britain*, op. cit., pp. 134–35; see also IWM, Women's Work Collection, MUN 12/4, 'Account of Welfare at the Cardonald Factory, Glasgow'.

103 L.K. Yates, *The Woman's Part*, op. cit., p. 9. See also IWM, Documents Collection, Catalogue No. 6399, 97/3/1, Diary, Mrs A. Purbrook, part IV, p. 7.

104 Samuel Hynes, *A War Imagined: The First World War and English Culture*, London: Bodley Head, 1990, p. 91.

105 Barbara Drake, *Women in the Engineering Trades*, op. cit., p. 77; Gail Braybon and Penny Summerfield, *Out of the Cage*, op. cit., p. 76.
106 Gail Braybon, *Women Workers in the First World War*, op. cit., pp. 162–63.
107 Monica Cosens, *Lloyd George's Munitions Girls*, op. cit., pp. 17, 108–9.
108 Angela Woollacott, *On Her Their Lives Depend*, op. cit., pp. 166–67.
109 Gail Braybon, *Women Workers in the First World War*, op. cit., p. 146; IWM, Women's Work Collection, EMP 55/22.
110 Barbara Drake, *Women in the Engineering Trades*, op. cit., p. 50; Gail Braybon, *Women Workers in the First World War*, op. cit., p. 67.
111 See G.D.H. Cole, *Labour in War Time*, op. cit., p. 241.
112 Gail Braybon, *Women Workers in the First World War*, op. cit., p. 74; Gerard DeGroot, *Blighty*, op. cit., p. 131; Gail Braybon and Penny Summerfield, *Out of the Cage*, op. cit., pp. 71–74; Ian Beckett, *Home Front 1914–1918*, op. cit., p. 86.
113 IWM, Women's Work Collection, EMP 48/2.
114 Deborah Thom, *Nice Girls and Rude Girls*, op. cit., pp. 116, 181–82; Angela Woollacott, 'Maternalism, Professionalism and Industrial Welfare Supervisors in World War I Britain', op. cit.
115 *Daily Mail*, 30th March 1916.
116 Gail Braybon, *Women Workers in the First World War*, op. cit., pp. 159–60.
117 *Daily Telegraph*, 14th February 1917.
118 IWM, Women's Work Collection, EMP 55/21, 'Press Cuttings in Regard to the Employment of Women in Office Jobs'.
119 Gail Braybon, *Women Workers in the First World War*, op. cit., pp. 167–68.
120 Madeline Ida Bedford, 'Munition Wages', in Catherine Reilly, ed., *Scars Upon My Heart: Women's Poetry and Verse of the First World War*, London: Virago, 1981, pp. 7–8.
121 Angela Woollacott, *On Her Their Lives Depend*, p. 108; *The Times*, 22nd February 1918, 26th November 1918.
122 Angela Woollacott, 'Maternalism, Professionalism and Industrial Welfare Supervisors in World War I Britain', op. cit., p. 30.

6 Society, family and welfare

In a country enduring an unexpectedly long war, Britons were never slow in taking time out to enjoy themselves. Amid an atmosphere of 'Oh! What a Lovely War', *The Times* reported in August 1915:

> From Hastings to Bognor … the hotels and lodging-houses are full; indeed, they are fuller than in most years. People are spending their money, too, pretty freely; perhaps not quite so lavishly as of old, but … there are bands playing, and singers singing; the theatres and cinematographs are doing well, and every place has its little troupe of Funs or Drolls or Merries, giving open-air entertainments.[1]

For those fortunate few who sheltered behind a wall of wealth, the war hovered on a distant horizon. The Bloomsbury Group – artists, poets, writers, pacifists one and all – had the means and motive to ignore the war. 'The "Bloomsburies" were all doing war-work of "National Importance"', commented Percy Wyndham Lewis, 'down in some downy English county, under the wings of powerful pacifist friends; pruning trees, planting goosebury bushes, and haymaking, doubtless in large sunbonnets.'[2] Yet the proclivity of some in the moneyed classes to let others make their sacrifices for them only emphasized the fact that wartime life for many ordinary home front Britons was becoming increasingly straitened. In their world the impact of war took many guises, sometimes in the shape of Zeppelin airship or Gotha bomber, or of shortages of fuel and food, and the disappearance of life's little luxuries, from a half-decent cigarette to muffins. Some Britons accepted these unfamiliar circumstances as a necessary sacrifice. Others wreaked their frustrations on the small numbers of German émigrés who had made Britain their home before the war. For the government, mobilizing the country pulled the state into areas of work and welfare that had previously been regarded as the individual's responsibility. In the meantime, the poor became less poor: the rich became less rich. Pre-war normalities were overturned. This was indeed an ironic war.

The shock of war

Wartime Britain quickly became a land of lost illusions. The idea that the conflict was something that would happen 'over there' took its first blow in December 1914 when a German naval squadron attacked Hartlepool, Whitby and Scarborough on the English north-east coast, claiming over 700 civilian casualties and heralding the onset of bombsite tourism with 10,000 sightseers visiting Scarborough to view the destruction.[3] Similar assaults were to follow on Yarmouth and Lowestoft in April 1916 and the Kent towns of Ramsgate, Margate and Dover in the spring of 1917. The second blow was delivered by the fearsome spectacle of aerial bombing unleashed by cigar-shaped, hydrogen-filled Zeppelin airships and, later, the frighteningly efficient Gotha bombers. Flying artillery weapons represented the strength of German technological prowess during the war, but in a military context the bombers were a blunt instrument. Inaccurate navigating and poor bomb-aiming techniques ensured that the 'legitimate' targets of dockyards, fuel depots and barracks were often missed, so inevitably bombs fell on heavily populated residential areas, terrorizing local communities and making German actions look brutal, callous and indiscriminate. Following the first Zeppelin raids on Great Yarmouth and King's Lynn in January 1915, German air attacks intensified. Hull was attacked in March 1915, and London experienced its first raid in May. By 1916 the Zeppelins had begun to reach towns in the Midlands and Scotland, until their vulnerability to air attack (77 out of a fleet of 115 had been lost by May 1917) forced the Germans to switch tactics by deploying purpose-built conventional aircraft, Gotha G.IVs, on bombing raids. The campaign was then extended to include day and night raids on London, which resulted in the worst atrocity to date, when a daylight sortie in June 1917 killed 158 civilians, including 18 children at a school in the East End district of Poplar. In all, the German air war against Britain involved 51 Zeppelin and 57 aircraft raids, killing some 1,413 people and injuring 3,407.[4]

The government's response to this aerial menace says much about the British way of war. Early improvised air-raid warnings, including the mass ringing of telephones and altering gas pressures to make household lights rise and fall in quick succession, were abandoned. Some attempted to humanize the experience through the use of language. Fine, moonless nights came to be known as 'Zeppelin weather'; the Government's Press Bureau described raids as 'visits'. But in 1915 the country's air-raid defence system was puny and ill-organized. Resistance consisted of a collection of obsolete aircraft and a shortage of ground weaponry, with responsibility for attacking raiders divided between the Army's Royal Flying Corps and the Navy's Royal Naval Air Service. However, by the late summer of 1916 improvements in wireless technology enabled telegraphy operators to track Zeppelin raiders in flight, and the development of an incendiary bullet proved spectacularly successful, as shown by Lieutenant W. Leefe Robinson's destruction of a Schütte-Lanz airship over Cuffley, Hertfordshire, in September 1915. On the ground, local

Figure 6.1 Zeppelin air-raid damage on Hull city centre, 6–7th June 1915

neighbourhoods were alerted to an imminent raid by cycling constables shouting 'Take cover!', alongside the usage of klaxons, hooters, football rattles, bells and whistles. Another aspect of air defence was, though, more enduring. The blackout (or more accurately 'the dim out'), namely the reduction of all household, street, shop and advertising illumination in urban areas during the night hours, became legally enforceable in October 1915. Windows in office buildings, for instance, were required to be covered with brown paper; household blinds and curtains were to be drawn at pre-arranged times; headlamps on motor vehicles were prohibited; buses, trams and trains were required to pull blinds over their windows and obscure their nightlights with black paint; tram destination boards had to be covered by a dark cloth, with route information being shown through one or two carefully cut holes; and street lamps in London and other cities were dimmed. One contemporary wrote that London pavements were reduced to 'a series of pools of light, each lamp throwing a circle of illumination about 3 yards in diameter carved out of the night upon the ground and no rays whatever thrown upwards', so that 'streets were tunnels of blackness on moonless winter nights'. However, the regulations were inconsistently applied. In some eastern towns (such as Cromer and King's Lynn) local councils ordered a complete blackout without exception. But one Hampshire town deployed the law only partially, and its residents could gaze at their fully illuminated neighbours in Dorset where the rules were not applied at all. Streetlamps in some coastal towns continued to shine, but were still covered with blue globes as a precaution against 'lurking submarines'.[5] Two years were to elapse before a systematic air-raid defence scheme would emerge, tying up 17,300 military personnel with anti-aircraft duties. In July 1917 an 'official' air-raid warning system was introduced, consisting of local constabularies firing maroons and Boy Scouts sounding the 'all clear' by bugle. By now, Britain's major cities had been connected to eight Early Warning Control Centres, which collected reports of impending raids from police stations and coastal lookouts and scrambled the Home Defence Squadrons. Searchlight batteries and anti-aircraft guns were established along a line of eastern Britain that stretched from Dover to Edinburgh. London itself was ringed by 353 searchlights, an 'apron' of balloons hooked together by lines of wire mesh, 266 anti-aircraft guns and 159 daylight fighter-planes supplemented by 123 night fighters, all co-ordinated from the central head-quarters of the London Air Defence Area (LADA).[6]

None of this could prevent the bombs from falling, and those (mostly urban) communities bereft of the physical infrastructure of protection were left to fend for themselves. Public shelters tended to be impromptu and makeshift. Railway arches were commandeered and lined with sandbags to offer protection. Church crypts were also popular. The people of Dover and Margate sought sanctuary in cliff-top caves or underground shelters.[7] Official government advice was not much help. People were warned to avoid top-floor rooms, place mattresses on the upper floor to cushion any impact, turn off

Figure 6.2 Policeman on air-raid warning duties, *c.* 1916

electricity and gas supplies and ensure that escape routes from cellars were kept clear if a house was struck. Londoners fled to the underground railway stations dragging along makeshift bedding, bags stuffed with life savings, small children cradled in 'mailcarts' and a small menagerie of treasured birds, dogs, cats and other pets (much to the annoyance of station masters).[8] Conditions could be foul. Choked with people, stations would become insanitary dens of dust, sweat and human excreta, raising fears among the authorities of an outbreak of typhoid or a plague of lice. Bored youths would spend the night travelling on trains, particularly on the Inner Circle Line, making unlimited circuits of the system. Bona fide passengers were often forced to step carefully over men, women and children sprawled randomly across platforms as they alighted from trains. In the face of nearly 300,000 frightened people regularly taking shelter in the underground system by 1917, any official attempts to impose controls on this mass movement of population risked severe social unrest.[9]

Demons

Popular reaction to air raids was mixed. Sylvia Pankhurst related stories of London's East End being flooded with sightseers viewing bomb-damaged properties. Liverpool's residents were reported as being cool and collected, but nonetheless greatly depressed.[10] Some shelters in London held impromptu concerts and 'dug-out dances': breaths of joy under the airborne nemesis.[11] The sensation of being attacked from the air was itself a remarkable, if not sobering, experience. An armaments worker in Woolwich recalled seeing a Zeppelin 'hovering about overhead', followed by a 'strange buzzing sound', a crash and a 'cold blast of air' as a bomb hit a factory storeroom. There were anecdotes of victims being decapitated by blast waves, while a young Hull girl who arrived at her school on the morning after a raid witnessed how:

> the Germans ... had simply destroyed the road down which I walked and there were bits of bodies all over and whole bodies and heads and arms and legs, bits blown into trees just everywhere ... I just walked into my classroom and sat down ... I could hardly speak at all.[12]

Anger and hatred remained the primary impulses, however. In Hull the outraged crowds who stoned a Royal Flying Corps vehicle the night after the city's first bombing raid targeted the airmen as scapegoats for the authorities' failure to protect civilians.[13] A group of angry citizens who descended on an anti-aircraft placement in Hyde Park demanding that the gunners open fire on a friendly aircraft overhead probably did so for the same reason.[14] Such random acts of street hostilities can be understood simply as crowds venting their rage on the nearest suitable target. Yet, in another context, they can be seen as part of a wider manifestation of anti-German feeling that air raids simply aggravated. From the war's outbreak, violence against German émigrés had been erupting sporadically across the country between 1914 and 1917, peaking between August and October 1914 and in May 1915, June 1916 and July 1917.[15] Much of the rioting was focused largely, but not exclusively, in the poorer working-class areas of Britain's main cities, although similar disturbances have been unearthed in more middle-class districts of London and southern England. The cities worst affected were Hull, where attacks on German shops and business premises were widespread; Liverpool, where four days of rioting in 1915 damaged 200 buildings causing an estimated £40,000 worth of damage; and in London's East End, where crowds numbered in thousands wrecked German-owned properties and attacked their occupants. In 1917 the Metropolitan Police reported that only two of the 21 districts within its jurisdiction had escaped disorder. Though the government was anxious to play down the riots as an isolated phenomenon, traditional notions of British tolerance towards foreign émigrés were undoubtedly damaged.[16]

Historians, being historians, of course are disinclined to take the riots at face value. Anti-German violence was a complex social dynamic that grew from different reasons and motives, amongst a class of people who were experiencing the worst of wartime conditions and suffering the heaviest military casualties. Scottish towns such as Greenock, Annan and Leith and the dockyard areas of Liverpool, Hull and London's East End, were areas of deep poverty, but with strong social communities where hardships were commonly shared, so it is perhaps not surprising that these areas suffered the most intense anger and ill-feeling.[17] The Hull riots of May 1915, for example, were said to have erupted from the agitation of four local women who had lost sons at the front. Furthermore, much of the unrest occurred in areas closely associated with the fishing community in the Hessle Road district, an area populated by trawlermen who fished constantly under threat from German mines and submarines, whilst some had been captured and interned in Germany. Other evidence suggests that the Hull disturbances were pre-planned and well organized, and the motive of revenge does not fully explain the more widespread riots that erupted across the city in 1917.[18] By the same token, local enmities fuelled by food shortages and rising prices may help to explain why grocers, bakers and pork-butchers were the rioters' first and sometimes only targets, although it would be simplistic to identify the disturbances solely as food riots. Shopkeepers of all kinds and nationalities were prone to intermittent attacks throughout the war, occasionally led by local businessmen keen to dish a German competitor, or those with a visceral lust for excitement.[19] Yet rioting also presented opportunities for the urban poor to embark on some unbridled larceny and plunder. Rioting crowds in Poplar, East London, took all they could from ransacked German-inhabited properties in what Sylvia Pankhurst described as 'the scarcity-born rage of loot'.[20] 'Here is wealth for the taking' reported *The Times* of one rioter, 'who had possession of several spring mattresses ... calmly driving his overloaded donkey-cart down C[h]risp Street'.[21]

Anti-German feeling also found other outlets. At times this reached the point of absurdity. Anyone who had the faintest connection with Germany came under suspicion; anything German was 'anglicized'. German shepherd dogs became Alsatians; German measles became Belgian Flush; the chemist shops of Boots felt the need to reassure their customers that their Eau de Cologne was made in Britain. City streets were renamed. Following the air-raid riots of 1917, even the Royal Family was quietly advised to change its ancestral surname of Saxe-Coburg-Gotha to Windsor, then, as now, a place of royal residence.[22] The mania plumbed new depths when Lord Haldane, a government minister and close friend of Asquith, was attacked mercilessly by the *Daily Mail* and *Morning Post*, mainly because of his fondness for German culture and a pet dog unfortunately named Kaiser. Another victim was the first sea lord, Prince Louis of Battenberg, who had the misfortune of having a German prince for a father. He resigned in October 1914 following a vindictive whispering campaign led by Lord Charles Beresford and subsequently changed his name to Mountbatten to secure a much-needed quiet life. Harassment of this kind continued through to September 1918, when a 1,000-strong crowd picketed the London residence of German-born and German-educated Foreign Office official Sir Eyre Crowe.[23]

And then there was the press. Starved of news from the front, yet angered by Germany's war methods and technologies, some popular newspapers had all the evidence they needed to depict *all* Germans as cultural demons. In Horatio Bottomley's jingoistic street rag *John Bull* (which regularly sold one or two million copies an issue) anti-German utterances were a given.[24] The *Daily Sketch*'s articles, penned by the euphemistic 'man in the street', were perhaps more common, consistently using gas attacks, air raids and the sinking of the Cunard Liner *Lusitania* (by U-boats off the southern Irish coast in 1915, killing 1,100 British civilians) to denounce the German race as a people detached from the constraints of civilized behaviour.[25] Similarly, Robert Blatchford (a 'Tory socialist') wrote in the *Weekly Despatch*:

> The Germans who sank the *Lusitania* are the same scoundrels as the Germans who poisoned the wells, who shelled Scarborough ... who used poison gas at Ypres ... [and] drop bombs on the crowded areas of London ... . How many Germans are living in this country ... and not in gaol?[26]

At the time such comments were not uncommon, nor were they considered extreme and, while reports of the *Lusitania*'s sinking have been pinpointed as a major factor in the May riots of 1915, the violence mainly occurred, as Adrian Gregory has noted, in areas of low newspaper readership.[27] As the main medium of wartime news and comment, the newspapers' influence on public opinion is difficult to prove conclusively. Be that as it may, it is hard to escape the impression that some newspapers during the war had become adept at dressing hatred with the voice of reason.

The press was certainly tuned to the so-called spy mania that gripped the country during the first months of the war. There were German spies in Britain in 1914, real ones, 21 of whom were arrested on the outbreak of war; 14 more were detained soon after. Eleven other spies who were apprehended during the war were imprisoned in the Tower of London and shot.[28] But, on the whole, the evidence for spy activity existed more in the public imagination. Not one of the 9,000 suspects who were investigated by the Metropolitan Police in September 1914 was ever brought to trial.[29] Yet this did not deter the great British public from taking on the role of spy-catcher. The hunger for espionage novels was cleverly exploited by William Le Queux, whose book *German Spies in England* sold 40,000 copies in just one week in 1915.[30] Elsewhere spies were seen surveying possible landing sites for an invading army or sabotaging telephone lines. In Hartlepool a local German band was reported for playing their music as a cover for covert operations. House roofs with weather vanes were said to be direction-finders for Zeppelins. There were whispers in south Essex that German spies had attempted to poison reservoirs at Chingford; German grocers in Hull were rumoured to be poisoning their foodstuffs; German barbers were suspected of sabotage. Perhaps the most ludicrous occurrence was the thrice-repeated arrest of a Suffolk Ordnance Survey worker employed in revising local maps. He eventually requested police protection so he could continue his work without disturbance.[31]

This was a time when anyone in Britain who had the misfortune to speak with a foreign accent, or be possessed of an overseas surname, was open to arbitrary arrest, restricted travel, internment or even deportation, with limited opportunities for appeal. The point was made with perfect clarity when the government's secret pre-war register containing the names and details of some 28,380 aliens (less than half of whom were German or Austro-Hungarian) formed part of the Aliens Restrictions Act, which was rushed through Parliament a day after war had been declared.[32] The act stipulated that all aliens of belligerent countries who were not of military age were to leave the country by 31st August or register with the police. Aliens (including Belgian refugees) were forbidden to own guns or signalling apparatus, move more than five miles from their home, or live on the east coast and were prohibited from frequenting military or naval bases. Compulsory permits were imposed upon any foreigner who wished to enter or leave the country, and further regulations banning overseas postal correspondence, the ownership of cameras, motor vehicles, wireless sets and military and naval maps soon followed. Any alien who wished to change their name now required Home Office permission, and by November all persons, alien or British, moving into hotels or boarding houses required police registration, while local authorities were later empowered to force the closure of restaurants, bars and other such premises that catered for alien customers. By September 1914 the number of internees had reached 13,600. All unnaturalized male Germans, Austrians and Hungarians of military age had been detained, interned or repatriated. Arrests on such a scale were unknown in Britain, and there were many cases of injustice. The

Home Secretary Reginald McKenna reasoned that imprisoning the innocent to catch the guilty was a gamble worth taking. Yet his policy took up valuable prison space, and the rapid internment rates interfered with the equally pressing need to find secure accommodation for prisoners of war. In December, McKenna agreed, against his better judgement, to release 1,000 prisoners on parole.[33]

The practice and mentality of 'Hun-hating' had a very long tail. Through the pens of right-wing journalists, Arnold White, Ellis Powell and Noel Pemberton Billing MP, Britons were asked to believe in a 'hidden hand' of spies and German sympathizers permeating all aspects of British life and deliberately inhibiting the possibilities of victory. On trial for libel in June 1918, Billing spoke of a 'Black Book' containing the details of 47,000 Britons, from Privy Councillors and the wives of Cabinet ministers, to members of the royal family and government, in whose sexual debauchery lay the source of Germany's successes in war. Corruption at the top was spread across the sexual activities of German agents and the imagined dangers of foreign influences and spilled over into enmity towards Jews, the Irish and other minority groups. An analysis of Arnold White's correspondence revealed that much of his support was drawn from affluent London suburbs, the Home Counties and the south coast of England, areas where an almost sanctified view of 'Englishness' had taken root, representing what one historian called 'a revolt of the middle class'. Against a backdrop of growing frustration over the lack of progress in the war, many were simply scratching around for solutions: they found them in a bundle of anti-alien and anti-German sentiments. Their one shining moment came when the British Empire Union merged with the Anti-German League (a group that defined its aims as 'NO German Goods, NO German Labour, NO German Influence' and 'Britain for the British') in January 1917 and began calling for the imprisonment of all enemy aliens, whilst inviting sponsors to support groups of vigilantes in seeking out foreign conspirators. Its rally in London on 13th July 1918 was followed by the delivery of a petition bearing 1.25 million signatures to Downing Street, protesting at what they saw as the huge numbers of enemy aliens on the loose in Britain. Perhaps the nadir had already been reached in 1917, with the release of the film *Once a Hun, Always a Hun*, which, amongst other things, advocated an embargo on all trade with Germany after the war.[34]

The government kept a light touch when confronted by alien baiting and rioting. After all, 'Hun-hating' provided proof of the public's commitment to the war, was a useful diversion from the lack of military success and kept a lid on more serious unrest.[35] Profiteering, however, was different. There was no doubt that the notion of hard-faced businessmen making money out of the war, while others sacrificed themselves at the workplace and on the battlefield, risked alienating the working classes. In the Labour press the profiteer was portrayed variously as 'The Vampire on the Back of Tommy' or the 'Brit Hun', whose greed contrasted with the noble sacrifices of the worker 'who had toiled in the industries so necessary for the successful prosecution of the war'. For some, such as Mr Ridley of the Railway Clerks' Association, profiteering breached the Treasury Agreement in a manner that emphasized 'the ... immorality of modern capitalism'.[36] The politically non-aligned *Co-operative News*, a voice of the nationwide Co-operative movement, commented on the wartime circumstances of the working classes: 'Conscription at a shilling a day for the private soldier; excess profits for the manufacturer and dealer. Suppression for the workers' papers; license for the Harmondsworth press; tall prices for producers; queues for consumers'.[37]

Was there a case to answer? For the government the issue of profiteering was wrapped up in notions of the wartime 'moral economy', and 'equality of sacrifice'. Without doubt the war provided an ideal climate for money making. Limitless demand, rising commodity prices, government contracts and captive markets ensured that many firms could simply set their own prices on products and services. A survey of wartime profits by *The Economist* in 1919 calculated that the ratio of profits to capital during the war increased from 8.2 per cent in 1914/15 to 11.2 per cent in 1918/19.[38] A government report admitted in 1915 that there were numerous cases of enormously increased profits, 'if businesses have done well *at all*, they have done *very well*'.[39] And this was confirmed when the profiteering 'culprits' settled around those industries – leather, wool and worsted, iron and steel, chemicals, food and food retailers, farming (which enjoyed the most considerable increases) and shipping – that especially benefited from wartime demand.[40] The performance of some companies was spectacular. Cammel Laird the shipbuilder, for example, increased its profits by 74 per cent after 1914; the profits of the Lewis Merthyr mining company, which showed a respectable annual average of £98,000 before the war, leapt to £200,000 between 1915 and 1918. For the government, the strength of public feeling precluded ignoring the issue, yet there was little room for manoeuvre. Profiteering was part of general wartime inflation, yet, while prosecution was an option, it would lend credibility to the public's belief that it was the profiteers who were driving up prices, while failure to pursue the profiteers would invite accusations of connivance.[41] In reality, ministers were left with only one choice – taxation. Following the introduction of Excess Profits Duty in the Finance Act of 1915, tax rates were levied at 50 per cent on all increased wartime profits; this was subsequently raised to 60 per cent in 1916 and 80 per cent by 1917.[42] Wartime chancellors came to regard the duty as of the same importance as income tax, but its effects were questionable. Clever accounting, coupled with the odd piece of malpractice here and there, meant that levies could easily be evaded. In spite of its overtures to curb profiteering, the government's actions could not be said to have been anything more than half-hearted.

Standards of living

The controversy over profiteering was a symptom of a much larger struggle that the population faced in coping with changing wartime living standards.

As a historical question, debates on this issue, until the 1980s, never travelled beyond the orthodox view that the war was, as summarized by one historian, 'an unmitigated disaster for the health and well-being of the nation'.[43] Jay Winter then attempted to open the closed doors by arguing that the war had thrown up a 'paradox'. Through an intensive statistical enquiry on mortality, health standards and incomes, Winter contended that, by and large, the health and well-being of families in some social groups, particularly the unskilled working classes, improved rather than declined during the war. Understandably, Winter's conclusions provoked a strong reaction, but the prima facie evidence of his case have changed the terms of subsequent analyses.[44]

The surprises begin in the realm of incomes. While the war affected the financial circumstances of all social groups, misery was felt most amongst Britain's social elite. The introduction of the 1915 Rent Act (discussed more fully on pages 182–3 and 294), which placed a ceiling on all incomes derived from land leases and tied properties, made it harder for many aristocratic landowners to meet the rising costs of estate management and general family maintenance from fixed assets.[45] The position was exacerbated first by death duties, then by Lloyd George's super tax, introduced in 1909, which imposed an extra levy on annual incomes over £10,000. In 1927 the Committee on National Debt calculated that property incomes rose by only 9.9 per cent between 1912/13 and 1922/3, whilst general wholesale prices were spiralling at nearly 90 per cent by 1917. The Inland Revenue estimated that real estate receipts, valued at 10 per cent of National Income in 1913/14, had slumped to 7 per cent by 1923/4. Those landowners who were active farmers, or exercised leasing rights on the mining of coal, iron-ore, minerals and precious metals on their land, undoubtedly benefited from the war. But many shared the experience of Lord Knaresborough, who protested to Bonar Law in January 1917 that 'the great majority of [us] are extremely hard hit by the present taxation following on the great fall of rent of late years'. Such 'Radical finance,' he complained, 'cunningly adapted to the purpose, is bleeding land-owners to death'.[46]

By contrast, middle-class incomes varied considerably. Middle-class employment tended to break down into two categories: the professions (medical practitioners and lawyers mostly); and the 'salariat' (normally those engaged in various avenues of white-collar occupations, mostly clerical, education and office work).[47] The Colwyn Committee on National Debt and Taxation calculated that the rise in incomes of doctors and dentists earning £1,200 or more annually in pre-war terms averaged around 45–50 per cent between 1913/14 and 1922/23. Yet the salaries of their colleagues who earned between £200 and £500 grew by anything between 76 and 101 per cent across the same period. Likewise, higher-earning lawyers with pre-war annual incomes of £1,600 experienced salary rises in the region of 58 per cent during the war, whilst the remuneration of their poorer colleagues with salaries of £500 per annum leapt by around 75 per cent. Accountants benefited the most from wartime conditions. Sustained by the huge growth in taxation and financial work since 1914, these 'new professionals' pulled in salary increases ranging from 96 to 169 per cent in the period between 1913/14 and 1922/23.[48] Similar trends are detected in the pay scales of the salariat. The incomes of bank clerks, for instance, traditionally regarded as the elite of the Edwardian clerical workforce, grew by a very modest 10 per cent during the period. Yet clerical officers in the civil service experienced a jump in income of 245 per cent between 1913 and 1924, while the pay growth of higher-grade civil service executive officers hovered around 96 per cent by 1924. The greatest gains, however, were made by male railway clerks, on the lowest step of the middle-class ladder, whose annual pay grew by 291 per cent on pre-war levels.[49]

A similar picture was evident in working-class incomes. Those who lost a husband or breadwinner to the armed forces were entitled to draw separation allowances, a very basic form of state benefit intended to ward off starvation and the workhouse, with payments related to family size and the husband's army rank. But the sums were paltry and had changed little since the end of the South African War, whilst bureaucratic inefficiency often meant long delays in distributing the benefits to needy households. For the majority of families, namely the wives of privates, corporals and sergeants, allowances were set at a daily rate of 1s 1d (approximately 5p); wives of 'colour' sergeants received 1s 4d a day (approximately 7p); while officers' wives were entitled to 2s 3d (approximately 11p a day). Payments were aligned with wartime inflation. By October 1917 allowances had been increased to a weekly sum of 23s (£1 15p) for the wife of a soldier with one child under the age of 14. By the end of the war the cost of separation allowances had reached nearly £420 million, spread amongst 1.5 million families.[50]

All the same, assessing working-class incomes as a whole during the war is a daunting historical exercise, particularly as pay-rates were closely related to trades and occupations.[51] Arthur Bowley, for example, observed that, when skilled engineering workers were awarded a 12.5 per cent weekly increase in earnings during 1917, the new rates were applied to blacksmiths, borers, coremakers, electrical fitters, gauge-makers, gear-cutters, grinders, hardeners and temperers, jig-makers, millers, millwrights, moulders, pattern-makers, planers, scientific instrument makers, shapers, slotters, toolmakers, toolsmiths and turners.[52] Another obstacle is unreliable evidence. Historians who rely on the wage statistics regularly published by the Board of Trade's *Labour Gazette* should be aware that the information submitted by employers was done so on a voluntary basis and only the wages of four out of a possible ten million workers were recorded. Moreover, wage rises in a trade at one plant were not necessarily replicated in others, or many deductions from pay packets went unregistered. Most important, nonetheless, as J.W.F. Rowe noted, pay rates differed hugely from earnings, if the diversity of piece-rates, time rates, overtime rates and bonuses were taken into account. For instance, piecework was fundamental in determining the earnings of engineering workers by 1916, where working weeks of 77 hours, with only one Sunday rest-day a month, was not uncommon in national fuse factories during 1915 and 1916. Male workers who worked an average of ten hours overtime a week increased their take-home pay by at least 20 per cent; women worked around seven and a half hours over their basic week, with many working-class family budgets supplemented by the wages of their adolescent offspring, many of whom happily relinquished education for the chance to earn some money in munitions work.[53]

Still, taking all these considerations into account, statistics show considerable differences in wage rates between the first and second periods of the war. Between 1914 and 1916 the upward movement in wage rates was slow and inconsistent, but averaged approximately 10 per cent annually. Wage rates in the years 1917–18, however, rose considerably: by around 30 per cent on average 1916 rates in 1917, increasing to 40 per cent over 1917 rates in 1918. By the Armistice, average overall earnings were roughly double 1914 levels. It should also be noted that earnings were determined by the position of an industry in relation to the war effort. If the wages of engineering workers rose in proportion to the wartime demand for munitions, then workers in the cotton industry commanded wage increases that in 1917 were only 19 per cent over their 1914 rates and contrasted sharply with the 55 per cent increases recorded for the entire wartime workforce.[54]

Across both the industrial and clerical spheres the trends were the same: in absolute and relative terms those workers who had been poorly paid before the war enjoyed the greatest earnings gains. The 75 per cent difference in pay for engineering turners over manual labourers in 1913 had been eroded to just 38 per cent by 1920, with coalminers, semi-skilled engineers, blast-furnace men and iron and steel workers receiving the largest increases, effectively levelling the pay gaps between skilled, semi-skilled and unskilled workers during the war. Unskilled workers clearly benefited from the policies of dilution and substitution.[55] Productivity improvements secured with the import of more-efficient American machinery simplified working techniques and gave unskilled workers greater scope to 'follow the money'. Female workers were just part of an increasingly mobile labour force that quickly surmized that moving from a trade not related to war production to one that was could enhance their incomes quite substantially. Noticing the trends, the *History of the Ministry of Munitions* remarked, 'the immense transfer of workers from one occupation to another and from one district to another accustomed individuals to wages they would never have commanded in their original occupations, and gave them conceptions of their economic value'.[56]

This did not necessarily make poorer families any more secure. Fed by the rapid growth in levels of government borrowing and expenditure, the innately inflationary character of the British economy guaranteed that steep price rises in domestic household items became a constant affliction. Bowley estimated that average price levels rose about 27 per cent annually between 1914 and 1917, representing a total increase of 125 per cent. A combination of government price controls, wage-fixing and increased taxation provided a temporary check towards the end of the war, yet wholesale prices were still 140 per cent above pre-war levels in 1918, ensuring that families needed £10 to buy what cost £4 in 1914, making the 20-shilling (100p) pound worth approximately 8s 3d (41p). What is more, some of the most basic items in the average household budget (food, clothing and fuel, for example) saw the sharpest price increases. A government committee reported that the price of bread had risen by 65 per cent between 1914 and 1916; fish and sugar prices had doubled until government controls brought some stability after 1917. The amount spent by working-class families on food was by then 39s a week (£1.95), a rise of 60 per cent. Prices of fuel and clothing went the same way. Severe shortages pushed up the index of expenditure on clothes by 65 per cent between 1900 and 1918, adding 3s (15p) or 4s (20p) to the weekly cost of living. Coal, the mainstay of heat, power and light in Britain, was priced at around 1s (5p) per hundred-weight in 1912 (although this price varied across the regions), yet its general price had by 1918 increased to an average of 1s 8d (approximately 8p), an increase of 67 per cent. Dorothy Peel wrote of coal queues becoming as long as food queues in London, and it became a punishable offence to discard ash and cinder waste, while newspapers published advice for making briquettes with clay and sawdust and using tar as fuel for cooking stoves.[57]

Thus, perhaps it is no surprise that, despite the upward trend in workers' wages, many families struggled to keep up with the inexorable pace of wartime inflation. Pemberton Reeve, in a revealing insight into the family wartime budget, exposed some uncomfortable realities:

> Mrs P., whose husband is a railwayman used to get 27 shillings before the war and now has 33 shillings. She has a new baby, which brings the number of her children up to five. Her rent for three rooms was 7 shillings, it is now 8 shillings for four rooms. She always paid a shilling a week each to a clothing and a boot club and this she continues to do. Her 'gramophone' ('the women are all buying a piano or gramophone') appears to be that she now buys twelve loaves a week instead of seven and pays 4 shillings instead of 1 shilling 5½ pence for it. Her coal costs her 10½ pence, her meat 2 shillings more and the rest of her expenditure is about 1 shilling 10 pence more than it was before the war. She therefore has ceased to buy fish, bacon, eggs, cocoa, jam and cow's milk altogether and buys less quantities of pot-herbs, margarine and sugar.[58]

Consumer expenditure on goods and services, alongside the average standard of living, fell by around 17 per cent. Consumption of drink and tobacco declined by 53 per cent; clothing by 24 per cent; and durable household goods by 23 per cent. Spending on food also declined, but only by 11 per cent.[59] Poorer families managed to keep their heads above water because of the insatiable demands for their labour, along with the benefits of high piece-rates, bonuses and abundant overtime, and relatively better wage deals than were afforded to skilled workers. This was sustained through changes to the wartime tax regime which, though catching some of the skilled workforce in its

Table 6.1 Retail prices and wages in the United Kingdom, 1914–1918

Year	Retail prices	Average weekly wage rates	Average weekly wage earnings
1914	100	100	100
1915	123	109	118
1916	146	119	134
1917	176	140	171
1918	203	180	212

Derived from: Department of Employment and Productivity, *British Labour Statistics: Historical Abstract*, London: HMSO, 1971, Table 89; J.M. Winter, *The Great War and the British People*, 2nd edn, Baskingstoke: Palgrave Macmillan, 2003, p. 233; C.H. Feinstein, *National Income, Expenditure and Output of the United Kingdom 1855–1965*, Cambridge University Press, 1972, Table 65; Peter Dewey, *War and Progress*, Harlow: Longman, 1997, p. 41

net, was now more sharply progressive, quietly redistributing income by taxing the wealthier classes more heavily. For some, the two pincers of the pre-war poverty trap – low wages and unemployment – were temporarily held in abeyance by wartime conditions.[60]

Even so, the perception of a prosperous working class benefiting at the expense of an impoverished middle class helped generate an atmosphere of cultural finger-pointing. *The Times* commented caustically in 1917 that 'Fur coats have become known as "munition overalls"', complaining that high streets were 'thronged with buyers' with picture palaces 'being crowded night after night', reflective of the prevailing view amongst the wealthier classes that the financial weight of the war had been unfairly placed on their shoulders. They saw *their* patriotism and losses in blood *and* money standing in sharp relief against the dissolute practices of the profiteers and avaricious workers.[61] Doubtless the real incomes of middle- and upper-class families had been adversely affected by the war, as a post-war study concluded.[62] Yet the notion of a wholesale shift in incomes across Britain's social classes was more illusory than real. Britain was far from becoming a 'born poor, die rich' society. That said, the war taught future policy makers that the questions of social and economic policy were closer than hitherto realized. The conscious redistribution of income as part of a long-term strategy of alleviating poverty and preventing social disorder was a trend that was checked only towards the end of the twentieth century.

Standards of life

While the war may have altered the living standards of many British people, in other aspects its effects were less clear. The conflict had little impact on the long-term decline in Britain's population growth, for example. Rates of increase slowed from 10.3 per cent in 1901–11 to just 4.7 per cent in 1911–21, a pattern that remained more or less constant until 1939.[63] Then again, the conflict interrupted the long-term downward trends in mortality rates (see Table 6.2). Aside from the military casualties, and the effects of the Spanish Flu pandemic of 1918 (which killed approximately 200,000 people), death

Table 6.2 Birth and death rates in England and Wales, 1910–1918 (per thousand of the population)

Year	Birth rate	Civilian death rate	'Natural' increase in population
1910	25.1	13.5	11.6
1914	23.8	14.0	9.8
1915	21.9	15.7	6.1
1916	20.9	14.3	6.7
1917	17.8	14.2	3.6
1918	17.7	17.3	0.4

Adapted from: J.M. Winter, *The Great War and the British People*, 2nd edn, Basingstoke: Palgrave Macmillan, 2003, p. 252; Peter Dewey, *War and Progress: Britain 1914–1945*, Harlow: Longman, 1997, p. 33; Brian R. Mitchell, *British Historical Statistics*, Cambridge: Cambridge University Press, 1988, pp. 43, 58–9

rates rose amongst men aged between 5 and 44 and women in the 10–24 and 75 and over age groups. Explanations for these appear to come down to poor working conditions and bad housing, which fostered increases in tuberculosis, pneumonia, bronchitis and other respiratory illnesses, but this view has proved contentious.[64] On the other hand, the war did not disrupt the longer-term declines in child mortality rates. Death rates for children aged 0–4 years declined from 33.3 to 26.3 per 1,000 females and from 40.3 to 31.8 per 1,000 boys during the war. Levels of infant death rates (those aged 0–1) fell too, from 108 to 96 per 1,000 in England and Wales. Jay Winter found that mortality rates of infants aged 2–3 months fell by 19 per cent between 1911/13 and 1918; deaths of those aged 4–6 months by 24 per cent; and those of infants aged 7–8 months by 13 per cent.[65] Similar patterns were detectable in Scotland, with the reduction in infant mortality being slightly less. The better survival rates of children have been put down to improved nutrition and sanitation and a decline in the virulence of potentially fatal diseases such as measles, whooping cough and scarlet fever; they appear to have been little affected by the scarcity of doctors and poor housing conditions.

The most striking feature of the war, however, was a weakening in infant birth rates. Declines in births were a notable feature in changing family structures before the war; but the fall gathered pace during the war years. The national average of live births per 1,000 head of population shrank from 25.1 in 1910 to 23.8 in 1914; to 20.9 in 1916; and to 17.7 in 1918, recovering quite sharply to 25.5 by 1920. This was reflected in declining family size. Numbers of children in the average mid-Victorian family measured anything between five and seven. Couples who married in 1910 were expected to give birth to 2.95 children; this had shrunk to 2.8 by 1914 and 2.45 by 1918.[66] The decline in family size was most noticeable amongst the wealthier classes and less marked in the poorer groups. Major differences emerged between manual and non-manual workers' families, where those at the bottom end tended to have families 40 per cent bigger than others.[67] Historians have accounted for this fall in births by citing the growing use of contraception during the war, combined with the collective decisions of many families to limit their numbers of children, and the prolonged separation of partners. Yet, wartime marriages surged. In 1914, England and Wales recorded marriage rates that jumped from 15.9 per 1,000 head of population to 19.4 a year later: a product maybe of hasty passions and beckoning wartime farewells. The rush to marry emerged only when expectations of a short war fell away and the emphasis of recruitment focused on unmarried young men.[68] Divorce rates also rose. The easier availability of legal aid, adulterous temptations during the long wartime separations of husband and wife and the growing social acceptability of divorce, especially amongst the wealthier classes, saw rates increase from approximately 1,000 petitions in 1913 in England and Wales to over 5,000 petitions six years later, approximately nine per 10,000 couples.[69]

Plummeting birth rates, fears of population decline and the high battlefield casualties prepared a fertile ground for the growth of a 'pro-natalism' movement after 1917, which campaigned to preserve infant life through improvements to the nation's pre- and post-natal care facilities. Eugenicists argued that the movement was wasting its time. The 'laws' of natural selection supplied the only 'solution' to a healthier nation by eliminating the 'unfit' and letting the strong survive.[70] By contrast, organizations and individuals as diverse as the jingoistic 'Babies of the Empire Society' (which proclaimed in 1917 that 'every effort must be directed to securing the future of the race') and the Local Government Board's Medical Officer (who argued that 'there is no insuperable difficulty in reducing the total deaths in childhood to one-half their present number') came together in a national obsession with 'the child'.[71]

This movement knew how to sell itself. In some respects, the ground had already been prepared by the work of pre-war voluntary organizations such as the National Association for the Prevention of Infant Mortality and the Association of Infant Consultations and Schools for Mothers, who managed around 160 infant welfare centres by 1916. Similarly, concerned professionals such as G.F. McCleary, Medical Officer of Health in Battersea, London, campaigned loudly for the establishment of a national chain of child welfare centres. Sir Arthur Acland, a former president of the Board of Education, formed an Infant Welfare Propaganda Fund from which paid organizers travelled the country drumming up support for infant welfare. Acland claimed responsibility for the creation of 200 health centres resulting from such work. Elsewhere pro-natalist themes were highlighted in a collection of pamphlets, cartoons and postcards that flew around bookstalls, magazines and newspapers, with infant welfare and parental fertility emphasized as dual priorities. Most prominent were the publicity drives organized by the National Baby Week Committee which conducted a week-long campaign highlighting the issue of infant mortality in 1917, opening with a rally at Westminster Central Hall attended by Queen Mary, and marches and meetings of young mums and their children in towns and cities across the country, in what was to become an annual event. Similarly motivated were a group of well-to-do 'public-spirited ladies' who in 1917 established the Children's Jewel Fund (headquarters in Bond Street, London) where money, jewels and other valuables were procured through sales, donations and sponsorship of various entertainments to fund infant welfare centres. An impressive £700,000 had been collected by the time of the fund's closure in 1920.[72]

Only the state, however, had the resources to transmute words into action. The Local Government Board (LGB), pushed along by successive reports of its Medical Officers and the terms of the Care of Mothers and Young Children Act of 1915, began issuing circulars to local councils advising them of the need to extend the network of infant welfare centres, which would handle ante-natal as well as post-natal care and focus on improving the survival chances of children aged between one and five years. Financial aid was provided by grants that paid up to half the running costs and salaries of health visitors.[73] Parents and medical attendants were legally compelled to inform the authorities of all births within a locality so that health visitors could monitor the health of new-borns, while encouraging mothers to attend infant welfare centres. By 1917, 396 local authority health centres had been established, along with the 446 infant welfare centres operated by charities. Yet the provision and quality of infant welfare varied greatly across different regions. Some councils argued that state provision undermined individual responsibility and furnished official intervention into essentially private matters,

Figure 6.3 Children outside Penny Kitchen, Bermondsey, East London, 1917

despite the best efforts of Arthur Newsholme, Chief Medical Officer at the Local Government Board, to batter recalcitrant authorities into compliance.[74] A Maternal and Child Welfare Act was eventually passed in 1918 to rectify the problem. But opposition arose from the insurance companies, who, as the administrators of the maternity benefits under the National Insurance Act, feared a decline in business through the loss of premiums. Even then, the Act fell short of outright compulsion. Local authorities were required rather than compelled to establish maternal and child welfare services, day nurseries and milk and food for disadvantaged mothers and infants, provided by a phalanx of fully qualified, salaried midwives and health visitors.[75] Local ratepayers must have winced, but what were a few extra pennies in tax when the future of the British race was at stake?

The helping hands given to children were not always extended to mothers. Contemporary social enquiries, as well as reports from women's organizations, suggested that as a group women suffered from lower standards of health than their spouses and official action in child and infant welfare was slow to recognize that the circumstances in which women bore and nurtured children were crucial to their well-being. In the Women's Co-operative Guild's 1915 book *Maternity* letters from working-class women exposed the problems of a life wrapped in poverty, pregnancy and sickness. It summarized:

> during the months of pregnancy, the woman must learn by experience and ignorance, usually being told that all her troubles are 'natural' …. If not working long hours in a factory, her home work may be more injurious, when ill or well, she washes, mangles, lifts heavy weights and may still be carrying an infant in arms. She may at the same time, have to nurse a sick husband or child. Up to the last minute before childbirth she has to wash and dress the children, cook the meals she's sometimes too tired to eat, and do all her own housework. At her confinement often only an untrained midwife is available, who sometimes has to make use of a child's help … . In the areas where bad housing causes the family in hundreds and thousands of cases to live in two or three rooms … privacy and quiet are impossible.[76]

Pioneering work in maternal health was undertaken at the St Pancras health centre in London.[77] But a major hindrance to progress hung as much upon class and attitudes towards sex as the question of improving facilities. Newspaper columns were filled with advice on 'mothercraft', given usually by well-meaning middle-class commentators and administrators whose backgrounds almost precluded them from being wholly objective about the lives of working-class mothers. Their advice usually amounted to groups of middle-class men addressing other men on how women should conduct themselves. More sympathetic words were likely from the mouths of female health visitors and some women doctors, but it still boiled down to middle-class women dispensing advice to working-class mothers in a mode that resembled a 'Lady

Bountiful' approach to infant welfare. This only succeeded in pushing considerable numbers of women away from formal help, while others resented the intrusion into their homes and lives. Hence, maternal welfare during the war was largely a half-built business. Meanwhile, more prosperous middle-class women, the most ardent consumers of the growing corpus of family care manuals, were denied the same access to welfare facilities provided for working-class mothers. As it was, the only significant help offered by the state came through the delivery of births, when the Midwives Act of 1902 was amended in 1916 to strengthen the training and regulation of midwifery. A more fully formed system of maternal welfare would be realized only well after the Armistice.[78]

This still left room for the occasional outbreak of moral panic, however. The country was made aware of the disturbing phenomenon of 'war nymphomania' and 'war babies' mostly from the pen of the MP Ronald McNeill who warned readers of the *Morning Post* in April 1915 about an impending spate of illegitimate babies borne by women who frequented soldiers in local barracks. McNeill's claims fuelled an immediate flurry of press anxiety, but the problem was exaggerated. Illegitimacy was in decline until 1915. When rates began to climb the following year, peaking in 1919 at 30 per cent above pre-war levels, they were shrugged off by the Registrar-General as a sign less of moral decline but of 'the exceptional circumstances [of war], including the freedom from home restraints of large numbers of young persons of both sexes'.[79] Conversely, single motherhood was approached with greater sensitivity. Traditionally 'bastardy' carried a deep social stigma for both mother and child that took a long time to live down. Yet, with every war baby now being seen as precious, illegitimacy was interpreted as an outcome of last-night flings between departing couples, or as a child born to a wife whose husband had been killed. This was probably why, in February 1915, the Archbishop of Canterbury, in a letter to the Prime Minister, urged that both married and single mothers should receive equal entitlements to separation allowances, whilst Bishop Joscelyne pleaded that unmarried mothers were now victims of war and that a 'problem of this character … needed watchfulness and loving care on the part of Christian womanhood in all parts of the land'. *The Times* dismissed such views as 'emotional nonsense', and complained that campaigners were in danger of glorifying 'human frailty as though it were praiseworthy'. But its leader column still agreed that the country needed to adopt 'a more charitable and more compassionate public opinion' towards this wartime phenomenon.[80]

General health care provision, however, was still problematic. Though the National Insurance Act of 1911 had furnished 12 million workers with access to a general practitioner and sickness benefit through 'approved societies' (which included trade unions and benefit clubs), their families were left to seek medical care through private insurance schemes and sick clubs. Others could apply to be included on a 'doctor's panel' managed by local insurance committees, which provided free consultations and prescriptions. All the same, beyond the basic levels, the quality of health care, even for insured patients, was uneven. While some schemes included fringe benefits such as hospital care and dental treatment, others did not. There were also protests that 'panel doctors' did not practise the same health standards for the poor as were provided to their wealthier fee-paying patients.[81] And while some industrial workers in government munitions factories received regular health checks, contact with a doctor was, for many families, sporadic. The supply of medics was badly affected by army recruitment. On average, military doctors cared for 476 soldiers; a 'civvy street' medic had to cope with 2,344 patients. Professor Winter contends that 20 per cent of the British population was without adequate medical coverage (defined as 4,000 patients a doctor) and that there were areas, such as Glasgow, where one doctor catered for more than 5,000 patients.[82] It was not until 1917, when the severity of the crisis was most acute, that the Central Medical War Committee (CMWC), which included most of the major officers of the British Medical Association, began an audit of available doctors – accounting for the needs of different localities – and established a system of industrial conscription for medical personnel. CMWC organizations across Ireland, Scotland, England and Wales contacted every physician, regardless of age, sex and experience, singled out those suitable for army service and balanced their numbers with the needs of the home population. In this way the supply of doctors was a matter kept firmly within the responsibility of the profession rather than the government, ensuring that both the Army and civilians had the doctors they needed. All were helped by the fortunate absence of any major epidemic until the Spanish Flu crisis of 1918.[83]

In the area of housing, family welfare took a backward step. Before the war, many urban Britons housed themselves in a patchwork quilt of Victorian villas, palatial suburbs, 'by-law' housing (a product of Victorian public health improvements), rows of small terraced workers' cottages, back-to-back housing, flats, tenements (houses or blocks of dwellings subdivided into separately occupied floors or single rooms) and poor-quality 'slum' property in variable states of dilapidation. For a lucky few there was a smattering of dream housing – well-built, well-equipped and expensive cottage-style accommodation – located in contrived semi-rural settlements (inspired by the Arts and Crafts Movement) such as Port Sunlight (in the Wirral); Bourneville (in Birmingham); New Earswick (near York); and Letchworth Garden City (in Hertfordshire).[84] Almost every house in Britain was privately rented, on weekly lets in England and Wales, but monthly and annual lets in Scotland. Quantities of local authority dwellings were small, just 1 per cent of the total, while the numbers of owner-occupiers drifted at around 10 per cent. Thus, the private landlord was the lynchpin of pre-war British housing. Predominantly, but not exclusively, drawn from the lower middle classes, many landlords were minor investors who built small amounts of accommodation using money raised from banks or, more commonly, solicitors, and incorporated the building and maintenance costs along with rates (a property tax levied by local authorities) into the rents.[85]

But, by 1914, this system was in crisis. At one level, housing was becoming less profitable. A combination of rising interest payments, new building regulations, increases in the cost of materials and swelling local authority rates (to meet new responsibilities in education and public health) meant that housing was no longer an attractive investment.[86] Some landlords sought better returns in government stocks ('consols') and foreign ventures in South America and Canada. Others directed their funds into the better yields offered by building societies. Many, however, attempted to restore profitability into their housing stock simply by increasing rents, sparking the formation of Tenants Defence Leagues across the country and the out-break of numerous rent strikes, notably in London, Wolverhampton and Birmingham, as families struggled to cope with an overall 14 per cent rise in their cost of living.[87] The most worrying aspect of the crisis, however, was a slow-down in house construction. New building declined by an average of 22,000 houses a year (5 per cent) between 1906 and 1914, with construction of working-class accommodation falling to just 47,000 by 1914.[88] Some commentators spoke of a 'house famine' in some parts of the country, and the shortages inevitably threw light on the overall condition of working-class accommodation. Reports of poor water supplies, bad sanitation and over-crowding were widespread. A survey of 1911 estimated that overcrowding on a standard of 'more than two per room' was affecting 10–12 per cent of the urban population in Britain, with conditions worst in Scotland where almost 10 per cent of the population were accommodated in one-roomed houses, with 55.7 per cent of Glaswegians (420,000) living more than two to a room.[89]

For both landlords *and* tenants then, housing offered poor value for money, yet the war merely intensified the crisis. Affected by shortages of materials and the loss of construction workers to the Army, numbers of new houses declined to just 17,000 by 1916, while the large-scale movement of families into the higher-paid munitions industries exacerbated shortages in local accommodation that were all too evident in industrial areas across the country. Nationally, the number of families sharing a dwelling increased from 15.7 per cent in 1914 to 20 per cent by 1918.[90] The numbers living on the 'box and cox' routine (whereby night-shift workers would occupy beds by day, succeeded by day-shift workers sleeping in the same beds at night: few were cleaned and aired) ran into thousands, and it was not uncommon to find nine or even ten workers sharing rooms.[91] The emergency encouraged many landlords to seize the opportunity of restoring the income value in their properties by imposing rent increases. Weekly rents in London increased from 9s 6d (approximately 48p) to 10s 6d (approximately 53p) in December 1914, and from 10s 6d to 12 shillings (60p) in September 1915. Quarterly rents on tenement houses in Glasgow rose in August 1915, adding £3 19s 4d to a yearly rental of £13 16s (£13.80), with the tenants given only a few days' notice of the rise. In their defence, landlords could declare that they, too, were feeling the pinch. If tenants could cast accusations of heartless profiteering, landlords could justifiably claim that they were acting within the terms of the market. But this was neither the time nor place to assert such a position.[92]

Throughout the autumn of 1915 newspapers were peppered with reports of rent strikes and protests in London, Birmingham, Coventry, the East Midlands, Liverpool and Birkenhead, where sharp rent rises were accompanied by an alarming growth in rent arrears and attempted evictions.[93] The tensions reached a climax in Glasgow where housing conditions were amongst the worst in Britain. The area had experienced its fair share of shortages, straitened conditions and successive stand-offs between landlords and tenants well before the outbreak of war. Yet popular indignation at rising food prices, profiteering, the effects of dilution and the Munitions Acts, and a deeply radicalized workforce, created a powder-keg atmosphere in the city. A host of companies specializing in shipbuilding, steel production, engineering and armaments huddled together along the Clyde valley had attracted a huge influx of migrants from Glasgow's hinterland looking for work and high wages. The number of vacant houses fell to less than 1 per cent of the total accommodation, and the building of new homes by private enterprise was reported to be 'more or less stagnant'.[94] Local rent rises had been met by sporadic agitations since January 1915. But, when landlords imposed further increases in rents of up to 10 per cent in the late summer, demonstrations and rent strikes broke out across the city. On 7th October 1915, 800 to 1,000 rent strikers, mostly women and children of the 'respectable working-class type', carefully marshalled by the Glasgow Labour Party, marched on the Town Council carrying banners proclaiming local landlords as 'the Prussians of Partick'.[95] Spontaneous actions against mass evictions and rent increases led by local activists, such as Mary Barbour in South Govan, reinforced the point.[96] The government responded by setting up a local enquiry led by Lord Hunter, which reported evidence of rent raising, evictions and an overall lack of maintenance, as well as a house famine. The flashpoint was reached on 17th November, when landlords brought 18 tenants to court for non-payment of increased rent, bringing 15,000 workers out on strike. The government, fearing a threat to war production, attempted to pacify the workforce by rushing through the Rent and Mortgage Interest (War Restrictions) Act, freezing rents at levels paid in 1914, with further limitations on increasing mortgage interest rates, and preventing investors from foreclosing mortgages for higher returns on government stocks.[97]

Ministers may have seen the rents legislation as a necessary intervention that would keep the housing problem in suspended animation until the war was over, but there was to be no escape from the housing quicksand. As long as a dearth of affordable accommodation remained (national housing shortages peaked at 805,000 by 1921), rent controls boxed the government into a very tight corner. Fear of social unrest sparked by rapidly rising rents in an unfettered market ensured that rent controls had to continue until shortages had eased; yet this was unlikely so long as the building trades remained in disarray and the legislation rendered new house building uneconomic. Thus, ministers had no option but to sponsor new house building by using public money, with local authorities given the responsibility for planning, construction and management. For better or worse, the state, in the shape of hundreds of municipal housing committees, became the nation's landlord.

In this, as in many other ways, the effects of the war burrowed deeper and deeper into the everyday lives of Britons who remained at home. While it is important to recognize the value of the historical debates over family welfare during the war, they should not be allowed to anaesthetize modern scholars from the realities of wartime life. Statistics imply that some classes benefited from improved living standards, better wages and relatively healthier lives, but they reveal only a half-open window on the social landscape of war. Anguish was widely felt over the fate of loved ones at the front, and the unrest of the period was possibly the only way in which the sense of frustration felt over deteriorating housing circumstances, food shortages and long hours of work in dangerous conditions could be conveyed. It may well have been 'Oh! What a Lovely War' for some, yet ultimately it was the pain of bereavement that united families across Britain's social spectrum. Bereavement is a universal experience, and no historian can convey the profound sense of grief felt by those families who lost loved ones at the front. The writer Alan Bennett related a tale of the Post Office telegram boy (uniformed in serge blue with red piping on his tunic) in his home city of Leeds, whose job it was to deliver transcripts of electric messages from the War Office about men who were missing or 'killed in action'. During the war these young Post Office lads were overworked. When they rode their bicycles into the working-class streets of Leeds, all the women would stand outside their front doors waiting to see which house would take delivery of the message. 'Page boys of death', Bennett called them.[98] Perhaps this tells us some real truths of family welfare in this 'war to end all wars'.

Sex and morality

The war undoubtedly disrupted British domestic life. The dislocation to family life was equalled by the transience that the conflict now brought to personal relationships. The demands of armed service, or long hours working in war industries, threatened traditional notions of personal morality, framed as they were by a Victorian religious code of sexual purity, public decency, family and marriage. Suddenly, for the small battalions of self-appointed moral guardians who took it upon themselves to discern what was acceptable and unacceptable behaviour, sex was everywhere, and it was women's rather than men's conduct that generated most concerns. The Army complained of young girls loitering around barracks on the pretence of collecting soldiers' washing. *The Times* was shocked at the numbers of prostitutes who openly accosted soldiers along streets and corners in the short stretch of road that ran between Stamford Street and the Old Vic theatre in London, with the back streets around Westminster Bridge Road and Blackfriars honeycombed with 'houses of accommodation'. Alarm bells rang over the influence of cinemas (or 'picture palaces' as they were more commonly known). Close seating, dark spaces and an intimate atmosphere provided ample opportunity, so moralists thought, for licentious behaviour and improper conduct. One organization estimated that there were at one time 60,000 prostitutes operating in London, mostly in cinemas, though this was news to the Metropolitan Police, who could find no evidence to support such claims. Music halls fared no better. The *Contemporary Review* spoke of 'Love, between the sexes, on the music hall stage frequently becomes lust. Peaceful domesticity becomes a butt of cynical jest, and ... harlotry is condoned.' The sense of shock was heightened when religious moralists and social purists were confronted by the casual nature of working-class relationships. One women's patrol expressed astonishment when confronted by a couple so consumed in the excitement of passion in a public park that 'daylight and people seem not to matter in the least. You come upon a heaped mass of arms and legs and much stocking and they are too absorbed to know we are there.' Wealthy eyebrows were raised when the government revealed the extent of common-law marriage amongst poorer groups. The Archbishop of Canterbury led a wave of protests when the government proposed to grant separation allowances to women in common-law wedlock, claiming that it endorsed immorality. Yet, at root, the problem lay in middle-class ignorance of poorer people's mores and attitudes. What was loose behaviour for some was just daily life for others.

Still, it became essential for young working-class people to be saved from themselves, lest their behaviour undermined society and threatened the war effort. To this end, a number of women's organizations initiated voluntary patrols to watch out for lewd behaviour in parks and open spaces, railway stations and streets, nooks, crannies and alleyways, befriending young girls who were behaving unsuitably, offering them advice, saving them from danger, whilst at the same time rescuing men from 'women of evil reputation'. Some 2,284 such patrols were operating throughout urban areas by 1917 with semi-official blessing from the Home Office. Groups such as the London Public Morality Council (who compiled reports on observed sexual activities of couples in London's parks and open spaces) rubbed shoulders with the less trusted Women's Police Service, led by the ex-suffragist Damer Dawson. As a well-to-do philanthropist, Dawson was helping Belgian refugees at Victoria Station when she hit upon the idea of recruiting and training women police officers and she was joined in her endeavours by Nina Boyle, another ex-suffragist concerned with helping women unjustly treated by the law, and Mary Allen, an ex-window-smashing suffragette. Professional differences between Boyle and Dawson over permanency of the new force saw two organizations emerge in 1915, the Women Police Volunteers, and Dawson's Women's Police Force. They shared the same goals: to create an organization of trained officers who dealt with women's cases and upholding women's rights. Eighteen-hundred women were eventually recruited, funded mainly by voluntary contributions, with additional help from local council 'watch' committees and police authorities. By 1917 policewomen were being recruited on full-time duties in seven counties and 24 cities, including London. Official blessing was given by the Ministry of Munitions, which in 1916 awarded Dawson's policewomen a contract to 'act as guardians' at munitions factories, monitoring the entry of women at factory gates, supervising them on their travels to and from work and handling complaints of harassment and improper conduct. In some localities female officers were charged with investigating instances of prostitution and social impurity, with powers to enter premises or land in pursuit of their duties. This, however, uncovered a hidden dilemma. Were women being used as adjuncts to the police, invading private domains, using the flexibility of the law to encroach upon and erode women's civil liberties? Public complaints were voiced of 'busybody' women police officers who pried behind trees, flashed torches at respectable citizens occupying park benches after dark and apprehended innocent young women on grounds of soliciting.

This only highlighted the difficulties that arose when state or quasi-state organizations tried to regulate private behaviour. The state had gingerly put its foot into the arena when it began terminating separation allowances to wives found culpable of irregular conduct or 'intemperance'. But the predicament was acutely revealed when sex became a question of public health. The Royal Commission on Venereal Disease, established in 1913, became a focal point for the moral purity lobby. Its 1916 report claimed that 'in a typical working class population of London at least 8–12 per cent of the adult males have acquired syphilis, and at least 3–7 per cent of the adult females'. The figures for gonorrhoea were even higher. Some commentators suspected that the figures were exaggerated over-estimates, but for the moralists the Commission's evidence quickly became a rallying call to combat what they saw as the collapsing social standards of wartime, while the press elevated the problem as a national outrage.

Perhaps the real scandal was the sharp differences in treatment between the classes. Syphilis remedies (Salvarsan) for the wealthy were readily available; the poor faced being refused hospital admission and loss of insurance benefits. Matters were confused even further when the government appeared to turn away from banning soldiers' use of *maisons tolérées* on the French front. A public outcry forced the government to put such places out of bounds. Although state regulation of vice was a step too far for a largely conservative public, state-funded pathology laboratories and special clinics in hospitals were established. Doctors were given free supplies of Salvarsan to minister to all, in or out of uniform, and this was to have a major impact on the control of venereal disease. But the onus of prohibiting the spread of sexual disease still remained with women. A new regulation preventing any infected woman from having intercourse with a serviceman was introduced in an amendment to the Defence of the Realm Act in 1916. The implications of this were nonsensical, as it became illegal for an infected wife to sleep with her husband, even if he was the source of her infection. But it revealed the dangers when the state becoming embroiled in questions of sexual morality.

In any event, what perhaps is not in doubt is that, although the war did not necessarily create a climate of greater permissiveness, it did make the world of sex and sexual relationships more visible. Whether this changed prevailing attitudes between the sexes is open to question. In 1916, Damer Dawson voiced her protest against the new regulations under the Defence of the Realm Act in which prostitutes who lingered in the vicinity of military camps could be prosecuted. 'They talk as if men were innocent angels, helpless in the hands of wicked women ... . In the realm of morals we have not advanced beyond Adam who was tempted by Eve.'

References

John Cowen, 'Music Halls and Morals', *Contemporary Review*, November 1916.
Cate Haste, *Rules of Desire: Sex in Britain World War I to the Present*, London: Vintage, 2002, pp. 32–38.
NA, HO 45/10806/309485, 'Women Police and Women Patrols'.
NA, HO 45/10526/141896, 'Indecency on Hampstead Heath, 1906–19'.
The Times, 22nd February 1917.
Jeffrey Weeks, *Sex, Politics and Society: The Regulation of Sexuality since 1800*, Harlow, Longman, 1981, pp. 214–15.
The Women's Police Service, *An Account of its Aims with a Report of Work Accomplished During the Year 1915*, London: St Clements Press, 1916.

Notes

1 *The Times*, 18th August 1915.
2 From Peter Vansittart, *Voices from the Great War*, London: Pimlico, 1998, p. 100.
3 Mrs C.S. Peel, *How We Lived Then: A Sketch of Social and Domestic Life in England During the War*, London: Lane, 1929, pp. 138–39; E. Sylvia Pankhurst, *The Home Front*, London: Cresset Library, 1932, pp. 114–16; Trevor Wilson, *The Myriad Faces of War*, Cambridge: Polity Press, 1986, pp. 156–57. See also NA, CAB 45/262, 'Raids on Coast of Great Britain: Scarborough Raid'; WO; 32/5265, Reports on Shelling of Scarborough and Whitby, Yorkshire by German Ships, 1914.
4 See Ian Beckett, *Home Front 1914–1918: How Britain Survived the Great War*, London: National Archives, 2006, pp. 191–94; Joseph Morris, *The German Air Raids on Great Britain 1914–1918*, London: 1925; Thomas Fegan, *The Baby Killers: German Air Raids on Britain in the First World War*, Barnsley: Pen & Sword, 2002; Andrew Hyde, *The First Blitz: The German Air Campaign Against Britain, 1917–18*, Barnsley, Pen & Sword, 2002; Trevor Wilson, *The Myriad Faces of War*, op. cit., pp. 389–93.
5 Ian Beckett, *Home Front 1914–1918*, op. cit., pp. 191–94; Peter Cooksley, *The Home Front: Civilian Life in World War One*, Stroud: Tempus, 2006, pp. 118–20.

6 NA, CAB 27/9, 'Air Raids: Air Policy'; NA, Air Ministry papers (hereafter 'AIR') 1/662/17/122/669, 'Home Defence: Reorganisation of London Air Raid Defence'.

7 Peter Cooksley, *The Home Front*, op. cit., pp. 98–99.

8 Mrs C.S. Peel, *How We Lived Then*, op. cit., p. 155.

9 See Peter Cooksley, *The Home Front*, op. cit., ch. 5.

10 Sylvia Pankhurst, *The Home Front*, op. cit., p. 193; Ian Beckett, *Home Front 1914–1918*, op. cit., p. 182.

11 See Peter Cooksley, *The Home Front*, op. cit., p. 98.

12 Ian Beckett, *Home Front 1914–1918*, op. cit., p. 182; Mrs C.S. Peel, *How We Lived Then*, op. cit., p. 161; Richard van Emden and Steve Humphries, *All Quiet on the Home Front: An Oral History of Life in Britain During the First World War*, London: Headline, 2003. p. 165.

13 See Douglas H. Robinson, *The Zeppelin in Combat*, London: G.T. Foulis, 1962, pp. 131–32.

14 Peter Cooksley, *The Home Front*, op. cit., p. 97.

15 Panikos Panayi, *The Enemy in Our Midst: Germans in Britain During the First World War*, Oxford: Berg, 1991, p. 223; Panikos Panayi, 'Anti-German Riots in London During the First World War', *German History*, vol. 7, no. 2, 1989; Colin Holmes, 'The Myth of Fairness: Racial Violence in Great Britain 1911–19', *History Today*, vol. 35, October 1985, pp. 41–45.

16 Panikos Panayi, *The Enemy in Our Midst: Germans in Britain During the First World War*, op. cit., pp. 223–24, 239; NA, HO 45/10787/298199, 'ALIENS: Alleged Maltreatment of German Women and Children in the United Kingdom, 1915–16'.

17 Adrian Gregory, *The Last Great War*, op. cit., p. 237.

18 Adrian Gregory, *The Last Great War*, op. cit., p. 236; D.G. Woodhouse, *Anti-German Sentiment in Kingston upon Hull: The German Community and the First World War*, Hull: Kingston upon Hull Record Office, 1990, pp. 36–40; David Bilton, *The Home Front in the Great War: Aspects of the Conflict 1914–1918*, Barnsley: Leo Cooper, 2003, pp. 45–49.

19 Adrian Gregory, *The Last Great War*, op. cit., pp. 237–38.

20 Sylvia Pankhurst, *The Home Front*, op. cit., p. 196.

21 *The Times*, 13th May 1915.

22 See NA, HO 144/22945, 'Titles, Styles and Precedence of Members of the Royal Family: Relinquishment of German Titles in Favour of British Titles; Adoption of Surnames Mountbatten and Windsor; Principles of Entitlement to the Style "Royal Highness" and the Case of the Duke and Duchess of Windsor, 1917'.

23 Trevor Wilson, *The Myriad Faces of War*, op. cit., pp. 642–43; David French, 'Spy Fever in Britain 1900–1915', *Historical Journal*, vol. 21, no. 2, 1978, pp. 355–70.

24 See Panikos Panayi, *The Enemy in Our Midst: Germans in Britain During the First World War*, op. cit., pp. 233–34; Adrian Gregory, *The Last Great War*, op. cit., p. 236.

25 *Daily Sketch*, 15th May 1915.

26 Panikos Panayi, 'Anti-German Riots in London During the First World War', op. cit., p. 191.

27 Adrian Gregory, *The Last Great War*, op. cit., p. 236.

28 NA, WO 94/103, 'Documents Concerning Prisoners Confined in the Tower for Espionage During the First World War, Including Those Executed 1914–18'.

29 David French, 'Spy Fever in Britain 1900–915', op. cit.

30 Panikos Panayi, *The Enemy in Our Midst: Germans in Britain During the First World War*, op. cit., p. 159.

31 David French, 'Spy Fever in Britain 1900–915', op. cit; *The Times*, 25th August 1914 (I am grateful to Mr Trevor Courtney for this reference); Richard van Emden and Steve Humphries, *All Quiet on the Home Front: An Oral History of Life in Britain During the First World War*, op. cit., pp. 67–69.

32 J.C. Bird, *Control of Enemy Alien Civilians in Great Britain, 1914–1918*, London & New York: Garland, pp. 38–39.

33 David Cesarani and Tony Kushner, *The Internment of Aliens in Twentieth-century Britain*, London: Frank Cass, 1993, pp. 34–36; David French, 'Spy Fever in Britain 1900–1915', op. cit.

34 This is discussed in much greater detail by Adrian Gregory, *The Last Great War*, op. cit., pp. 238–48; Trevor Wilson, *The Myriad Faces of War*, op. cit., pp. 641–43; Richard van Emden and Steve Humphries, *All Quiet on the Home Front: An Oral History of Life in Britain During the First World War*, op. cit., pp. 59–60; IWM Collections, Printed Books, Catalogue no. 78406, 'The British Empire Union Founded During the First Year of the Great War to Destroy German Influence, Prohibit German Labour, Boycott German Goods Within the British Empire Now and After the War'.

35 See Nicoletta F. Gullace, 'Friends, Aliens and Enemies: Fictive Communities and the *Lusitania* Riots of 1915', *Journal of Social History*, vol. 39. no. 2, Winter 2005, pp. 351–54.

36 Bernard Waites, *A Class Society at War: England 1914–1918*, Leamington Spa: Berg, 1987, p. 68.

37 *Co-operative News*, 26th May 1917, in Bernard Waites, *A Class Society at War: England 1914–1918*, op. cit., p. 71.

38 *The Economist*, 26th July 1919, pp. 124–26; Bernard Waites, *A Class Society at War: England 1914–1918*, op. cit., p. 99.

39 NA, Inland Revenue papers (hereafter 'IR') 74/70, 'Exceptional Profits Due to the War', 16th March 1915, report by J.C. Stamp.

40 See NA, T 170/105, 'Note on the Subject of "Profiteering" During the War', 12th September 1916, report by R.V. Hopkins; NA, T 170/105, 'Profiteering', report by Sir John Bradbury.

41 Bernard Waites, *A Class Society at War: England 1914–1918*, op. cit., p. 101; *Manchester Guardian*, 19th June 1916. See also the discussion by Adrian Gregory, *The Last Great War*, op. cit., pp. 138–40.

42 Josiah C. Stamp, *Taxation During the War*, London: Milford, 1932, pp. 213–14. See also the comments made in Arthur L. Bowley, *Some Economic Consequences of the Great War*, London: Butterworth (reprinted by Hyperion Press, 1979), pp. 106–7; Bernard Waites, *A Class Society at War: England 1914–1918*, op. cit., p. 101.

43 Helen Jones, *Health and Society in Twentieth-century Britain*, Harlow: Longman 1994, p. 34.

44 See J.M. Winter, *The Great War and the British People*, 2nd edn, Basingstoke: Palgrave Macmillan, 2003, 'Introduction' and parts II and III; J.M. Winter, 'Aspects of the Impact of the First World War on Infant Mortality in Britain', *Journal of European Economic History*, vol. xi, 1982, pp. 713–38; J.M. Winter, 'The Impact of the First World War on Civilian Health in Britain', *Economic History Review*, 2nd series, vol. 30, no. 3, 1977, pp. 489–504; J.M. Winter, 'Military Fitness and Public Health in Britain in the First World War', *Journal of Contemporary History*, vol. 15, no. 2, 1980, pp. 211–44. For the riposte see Linda Bryder, 'The First World War: Healthy or Hungry?', *History Workshop Journal*, vol. 24, 1987, pp. 141–57; Bernard Harris, 'The Demographic Impact of the First World War: An Anthropometric Perspective', *Journal of the Society for the Social History of Medicine*, vol. 6. no. 3, 1993, pp. 343–66. For a riposte to the riposte see J.M. Winter, 'Public Health and the Political Economy of War, 1914–18', *History Workshop Journal*, no. 26, Winter, 1988, pp. 163–73.

45 See David Cannadine, *The Decline and Fall of the British Aristocracy*, London: Macmillan, Papermac edn, 1996, ch.2.

46 NA, T 172/970, Knaresborough to Bonar Law, 26th January 1917; David Cannadine, *The Decline and Fall of the British Aristocracy*, op. cit., pp. 90–125; Peter

Dewey, *War and Progress: Britain 1914–1945*, Harlow: Longman, 1997, p. 27; Bernard Waites, *A Class Society at War: England 1914–1918*, op. cit., pp. 92–95.

47 Bernard Waites, *A Class Society at War: England 1914–1918*, op. cit., p. 90.

48 *Report of the Departmental Committee on National Debt and Taxation*, London: HMSO, 1927, Cmnd 2800, Appendix XI; Bernard Waites, *A Class Society at War: England 1914–1918*, op. cit., pp. 90–92.

49 Report of the Departmental Committee on national debt and taxation, op. cit.; Bernard Waites, *A Class Society at War*, op. cit.

50 J.M. Winter, *The Great War and the British People*, 2nd edn, op. cit., pp. 240–41; Gerard DeGroot, *Blighty: British Society in the Era of the Great War*, Harlow: Longman, 1996, p. 206; Sylvia Pankhurst, *The Home Front*, op. cit., pp. 24–25.

51 J.M. Winter, *The Great War and the British People*, 2nd edn, op. cit., p. 230.

52 Arthur L. Bowley, *Prices and Wages in the United Kingdom, 1914–1920*, Oxford: Humphrey Milford, 1921, p. 99.

53 J.W.F. Rowe, *Wages in Practice and Theory*, London: Routledge, 1928, ch. 1; Bernard Waites, *A Class Society at War: England 1914–1918*, op. cit., pp. 133–36.

54 Bernard Waites, *A Class Society at War: England 1914–1918*, op. cit., pp. 134–36; J.W.F. Rowe, *Wages in Practice and Theory*, op. cit., pp. 53–55; Peter Dewey, *War and Progress: Britain 1914–1945*, op. cit., p. 42; Arthur L. Bowley, *Prices and Wages in the United Kingdom, 1914–1920*, op. cit., pp. 87–104.

55 Bernard Waites, *A Class Society at War: England 1914–1918*, op. cit.; J.W.F. Rowe, *Wages in Practice and Theory*, op. cit.; Peter Dewey, *War and Progress: Britain 1914–1945*, op. cit.; Arthur L. Bowley, *Prices and Wages in the United Kingdom, 1914–1920*, op. cit.

56 *History of the Ministry of Munitions*, vol. 5, part 1, p. 232; Bernard Waites, *A Class Society at War: England 1914–1918*, op. cit., p. 134.

57 Arthur L. Bowley, *Prices and Wages in the United Kingdom, 1914–1920*, op. cit., ch. 3, and pp. 63–66; NA, BT 13/73, 'Departmental Committee on Prices: Second Interim Report, Dec. 1916'; Mrs C.S. Peel, *How We Lived Then*, op. cit., pp. 56–57.

58 Cited in Adrian Gregory, *The Last Great War*, op. cit., p. 196.

59 J.M. Winter, *The Great War and the British People*, 2nd edn, op. cit., pp. 229–30.

60 Peter Dewey, *War and Progress: Britain 1914–1945*, op. cit., pp. 31–32.

61 *The Times*, 5th March 1917. See also C.F.G. Masterman, *England After War*, London: Hodder & Stoughton, 1922, pp. 24–67.

62 A.L. Bowley and J.C. Stamp, *The National Income 1924*, Oxford, 1927, pp. 58–59.

63 See B.R. Mitchell, *British Historical Statistics*, Cambridge: Cambridge University Press, 1988, table 13; Peter Dewey, *War and Progress: Britain 1914–1945*, op. cit., p. 33.

64 J.M. Winter, *The Great War and the British People*, 2nd edn, op. cit., pp. 119–33.

65 Bernard Harris, 'The Demographic Impact of the First World War: An Anthropometric Perspective', op. cit., pp. 347–49; J.M. Winter, *The Great War and the British People*, 2nd edn, op. cit., pp. 251–54.

66 Ronald Fletcher, *The Family and Marriage in Britain*, 3rd edn, Harmondsworth: Penguin 1973, p. 124; Royal Commission on Population, *Final Report*, London: HMSO, 1949, Cmnd 7695; J. Lewis-Faning, Royal Commission on Population, *Papers*, vol. I, *Report of an Inquiry into Family Limitation and Its Influence on Human Fertility in the Past Fifty Years*, London: HMSO, 1949; Peter Dewey, *War and Progress: Britain 1914–1945*, op. cit., pp. 52–53.

67 Peter Dewey, *War and Progress: Britain 1914–1945*, op. cit., p. 52.

68 See article by 'R.J', *The Times*, 30th April 1915.

69 J.M. Winter, *The Great War and the British People*, 2nd edn., op. cit., pp. 251, 261–64.

70 See Jane Lewis, *The Politics of Motherhood: Child and Maternal Welfare in England, 1900–1939*, London: Croom Helm, 1980, pp. 28–31.

71 IWM, Women's Work Collection, Welfare 1/4, *Babies of the Empire Society 'For the Health of Mothers and Babies'*; *Forty-fifth Annual Report of the Local Government*

Board 1915–16: Supplement Containing the Report of the Medical Officer 1915–1916, London: HMSO, 1917, p. iv; J.M. Winter, *The Great War and the British People*, 2nd edn, op. cit., pp. 189–90.

72 J.M. Winter, *The Great War and the British People*, 2nd edn., op. cit., pp. 191–93; Jane Lewis, *The Politics of Motherhood: Child and Maternal Welfare in England, 1900–1939*, op. cit., p. 34; *The Times*, 2nd July 1917.

73 Jane Lewis, *The Politics of Motherhood: Child and Maternal Welfare in England, 1900–1939*, op. cit., pp. 34–35.

74 See J.M. Winter, *The Great War and the British People*, 2nd edn., op. cit., pp. 198–204.

75 J.M. Winter, *The Great War and the British People*, 2nd edn., op. cit., pp. 194–96.

76 Helen Jones, *Health and Society in Twentieth-century Britain*, op. cit., p. 41; Jane Lewis, *The Politics of Motherhood: Child and Maternal Welfare in England, 1900–1939*, op. cit., pp. 35, 41–42.

77 Jane Lewis, *The Politics of Motherhood: Child and Maternal Welfare in England, 1900–1939*, op. cit., p. 35.

78 J.M. Winter, *The Great War and the British People*, 2nd edn., op. cit, pp. 189–90.

79 Cate Haste, *Rules of Desire: Sex in Britain, World War I to the Present*, London: Vintage, 2002, pp. 41–42.

80 Cate Haste, *Rules of Desire: Sex in Britain, World War I to the Present*, op. cit. See also *The Times*, 19th April 1915, 21st April 1915, 19th August 1918.

81 John Stevenson, *British Society 1914–45*, Harmondsworth: Penguin, 1984, p. 212; Peter Dewey, *War and Progress: Britain 1914–1945*, op. cit., p. 148.

82 Gerard DeGroot, *Blighty*, op. cit., p. 212; J.M. Winter, *The Great War and the British People*, 2nd edn, op. cit., pp. 178–87.

83 J.M. Winter, *The Great War and the British People*, 2nd edn, op. cit., pp. 154–78.

84 See *Report of Board of Trade Inquiry into Working-class Rents and Retail Prices in Industrial Towns of the United Kingdom*, London: HMSO, 1913, pp. xvii–xviii; John Burnett, *A Social History of Housing, 1815–1985*, 2nd edn, London: Routledge, 1986, p. 64, and chs. 5–7.

85 See M.J. Daunton, *A Property-owning Democracy? Housing in Britain*, London: Faber & Faber, 1987, ch. 2.

86 *The Land: The Report of the Land Enquiry Committee*, vol. II, *Urban*, London, 1914, pp. 84–86. See also *Report of Committee Appointed by the Secretary for Scotland to Enquire into Circumstances Connected with the Alleged Recent Increases in the Rental of Small Dwelling-houses in Industrial Districts in Scotland*, Cmnd 8111, British Parliamentary Papers, vol. XXXV 1914–16, pp. 6–7; Ministry of Reconstruction, *Report of the Committee on the Increase of Rent and Mortgage Interest (War Restrictions) Acts*, London: HMSO, 1919, Cmnd 9235, British Parliamentary Papers, vol. XII 1919, p. 5.

87 See David Englander, *Landlord and Tenant in Urban Britain 1838–1918*, Oxford: Oxford University Press, 1983, ch. 4.

88 *The Land: The Report of the Land Enquiry Committee*, vol. II, *Urban*, op. cit., pp. 78–88; see also A.K. Cairncross, *Home and Foreign Investment 1870–1913*, Cambridge, 1953, p. 45; M.J. Daunton, *A Property-owning Democracy?*, op. cit., p. 38.

89 Richard Rodger, 'Political Economy, Ideology and the Persistence of Working-class Housing Problems in Britain, 1850–1914', *International Review of Social History*, vol. XXXII, 1987, pp. 109–43; Enid Gauldie, *Cruel Habitations: A History of Working-class Housing, 1780–1918*, London: Allen & Unwin, 1974, p. 168; *The Land: The Report of the Land Enquiry Committee*, vol. II, *Urban*, London, op. cit., p. 28; *The Times*, 19th November 1902.

90 J.M. Winter, *The Great War and the British People*, 2nd edn, op. cit., p. 243; Commission of Inquiry into Industrial Unrest, No. 1 Division, *Report of the Commissioners for the North-western Area, Including a Supplemental Report on the*

Barrow-in Furness District, Cmnd 8663, pp. 31–33, British Parliamentary Papers, vol. XV, 1917–18.

91 Commission of Inquiry into Industrial Unrest, No. 1 Division, *Report of the Commissioners for the North-western Area, Including a Supplemental Report on the Barrow-in Furness District*, Comnd 8663, op. cit., p. 32; *History of the Ministry of Munitions*, vol. V. part V, ch. 1, pp. 1–2; Commission of Inquiry into Industrial Unrest, No. 1 Division; *Report of the Commissioners for the North-Eastern Area* Cmnd 8662, p. 4, British Parliamentary Papers, vol. XV 1917–18.

92 *History of the Ministry of Munitions*, vol. V, part V, ch. IV, pp. 33–34; *Report of Committee Appointed by the Secretary for Scotland to Enquire into Circumstances Connected with the Alleged Recent Increases in the Rental of Small Dwelling-houses in Industrial Districts in Scotland*, Cmnd 8111, pp. 5–7, British Parliamentary Papers, vol. XXXV, 1914–16; see also Laurence F. Orbach, *Homes for Heroes: A Study of the Evolution of British Public Housing, 1915–1921*, London: Seeley Service, 1977, p. 142.

93 Laurence F. Orbach, *Homes for Heroes*, op. cit., p. 15; *The Times*, 11th October 1915. See also *History of the Ministry of Munitions*, vol. V. part V, ch. 1; *The Times*, 18th September 1915, 8th October 1915, 14th October 1915; Trevor Wilson, *The Myriad Faces of War*, op. cit., pp. 806–7.

94 *Report of Committee Appointed by the Secretary for Scotland to Enquire into Circumstances Connected with the Alleged Recent Increases in the Rental of Small Dwelling-houses in Industrial Districts in Scotland*, Cmnd 8111, p. 4, British Parliamentary Papers, vol. XXXV, 1914–16.

95 Joseph Melling, *Rent Strikes: People's Struggles for Housing in West Scotland 1890–1916*, Edinburgh: Polygon, 1983, pp. 60–66.

96 *The Times*, 8th October 1915. For a succinct overview of Mary Barbour's life and political career, see Michael Byers, 'Mary Barbour (1875–1958)', in http://gdl.cdlr. strath.ac.uk/redclyde/redclypeobyebar.htm.

97 David Englander, *Landlord and Tenant in Urban Britain, 1838–1918*, op. cit., p. 233. See also Joseph Melling, 'Clydeside Housing and the Evolution of Rent Control, 1900–1939', in J. Melling, ed., *Housing, Social Policy and the State*, London: Croom Helm, 1980, pp. 139–67; Trevor Wilson, *The Myriad Faces of War*, op. cit., pp. 806–09.

98 Alan Bennett, BBC TV Broadcast, introduction to 'A Day Out', 5th December 2009.

7   Food, farming and rural society

Mention 'food' and historians of the British war effort between 1914 and 1918 will voice their agreement as to its critical role in her struggle against the Central Powers. In his memoirs, Lloyd George emphasized food supplies as the one decisive factor between victory and capitulation.[1] It had been Germany's failure to maintain adequate food stocks that had undermined her people's will to fight and accelerated the country's defeat. In Britain, the food issue boiled down to a question of feeding the vastly expanded armed services whilst maintaining supplies for her workers and families. This was a challenge of some magnitude. British farming was, by comparison with that of her enemies, relatively small and under-prepared to meet national needs. Before the war much of Britain's food was imported. It was said that four out of every five slices of bread eaten by Britons was made from foreign flour; and, despite her naval dominance, the shipment of essential supplies of 'staple' foods, principally from the Americas and Australasia, was vulnerable to attacks from German submarines.[2] Thus, once again, dangerous circumstances compelled the government to act. British agriculture had to be mobilized to expand domestic sources of basic foodstuffs, home demand had to be controlled and shipping lanes had to be safeguarded. The outcome was broadly successful. The country did not starve, although distribution and galloping price inflation were major problems. But at least Britons were kept working and fighting, while the effects of growing state intervention in the countryside blew the wind of reform (for a short while) on to Britain's fiercely independent farming industry and the rural communities on which it depended. It seemed a small price to pay for national survival.

Laissez-faire modified

In 1914, Britain was conspicuous amongst the belligerent countries in her heavy reliance on imported food. Over 70 per cent of the wheat and 60 per cent of meat consumed came from overseas.[3] Despite the expansion of meat and dairy farming during the Edwardian years, British agriculture had long lost its capacity to feed the nation. Since the agricultural depression of the 1870s, areas of arable cultivation had shrunk from 24 million acres in 1872 to

19.5 million by 1913.[4] The numbers of agricultural workers in England and Wales too had declined from 1,013,150 in 1871 to around 668,000 male and 36,000 female workers by 1914, representing just 11.5 per cent of the national workforce.[5] Yet the diversity of Britain's farms and farmers remained considerable. Generally, those farms located north of a line drawn from the Bristol Channel to the Wash in East Anglia remained small (about 50 acres) and were dominated (particularly in the northern uplands of England and the Welsh and Scottish highlands) by rough grazing and the husbanding of sheep and, to a lesser extent, goats; whilst in lowland areas farms could be up to 70 acres in size and were largely taken up by arable, pasture and livestock husbandry.[6] Moreover, what constituted a 'farmer' could be anything from a cottager keeping pigs and growing vegetables on a small plot, to a prosperous tenant farmer managing an agri-businesses of over 500 acres, or a 'territorial magnate' (in Alun Howkins's words), 7,000 of whom owned four-fifths of the territory in the British Isles.[7] Living in their shadow were the more humble, but no less noble, rural working class. Agricultural employees were broadly divided into two camps. In England's northern counties many worked on Farm Service contracts, living on or close to a farm and engaged in ploughing, milking and harvesting tasks and earning wages through six-month or annual 'terms'. Much more predominant, however, were agricultural labourers, who made up 80 per cent of the rural workforce in England before the war (40 per cent in Wales). This group subdivided itself through earnings, status, trade and locality. Those in charge of animals – managing dairy herds, shepherding and leading plough teams – enjoyed the highest prestige; ploughboys were much less regarded. For all that, a feature common to all rural work was poor wages and prospects. Average weekly incomes could vary from as much as 20s in Northumberland to 14s in Oxfordshire. Once a worker had mastered the necessary rural skills by the age of 21, there were very few opportunities for social betterment and higher wages. This, and the changes in farming practices, which often required fewer labourers, prompted many rural workers to migrate into the towns or overseas. Indeed, labour shortages became the one perennial complaint amongst agricultural employers before the war.[8]

Although a Royal Commission on food supplies in 1905 had warned of possible wheat shortages, price inflation and panic buying on the outbreak of war, the British government had no contingency plans for domestic production in 1914. Confidence was placed in the Royal Navy's ability to safeguard international shipping lanes to sustain import flows, along with the insistence of the Board of Trade President Walter Runciman that supplies could still be maintained through existing commercial channels and that price increases would be pegged back once new food sources had been secured.[9] Nevertheless, Asquith was sufficiently concerned to establish a Cabinet Committee on Food Supplies in August 1914 (one of five that would be dealing with food resources by January 1915), with a remit to secure a steady supply of food at reasonable prices and deflect the risk of wildfire public panic.[10] Three commodities mattered most: wheat, meat and sugar. In November 1914 the Cabinet approved the formation of a Grain Supplies Committee led by Sir Henry Rew (a prominent Board of Agriculture official). Rew faced a tightening world market. His plan to buy enough wheat to feed the military and build a reserve stock of 1.5 million tons of wheat (and 500,000 tons of flour) was threatened by competition from other belligerent countries; a failing Australian crop; Turkey's closure of the Dardenelles (blocking supplies from Russia and the Balkans); and the Indian government's requisitioning all of its wheat surpluses in an attempt to restrain its own domestic prices.[11] Such obstacles were offset to an extent by bumper harvests across the northern hemisphere, allowing British farmers to accrue enough wheat stocks to keep the country supplied for 21 weeks. Yet shortages were expected by the spring of 1915. Board of Trade officials calculated that reserves would be down to eight weeks by May, with further shrinkages by August, without taking account of the effect of enemy attacks on Allied shipping.[12]

Similar challenges were faced in obtaining supplies of meat. Here the Food Committee's problems were complicated by the War Office commandeering all the meat on the London markets for the Army, whilst simultaneously seeking contracts for shipments of frozen meat from Argentina. Fears of jeopardizing its neutrality made the Argentine government wary of trading directly with the British War Office, and the Board of Trade was forced into purchasing supplies through an agent without seeking parliamentary approval, making its buying operations technically illegal. Yet this did not deter the Board from adopting this method when it appointed, in October 1914, Sir Thomas Robinson, Agent General for Queensland, to buy on the government's behalf 15,000 tons of meat monthly, channelling 10,000 tons for the Army, with a surplus secured for domestic supplies. The Board of Trade subsequently assumed responsibility for all frozen meat imports from South America, buoyed by agreements with the Australian and New Zealand governments to requisition their entire meat exports at fixed prices.[13]

The government, however, lost no time in satisfying the nation's sugar needs by appointing, on 20th August 1914, a Royal Commission on Sugar Supplies, which immediately took over all trading activities, buying up imports on the state's account. As a source of nutrition, sugar was regarded as equally important to wheat. Britain was the world's leading consumer. Some MPs spoke of sugar as a 'valuable food', and British scientists held sugar to be a cheap form of calorie intake, generating vital energy in workers and critical for providing poorer children with sufficient nourishment for their health and survival. Yet sugar was a commodity that was almost entirely imported. Two-thirds of the country's supplies were shipped as beet sugar (a root crop) from Germany and Austria–Hungary before the war, and the sudden loss of European supplies forced the commission to search for cane sugar in the Caribbean, Java, Mauritius and the Philippines. In the event, the Sugar Commission was one of the Asquith government's few successes. Its buying operations had secured nearly one million tons by 1915, almost half the country's annual consumption, and problems over further supplies did not emerge until the end of that year.[14]

This was the moment when the government's best-laid plans went awry. The multiplicity of Cabinet food committees had already knocked the official laissez-faire policy off-guard, but it was further undermined when the Cabinet was forced to rush through Parliament the Unreasonable Withholding of Foodstuffs Act in August 1914 (which empowered the Board of Trade to seize stocks from any retailer suspected of profiteering), in an attempt to stem the rising wave of hoarding and panic buying of foodstuffs that had erupted across the country at the outbreak of war.[15] Panic buying fell away spontaneously, but prices did not. Rising home demand and increasing international competition for limited supplies on world markets sparked rapid inflation. The price of sugar, for example, rose to around 80 per cent of its pre-war level in August 1914, settling back to 67 per cent by January 1915; wheat prices jumped by 80 per cent; and meat prices by 40 per cent in the same period.[16] Sugar traders identified the Commission's lack of business sense as the main problem, pointing to Henry Tate's practice of paying inflated rates for sugar in his anxiety to secure supplies and dealing in far-flung markets, which inevitably meant higher freight charges.[17] And the government's reluctance to take control of merchant shipping left both the military and the Admiralty free to requisition civilian vessels almost at will, creating severe shortages of cargo-space for food imports.[18]

Labour organizations and women's groups lobbied the government to impose a scheme of 'maximum prices' on basic necessities and for a short time the Food Committee obliged: lists of maximum prices were being published in the press throughout the autumn of 1914.[19] They were not legally binding, however, and the figures quoted were based more on traders' estimates of a profitable return rather than a fair price for consumers. Even then, smaller retailers complained that the quoted prices were set too low for them to make a living. Hence 'maximum prices' became government prices and many shopkeepers simply interpreted them as a new minimum and charged accordingly.[20] In Parliament, Asquith highlighted the German experience of price fixing that had helped create a thriving black market in food. In Cabinet, Walter Runciman warned that Britain's reliance on imported food made price fixing extremely treacherous, as it would drive her overseas suppliers to seek better prices elsewhere and deprive Britain of much-needed provisions. Ministerial inertia thus ensured the high cost of food became a problem that simply refused to fade away. Offering solace to the population, Asquith told MPs that food costs were no higher than those experienced during the Franco-Prussian war of 1870. But running a wartime food policy that relied on a hope that things would soon become better could not endure for very long.[21]

Faint signs of a shift in policy emerged when Asquith formed his first coalition government in May 1915. The subsequent ministerial reshuffle saw the Earl of Selborne (a Tory peer and one-time advocate of tariff reform) brought in as President of the Board of Agriculture, replacing the masterly inactive Lord Lucas, a man who, according to one of his colleagues, was only 'industrious after 11 a.m'.[22] Selborne realized from the outset the strategic hazards of the country's reliance on foreign food. Yet it was a difficulty that could be overcome if a more interventionist approach in agriculture was adopted that would rapidly increase the supply of home-grown produce. Selborne's views did not sit well with his Cabinet colleagues, but at least they found favour with his friend Lord Milner, who had long advocated state support for agriculture.[23] Selborne had no hesitation in appointing Milner as head of a cross-party Board of Agriculture committee in June 1915 to investigate the possibilities of increasing food production in England and Wales. Appropriate committees for Scotland and Ireland were established a few days later. Milner's committee took just one month to produce an interim report, which recognized that farmers could be persuaded to plough up unsuitable land for wheat or cereals only if they could make a monetary return from the crop. Thus, Milner proposed first a 'plough policy', which involved turning over poor and unprofitable grassland to arable cultivation; second, this was supported by the introduction of a state price guarantee for wheat. Milner thought this could be achieved if farmers received 'deficiency payments' when the wholesale price of wheat dipped below 45 shillings a quarter. The method was effectively a state subsidy and was conditional on farmers having increased their arable acreage by one fifth of that in October 1913. Milner's scheme was not compulsory: intervention would only be necessary to make the market work more efficiently.[24]

Selborne faced an uphill struggle to persuade Asquith's Cabinet to accept the proposals. Milner admitted that his committee had been 'a set of men absolutely divided' over the proposals.[25] In Cabinet, Selborne faced intense opposition from McKenna, whose Treasury advisers were convinced that state expenditure in agriculture represented an unwanted and unnecessary level of interference that could not be countenanced. Selborne's position was further undermined by Bonar Law's reluctance to declare himself on the issue and Balfour's denial (as First Lord of the Admiralty) of any threat to domestic supplies. Lloyd George, however, fully supported Selborne, but was outnumbered as the Cabinet swung against Milner's scheme.[26] When the Committee's final report was published in October 1915, the price guarantee had been diluted into a set of alternative proposals for food production.[27]

Selborne was left appealing to 'the self-interest of farmers and to their patriotism' to increase their production and he eventually resigned in June 1916 over the government's Irish policy.[28] Even so, Selborne left an important legacy. Milner's 'plough up' policy and system of guaranteed prices would provide a working blueprint for the government's agricultural regime in the second half of the war.[29] And his creation of the County War Agricultural Committees, locally appointed bodies of county landowners, farmers and agriculturalists, formed the spine of the food production committees of 1917 and 1918.[30]

In a sense, the Cabinet's rejection of Selborne's schemes was understandable. Fears of national starvation had been more than adequately assuaged by the abundant harvest of 1915. Higher prices and good weather had produced yields in the United Kingdom 31 per cent greater than any year since 1904. Supplies were boosted further by the Canadian harvest of 11.6 million tons (more than double pre-war averages) and the record-breaking results from the United States of America of 27.9 million tons, of which 66 per cent was available for export. The news was greeted with a tinge of smugness within Asquith's Cabinet. One could almost imagine its ministers, leaning back in their office chairs, hands behind their heads, crossed legs and feet planted firmly on their desks, sighing 'Food crisis? What food crisis?'[31]

War and the countryside, 1914–16

Despite the question mark that hung over British agriculture's ability to increase its contribution to the national larder, the farming industry more or less held its own in the first two years of the war. Rising prices had tempted many farmers back into cereal production just before and immediately after the outbreak, and the harvest of 1915 revealed increases of 20 per cent in wheat and 8 per cent in oats. Milk production rose in 1914 to 1.24 million gallons (slipping back to 1.17 million gallons in 1915), and potato output peaked at 4 million tons in 1914, falling (thanks to bad weather, particularly in Scotland) to 3.8 million tons a year later. The national flock of sheep, at 25 million at the beginning of 1916, was 4 per cent higher than pre-war, though the national pig stock had declined by around 7 per cent of its 1913 total, a decline attributable largely to the increasing shortages of barley and brewers' grains which were beginning to be affected by the legislative controls on the production (and consumption) of alcoholic liquor. Overall, Britain's home-grown food supplies remained constant, and British farmers were benefiting from rising incomes.[32]

The war brought other urgencies to the countryside. The War Office's struggle to accommodate the huge numbers of army volunteers spawned a proliferation of makeshift camps springing up across many rural areas, drafting in villagers to help with their construction, whilst generating good business for local shops from wandering soldiers with money to spend. Village housewives gained much-needed income by taking in military laundry and accommodating officers and soldiers.[33] In other respects, the Army was less welcome. Large-scale mobilization brought significant requisitioning of horses both for riding and the transport of armoury, munitions and provisions. For many rural people the loss of farm horses was sorely felt. Horses were an integral part of a farm's power supply, the conveyance of people and produce, and an invaluable source of manure. Numbers of agricultural horses fell markedly from 926,820 in 1914 to 858,032 in 1915. The farm-horse population only began to recover once mobilization was complete and the Army looked to meet its needs with imported horses. Even so, while numbers of farm horses recovered to 906,233 by 1916, this was still below 1914 levels.[34]

More dramatic was the impact of army recruitment. Like their urban counterparts, Britain's agricultural manhood walked into the recruiting stations in 1914 for pay, patriotism, job security and a short war. In rural Scotland recruitment rates were higher than elsewhere: 93 per 10,000 population according to Adrian Gregory, with 507 men from the isolated Highland parish of Gairloch volunteering for military duty from a total population of 3,317 (15.3 per cent). Poverty and poor job prospects were doubtless important factors, yet patriotism ran deeper in Scottish than English culture. Deeply imbued with an ancient national memory of the warrior, Scottish country boys went to war in honour of the men who 'had bled with Wallace and fought for the Bruce', and Robert Burns's poetic chant, 'A man's a man for a' that', could not have been far from Scottish recruits' minds.[35] In England rural recruitment in 1914 was a tale of two cultures. The first played heavily on the traditional values of patriotism, deference and a deeply paternalistic system of social relationships that were wrapped in notions of privilege, duty and responsibility. For many land-owning families an army career was seen as respectable. Its sons, brothers and husbands were well schooled in military culture. And some rural elites exercised their position within local communities to press men into army service, threatening their workers with dismissal and eviction if they refused to join up.[36] The second relied more on the influence of urban cultures. Local landowner and MP Claude Lowther, owner of Herstmonceux Castle in Sussex, adopted a 'Pals' principle to raise a corps of men, emphasizing a sense of place and locality rather than the ambiguous notions of paternalism and duty. Exploiting the dominant feature of the local landscape (the South Downs) to cut across the divides of class and locality, Lowther appealed to men 'from the shop as well as the sheepfold' to 'join the Southdowners', in a manner that denied the older social structures shaped by the indigenous gentry.[37] Estimates of the numbers of farm workers lost to the Army and other occupations by 1916 vary. Edith Whetham estimated that the figures touched 150,000 in England and Wales. Contemporary estimates from the Board of Trade put the numbers closer to 216,000. The Board of Agriculture's calculations were greater still, with 350,000 men said to have left agriculture in England and Wales since the start of the war, some 23–45 per cent of the pre-war workforce.[38]

A side-effect of rural recruitment was labour shortages. Farmers bemoaned the loss of farm labour to the armed forces and higher-paid occupations, though their own central role in the war effort made them virtually 'unrecruitable'.[39] The War Office recognized the problem early in May 1915, when it forbade the enlistment of skilled farm workers. By the autumn specific agricultural trades – bailiffs, shepherds, stockmen and horsemen, as well as thatchers, engine drivers and mechanics, and threshing machine operatives – had all become 'starred' occupations, leaving the bulk of army recruitment to be drawn from unskilled and semi-skilled farm labourers.[40] This meant that the agricultural workforce had to be refreshed from other sources. School children were one source. Farming had a long tradition of employing youngsters on menial labouring tasks and during the war they were still regarded as legitimate cheap labour. Existing legislation allowed children who had reached an acceptable educational standard to finish their schooling a year before the official leaving age of 13, and it was possible for them to be withdrawn in the case of sickness 'or any other unavoidable cause'.[41] In Parliament, Asquith gave his blessing when he declared his support for the recruitment of boys aged between 11 and 14 on farming operations during the autumn and winter months, whilst many local education authorities consented to the early release of children for farm work. Between September 1914 and January 1915, 38 authorities in England and Wales allowed 1,413 children to leave school for the farm. By January 1916, this figure rose to 8,026 in 54 authorities, a number that grew to 14,915 by the time the government stopped counting in October 1916.[42]

Soldiers were another font of labour supply. Farmers viewed soldier-labour as extremely flexible. They were physically fit, came in an abundant supply, and could be employed on an *ad hoc* basis, with no conditions made over the nature of the work. But soldiers were expensive. They often lacked the necessary skills, were not easily secured and were subject to strict military conditions as to their usage. Daily wage costs averaged around 4s (20p), or 2s 6d (12.5p) if the farmer provided board and lodging, well above ordinary labourers' rates, and soldier workers were obliged to be paid 'wet time' when bad weather prohibited outdoor tasks. Hence, for the first two years of the war the use of soldier-labour was relatively modest. The War Office's first release of soldiers was to help with the hay harvest in 1915, and eventually around 23,000 were deployed as temporary farm workers between October 1915 and August 1916, with few being employed for more than four weeks.[43]

This left women as the only other viable source of farm labour. The presence of 'village' women employed in agriculture was not new, though many farmers considered women incapable of undertaking dirty or heavy jobs, or working with animals, and inclined to down tools in bad weather. Even in 1918, Hampshire agriculturalists were said to 'take on anything that comes along, boys, old men, cripples, mentally deficient, criminals, or anything else … they will not have women'.[44] For their part village women were reluctant to take on work that was regarded as demeaning and unfeminine, and separation allowances for the wives of enlisted men, though far from satisfactory, were usually sufficient to provide for daily needs before 1916. Moreover, with new, better-paid opportunities emerging for women in munitions work and other urban-based occupations, outdoor working for grumpy and unappreciative farmers hardly presented an appealing prospect. For a countrywoman whose father took home a weekly wage of 14s in 1914, the chance to earn 52s a week as a tram conductress (plus holiday and uniform) must have been very tempting.[45] Therefore it is not surprising that, for the first years of the war, the numbers of women working in British agriculture fell below pre-1914 levels, dipping to 111,000 by 1915. The Board of Agriculture tried to inject some life into women's agricultural employment by instituting training schemes in milking and light farm work at local agricultural colleges. Women were then placed in work by Labour Exchanges about 2–4 weeks after finishing their course. This method of gentle persuasion was stepped up by the formation of Women's War Agricultural Committees, which were briefed to register countrywomen who were ready to work and place them in suitable posts with local farmers. The government claimed that 140,000 such women had been registered across the country by 1916, but subsequent analyses have reported that around 72,000 were certificated to work in farming occupations during this period, with 62,000 completing the 30 days' approved service. Only 29,000 women were working on farms during the 1916 harvest.[46]

Hungry days

In its first two years, then, the war largely filtered its effects more through rural society than the farming industry, yet the need for Britons to take the food issue seriously sprang almost from nowhere. In October 1916, Lord Crawford, head of the Wheat Commission (and Selborne's replacement at the Board of Agriculture), circulated a Cabinet memorandum detailing an 8 per cent weakening of British harvest yields on pre-war levels. Grain production had fallen to 1913 totals; the potato crop had shrunk by 25 per cent; milk supplies by 13 per cent; and there was 8 per cent less meat available for retail. The country's annual fish catch had dropped by one-third, thanks largely to the Admiralty requisitioning 80 per cent of the national trawler fleet, and production of 'fat stock' meats from cattle, sheep and pigs was threatened by the agricultural labour shortage. The picture was worsened by shortfalls in the North American wheat harvest, which fell to 24.5 million tons in 1916, and the mounting losses of Allied merchant shipping to German U-boat action, which Admiral Jellicoe warned were so great that Britain could be forced to sue for peace, regardless of the military position on the Western Front.[47] Outside Westminster the British public needed no reminding of the country's food problems. Rising prices were a constant irritant. Food expenditure took two-thirds of the average working-class family's weekly wage; prices of cheaper foods, particularly frozen imported meat, tended to rise at higher rates than better-quality produce, and the lack of storage space in poorer homes meant that housewives had to buy smaller quantities and more often.[48]

By 1917 food shortages were beginning to show, as empty shelves in retail shops and the emergence of the food queue became a common sight. *The Times* reported 'queues in the fog' in December. In some parts of London women were beginning to form lines for margarine (and other items, including tea, condensed milk, rice and butter) at dairy shops as early as 5 a.m., with some queues numbering between 1,000 and 3,000 across parts of the East End.[49] Dorothy Peel recalled women and children waiting outside 'shabby shops common to the poor districts of all towns' carrying 'baskets, string bags, fish basses, bags made of American cloth … . Women used to go from shop to shop trying to find one at which they could buy meat or margarine, tea and possibly a little extra sugar.'[50]

By 1918, queues were threatening public order and civilian morale. Munition workers stopped working to assist their wives in queuing or raided shops known to be withholding supplies. Writing to her husband from Walthamstow, Edie Bennett described how 'we are being slowly starved out, we have to line up for everything now … tea, sugar, marg and joint of meat is a thing of the past'.[51] In places as far apart as Glasgow and Leytonstone, crowds of workers' wives looted closed shops to secure supplies of bread and potatoes before being brought under control by the military. In Wrexham, a cartman selling potatoes had been 'surrounded by hundreds of clamouring people, chiefly women, who scrambled on to the vehicle in the eagerness to buy'.[52] In Maryport, Cumberland, housewives ransacked farmers' carts when the sellers resisted calls to sell potatoes at a 'fair price'. Farmers retaliated by blockading the town, leaving residents without supplies of potatoes and butter for nearly a month.[53]

In a sense, food shortages were a two-headed coin. While bread was always freely available, deficiencies in some commodities came and went. The supply of potatoes, for example, nearly dried up in the first half of 1917, but a bumper harvest later in the year produced greater quantities than retailers could handle.[54] Sugar and butter, on the other hand, were constantly in short supply, with shops in smaller towns and rural districts receiving few or no supplies for weeks. Deficiencies in other foodstuffs, such as meat and tea, became more intense as the war progressed. Then again, some food shortages were occasioned by the British consumer's innate conservatism. Working-class tradition determined that the male breadwinners in the family took first priority in times of shortage, consuming the lion's share of available meat, bread and vegetables, with spouse and children scrambling for leftovers from the plate. Customer resistance to new foods ensured that some items, such as horsemeat and tinned fish, both of which were in plentiful supply, remained on the shelves, regardless of the government's campaign to entice the public into eating unfamiliar fare.[55]

Food shortages also magnified Britain's deep social inequalities. Rumours of the wealthy hoarding food provoked rowdy demonstrations in Yorkshire.[56] Some retailers exploited the sugar scarcity for profit, denying availability to poorer customers whilst selling it as a luxury item to wealthy patrons. And there appeared to be no scarcity of fodder for hunters, race-horses and polo-ponies amid the lengthening queues, and reports of shopkeepers closing their premises to waiting customers while supplying provisions by delivery to their favoured wealthier patrons caused widespread offence. Some of London's East End families survived on a diet of tea, bread, potatoes and cabbage leaves, as the *Daily Herald* revealed in November 1917 that diners at London's Ritz Hotel were able to consume six-course dinners of fish and meat entrées, smoked salmon, a choice of soups and desserts and limitless servings of cheese and cream.[57]

Of course Britain's food supply was dysfunctional. In war this was to be expected. Yet neither the government nor producers were giving the public a fair deal. Plain greed partly explains farmers' attempts to cash in on rising cereal prices, sewing the same fields with wheat in consecutive years and omitting the 'root break' (the sewing of root crops to replenish nutrients in the soil) in the cultivation cycle. Yields of wheat, a crop that rapidly absorbs soil fertility, not surprisingly, nearly collapsed in 1916, a near catastrophe for which farmers alone should bear responsibility.[58] In a similar vein, only unforgivable incompetence can explain the government's failure to prevent the reckless commandeering by the military of shipping and food supplies. Ministers who needed reminding of the effects of their inaction could look no further than the Australasian trade, where shipping shortages caused by naval practices had forced owners to concentrate their vessels in the more profitable North Atlantic routes, with ships transporting thrice as much cargo than on a return voyage to Australia. Valuable produce was left to rot in southern dominion ports through lack of shipping space. Nearly two million sheep and cattle carcasses from New Zealand were being stacked in cold storage by June 1915, at a time when civil servants were forecasting a 133,000-ton deficit in British meat stocks for that year.[59]

The *coup de grâce* came over price controls, where the government's haste to limit the retail price of food in 1917 without taking control of its supply led to a near breakdown of distribution channels. With high street prices now regulated, yet wholesale and supply prices still set at market rates, retailers, at a time of rapid inflation, were reduced to selling produce at a loss, or not at all, while wholesalers could withdraw specific foodstuffs in search of better returns, or direct them to fewer outlets. Moreover, retailers who were located at some distance from distribution centres, struggled to compete against those who were situated closer and benefited from lower transport costs. The upshot was severe local shortages. Food supplies to the poorer areas of Liverpool, mining communities in north-east England and poorer districts in north London were reported to be at starvation levels in 1917. In the localities of Usworth and Washington, school strikes were being reported over the issue of inadequate food supplies.[60] When prices were fixed on imported butter, Dutch and Danish producers redirected their output to other countries. Margarine, bacon, tea and cheese supplies likewise followed the route to maximum profit over the autumn and winter seasons of 1917–18. Administrative confusion over the setting of meat prices in 1917 produced severe shortages, particularly in London, as butchers, located far from wholesale markets, stared at empty counters, whilst harassed government ministers declared two meatless days a week. Food had become a mid-war crisis for the government. Clinging to a laissez-faire 'solution' was now creating larger problems. The majority of

British citizens already ate less than was necessary for their daily physical needs. And the near chaos in distribution networks could be resolved only by the assumption of central control and co-ordination of food supplies. Persuading ministers to grasp this reality would be an achievement in itself.[61]

Enter Lord Devonport

There was not, however, to be a headlong rush to control. Asquith made some token gestures by appointing a Wheat Commission in October 1916 and giving the Board of Trade new powers over food. But it was not until Lloyd George took charge in Downing Street that a new Ministry of Food was established, led by Lord Devonport as a 'food controller'. As a retailer and business partner in one of London's leading tea importers, Devonport regarded the educated classes with contempt, and his civil servants as 'molluscs', and chose to staff the ministry with personnel of a similar disposition, including the 'dynamic' William Beveridge and Isidore Salmon, a director of Lyons Corner Houses.[62] Despite these overtures, Devonport proved no more willing to introduce food controls than his predecessors. Both the retailing and farming industries strongly resisted anything that smelt of state regulation and the ministry shared Arthur Henderson's concern that food controls could stir widespread labour unrest.[63] Consequently, Beveridge's carefully laid plans for a nationwide rationing system were sidelined in favour of a 'voluntary rationing' campaign: essentially a Derby scheme for food. If the public did not regulate their consumption voluntarily, then compulsion would follow.

The campaign had several limbs. One was directed at hotels, restaurants and other public eating-places. The Public Meals Order issued in December 1916 restricted diners to two courses for lunch and three at dinner, informing restaurant-goers 'Today the true patriot who can afford it will eat asparagus, not potatoes.'[64] This was followed by an exhortatory (and short-lived) 'go-without' campaign, with ministers imploring the public to have one 'meatless day' a week and to 'eat less bread', with Devonport calling upon every family to make its own sacrifices ensuring that 'not a crust or crumb is wasted'.[65] The ministry hired female staff to give 'war cookery' demonstrations and promote the use of obtainable (but disliked) foods such as horsemeat and lentils. For many Britons a future of scrag-end, soggy potato, stewed cabbage and watery gravy now beckoned. Having been asked to sacrifice meat for bread in their meals, they were now expected to forego both meat *and* bread. A soldier writing from France in September 1916 told his family 'Shall we have MEATLESS DAYS? If so I will stay out here!'[66] Ministerial economy drives were backed by initiatives to stretch existing wheat stocks by adding flour substitutes, particularly potatoes, maize and barley, into bread. The white loaf of pre-war years was replaced by 'Government bread' – a black loaf full of potato segments that would shoot out during cutting, memorably described by one historian 'as digestible as a howitzer shell and probably as lethal'.[67]

The campaign's success, however, depended upon shameless publicity. Pooling ideas with the National War Savings Committee, the ministry launched a major promotion campaign in March 1917 with churchgoers being the first to receive the gospel of economy through sermons given by their local clergy. Requests were made to cinemas to screen specially produced films on the food question. Speakers were recruited, including the popular music-hall comedian Harry Lauder, to tour lecture halls and theatres extolling the patriotic virtues of food economy. Details of convictions under new laws outlawing food waste were published in the press. The ministry also produced a set of posters proclaiming 'Save the Wheat, Help the Fleet', along with a series of leaflets and handbooks, with titles such as *Mr Slice o' Bread* which claimed that 48 million slices were being wasted daily, and the *Food Economy Handbook* containing advice about nutrition and weekly budgeting on food spending. The campaign was supported by 1,000 local food committees created by the ministry to implement orders and restrictions conferred on local authorities by the Defence of the Realm Act. A Royal Proclamation was issued whereby families could demonstrate their commitment to reducing their bread consumption by acquiring a Householder's Pledge card (signed by the King) and reciting a campaign song:

Back up the lads who fight for you, with all the might you can
And sign the pledge that shows you mean to thwart the German plan
Let the little purple ribbon have its silken length unfurled
Till it brings eternal freedom to a battle-weary world.[68]

Enter Lord Rhondda

Devonport's campaign met with widespread public indifference. The government's calls for restraint could not surmount the resentment felt over sugar shortages, high prices and hoarding. When government enquiries cited food problems as one of the main factors behind the industrial militancy of 1917, Lloyd George decided that a change of Controller was required and in May appointed Lord Rhondda (formerly D.A. Thomas), another millionaire minister with extensive business interests in Britain and America. As an 'applied economist' and reluctant interventionist, Rhondda's remit extended beyond direct ministerial responsibilities.[69] He co-ordinated the policies of the Board of Trade's Wheat and Sugar Commissions; advised delegates on the Inter-Allied Food Authorities (a set of international commissions set up to co-ordinate the food policies of Britain's wartime partners); and reduced the Board of Agriculture's influence on ministry procedures. A number of regional commissioners and local Food Control Committees were founded, staffed by farmers, traders and local unions; a Consumers' Council was established to voice the concerns of customers and the 'organized working class' through representatives appointed by the trade unions and the Co-operative movement.[70] Henceforth, wartime food policy would develop along two lines: food

Figure 7.1 Lord Rhondda helping out in a National Kitchen, March 1918, shortly
 before his death

production, through greater regulation of agriculture; and food supply by
statutory controls on retailing, pricing and distribution.

The question of food production began (and ended) at home. Allotment-
holding expanded greatly during the war, from 570,000 in 1914 to over 1.4
million by the summer of 1918.[71] Common and unused private land was dug
up for vegetable cultivation. The King had the Buckingham Palace gardens
turned over to horticulture. Nevertheless, the brunt of the new policy was to
be shouldered by the agriculturalists. Amid political calls for greater regulation and centralized co-ordination, Rowland Prothero (later Lord Ernle), the
new President of the Board of Agriculture, announced in December 1917 a
campaign (borrowing heavily from the Milner report) to inject new vigour
into farming which was quickly dubbed the 'plough policy'. One side of the
policy – compulsion – was already in operation. Under Regulation 2L of the
Defence of the Realm Act authorities could demand right of access to unoccupied land. This was reinforced by Regulation 2M which gave them power
to inspect land, enforce cultivation orders and requisition a farm if the tenant
or owner was unwilling to co-operate. The new administrative structure was
overseen by a new Food Production Department (FPD) at the Board of
Agriculture led by T.H. Middleton. The policy was sweetened by a system of
price guarantees for farmers, on condition that they accept the right of the
state to enforce cultivation of dormant or uneconomic land, with a new

minimum weekly wage of 25 shillings (£1.25) for farm workers and rent controls on tenanted cottages. The new order formed the backbone of the Corn Production Act passed by Parliament in August 1917.[72]

The FPD was not intended to be a farming dictator. It would rely mainly on devolving its powers by reforming Selborne's County War Agricultural Committees into a beehive of County War Executive Committees. Staffed by four to seven people, predominantly farmers, land owners and their agents (in Scotland the duties were mostly allocated to government employees), the Committees were empowered to enter and survey land, ignore any restrictive covenants on husbandry placed by landowners, issue instructions for the type of crops to be grown and devise schemes for the cultivation of dormant land. Their methods relied heavily on local persuasion: a friendly 'word in the ear', an appeal to patriotic duty, or making offers that could not be refused. Recalcitrant occupiers who refused to 'raise their husbandry standards', faced eviction, forcible requisitioning of the land by the Committee, fines or even imprisonment.[73] Some farmers complained that the policy was being run by 'plough maniacs', ordering tilling on land that was suitable only for grazing, inviting unwelcome pests.[74]

But with the stick came carrots. The FPD worked hard to overcome a shortage of fertilizers caused by the loss of German imports. Working with the Ministry of Munitions, the FPD produced a suitable replacement, sulphate of ammonia, which was offered to farmers at a reduced price of £16 a ton. It had tripled in usage by 1918. Farmers were even offered favourable credit facilities by commercial banks to help buy extra fertilizers and equipment.[75] A more visible advance was seen in the push for greater mechanization. In December 1916, Prothero managed to squeeze a £442,000 grant from the Treasury, specifically for buying new machinery, much of which would be allocated to the County Committees and hired to farmers on generous terms.[76] Mechanization was not unknown in British agriculture. At one level it was found that small, simple changes in technique could generate considerable improvement. Using three horses and two furrows in a plough team, for example, could double the acreage turned over by one man in one day.[77]

Table 7.1 Agricultural production in the United Kingdom, 1914–1918 ('000 tonnes unless otherwise stated)

Year	Cereals (wheat, barley & oats)	Root crops (potatoes, turnips & swedes)	Legumes (peas & beans, – 'ooo qrs)	Dairy (milk, mn gallons)	Livestock (cattle, pigs & sheep)
1914	5,106	23,793	1,486	1,243	14,721
1915	5,115	23,170	1,219	1,175	14,839
1916	4,769	21918	1150	1,104	15,068
1917	5,103	24,668	743	1,026	14,646
1918	6,992	22,892	1,361	915	13,374

Adapted from: Peter Dewey, *British Agriculture in the First World War*, London: Routledge, 1989, p. 244; William Beveridge, *British Food Control*, London: Humphrey Milford, 1928, pp. 360–1

And the introduction of new automated threshing and reaping machines, and petrol-engine cultivators, fuelled improving production levels. Moreover, steam ploughing, a technique that could break up even the toughest grasslands, was still in widespread use throughout the war.[78]

Much of the new agricultural machinery was American-built. Imports totalled £3.56 million in 1917, rising to £5.69 million by 1918. However, the most visible sign of farm mechanization was the tractor. Out of the Treasury grant £350,000 was allocated to the purchase of imported American tractors in 1917. Models with ostentatious names such as the Titan, the Mogul and the more prosaic Caterpillar tractors were already operating on some farms by 1915. But the market was overturned in 1917 by the introduction of the Ford Motor Company's Fordson tractor. Small, lightweight and cheap (it cost US $795 compared to the average price of $2,000), mass-produced Fordsons were the Model T's of the farmyard. The FPD placed an order for 6,000 to be built under licence in Britain, but squabbles with the Ministry of Munitions over production space meant that the majority of Fordsons had to be imported, and there were many delays before supplies eventually arrived in the spring of 1918, too late for the 1917–18 ploughing season. Tractors had their drawbacks. Some struggled on the sloping fields and different soil conditions in Britain, and many could be used only for light work, such as turning over stubble or harvesting on the larger flat fields.[79] Nevertheless, the introduction of Fordsons brought a quiet revolution into the countryside. In his memoirs, Harry Reffold, a farmhand working in the East Yorkshire Wolds, remembered the Fordson's steel wheels, their small size and manoeuvrability, lamenting:

> when I think of the reception given to the innovation of the first of the threshing machines, all of which had caused near riots, the advent of the tractor, which was to cause the loss of thousands of jobs and alter the whole of farming life and methods for ever, caused barely a ripple.[80]

Farmers, meanwhile, could take comfort from the Corn Production Act's system of price guarantees. The intention of course was to keep farmers cultivating the important foodstuffs (principally wheat and oats) with the assurance that their produce would still be bought at a price underwritten by the government, even during periods of falling values. Wheat prices were set at 60 shillings (£3) per quarter in 1917; 55 shillings (£2.75) for 1918 and 1919; and 45 shillings (£2.25) from 1920 onwards. Oat prices were fixed at 38s 6d (approximately £1.93) per quarter in 1917; 32 shillings (£1.60) in 1918 and 1919; and 24 shillings (£1.20) from 1920 onwards.[81] The effect was to boost farmers' incomes (which had been on an upward trajectory since the start of the war) even further. Relentless demand, rising prices, a liberal tax regime and freedom to raise crops and livestock that offered the best returns saw farm incomes rise sharply. Peter Dewey estimated that the farmers' share of national agricultural incomes rose from about two-fifths before the war to almost two-thirds in 1917–18.[82] Gross profits per acre increased by 477.1 per cent in 1915–16; and by 445.7 per cent in 1916–17.[83] Profits were pegged back in the last year of the war. Ministry regulations, the rising costs of fertilizer, seed and machinery, and the imposition of direct taxation in 1918 all combined to temper growing fortunes. But farmers rode their luck. Dubbed 'the real kings of profit-making' by one historian, farmers were seen as 'Britain's saviours' and escaped the national vitriol poured on industrial and commercial profiteers.[84] Instead, farmers revelled in prosperity. In 1932, A.G. Street wrote of these years:

> I was as bad, or as daft or, possibly more truthfully, as criminally extravagant as any one. I kept two hunters, one for myself and one for my wife; and glorious days we had together with the local pack … . We went to tennis parties nearly every fine afternoon in the summer, and, in our turn, entertained up to as many as twenty guests on our own tennis-court, and usually supper afterwards … . In short, farmers swanked.[85]

Everything, however, depended on labour. Indigenous agricultural labourers, though theoretically protected from army recruitment, were a workforce in limbo.[86] In spite of the presence of a new government agency, the Agricultural Wages Board (set up to monitor workers' incomes and enforce minimum wage levels), the fortunes of agricultural labourers constantly lagged behind their industrial counterparts. Farm wages had increased by 56–61 per cent on 1914 rates, but when average family spending on food had grown by 86 per cent by the spring of 1918, any sense of improvement was highly relative, and farm workers were denied the opportunities to supplement their incomes through overtime and bonuses as their labouring hours were ruled by rural customs and seasonal work.[87] But, with virtual full employment in agriculture, many farm workers' growing sense of power and self-worth was reflected in the growth of agricultural trade unionism. Fifty per cent of labourers were union members in 1918. Membership of the National Agricultural Labourers' Union increased from 9,000 in 1914 to 170,000 by the Armistice; the agricultural branch of the Workers' Union had grown to 100,000 members in the same period. County Wage Boards, established to set local wage rates under the Corn Production legislation, now included farm workers' representatives, and unions took over responsibility for wage bargaining.[88] This did not protect farm labourers from the call-up and occasional 'recruitment shock'. Approximately 300,000 farmworkers in England and Wales were lost to the Army during the war, with 30,000 men conscripted for the Passchendaele campaign in June 1917 and the desperate 'comb out' in May 1918 to resist the German offensive in France. All the same, the perennial difficulty with agricultural labourers was their scarcity. Tons of agricultural supplies and government-owned machinery, along with thousands of horses, stood idle at local depots for want of farm workers.[89]

In such circumstances it is hardly surprising that the search for extra farm hands took over from where it left off in 1916. In January 1917 the War Office volunteered the services of 11,500 soldiers considered unsuitable for overseas duties. Brought together as Army Agricultural Companies, the first priority of this soldier-labour was to help with the spring planting and autumn harvesting seasons, yet the initiative was slow to take effect. Just 9,800 had been assigned at the end of June, and these had to be supplemented by 12,500 Home Defence Force troops and the recall of 18,000 ploughmen from the front in the spring. By the beginning of July, they had been replaced by a further contingent of 17,000 soldiers, and the numbers of infantrymen on farms grew significantly thereafter. Some 63,000 soldiers were working in agriculture by March 1918, and the numbers had peaked at the time of the Armistice to 79,000.[90] Military men on farms created unexpected tensions. East Riding farmers grumbled over the qualities of southerners employed on their land. Growers in Herefordshire found that their workforce now consisted of lift attendants, ship's painters, brass polishers, chocolate makers and a ladies' tailor.[91] Local enmities were heightened further by the influx of prisoners of war. Farmers took on prisoner-labourers because they were cheap, and in the case of Saxons, Schleswig-Holsteiners and Poles, possessed vital agricultural skills. Prussians, however, were seen as 'brutal, unkind and uncouth'.[92] Although the Board of Agriculture gave the practice its official blessing in 1916, it was not until the spring of 1917 that the numbers of prisoner-farm workers began to expand. Localized hostilities and fears of possible escape attempts led many County Committees to allow prisoner employment predominantly in 'gangs' monitored by guards, performing specific tasks such as potato harvesting, timber felling and drainage work.[93] However, by the spring of 1918, as local antagonisms subsided, villagers in some districts could be found offering extra food to supplement the prisoners' meagre rations of 4 ounces of broken biscuits, a piece of bread and 1 ounce of cheese.[94] By the end of hostilities the prisoner workforce stood at 30,000.[95]

The search for labour inevitably encompassed women. Traditional rural prejudices were overridden as the Board of Agriculture sought to recruit a new female workforce. One source drew heavily on the traditional supply of village women. In 1916 the Board encouraged local Women War Agricultural Committees to step up recruitment drives in rural districts, followed by a more organized campaign co-ordinated by the Women's Branch of the Board of Agriculture in January 1917. In the villages, women signed up more from the need to compensate for the deep bites that wartime inflation had taken into the value of their separation allowances than duty and patriotism, and family commitments ensured that part-time workers were more abundant than full-timers. Estimates of the total numbers of female labourers varied from the Board's figure of 230,000, to the War Cabinet's 300,000, and the FPD's figure of 180,000.[96] Village women were employed mainly on familiar routine farm tasks, but in a number of districts their work was expanded to take on cultivating waste land and allotments, even to the point of taking over derelict farms and turning them into working enterprises.[97] The one enduring aspect of village women's work was the founding of the Women's

Institute movement in 1915. Founded originally in Anglesey during September 1915, and taking a lead from a similar organization formed in Canada during the 1890s, Women's Institutes were primarily concerned with food conservation and production, notably preserving fruit and vegetables and jam making, and encouraging garden cultivation. Forty such institutes had been established by 1917, each providing a secular forum for village women to confer on common interests and problems within an apolitical atmosphere. Their success was exploited and encouraged by the Women's Branch of the Board of Agriculture, who actively nurtured the movement throughout the war. Indeed the institutes were one of the few women's wartime associations that would survive and prosper after 1918.[98]

Whatever the contribution of village women, the Board was anxious to attract their middle-class 'educated' counterparts into farm work. Initial attitudes held that middle-class girls should be deployed in supervisory occupations, mainly in dairies and gardens, and possibly lecturing. This was certainly the ambit of voluntary organizations such as Lady Londonderry's Women's Legion and Mrs Dawson Scott's Women's Defence Relief Corps, which were formed to train new recruits and dispatch them to needy farmers. But they were not deemed a success. The Women's Defence Relief Corps placed fewer than 500 women workers, mainly on light farming tasks such as hop and fruit picking in 1916–17, and was constantly beset by funding problems and complaints of poor pay and working conditions.[99] In January 1916 the Board attempted to revive the campaign by financing the training schemes organized by the Women's Farm and Garden Union, whilst at the same time bringing the organization into union with a little-known movement from Essex, the Women's National Land Service Corps, organized by Mrs Rowland Williams. The objective was to exhort middle-class women into working to preserve the national food supply and instil a change of attitude towards women's agricultural work in sceptical farmers. In spite of its initial success – 2,000 women were recruited, trained and sent out to farms in the first year of operation – the Union's achievements were less than its expectations, and in March 1917 the Board decided to reorganize the enlistment of female labour by forming the Women's Land Army (see Chapter 5 text box, Land Army).[100]

Government controls, price guarantees, subsidized wages, controlled rents and soaring profits: was this a brave new world for British agriculture? When the lamps were lit again in 1918 the rural world was conspicuously more prosperous for some, and farmers were seduced into thinking that their industry had entered a new 'golden age', before the subsidy axe fell in the 1920s.[101] But success was relative. On its own terms, the plough policy fell short. The cultivated area of Britain had increased by 12.36 million acres by 1918, an average rise of 18 per cent on pre-war levels, but the programme progressed only two-thirds towards the government targets set in 1917 (three-quarters, for Scotland). Supplies of meat and milk also declined as the government's policy of emphasizing cereals over meat production took hold. Moreover, the total amount of land in agricultural use in Britain, at

Figure 7.2 Hard work on the farm for a Land Army girl

31.75 million acres, had declined from the pre-war total of 32.06 million acres. Then again, the production of wheat, oats and potatoes reached a peak in 1918, averaging about 40 per cent above 1904–13 levels, and increases in calorific values of foodstuffs of around 24 per cent helped to keep the threat of national starvation at bay.[102]

Dragged into rationing

None of this mattered unless the government regulated both the consumption and distribution of the country's food. It is easy, in retrospect, to assume that the onset of rationing was the culmination of a series of carefully planned steps, each designed as part of an agreed objective. But this would simply flatter to deceive. Instead, ministers were dragged into rationing by a combination of fear about the administrative leviathan needed to operate a centralized food distribution system, and dread of the British public's reaction to food controls.[103] Elements of food control were thus introduced as dictated by circumstances: when the perceived risks of introducing regulation were outweighed by the perils of inaction. One critical element was shipping. After the chaos caused by naval and military requisitioning, submarine warfare and an industry left free to put its profits over patriotism, improvements came in December 1916 with the appointment of Joseph Maclay as head of a new Ministry of Shipping. Maclay promptly extended the government's requisitioning powers to all British merchant vessels, at fixed prices, and with strict rules on allocating cargo space. Considerable efforts were also made to expand the construction rates of new ships and the purchasing and import of replacement vessels for those sunk by U-boats. Over 1,300,000 tons of new shipping was launched in 1917, doubling the totals of the previous year. Maclay ordered greater co-ordination between docks and railways across the country in the interests of rationalizing the use of dockyard labour. In February 1917, Maclay established a Tonnage Priority Committee, comprising representatives of the importing industries, with a brief to prioritize space for commodities on vessels in accordance with their importance to the war effort (carrying wheat as milled flour was the one shining example).[104]

Just as essential was Rhondda's decision to subsidize bread prices. In the spring of 1917, with the U-boat campaign at its height, wheat shortages pushed up the cost of a 4lb loaf from 10d to 1 shilling. Bread was commonly regarded as an indispensable food. Surveys revealed that working-class families consumed 4–10 lbs daily. And this was a difficult time. Food shortages and lengthening queues, along with civil unrest and industrial troubles, combined to create an atmosphere of crisis. Three million working days were lost in the second half of 1917; 50,000 Lanarkshire miners walked out in protest against high food prices. News of the food crisis even began to affect troop morale in France.[105] And, as the *Daily Herald* commented, was it not true that 'almost all revolutions start because people wait in crowds for food?'[106] In the event, Rhondda gained Cabinet approval in September 1917 to reduce the cost of a 1-shilling loaf (5p) to 9d (4p), extending the subsidies to milled flour to retain profitability in the milling industry.[107] This accompanied the extra powers granted to Rhondda under DORA to introduce a state takeover of food imports and domestic products, together with ministerial control of every stage of food distribution from market, to wholesaler, to corner shop, and 'a ladder of prices' set for cereals, meat, sugar, cheese, margarine, condensed milk and imported bacon. Eventually, 90 per cent of all food consumed throughout the country was affected by price fixing in a system that Beveridge summarized as 'the more important the food, the more complete … [was] the control'.[108] However, bread subsidies only made the case for rationing more compelling. Circumstances would eventually force the War Cabinet's hand. Yet the ministry still regarded food controls as a leap in the dark.

The government's next step towards rationing bordered on the chaotic. In 1916, uncertainty over supplies compelled the Sugar Commission to introduce trade rationing, where quotas were allocated to wholesalers and retailers based upon pre-war sales. This 'datum' system was far from efficient. Population movements due to war work had given rise to a great deal of injustice. Some traders received sugar supplies out of all proportion to their customer numbers, while those who traded in the new armaments centres received very few supplies. Some retailers, without any guidance on how sugar rations were to be allocated to customers, adopted a method whereby amounts of sugar were sold in direct proportion to customers' overall purchases, which invariably benefited wealthier patrons at the expense of the poor.[109] The ministry's second scheme, agreed in the spring of 1917, required entire families to register with a local retailer, who in turn would draw supplies from a central wholesaler who then informed the Sugar Commission, so that provisions were then allocated in line with existing stocks and density of population. The administrative apparatus for this scheme was in place when Rhondda decided to change the plan in September, moving the emphasis of registration from families to individuals. The switch prompted a national tearing up of old forms and much confusion over the completion of new documents. Many families were unaware of the need to reapply, and those who did struggled with the arcane rubric of the new forms. Consequently, thousands sent forms to the ministry using the fictitious information given in the explanatory leaflet; thousands more were left without rations when the new scheme was finally introduced, including the Prime Minister. Rhondda's officials were hopelessly unprepared for the planned launch of sugar rationing on 1st January 1918, and the system was abandoned by the spring of that year.[110]

The final prod into rationing came not from the ministry, but from local initiatives. Frustrated at waiting for a ministry scheme, some local authorities began to introduce their own municipal schemes. Gravesend began rationing sugar in November 1917, swiftly followed by rationing of butter, tea and margarine in December, and of meat in January 1918. Birmingham followed suit. Although these local plans differed in detail – Gravesend issued cards to individuals; Birmingham issued them to households – both schemes required customer registration with one retailer. Left alone, there was a good chance that the country would have been covered by such *ad hoc* municipal schemes, making any state system look superfluous.[111] All the same, in December 1917, Rhondda decided to use the local authority apparatus to implement a Food Control Committees (Local Distribution) Order. Local councils were granted powers to impose food controls in their areas, with the requirement that they first received ministerial approval, and that their weekly food allowances did not exceed the maximum limits laid down by the Food Controller. On 30th January 1918 the War Cabinet finally approved the Order for national compulsory rationing based on a 'scale of rations' covering bread and flour, fats (butter, margarine and lard) and sugar, as recommended by Beveridge's committee.[112] Bread rationing, in the event, was never enforced, but butter and margarine were limited to a weekly allowance of 4 ounces, and lard, of 2 ounces. Meat rationing, introduced in February, was allocated on the basis of monetary value rather than weight, and worked out to around one pound of meat weekly; bacon was rationed to between 4 and 8 ounces. Those employed on heavy industrial work, however, received supplementary rations of bacon, whilst others received extra meat in relation to wholesale supplies. Children aged under six were allowed 50 per cent of the adult allocations. All customers were required to register with a retailer and offer the appropriate ration card when making a purchase, while the shopkeeper was legally obliged to produce the counterfoils as proof of the amounts sold. Restaurant-goers had to submit their coupons upon ordering.[113] This way, both supply and distribution were effectively controlled, benefiting both purchaser and retailer. Ration cards had been issued for all meats in February 1918, and ration books for all foods in short supply were distributed in July.[114] The scheme was both successful and universally popular. Food queues disappeared and, while people did not take to dancing in the streets, housewives could at least count on being able to obtain their prescribed rations at any time during opening hours. Ultimately, rationing drew its strength from playing on the British sense of fair play. Food coupons were honoured like bank notes, according to Beveridge.[115] Public hunger was abated and the government had been saved from itself. All that remained was to win the war.

In the short run, Britain's food policy was broadly successful. Home-grown supplies in 1918 rose 47 per cent on pre-war levels, and there was little evidence that the nation as a whole was underfed during the conflict. Dewey reports that, though the average daily calorie intake for individuals fell from 3,418 in 1916 to 3,358 in 1918, this did not affect vitamin intake. Indeed, some evidence suggests that the physical health of Britons improved during the war, whilst rationing helped to improve the health of poorer families whose earnings before 1914 were insufficient to obtain an adequate diet.[116] What was remembered, however, were the imposed changes to British eating habits. Consumption of butter, fresh meat and sugar fell by around 40 per cent; milk consumption decreased by around 25 per cent. The national ingestion of bread, potatoes, lard, margarine and ham rose appreciably as part of government policy to lessen the national addiction to imports. In the final reckoning, as Hardach tells us, in spite of all the muddle, complacency, fear and incompetence, Britain's wartime governments managed to keep the country fed thanks to a policy of keeping enough shipping space for food imports, belatedly introducing a rationing system that was patently fair and successfully mobilizing the agricultural industry through the pull of patriotism and the push of subsidy.[117] Against this background shone the stoicism of a British public who, in spite of the queuing, the occasional riot and the petty regulations over food waste (leaving a loaf of bread on a kitchen shelf when moving house became a prosecutable offence for example), were prepared to tolerate hardships with, in the words of the official history, 'exemplary goodwill'.[118] Perhaps this was just as well. In little over 20 years hence they would be asked to make similar sacrifices when the stakes for national survival were much higher.

Drink

During the First World War it soon became obvious to the government that, prominent amongst its many concerns, was a need to constrain and regulate the country's drinking habits. 'War means whisky' pronounced an Oxford don in 1914; 'more war means more whisky', he stated a year later. It was said that the average worker drank a pint of beer at breakfast, one at lunch, another in the afternoon and one more immediately after work. Investigations into the shipyard disturbances on Clydeside in 1915 discovered that one street in the district contained no fewer than 30 pubs within a half-mile radius; the yards and works were surrounded by bars and drinking places where 'every possible facility is offered for obtaining drink for consumption both on and off the premises'. The drinking customs of Clyde workers were characterized by the imbibing of a gill of whisky followed by a 'chaser', a schooner of beer (around one-third of a pint). English workers drank likewise, although their preference was for 'ale' rather than the darker 'heavy' beers drunk by the Glaswegians. All, however, shared a taste for heavy drinking, particularly after days filled with hard manual labour. Meanwhile, their hard-pressed housewives took solace in a drop of 'mothers ruin' – gin. The prominence of the Temperance movement across England, Wales and parts of Scotland perhaps belies the image of wartime Britain as a drink-sodden society. But the question was compelling enough to legitimize strong and occasionally punitive government action between 1914 and 1918. The demands of war barked loudly for intervention.

Drink was one of those 'damned if we do; damned if we don't' issues that struck at the heart of British society. Fears of social unrest resulting from constraining national drinking practices subsided amongst worries that the extra wages earned in the war industries would find their way across the bar, resulting in increasing drunkenness and violence, indiscipline across the armed forces and reduced productivity. While Kitchener implored the public to refrain from buying drinks for soldiers in pubs, the armed forces' chiefs were empowered under the Defence of the Realm Act in 1914 to restrict (or close, in the case of an emergency) pub opening hours in naval and military areas and prohibit the carrying of liquor in dockyards.

This was followed by the passing of the Intoxicating Liquor (Temporary Restriction) Act, passed at the end of August 1914 giving Justices of the Peace powers (on the advice of the police) to limit opening hours of drinking places in their respective localities. In all, 427 out of the 1,000 licensing districts in England and Wales found themselves subject to such restrictive orders in the space of six months. Lloyd George led the drive towards national sobriety by claiming during a speech at Bangor, North Wales, in February 1915 that drunkenness among workers was impairing their strength and efficiency. A month later, at a meeting of shipyard employers, he went further, stating famously that the country was fighting 'Germany, Austria and Drink; and as far as I can see the greatest of these deadly foes is Drink'. Even the King publicly 'took the pledge' to abstain from alcohol on 11th April 1915 and was disappointed that other public figures (including Lloyd George) failed to follow suit.

In May 1917, Parliament approved the establishment of the Central Control Board (Liquor Traffic) with powers to control the sale and consumption of alcohol in any area where excessive drinking was deemed to be impeding the war effort. The Board's powers grew in strength as the war progressed. Its first action was to place seaports under its control. The Sussex port of Newhaven was the first, in June 1916, followed by Southampton, Liverpool and Bristol in August. Industrial centres across the Midlands, Yorkshire and the London region soon followed. By 1917, 93 per cent of people in Britain were subject to the Board's liquor controls. The Board's influence took many forms. Initially the emphasis was on regulating opening hours of pubs and bars – limiting drinking times to two hours at lunchtime and two to three in the evening. Where pubs previously opened daily for around 18 hours, no sales could now take place before 12.30 p.m. or between 2.30 p.m. and 6 p.m. Sunday opening times in England were restricted to five hours from the previous seven. In Wales and Scotland the laws prohibiting pubs to open 'on the Sabbath' were upheld. The sale of liquor to be consumed 'off the premises' (through 'off-licences' as they became known) was restricted to just two-and-a-half hours during the week, with enforced weekend closing. The drinker's pain was worsened when the Board outlawed the buying of drinks for servicemen and the working-class custom of buying 'rounds' of drinks for friends; prohibited the canvassing of liquor orders; banned the granting of credit facilities for drink (putting drinks 'on the slate'); and pre-vented landlords from enacting the 'long pull', that is, over-measuring their beer so as to draw trade into their house. Spirits sold in bottles of less than one quart were banned, making consumption less rapid and their transport more difficult.

More controversially, the Board initiated the state take-over of all licensed premises and the liquor trade, and imposed strict controls in areas regarded to be of 'supreme importance to the national war effort'. Nationalization of the pubs in this manner moved slowly at first. The Board's initial actions were to buy a group of pubs, bars and off-licences around the Royal Small Arms Factory at Enfield, North London, in 1916. The Board then went on to adopt similar measures around the base of the Grand Fleet at Cromarty Firth in Scotland (which later became a base for American forces). The largest state purchase was at Gretna on the Scottish border, where the enormous government explosives factory (eventually drawing in a wartime population of 140,000 people) had sparked concerns amongst local authorities and factory managers over increasing drunkenness, absenteeism and 'broken time' amongst its workers. Pubs immediately adjacent to the National Factory were the first to be 'acquired'. Continuing anxieties pulled the Board into purchasing premises across the towns of Annan and Gretna in Dumfriesshire, the city of Carlisle and the town of Maryport in Cumberland (it was not until the 1970s that Carlisle's pubs were finally restored into private hands). Here, the state came to own five local breweries (three of which were subsequently closed) and 342 bars and pubs, whilst also imposing a severe reduction in off-licences. Further regulations prohibited the sale of spirits on Saturdays and all liquor advertising outside licensed premises; enforced closing of all pubs on Sundays, north and south of the border, came later. Even so, state takeover of local pubs did bring improved pay and working conditions for pub employees, who were no longer reliant upon drink sales for their wages. The Board also encouraged the sale of food and soft drinks in pubs, with commission rates being paid to managers. Licensed restaurants with recreational facilities were also established alongside 'tea-rooms' at country inns. The pub, at least in the Solway area, was being dragged away from its Victorian 'drinking den' reputation.

The Board saw itself as doing the country a huge favour. The War Cabinet reported in 1918 that weekly convictions for drunkenness in England and Wales, which had averaged 3,388 in 1914, had fallen to 449 by 1918. In Scotland weekly averages declined from 1,485 in October 1915 to 355 three years later. Incidences of drunkenness in women decreased from 40,815 in 1914 to 20,206 in 1916. The *Brewers Gazette* noted that, as a result of the early closure of pubs, areas like the Elephant and Castle, south London, where immense crowds would lounge about until 1 a.m., 'have suddenly become peaceful and respectable'. In other ways the Board saw itself as an agency of social reform. Teams of physiologists, psychologists and pharmacologists were instructed by the Board to conduct experiments on the effects of alcohol on the human body, producing in 1918 a pamphlet, 'Alcohol: Its Action on the Human Organism', which was still regarded as an authority on the issue in the 1930s. Another innovation was the Board's venture into the establishment of industrial canteens in munition factories. Its Canteen Committee under Sir George Newman encouraged employers to provide places away from pubs where cheap and nutritious meals could be purchased and 'at a reasonable price under good conditions', offsetting the costs against tax. Between 800 and 900 canteens were provided by 1918, 95 per cent of which were 'dry'; the rest had beer available if served with a meal.

What regular drinkers thought of the Board's activities was another matter. They experienced a sharp rise in the price of alcohol after 1915, thanks largely to punitive taxation. A pint of beer increased from 3d to 10d between 1916 and 1918. Spirits became luxury items as duty was raised from 3d a glass in 1914 to nearly five times that figure by 1920. Perhaps the final insult was the reduction of the alcoholic content in spirits and ale. The potency of spirits was pegged at 70 per cent proof (today it is just 40–45 per cent), and beer drinkers would talk of 'government ale' or 'Lloyd George's beer'. 'Dip your bread in it, shove your head in it, from January to October, And I bet you a penny you will still be sober'.

References

Henry Carter, *The Control of the Drink Trade: A Contribution to National Efficiency 1915–17*, London: Longmans Green, 1918.
Gerard DeGroot, *Blighty; British Society in the Era of the Great War*, Harlow: Longman, 1996, pp. 237–38.

Arthur Marwick, *The Deluge: British Society and the First World War*, 2nd edn, Basingstoke: Macmillan, 1992, pp. 102–08.

NA, CAB 24/31, GT 2600, 'Control and Purchase of the Liquor Trade', 13th November 1917.

Michael E. Rose, 'The Success of Social Reform? The Central Control Board (Liquor Traffic) 1915–21', in M.R.D. Foot, *War and Society: Historical Essays in Honour and Memory of J.R. Western 1928–71*, London: Paul Elek, 1973, pp. 71–84.

Arthur Shadwell, *Drink in 1914–22: A Lesson in Control*, London: Longmans, 1923.

The Times, 30th March 1915.

National Kitchens

Between 1917 and 1918 hungry Britons seeking a cheap but nutritious meal could occasionally find succour in a National Kitchen (also known as National Restaurants) where cost-priced, subsidized food could be bought either as a ready-cooked take-away snack or served to the plate through a canteen/cafeteria-style service. As one of Lord Rhondda's more eager initiatives, National Kitchens sprang from the Food Controller's rising irritation at the public's refusal to budge from its favoured 'meat and two veg' diet and embrace more exotic (and readily available) foods such as rice, cornmeal, dried beans and tinned fish. The idea was not new. Communal kitchens, run mostly by voluntary organizations (such as the Salvation Army), had been operative since 1914, offering culinary solace to the 'respectable poor' caught by rising food prices. Rhondda moved the concept a step further by emphasizing National Kitchens as a way of raising the British public's gastronomic horizons as well as offering value for money. Ministry of Food specialists reckoned that, if the restaurants proved popular, a 10–25 per cent saving on normal food consumption was possible. Nourishing food would be served in hygienic surroundings; economies could be secured in soap, towels, utensils and crockery; housewives would be freed from the daily grind of domestic cooking (presumably to take up work in the war industries); and restaurant and retailing staff would be released for service in the armed services. The waste of a 'thousand homes and a thousand gas and coal fires' could be averted, Lord Rhondda proclaimed, and the halleluja chorus of opportunity was completed by his promise to deliver the provision and management of National Kitchens into the hands of local authorities across Britain where municipal experts and businessmen would run them as commercial enterprises, supported by Treasury grants. The ambition was to promote National Kitchens as a shared war experience, where folk of all classes would eat together in anticipation of the new post-war mass democracy. It was even suggested that National Travelling Kitchens could be initiated, where tramcars and buses could be equipped with heating appliances to bring hot food to the city street and rural byway. Typical

National Kitchen fare included soup, fish rolls, cold roast beef, shepherds pie, fig pudding, stewed apples and custard, and suet pudding. The first establishment opened to a great fanfare on 21st May 1917, and Queen Mary herself took a hand in serving the meals. Sadly, Rhondda's high hopes for National Kitchens floundered on the rock of public indifference. Whatever the quality of the food, however clean and comfortable the atmosphere, National Restaurants could not escape their soup kitchen origins with all the connotations of poverty, destitution and lack of respectability. Hence the working classes shunned them; the wealthy viewed them as the embodiment of their distaste for social levelling, communism and a rejection of the actualities of class, rank and money. Egalitarian eating was not something that appealed to many British people during the war. It seems that the prospect of dining alongside the 'great unwashed' represented a step too far along the dubious road of equality.

References

L. Margaret Barnett, *British Food Policy During the First World War*, London: Allen & Unwin, 1985, p. 151.

The Times, 22nd May 1917, 5th February 1918, 23rd February 1918, 27th March 1918, 15th May 1918.

Notes

1 *War Memoirs of David Lloyd George*, vol. III, London: Nicholson & Watson, 1934, p. 1269.
2 Gerd Hardach, *The First World War*, London: Allen Lane, 1977, p. 109.
3 T.H. Middleton, *Food Production in War*, Oxford: Clarendon Press, 1923, p. 87; Sir William Beveridge, *British Food Control*, London: Humphrey Milford, 1928, p. 359; Jose Harris, 'Bureaucrats and Businessmen in British Food Control, 1916–19', in Kathleen Burk, ed., *War and the State: The Transformation of British Government, 1914–1919*, London: Allen & Unwin, 1982, pp. 135–36; L. Margaret Barnett, *British Food Policy During the First World War*, London: Allen & Unwin, 1985, pp. 2–3; Peter Dewey, *British Agriculture in the First World War*, London: Routledge, 1989, p. 17.
4 L. Margaret Barnett, *British Food Policy*, op. cit., p. 3; Alun Howkins, *The Death of Rural England: A Social History of the Countryside since 1900*, London: Routledge, 2003, p. 9. See also Pamela Horn, *Rural Life in England in the First World War*, Dublin: Gill & Macmillan, 1984, pp. 1–2, and Appendix 2, pp. 240–41; T.W. Fletcher, 'The Great Depression in English Agriculture 1873–96', *Economic History Review*, 2nd series, vol. 13, no. 3, 1961, pp. 417–32.
5 L. Margaret Barnett, *British Food Policy*, op. cit., p. 4.
6 Alun Howkins, *The Death of Rural England*, op. cit., pp. 7–8; Peter Dewey, *British Agriculture in the First Word War*, op. cit., pp. 7–9.
7 Alun Howkins, *The Death of Rural England*, op. cit., p. 11. See also Pamela Horn, *Rural Life in England in the First World War*, op. cit., p. 3; Madeleine Beard, *English Landed Society in the Twentieth Century*, London: Routledge, 1989, ch. 1;

David Cannadine, *The Decline and Fall of the British Aristocracy*, Basingstoke: Macmillan, 1992, p. 23.

8 Alun Howkins, *The Death of Rural England*, op. cit., pp. 14–20; Alun Howkins, *Reshaping Rural England: A Social History 1850–1925*, London: Routledge, 1992, ch. 9; Edith H. Whetham, *The Agrarian History of England and Wales*, vol. 8, *1914–39*, Cambridge: Cambridge University Press, 1978, pp. 1–17; Peter Dewey, *British Agriculture*, op. cit., p. 16.

9 *Royal Commission on Supply of Food and Raw Material in Time of War*, first report, Cmnd 2643, vol. I, London: HMSO, 1905, pp. 15–25, 35; NA, CAB 38/26/7, 'Report of the Standing Sub-committee of the C[ommitee of] I[mperial] D[efence] on Supplies in Time of War', 12th February 1914, op. cit., pp. 25–27; Jose Harris, 'Bureaucrats and Businessmen in British Food Control, 1916–19', op. cit., pp. 136–37.

10 T.H. Middleton, *Food Production in War*, op. cit., ch. 4; Sir William Beveridge, *British Food Control*, op. cit., pp. 7–8, 13–15; L. Margaret Barnett, *British Food Policy*, op. cit., pp. 21–23; Jose Harris, 'Bureaucrats and Businessmen in British Food Control, 1916–19', op. cit., pp. 136–37.

11 David French, *British Economic and Strategic Planning, 1905–1915*, London: Allen & Unwin, 1982, p. 102; L. Margaret Barnett, *British Food Policy*, op. cit., pp. 27–28.

12 L. Margaret Barnett, *British Food Policy*, op. cit., pp. 28–30.

13 NA, Department of Agriculture papers (hereafter 'MAF') 60/93, Control of Meat: Minutes and Memoranda on the Transfer of Organisation for the Purchase of Meat and Cheese from the BOT to the MOF'; E.M.H. Lloyd, *Experiments in State Control at the War Office and the Ministry of Food*, Oxford: Clarendon Press, 1924; L. Margaret Barnett, *British Food Policy*, op. cit., p. 33.

14 L. Margaret Barnett, *British Food Policy*, op. cit., pp. 30–31; Sir William Beveridge, *British Food Control*, op. cit., pp. 125, 121–22, Christopher Addison, *Four and a Half Years*, vol. 2, London: Hutchinson, 1934, p. 422; C.S. Peel, *How We Lived Then, 1914–1918: A Sketch of Social and Domestic Life in England During the War*, London: The Bodley Head, 1929, p. 82.

15 Gerard DeGroot, *Blighty: British Society in the Era of the Great War*, Harlow: Longman, 1996, p. 58.

16 L. Margaret Barnett, *British Food Policy*, op. cit., p. 31; Arthur Marwick, *The Deluge: British Society and the First World War*, 2nd edn, London: Macmillan, pp. 165–66, 201; Jose Harris, 'Bureaucrats and Businessmen in British Food Control, 1916–19', op. cit., pp. 136–37.

17 NA, CAB 37/131/30, 'Interim Report of the Departmental Committee on the Home Production of Food', 15th July 1915; NA, T 171/109, First Budget; Treasury Memoranda, part 1, undated; David French, *British Economic and Strategic Planning, 1905–1915*, op. cit., p. 102.

18 NA, CAB 1/11/9, 'Report by the Director of Transports, Admiralty, on the Memorandum on the Shortage of Merchant Shipping Tonnage prepared by the Board of Trade', 16th January 1915; NA, CAB 1/11/7, 'Shortage of Merchant Tonnage', 11th January 1915; David French, *British Economic and Strategic Planning, 1905–1915*, op. cit., pp. 104–05.

19 *The Times*, 11th August 1914.

20 NA, CAB 37/123/51, 'Wheat Prices', 26th January 1915; L. Margaret Barnett, *British Food Policy*, op. cit., pp. 37–38, 40.

21 L. Margaret Barnett, *British Food Policy*, op. cit., p. 40; David French, *British Economic and Strategic Planning, 1905–1915*, op. cit., p. 99.

22 E. David, ed., *Inside Asquith's Cabinet: From the Diaries of Charles Hobhouse*, London: Murray, 1977, p. 231.

23 L. Margaret Barnett, *British Food Policy*, op. cit., pp. 50–51.

24 L. Margaret Barnett, *British Food Policy*, op. cit., pp. 50–51. See also Board of Agriculture and Fisheries, *Departmental Committee on the Home Production of Food (England and Wales), Interim Report*, Cmnd 8048, London: HMSO, 1915; Peter Dewey, *British Agriculture in the First World War*, op. cit., pp. 25–26.

25 L. Margaret Barnett, *British Food Policy*, op. cit., p. 51.

26 L. Margaret Barnett, *British Food Policy*, op. cit., pp. 52–54; Peter Dewey, *British Agriculture*, op. cit., p. 26; NA, CAB 41/36/37, Asquith to the King, 5th August 1915.

27 Board of Agriculture and Fisheries, *Departmental Committee on the Home Production of Food (England and Wales), Final Report*, Cmnd 8095, London: HMSO, 1915, p. 3.

28 NA, CAB 24/2, GT.65, 'The Food Supply of the United Kingdom: Memorandum by the Earl of Selborne', 16th March 1916; NA, CAB 24/2, GT.60, 'Food Supply and Production; Memorandum by the Earl of Selborne', 2nd March 1916.

29 NA, CAB 24/2, GT.65; NA, CAB 24/2, GT. 60, op. cit.

30 NA, MAF 39/23, 'War Agricultural Committees, Formation of' (1915).

31 L. Margaret Barnett, *British Food Policy*, op. cit., p. 56.

32 Peter Dewey, *British Agriculture in the First World War*, op. cit., pp. 79–83.

33 Pamela Horn, *Rural Life in England in the First World War*, op. cit., pp. 33–34; see also IWM, Robert Saunders to William Saunders, 11th October 1914, 14th February 1915, 'Private Papers of R Saunders', 657079/15/1.

34 Pamela Horn, *Rural Life in England in the First World War*, op. cit., pp. 90–92; Peter Dewey, *British Agriculture in the First World War*, op. cit., p. 61.

35 Adrian Gregory, *The Last Great War: British Society and the First World War*, Cambridge: Cambridge University Press, 2008, pp. 82–85.

36 Pamela Horn, *Rural Life in England in the First World War*, op. cit., pp. 27–30; Peter Simkins, *Kitchener's Army: The Making of the New Armies 1914–1916*, Barnsley: Pen & Sword, 2007, p. 174; G. Slater, ed., *My Warrior Sons: The Borton Family Diary, 1914–1918*, London: Peter Davies, 1973, pp. 11–12; Alun Howkins, *The Death of Rural England*, op. cit., pp. 28–29.

37 See Keith Grieves, 'Lowther's Lambs: Rural Paternalism and Voluntary Recruitment in the First World War', *Rural History*, vol. 4, no. 1, 1993, pp. 55–75.

38 Peter Dewey, *British Agriculture in the First World War*, op. cit., p. 40; Alan Armstrong, *Farmworkers: A Social and Economic History 1770–1980*, London: B.T. Batsford, 1988, p. 159.

39 Peter Dewey, *British Agriculture in the First World War*, op. cit., p. 44.

40 Peter Dewey, *British Agriculture in the First World War*, op. cit., p. 39.

41 See NA, Ministry of Education papers (hereafter 'ED') 91/137, 'Children (Employment and School Attendance Bill) 1914'; Board of Education, *School Attendance and Employment in Agriculture: Summary of Returns Supplied by Local Authorities*, Cmnd, 7881, London: HMSO, 1914–16; Peter Dewey, *British Agriculture in the First World War*, op. cit., p. 48.

42 Pamela Horn, *Rural Life in England in the First World War*, op. cit., pp. 166–70; Pamela Horn, 'The Employment of Elementary School-children in Agriculture, 1914–18', *History of Education*, vol. 12, no. 3, 1983.

43 J.K. Montgomery, *The Maintenance of the Agricultural Labour Supply in England and Wales During the War*, Rome: International Institute of Agriculture, Bureau of Economic and Social Intelligence, 1924, pp. 22–23; Peter Dewey, *British Agriculture*, op. cit., pp. 48–49; Pamela Horn, *Rural Life in England in the First World War*, op. cit., pp. 94–95.

44 NA, Ministry of National Service papers (hereafter 'NATS') 1/215, T.M. Taylor to Major Lloyd Graeme, 1st January 1918, 'Dilution of Agricultural Labour 1918'.

45 Alun Howkins, *The Death of Rural England*, op. cit., p. 30.

46 Alun Howkins, *The Death of Rural England*, op. cit., p. 31; Peter Dewey, *British Agriculture in the First World War*, op. cit., pp. 51–53. See also NA, MAF 59/1, 'Women's County Committees: Organisation of Women's Labour', 1916.

47 NA, CAB 42/22/12, 'Food Prospects in 1917', Memorandum by Lord Crawford, 30th October 1916; L. Margaret Barnett, *British Food Policy*, op. cit., pp. 87–88; T.H. Middleton, *Food Production in War*, op. cit., p. 160; Peter Dewey, *British Agriculture*, op. cit., p. 31. See also Gerd Hardach, *The First World War*, op. cit., pp. 42–43; L. Margaret Barnett, *British Food Policy*, op. cit., p. 87.

48 L. Margaret Barnett, *British Food Policy*, op. cit., pp. 77–78.

49 *The Times*, 10th, 17th, 20th December 1917; Sir William Beveridge, *British Food Control*, op. cit., pp. 193–94.

50 C.S. Peel, *How We Lived Then*, op. cit., pp. 96–98.

51 IWM, Private papers of E.S. Bennett, 3695 96/3/1, quoted in Adrian Gregory, *The Last Great War*, op. cit., p. 215.

52 Ian F.W. Beckett, *Home Front 1914–1918: How Britain Survived the Great War*, London: National Archives, p. 116.

53 L. Margaret Barnett, *British Food Policy*, op. cit., p. 118; Trevor Wilson, *The Myriad Faces of War: Britain and the Great War, 1914–1918*, Oxford: Polity Press, 1986, pp. 513–14; NA, MAF, 60/243, 'Food Queues: Notes and Memoranda on their Prevention: Dec. 1917–Apr. 1918'.

54 See 'Weekly Bulletin', in NA, Papers of the National Savings Committee (hereafter 'NSC') 7/37, 'War Finance Campaign: Food Control Campaign, 1916–17'.

55 Trevor Wilson, *The Myriad Faces of War: Britain and the Great War, 1914–1918*, op. cit., p. 514; Richard van Emden and Steve Humphries, *All Quiet on the Home Front: An Oral History of Life in Britain During the First World War*, London: Headline, 2003, pp. 195–96.

56 House of Lords Record Office, Lloyd George papers, F/6/49, Dr Macnamara to Prime Minister, 27th November 1917.

57 *Daily Herald*, 24th November 1917; L. Margaret Barnett, *British Food Policy*, op. cit., p. 142.

58 See Peter Dewey, *British Agriculture in the First World War*, op. cit., pp. 80–81.

59 NA, Board of Trade papers (hereafter 'BT') 13/63 'Meat Supplies – Australasian Requisitioned Space – use of, 1915'; NA, Public Record Office papers (hereafter 'PRO') 30/30/4, RHR, 'Note on Meat Supplies', 14th June 1915, p. 72.

60 Richard van Emden and Steve Humphries, *All Quiet on the Home Front*, op. cit., p. 159.

61 NA, MAF 60/105, 'Home Food Supplies and Price Regulation', 1916–20; Sir William Beveridge, *British Food Control*, op. cit., pp. 162–81; L. Margaret Barnett, *British Food Policy*, op. cit., pp. 140–42; Adrian Gregory, *The Last Great War*, op. cit., p. 215.

62 Jose Harris, 'Bureaucrats and Businessmen in British Food Control, 1916–19', op. cit., p. 139; Frank H. Coller, *A State Trading Adventure: the Ministry of Food 1917–21*, London: Oxford University Press, 1924, p. 37.

63 *War Memoirs of David Lloyd George*, vol. III, op. cit., p. 1320; vol. IV, p. 1955; Viscount Kearley (Lord Devonport), *The Travelled Road: Some Memoirs of a Busy Life*, Rochester: privately published, 1935, p. 215.

64 Gerard DeGroot, *Blighty*, op. cit., p. 210.

65 L. Margaret Barnett, *British Food Policy*, op. cit., p. 115; Richard van Emden and Steve Humphries, *All Quiet on the Home Front*, op. cit., p. 194.

66 IWM, Private papers of E.F. Chapman, 1799, and 93/3/1, Letter, May 1917.

67 Gerard DeGroot, *Blighty*, op. cit., p. 89; Richard van Emden and Steve Humphries, *All Quiet on the Home Front*, op. cit., pp. 196–97.

68 NA, 7/37, 'War Finance Campaign', 'Food Control Campaign, 1916–17'; Ian F.W. Beckett, *Home Front 1914–1918*, op. cit., pp. 115–16.
69 NA, CAB 17/198, 'Lord Rhondda on Food Supply', 1918; Jose Harris, 'Bureaucrats and Businessmen in British Food Control, 1916–19', op. cit., p. 140.
70 Jose Harris, 'Bureaucrats and Businessmen in British Food Control, 1916–19', op. cit., p. 141; also discussed fully in L. Margaret Barnett, *British Food Policy*, op. cit., pp. 153–57.
71 NA, MAF 42/8, 'FPD Report for the Year', 1918.
72 See Peter Dewey, *British Agriculture in the First World War*, op. cit., pp. 92–96; Edith H. Whetham, *The Agrarian History of England and Wales*, vol. VIII, *1914–39*, op. cit., pp. 94–97.
73 Peter Dewey, *British Agriculture in the First World War*, op. cit.; NA, MAF 39/23, 'Formation of War Agricultural Committees'; West Sussex Record Office, (hereafter 'WSRO'), 'War Agricultural Committee Minutes', WOC/CM80/1/1, 19th February 1917.
74 Pamela Horn, *Rural Life in England in the First World War*, op. cit., pp. 52–53.
75 T.H. Middleton, *Food Production in War*, Oxford: Clarendon Press, 1923, pp. 228–29; Edith H. Whetham, *The Agrarian History of England and Wales*, vol. VIII, *1914–39*, op. cit., pp. 101–2.
76 L. Margaret Barnett, *British Food Policy*, op. cit., p. 199.
77 See Harry Reffold, *Pie for Breakfast: Reminiscences of a Farmhand*, Beverley: Hutton Press, 1984, p. 77.
78 L. Margaret Barnett, *British Food Policy*, op. cit., p. 200. Steam ploughing was a technique introduced in the 1850s whereby traction engines would be placed on opposite sides of a field, and would pull a plough connected to a cable back and forth across the land.
79 Peter Dewey, *British Agriculture in the First World War*, op. cit., pp. 148–60; Peter Dewey, *Iron Harvests of the Field: The Making of Farm Machinery in Britain since 1800*, Lancaster: Carnegie, 2008, pp. 175–78; Edith H. Whetham, *The Agrarian History of England and Wales*, vol. VIII, *1914–39*, op. cit., pp. 106–07.
80 Harry Reffold, *Pie for Breakfast*, op. cit., pp. 77–78.
81 Peter Dewey, *British Agriculture in the First World War*, op. cit., p. 93.
82 Peter Dewey, *British Agriculture in the First World War*, op. cit., p. 236.
83 Pamela Horn, *Rural Life in England in the First World War*, op. cit., pp. 56–57; Peter Dewey, 'British Farming Profits and Government Policy During the First World War', *Economic History Review*, New series, vol. 37, no. 3, 1984, pp. 373–90.
84 Adrian Gregory, *The Last Great War*, op. cit., p.141.
85 A.G. Street, *Farmer's Glory*, London: Faber & Faber, 1932, p. 223, in Alun Howkins, *The Death of Rural England*, op. cit., p. 37.
86 See NA, CAB 24/7, GT.174, 'Agricultural Labour', 12th March 1917.
87 Peter Dewey, *British Agriculture*, op. cit., pp. 110–11.
88 Alun Howkins, *Reshaping Rural England*, op. cit., pp. 267–69; Alun Howkins, *The Death of Rural England*, op. cit., p. 35.
89 Alan Armstrong, *Farmworkers*, op. cit., pp. 159–60; Peter Dewey, *British Agriculture in the First World War*, op. cit., p. 106; Edith H. Whetham, *The Agrarian History of England and Wales*, vol. VIII, *1914–39*, op. cit., pp. 99–101; NA, MAF 60/93, 'Committee of Imperial Defence, Food Supply in War', 1923.
90 NA, CAB 23/1 42 (6), Meeting of the War Cabinet, 23rd January 1917; NA, CAB 23/1 39 (1), Meeting of the War Cabinet, 19th January 1917, Appendix I; NA, CAB 23/3 170 (1), Meeting of the War Cabinet, 27th June 1917; NA, CAB 23/4/287 (3), Meeting of the War Cabinet, 29th November 1917; Peter Dewey, *British Agriculture*, op. cit., pp. 113–18; Pamela Horn, *Rural Life in England in the First World War*, op. cit., pp. 102–04; WSRO, 'War Agricultural Committee Minutes', WOC/CM80/1/1, Labour Sub-committee Minutes, 13th May 1918.

91 Alan Armstrong, *Farmworkers*, op. cit., pp. 161–62.
92 Pamela Horn, *Rural Life in England in the First World War*, op. cit., p. 154.
93 Alan Armstrong, *Farmworkers*, op. cit., p. 163.
94 Pamela Horn, *Rural Life in England in the First World War*, op. cit., p. 154.
95 Peter Dewey, *British Agriculture in the First World War*, op. cit., pp. 120–27; Pamela Horn, 'Prisoners on the Farm', *The Countryman*, vol. 88, no. 4, 1983; NA, NATS 1/1332, 'Prisoner of War Employment Committee'; NA, NATS 1/570, 'Prisoners of War: Rations for Prisoners Engaged in Heavy Manual Work; Policy File 1918'.
96 War Cabinet, *Report for the Year 1917*, Cmnd 9005, London: HMSO, 1918, pp. 160–61; Peter Dewey, *British Agriculture in the First World War*, op. cit., pp. 128–30; see also Peter Dewey, 'Agricultural Labour Supply in England and Wales During the First World War', *Economic History Review*, New series, vol. 28, no. 1, 1975, pp. 100–112.
97 Pamela Horn, *Rural Life in England in the First World War*, op. cit., pp. 135–36; IWM, Women's Work Collection, 'War Service for Country Women', LAND 1/25.
98 Pamela Horn, *Rural Life in England in the First World War*, op. cit., pp. 136–38; Ian Beckett, *Home Front, 1914–1918*, op. cit., p. 77.
99 IWM, Women's Work Collection, 'Report of the Women's Defence Relief Corps: 1914–16', LAND 1/24; 'The Women's Farm and Garden Union', LAND 5/1/8; NA, MAF 59/1, 'Women's County Committees: Organisation of Women's Labour'; Pamela Horn, *Rural Life in England in the First World War*, op. cit., pp. 118–19.
100 Pamela Horn, *Rural Life in England in the First World War*, op. cit., p. 122; Alan Armstrong, *Farmworkers*, op. cit., pp. 163–64; Alun Howkins, *Reshaping Rural England*, op. cit., pp. 261–65.
101 Alun Howkins, *The Death of Rural England*, op. cit., pp. 36–38; Edith H. Whetham, 'The Agriculture Act, 1920 and Its Repeal – the "Great Betrayal"', *Agricultural History Review*, vol. 22, part 1, 1974.
102 Peter Dewey, *British Agriculture in the First World War*, op. cit., pp. 211–13; P. E. Dewey, 'Food Production and Policy in the United Kingdom, 1914–18', *Transactions of the Royal Historical Society*, fifth series, vol. 30, 1980, pp. 71–89.
103 See Kevin Manton, 'Sir William Beveridge, The British Government and Plans for Food Control in Time of War, c.1916–41', *Contemporary British History*, vol. 23, no. 3, September 2009, pp. 363–85.
104 L. Margaret Barnett, *British Food Policy*, op. cit., p. 104; J.A. Salter, *Allied Shipping Control: An Experiment in International Administration*, Oxford: Clarendon 1921, pp. 81–82; NA, CAB 1/23/21, 'Merchant Shipping, 1917'; NA, CAB 1/24/3, 'Position of Shipping in 1917'; *War Memoirs of David Lloyd George*, vol. III, op. cit., pp. 1222–23, 237–47; Gerard DeGroot, *Blighty*, op. cit., pp. 87–88.
105 NA, MAF 60/243, 'The Effect of Food Queues at Home on Men at the Front', 16th April 1918.
106 *Daily Herald*, 21st February 1918; NA, CAB 24/27, 'Food Control and Labour Unrest, GT.2132, 20th September 1917; NA, CAB 24/38, 'The Labour Situation', 9th January 1918; L. Margaret Barnett, *British Food Policy*, op. cit., p. 143.
107 NA, MAF 60/3, 'Bread Subsidy', 1917.
108 Sir William Beveridge, *British Food Control*, op. cit., p. 164; L. Margaret Barnett, *British Food Policy*, op. cit., pp. 135–36.
109 Sir William Beveridge, *British Food Control*, op. cit., pp. 184–86; Gerd Hardach, *The First World War*, op. cit., p. 129.
110 NA, NSC 7/37, 'Ministry of Food: Sugar Distribution Scheme'; L. Margaret Barnett, *British Food Policy*, op. cit., pp. 137–39.
111 NA, MAF 60/243, 'The Prevention of Queues', 19th December 1917; L. Margaret Barnett, *British Food Policy*, op. cit., p. 147.

112 NA, MAF 60/108, 'Rhondda: Compulsory Rationing', 24th January 1918; NA, CAB 24/31, 'Compulsory Rationing and Distribution of Essential Foods', (Rhondda), 9th November 1917; NA, CAB 23/5 (73–74), Meeting of the War Cabinet, 30th January 1918; Sir William Beveridge, *British Food Control*, op. cit., pp. 199–200; L. Margaret Barnett, *British Food Policy*, op. cit., p. 148.

113 L. Margaret Barnett, *British Food Policy*, op. cit., p. 148; Gerard DeGroot, *Blighty*, op. cit., p.203.

114 Gerd Hardach, *The First World War*, op. cit., p. 130.

115 NA, MAF 60/243, 'The Effect of Food Queues at Home on Men at the Front', 16th April 1918; Sir William Beveridge, *British Food Control*, op. cit., p. 200.

116 Peter Dewey, 'Nutrition and Living Standards in Wartime Britain', in Richard Wall and Jay Winter, eds, *The Upheaval of War: Family, Work and Welfare in Europe, 1914–1918*, Cambridge: Cambridge University Press, 1988, pp. 206–10; Sir William Beveridge, *British Food Control*, op. cit., table XX; Working Classes Cost of Living Committee, *Report*, London: HMSO, 1918, para. 23.

117 Gerd Hardach, *The First World War*, op. cit., p. 131.

118 Sir William Beveridge, *British Food Control*, op. cit., pp. 238–39.

8 A question of propaganda

Cate Haste informs us that the term 'propaganda' originated during the ministry of Pope Gregory XV in 1622, when he founded a Congregation *de propaganda fide* to instruct trainee Catholic clerics to extend the Christian faith and gospel across the Asian and African continents.[1] The twentieth-century experience has taught modern scholars to view propaganda primarily as a political and government activity aimed at the management of public opinion. At the opening of the First World War the British government regarded propaganda as a rather distasteful activity, and preferred to leave the task of generating pro-war feelings to a variety of voluntary and religious bodies, commercial advertisers, patriotic organizations, public rumour and gossip and, of course, the press. Even when the prolonged war finally pulled the government into the propaganda business, it still attempted to hide its presence behind the facade of a cross-party organization. But the need to counter the spread of war-weariness and pacifism, and the dangers of civil and industrial unrest, dragged ministers into the hitherto unknown arena of attempting to influence the everyday activities and attitudes of its citizens. Shifting circumstances thus brought shifting imperatives. What began in 1914 as an effort to emphasize the values of duty and patriotism, defending the weak and dehumanizing the enemy, became, by the war's end, a sophisticated state machine designed to both sustain support for the war and guide people's behaviour, with government leaders treating propaganda as a new war weapon and 'truth' becoming a concept relative to wartime priorities and the national interest.[2]

'Forced upon us'

In 1914, 'propaganda' to the British government was a rather embarrassing concept alien to its liberal instincts, and early efforts rarely ventured far beyond extolling the virtues of patriotism and duty and the defence of what Asquith called 'international good faith'.[3] But ministers still had to face the uncomfortable fact that they had declared war without clearly identifying its causes or enunciating its purpose, and the German army's march into neutral Belgium was quickly grasped as an opportunity to portray Britain as a peace-loving nation stirred to action by the threat of brute force and in defence of her national honour. 'The war has been forced upon us', Asquith told the House of Commons on 27th August. It was only when we had to make a choice between 'the discharge of a binding trust' and a 'shameless subservience to naked force' that we 'threw away the scabbard'.[4] This 'defensive' theme was soon picked up on the streets, inspiring the crowds gathering around army recruitment offices and rousing some of the nation's intelligentsia into dancing around the patriotism maypole.[5] Fifty-three prominent writers, including such luminaries as Arthur Conan-Doyle, H.G. Wells, John Masefield and Arnold Bennett, put their signatures to a public statement, published in a September edition of *The Times*, declaring their support for a war in which Britain was 'compelled to take arms' to rescue Europe from the 'Blood and Iron' rule of a 'military caste'.[6] Other writers (Thomas Hardy, Henry Newbolt and Gilbert Murray amongst them) showed their patriotism by gathering in Sir Frances Younghusband's 'Fight for Right' group, which published an evangelizing manifesto claiming 'Faith in the righteousness of our Cause' and extolling 'the efforts and the sacrifices of men and women who mean to *make* it prevail'.[7]

The room for intellectual doubt was small. George Bernard Shaw made plain his doubts in a pamphlet, *Common Sense About the War*, published in November 1914. Hardy too, after flirting briefly with patriotism through his early war poetry, became more darkly pessimistic towards the conflict after Christmas 1914.[8] Elsewhere, distinguished classical scholars Gilbert Murray and Lord Wearmouth, leading figures in the pre-war pacifist movement, strove to occupy the moral high ground of neutrality, yet were driven towards accepting the war when faced with the enormity of circumstances. Murray, a member of the Neutrality Committee and author of the pamphlet *How Can War Ever Be Right?*, commented to a friend, just hours after the declaration on 4th August, that he found 'it very difficult to oppose Government action when the German government has plainly run amok'.[9] Wearmouth similarly recognized the 'Germanic ... disregard of treaties, solemn obligations or humanitarian considerations', hoping that the war would sweep away the thrones of the Hapsburgs and Hohenzollerns.[10] H.G. Wells, just beginning his long conversion to war sceptic, tried to smother his doubts by dubbing the conflict 'The War that will end War', arguing in the *Daily News* that 'We are ... fighting to release Germany and all the world from the superstition that brutality and cynicism are the methods of success.'[11] Applying an intellectual backbone to the war, six Oxford academics attempted to trace the course of German history in order to prove that country's culpability. Their views, published as the 'Oxford Pamphlets' in 1914, summarized the war 'as a struggle between two nations, one of which claims a prerogative to act outside the public law of Europe in order to secure the "safety" of its own State, while the other stands for the rule of public law'. In essence this was history mobilized as reasoned propaganda.[12]

Similar bouts of conscience-wrestling could be witnessed in the attitude of the Church towards the war. Religion mattered to many Britons in 1914. It was said that the Church 'had the ear of the nation'.[13] Political beliefs often went hand-in-hand with denominational affiliation.[14] Upper- and middle-class Conservatives largely aligned themselves with High Church Anglicanism; Liberals, socialists and some business leaders settled into Nonconformity, namely those branches of protestant Christian practice that had detached themselves from mainstream Anglicanism at the end of the eighteenth century, which was particularly strong in rural and industrial communities across Wales, Scotland and Northern England. In all, 30 million people belonged to one of the major religious denominations, about 90 per cent of the national population. Therefore clerical attitudes towards the war carried their own importance as pastors, preachers and clergymen struggled to justify the un-Christian act of killing other (enemy) Christians.[15]

Some English Presbyterians had few doubts about the worthiness of the war. One minister in Liverpool could quite easily deliver sermons claiming that Germany represented a 'moral menace to civilization'.[16] Yet the Church of England's ethical ambivalence towards the war was reflected in the Bishop of Chelmsford's attempt to resolve his own spiritual dilemma by urging his congregation to be 'calm and quiet', neither falling into depression if defeat should befall the nation, nor erupting into 'undue and unworthy exaltation if God gives us victory', reminding his parishioners that the Christian God was the Father not only of the British, but also of 'the men with whom we are at war'. The Bishop's attempt, however, to frame the war within a Christian–humanitarian outlook failed to rub off on one Essex clergyman who preached 12 'recruiting sermons' over the first six weeks of the war, or one Wimbledon clergyman's view that German invaders would 'destroy every male child' in England.[17] Few, however, were ready to support the call of the Bishop of London, A.F. Winnington-Ingram, 'to kill Germans, … not for the sake of killing, but to save the world … to kill the young men as well as the old … lest the civilization of the world should itself be killed'. Coming after a series of German air raids on London, the emotional violence of the Bishop's comments can be understood.[18] Even so, many churchmen probably allied themselves with William Temple, son of an Archbishop of Canterbury, who strongly believed that the war presented the Church with an opportunity to spiritually cleanse the country, undoing the damage done by the growing materialist values and consumerist cultures that had gripped its people in the pre-war years. Temple contended in a series of pamphlets that the war could be invoked as a modern crusade, re-evangelizing the nation, taking the word to the industrial working classes. Supporters agreed with his view that the war presented an opportunity to undertake the 'real' Christianization of the people, the beginning of a process to reconstruct the nation's moral life through the living Christ.[19]

Recruitment propaganda

In their efforts to construct a clerical and scholarly justification for the war, intellectuals were a rather forlorn bunch. Attempts to rationalize the conflict as a question of ideals and moral rectitude mattered little amid an atmosphere of emotion and instinct. The country did not need lofty ideals; it needed patriotism and hatred: notions easily understood by people from ordinary backgrounds, and easily tailored to the recruitment drive.

The creation of Kitchener's volunteer army lent recruitment propaganda a special quality that would distinguish it from others, even if the War Office's initial outpourings had a distinctive whiff of the amateur around them. Relying heavily on typescript advertisements (in the press and public displays), the activities of recruiting officers, and public meetings in town halls, squares and on street corners, the Army's early messages, as refined by the Caxton Advertising Agency, focused exclusively on promoting the desirability of army life. 'What the Army Offers' became a common theme, distilling later into 'Your King and Country Need You' as the demands of war took hold.[20] The message was spread by an innumerable array of voluntary bodies such as the Cobden Club, the Atlantic Union and the Victoria League, co-ordinated by the Central Committee for National Patriotic Organizations formed in August 1914, with Asquith as its President, assisted by Balfour and the Earl of Rosebury.[21] Against a backdrop of the early war recruitment rush, the effectiveness of these initial propaganda efforts is difficult to assess. But the subsequent emergence of the Parliamentary Recruiting Committee (PRC) formed, as we have seen, to stimulate army recruitment at a time when volunteer numbers were weakening, took recruitment propaganda to another level. In the first place, the PRC's efforts were more diverse. Propaganda output extended across a number of differing activities, from household canvassing, to nightly meetings, rallies addressed by well-known public figures and music hall concerts held amid much flag-waving and patriotic singing.[22] Second, the propaganda message was carried by new technologies. Both the PRC and the War Office attempted to reinforce the recruitment themes through phonograph disc recordings in what was perhaps the first use of saleable audio propaganda. Phonographs struck a chord with the public. Harnessing the skills of actors and music hall stars of the era, the recordings (called 'descriptive sketches') encompassed blatant tear-jerking patriotism, with celebrated singers such as Edna Thornton giving renditions of the recruiting song 'Your King and Country need you'. Others re-enacted battles at the front, speeches from generals or even depictions of air raids, complete with the sounds of German bombers, reactions of a frightened crowd and the calls of constables on air-raid warning duty. What was dressed as light-hearted entertainment carried at its core the message of impressing upon reluctant men the need to join the services.[23]

The dexterous appeal of the phonograph was matched by the picture poster. After its emergence as a respectable art form in the late nineteenth century, social analysts have identified posters as being part of a new visual media whose usage was given new life by the conflict. The PRC alone produced over 200 designs before the onset of conscription in 1916, with themes that ranged from the crass to the complex. As a recruitment stimulant, nothing worked better than the shameless patriotic appeal, epitomized perhaps by Alfred Leete's representation of Lord Kitchener which, after being cleverly exploited by Hedley le Bas of the PRC, first appeared in the autumn of 1914. As a popular imperial war hero, Kitchener's image embodied Britain's strength and resolve. But the poster derived its power from its capacity to act as psychological blackmail. Little attention was paid to the barriers of social class, occupation and background: all men were targeted, and it was impossible for the viewer to escape the Field Marshal's piercing gaze and pointing finger.[24]

The poster lent a new sense of status to the notion of army service, which hitherto had been regarded by the respectable working classes as a job for the feckless, the criminal, the unemployed and unemployable. In other instances the poster repackaged older visual languages. Peer pressure and sexual humiliation became common currency in early war posters as a way of encouraging women to apply moral pressure on their menfolk to fight. In some instances, such as the PRC poster of a mother addressing her son with the caption 'GO – IT'S YOUR DUTY LAD', the appeal was relatively innocuous. Yet the sub-text of many posters was inviting women to question the sexual virility of their men if they refused to volunteer. 'If he does not think that you and your country are worth fighting for – do you think he is *worthy* of you?' screamed one poster, while others proclaimed, 'If your young man neglects his duty to his King and Country, the time may come when he will NEGLECT YOU'. Such messages blatantly placed sex at the heart of recruitment and were successfully exploited in music hall meetings and phonograph recordings (see also Chapter 9). Army service was a matter of erotic power, sexual attraction and manliness, although how far these assertions were borne out by experience is harder to ascertain.[25]

Shackling the press

The role of the press as a propaganda source was more ambiguous. As an independent medium, the wartime power of newspapers was without parallel. They provided their readers with valuable information (if not necessarily wisdom) about the world, conveyed in a language that was readily understood. Public hunger for the written text was seemingly insatiable. Sixteen daily newspapers served London alone; almost every metropolitan community across the country had at least one local paper (both morning and evening); and the circulation figures of national popular titles such as the *Daily Mail* and *Daily Mirror* were around a million. Yet many newspaper proprietors inhabited the same social class as the politicians. They frequented the same clubs, ate at the same restaurants, shared similar outlooks and broadly concurred on what the public should know. In a democracy, of course, the press was not an organ of government. Yet proprietors who held fast to their role as the clarions of free speech, reserving the right to praise and condemn the government, war or no war, invited accusations of disloyalty. And ministers who withheld information from the press, or attempted to constrain journalistic freedom through fear of revealing sensitive secrets to the enemy, risked claims of subverting liberty. Hence, the relationship between politicians and the press during the war was never easy. Most of the national dailies (apart from the *Daily Herald*) broadly supported the war, and many provided a valuable bridge of communication between government and the people, allowing the public to interpret how the war was being conducted, whilst enabling politicians to gauge the public mood. But there was always a tacit agreement between reporters and politicians that too much knowledge was a dangerous thing.[26]

Censorship exposed this awkward relationship most clearly. All newspapers were subject to the sweeping regulations of the Defence of the Realm Act (DORA), which prohibited the collection and publication of any military and naval material deemed to be useful to the enemy and outlawed the spreading of false reports likely to cause disaffection in the armed forces or prejudice relations with Britain's allies. DORA also gave the military the power to search any publishing premises where a breach of these conditions was suspected; all offences were to be tried by court martial, with possible life imprisonment for convicted wrongdoers. However, the regulations were infrequently used, and prosecutions were rarely successful, as the government's attempt to suppress the right-wing newspaper *The Globe* in November 1915, for publishing a fabricated report of Kitchener's resignation, proved.[27]

Nevertheless, both press and politicians agreed that censorship should be managed. In 1914 an agreement between the Armed Services Chiefs, the Newspaper Proprietors' Federation and the Newspaper Society established a Joint Standing Committee to arbitrate on the publication of 'sensitive' information. Under its terms, editors were obliged to forward sensitive stories to the Service departments for clearance. In return, criticism of government would remain an editorial prerogative, with no constraints on the availability of news.[28] However, this atmosphere of mutual back-scratching was poisoned at the outset by the distrust and dislike of the press within the military and naval hierarchies. Kitchener's well-known loathing of journalists (a legacy of his time in the Sudan, when he famously referred to reporters as 'drunken swabs') probably explains his immediate and unexplained ban on allowing correspondents anywhere near the Western Front.[29] Worse was to come when the government commandeered the entire land telegraph network, submarine cables and wireless stations and installed a military censor at the Central Telegraph Office to vet and monitor all messages sent and received across the wires. The subsequent 'news blackout' resulted in no information being released on the embarkation and movements of the British Expeditionary Force until 18th August 1914, and reports of increased armaments production at Woolwich were kept from publication. Caught in a news vacuum, reporters reverted to their time-honoured practices of invention and speculation.[30]

It was amidst the subsequent glut of exaggerated reports and wild rumours that Churchill instigated the setting up of a government Press Bureau, headed by the occasionally abusive Conservative MP F.E. Smith, to secure 'a steady stream of trustworthy information supplied by both the War Office and the Admiralty'.[31] The Bureau was essentially an experiment, with Smith's role hemmed in by a Bureau staff comprised mostly of officers seconded from the War Office and the Admiralty.[32] Newspapers were not slow in their complaints about government 'news management'. However, following Smith's clumsy handling of a sensational report of the British Army's retreat from Mons that appeared in *The Times* on 31st August 1914, the more reliable Sir Stanley Buckmaster was appointed as Director, bringing much-needed stability.[33] As Solicitor-General, Buckmaster knew the value of keeping secrets secret, whilst making the news more publicly palatable, even if it meant disconnecting information from the truth and keeping reports of disasters as far as possible from a news-hungry press. Buckmaster adroitly consolidated the Bureau by relocating its offices from Charing Cross Road in London back to Whitehall and reorganizing the administrative structure into four new sections: Issuing, which dealt with all official information and government notices; Cable, which handled the compulsory censorship of press cablegrams; the Press Department, to which all 'sensitive' news reports were voluntarily referred; and finally the Naval Room, which took responsibility for matters relating to Admiralty censorship.[34]

But the reforms did little to lessen the tensions between ministers and the Press. Buckmaster became acutely aware that his role as Censor-in-Chief was caught between two poles. Although it was his job to prevent secretive material from leaking into the public domain, it was not his job to save the government from its own embarrassments, as Churchill discovered when he tried to silence newspaper criticism of his role in the Antwerp evacuation in 1914. Yet Buckmaster became adept at refining the 'D' (Defence) notice system, which issued private and confidential notices to editors restricting news reporting of sensitive topics and major events. Newspapers resented, but tolerated, D-notices. They went along with the system, partly in fear of prosecution under the DORA regulations and partly to ensure that the other side of the censorship deal – guaranteeing the freedom of critical commentary on the war effort – remained untouched. But journalists must have been sorely tested as the war unfolded, particularly when the government extended the usage of D-notices to cover all aspects of war reporting on the Home Front, from food shortages, to shipping losses and air raids, industrial disputes and military setbacks. Editors came to regard the brusque and opaque D-notices as another form of home propaganda, or news as the government liked to see it.[35]

The government still kept the upper hand, though. Its complicity in the military's desire to strangle war news by silencing war correspondents meant that any reporter caught in France was liable to arrest and imprisonment, and possible execution. Kitchener attempted to assuage the public by appointing

Colonel Sir Ernest Swinton to write the Army's version on the progress of the war. Swinton's despatches were heavily vetted by Army High Command and appeared in the press under the byline, Eye-witness; they were never taken seriously by Fleet Street.[36] On the other hand, some correspondents, such as Philip Gibbs (correspondent for the *Daily Telegraph* and *Daily Chronicle*), went to great lengths to move closer to the fighting, enrolling as a special commissioner in the Red Cross before being arrested and warned by Kitchener that he risked being shot by firing squad if caught near the front again.[37] The political-military consensus on secrecy aimed at securing complete control of war news, before being reminded, in January 1915, through the former American President Theodore Roosevelt's letters to the Foreign Office, that banning correspondents from the front was handing the Germans a free rein to conduct their own propaganda campaign in the United States of America with little hindrance.[38]

Thus, consensus began to fray at the edges. Two new co-directors at the Press Bureau, E.T. Cook and Frank Swettenham, adopted a more flexible approach, introducing weekly ministerial press conferences in February 1915, supported by the Foreign Office's encouragement of regular meetings between journalists and senior military and naval personnel.[39] In May the Cabinet loosened constraints on war correspondents reporting from the front, sanctioning High Command to permit six selected journalists from the better-known newspapers to become 'embedded' with the Army in France. These journalists joined as officers, wore uniforms with a correspondent's 'green sash' on their shoulders, were given orderlies and batmen, frequented the officers' mess, worked within tight regulations governing their activities and found themselves constantly accompanied by the Army's 'travelling censors'. Correspondents were tolerated on condition that no regiment would be cited by name, only vague references were made to places of battle and all mention of officers, except for the Commander-in-Chief, was prohibited. The Army's Chief of Intelligence, General J.V. Charteris, summed up the new policy as 'Say what you like old man. But don't mention any places or people.'[40]

Not surprisingly, the style of reporting during the war settled into a pattern of accentuating the positive, eliminating the negative. Rather than challenge the censors, editors became as terrified of revealing sensitive information as the military. Desperate to obtain news of the war, those war reporters who were allowed near the front tended to bury their grievances and play to the Army's agenda of providing colourful stories of valour and brilliance, and safeguarding the reputations of the High Command. Gibbs recalled in his memoirs, 'We identified ourselves absolutely with the Armies in the field … . We wiped out of our minds … all temptation to write one word which would make the task of officers and men more difficult or dangerous … . We were our own censors.'[41] While this fell short of the journalist acting as war propagandist, the issuing of distorted reports for the Home Front hid the true reality of the war from the public eye.[42] Fear that revealing the truth would shake opinion at home and fatally undermine popular support was reflected in Gibbs account of the Battle of the Somme:

> My dispatches tell the truth … . But they do not tell all the truth. I have had to spare the feelings of the men and women whose sons and husbands are still fighting in France. I have not told all there is to tell about the agonies of this war, nor given in full realism the horrors that are inevitable in such fighting. It is perhaps better not to do so, here and now, although it is a moral cowardice which makes many people shut their eyes to the shambles, comforting their souls with fine phrases about the beauty of sacrifice.[43]

Fictions and hatreds

During the first two years of the war the British public were confronted with their own 'truths' – managed, shaped and exploited by the press and government, in which tales of heroism, stoical deeds and modest progress were mingled with stories and rumours of the 'beastly Hun', a cultural construction that caricatured Germany and Germans as a debasement of humanity and an affront to civilized behaviour. Cultivated mythical heroisms and hatreds had their uses. They gave solace to anxious families waiting for news of their loved ones; and they helped Britons understand the war by knowing their enemy. The press certainly played a role in the process. Two of the better-known stories of the war originated in newspapers. Perhaps intended as spiritual balm for fretful families, they quickly became popular truths. Arthur Machen's romantic tale of ghostly Agincourt bowmen, aiding beleaguered British battalions retreating from Mons by firing arrows that killed German soldiers without leaving a wound, was intentionally fictional. Yet, with its publication in the *Evening Standard* in September 1914, Machen's account of 'long lines of shapes, with a shining about them' rapidly grew into a factual tale of believable angels. Given credence by the clergy, the 'Angels of Mons' story became an expression of patriotism. It became almost treasonable to doubt it.[44] Just as persuasive was 'news' of 20,000 to 40,000 Russian troops arriving in the country (the numbers varied like a Chinese whisper), with 'snow on their boots' en route to France. This was a story that required no verification. Someone knew somebody who had heard the story from a passenger on a train, a housewife in a queue, a man in the street. Perhaps that wasn't the point. 'The thought of the Russians did much to cheer us up', wrote one diarist in 1914, especially when 'we all had a bad attack of the glooms'.[45]

Comfort rumours had their use in allaying the public's nervousness, but they also seduced wartime Britons into believing the nastiest stories about the enemy. Some atrocity tales, which began to circulate almost the moment the German army invaded Belgium, were nourished by elements of truth and appear to have grown off the back of intermittent and vague reports of enemy war crimes that appeared in the early weeks of the war. German troops' fear of Belgian terrorists (the *francs-tireurs*) was probably responsible for the deliberate killing of over 4,000 Belgian civilians during the war. News of this, along with the destruction of the university library of Louvain and Rheims Cathedral, appeared to confirm Britons' worst fears of 'the Hun' as the destroyer of civilization.[46] Accounts from British soldiers, elaborated by an anxious and over-active popular imagination, created a public ready to believe rumours of babies being impaled on soldiers' bayonets, raped nuns, enslaved and murdered priests, innocent children with their hands cut off, civilians being used as human shields, crucified soldiers and the breasts of gallant nurses being sliced away. All hummed with the language of 'violation' or forced entry that paralleled the German invasion of Belgium. Many of the stories were mythical; some were embroidered truths. But all seemed unconsciously to serve the propaganda purpose of demonizing the enemy.

Convinced of a market for atrocity stories, the press certainly added its penny-worth to the national rumour machine. Versions of a forged story about a defiled and mutilated British nurse caught in a Belgian hospital by German troops appeared in the *Evening Standard*, *Pall Mall Gazette* and *Westminster Gazette* in September 1914 without authentication. *The Times*, around the same time, published a letter from a London vicar about his son serving in the BEF, reporting the rape of three young girls by German soldiers, under the headline, 'Victims of German Barbarism', prompting questions as to its factual legitimacy.[47] *The Times* was to plumb the depths of popular taste some three years later in April 1917 when it published an entirely fictional account of a German 'corpse factory', where the bodies of dead soldiers were being smelted down to make fats and glycerines for armaments manufacture.[48] Later studies have identified the story as a product of a British general's over-active imagination, though Adrian Gregory points the finger at Siegfried Sassoon playing poetry with a known urban myth.[49]

It was, however, the *Daily Mail* that occupied the premier position in the array of newspaper anti-Germanism. The paper's credentials were already established before the war with its notorious 'Made in Germany' anti-dumping campaigns and its infamous role in stoking popular anti-German feelings over the Dreadnought scare. For the *Mail*, the behaviour of the German army in Belgium only confirmed its suspicions about the true nature of the Teutonic beast, and its printing of atrocity stories began in earnest once the war had broken out. In fairness, the *Mail* always walked carefully between truth, hyperbole and invention. Reports of German outrages formed a small proportion of its daily news output. Its coverage of the massacre of 400 peasants in November 1914 and the sacking of Dinant (in Belgium) by the German army were broadly accurate. And the paper's editorials were prepared to accept contradictory accounts alongside sceptical commentary from its own reporters. But, occasionally, these acted as totems for the *real* story, as instanced by Hamilton Fyfe's reports of 'The Barbarity of German Troops' in the editions of 21st August 1914, where, despite the reporter's initial doubts about the stories, the evidence was such that the truth *had* to be told.[50]

In any event, if the public wanted proof of such stories, they need look no further than the pages of the Bryce Report. Set up by Asquith in December 1914, Lord Bryce, a former ambassador to Washington, led a commission of highly respected lawyers and historians to authenticate claims of war crimes and outrages committed by the German army in Belgium. Bryce, a self-declared Germanophile, had opposed the war at the outset. Yet, once his team had painstakingly drawn evidence from 1,200 Belgian refugees, he concluded that Germany was guilty of 'murder, lust and pillage ... on a scale unparalleled in any war between civilized nations during the last three centuries'. These were crimes that could be explained only as part of 'a system and in pursuance of a set purpose'.[51] Historians agree that the Bryce Report was flawed. Testimony was not taken under oath, interviewees were not cross-examined (no hard evidence could be found of hand amputation for example) and any doubts that commission members had over the integrity of the findings were not acknowledged.[52] Yet few cared. Questioning the report's integrity risked accusations of being unpatriotic. For the government, the real value of the Bryce Report was in its timing. It sold in its thousands and, published in Britain and the United States of America just one week after the sinking of the *Lusitania*, strengthened Britain's case for German war guilt and helped sway American opinion towards the Allies, whilst giving a febrile public an official and respected endorsement of what they knew all along: Britain was at war to save the world from German barbarity.

And yet, perhaps, in the final reckoning, the British obsession with German atrocities was more a matter of what one historian sees as 'cultural relativism'. German armies fought wars with an assumption that both soldiers and civilians were combatants. Indeed, poison gas and flame throwers, using cathedrals as lookout posts to direct shelling, bombing raids on enemy cities, and the sinking of Allied ships on the high seas were all legitimate ways of winning and *shortening* the war: a very modern approach that would take another generation, and another global conflict, for the British to understand. Caught as they were in a period of cultural conservatism and naivety, many approached war essentially as a gentleman's duel, bound by the immovable and universal rules of law and custom and respect for humanity. Thus, the shelling of innocent civilians in Scarborough, Whitby and Hartlepool, the U-boat campaign and air raids were an affront to civilization and a violation of an unwritten code of honour, confirming the bestiality of the enemy. For Britons, such cruel attacks on defenceless people justified the fight. Equally, Germany could legitimize her war methods in the face of a British naval blockade that was attempting to strangle her war effort and starve innocent German citizens. So, what was the difference?[53]

Three episodes highlighted this culture gap. One was the largely forgotten case of Captain James Fryatt, a British merchant seaman who rammed a German U-boat in March 1915 following the declaration of unrestricted submarine warfare. Fryatt, who was awarded a gold medal for his actions by the Admiralty, was subsequently captured by a German flotilla in June 1916 and executed on 27th July. The Germans saw Fryatt as a '*franc-tireur* of the sea'; the British saw the incident as a 'new German atrocity': a British seaman murdered for doing his duty. In 1919, Fryatt's body was repatriated and given a state funeral at St Paul's Cathedral, with a commemorative memorial erected at the entrance to Liverpool Street Station in London. His tombstone at All Saints church in Dovercourt was marked by the epitaph 'Illegally executed by the Germans'.[54] Fryatt's death exemplified the differing British and German cultural attitudes to 'duty': something that echoed the execution of the British nurse Edith Cavell in October 1915. Cavell's actions in helping stranded Allied soldiers caught behind German lines was seen in Britain as an act of heroism; the Germans, by contrast, interpreted her deeds as espionage. Strictly speaking, their capture of Cavell and her subsequent death by firing squad was legitimate, but it provided the British with yet more proof of German savagery. Nevertheless, Cavell's martyrdom was achieved without revealing that she had indeed been managing a clandestine operation in Belgium and was aware of the consequences if caught. But German officers failed to understand that the application of a little clemency in this regard would have turned the propaganda message in their favour.[55] Instead, their actions only hardened British perceptions, which were already boiling following the sinking of the passenger ship the *Lusitania* by a U-boat off the coast of Ireland in May 1915. The loss of over 1,000 innocent civilian lives, 124 of them neutral Americans, was characteristically viewed by the British press as one more chapter in a growing catalogue of German war crimes, especially as 94 of the victims were children. Yet, Germany's warnings about her policy on unrestricted submarine warfare and her suspicions that the *Lusitania* was carrying a shipment of arms (which was true) were practically ignored in the ensuing propaganda battle. What shocked British and American opinion was that the sinking was celebrated in Germany. The U-boat crew were decorated for their actions, and Munich craftsman Helmut Goetz's production of a *Lusitania* medal, originally intended as a satirical comment on the German government's claims that the vessel was transporting contraband cargoes, was taken, replicated and sold in thousands in Britain and the United States of America, caricaturing the German action as 'Another triumph for our Glorious Navy'. Britons, already soaked by propaganda messages that the British people bore no responsibility for the war, were now convinced (and had convinced themselves) that there was something fundamentally immoral with the way Germany was prosecuting the war, which made the fight against her all the more necessary. As DeGroot has commented, despite their claims of British hypocrisy, Germans had become adept at making themselves look evil. Their methods of warfare had become the principal driving force in the 'political and cultural self mobilization' of the British by 1915. It was a position from which Germany would never quite recover.[56]

The touch of government

Britain's *ad hoc*, improvised and fragmentary propaganda effort held together, more or less, until the end of 1916. But it could not withstand a longer war. When Lloyd George's new government took office, the Prime Minister looked at reorganizing the administration of British propaganda, but Cabinet opposition drove him to settle instead for the establishment of a Department of Information, under the directorship of the novelist John Buchan, which took over responsibility for overseas propaganda from Charles Masterman's bureau at Wellington House.[57] Home propaganda fell under the auspices of the National War Aims Committee (NWAC), launched in August 1917. These bodies, as well as the publicity sections of some government departments, were merged into a new Ministry of Information created on 4th March 1918, headed by Lord Beaverbrook. The new system was bounded by three concerns. The first was raised by MPs sceptical of Lloyd George's motives in creating an addition to the wartime state that was accountable only to him, rather than Parliament. A government department that existed outside democratic control was, some felt, a dangerous precedent.[58] A second concern was raised over Lloyd George's inclination to stock the administrative staff of the propaganda system with pressmen. His fondness for the company of press lords over politicians was common knowledge. Besides, in a body dedicated to spreading a message extolling the righteousness of the British cause in this war, why not employ the services of such masters of mass communication? Men like Robert Donald, editor of the *News Chronicle*, C.P. Scott (another of Lloyd George's confidants), editor of the *Manchester Guardian*, and Northcliffe had all sat on an Advisory Committee within the Department of Information.[59] Northcliffe especially had shown an interest in propaganda from the war's beginnings. He advocated to the War Office the value of dropping leaflets from aircraft over enemy territory in September 1914. Yet, Lloyd George knew the power of the press to be both a friend and enemy. His attempt to embrace Northcliffe within the bosom of the government was one way of muzzling the press lord's inclination to publicly criticize Lloyd George's conduct of the war through the pages of the *Daily Mail* and *The Times*. Beaverbrook's appointment, ostensibly out of recognition of his success in organizing Canadian propaganda, could have been for similar underlying reasons.[60] Perhaps Lloyd George felt that by keeping his friends close, he could keep his enemies closer.

The most critical concern, however, was fear of a changing public mood. In the absence of opinion polling or scientific techniques, wartime politicians had few tools to gauge and understand public opinion, and the social effects of changing situations on the Home Front were largely unknown.[61] Since the beginning of 1916 the public had had to swallow the introduction of conscription; rising prices and higher taxes; loss of rights at the workplace; bombing raids; and shortages of food and fuel. War-weariness and public disquiet about both domestic conditions and faith in the military's ability to win spilled over into industrial unrest and anger over profiteering and the inequality of sacrifice. For ministers, these were foreseeable threats to national morale. Less certain was how far the rising voices of the pacifist movement would permeate the public consciousness and how lethal would be the backwash from the Bolsheviks' takeover in Russia.

Despite the need, the creation of a body responsible for home propaganda happened almost by default. In May 1917, John Buchan, in a report to the Cabinet, admitted that, because of his Department's preoccupation with foreign propaganda, the Home Front had been overlooked. Buchan acknowledged the necessity for 'the direction of British opinion' against Britain's enemies, but, given the scale of unrest in industrial areas and continuing failures at the front, he confessed that 'I am very strongly of the opinion that it is necessary to do a considerable amount of propaganda in Britain itself'. Buchan suggested a series of lectures and addresses 'in all the chief centres', with visits of workers' delegations to sections of the front, who could pass on their experiences to colleagues at home.[62]

The resulting NWAC took nearly three months to set up and was never recognized as a ministry of state. Instead, it assumed the credentials of an improved version of the Parliamentary Recruiting Committee, run by an all-party executive with Asquith as President and G.N. Barnes and Bonar Law as vice-presidents. It relied heavily on the branches of the Central Committee for National Patriotic Organizations, local political party infrastructure and press contacts for the dissemination of material and organization of propaganda events; it was staffed by volunteers and funded largely by voluntary donations, until Parliament approved a £240,000 grant to finance its activities in November 1917. By the spring of 1918, the NWAC had effectively become the main controlling body of all propaganda output in Britain, yet it operated in a policy vacuum. With its aims defined as counteracting 'the insidious and specious propaganda of pacifist publications', urging the public to uphold the ideals of 'Liberty and Justice', and maintaining the struggle to a victorious end, the NWAC could elucidate what the war was against; but it could not state with any confidence what the war was meant to achieve.[63]

Once born, however, the NWAC was not long in taking its strides. Campaigns were conducted through a network of smaller local committees and constituency party organizations, each composed of party workers represented in equal numbers, 'together with citizens of every shade of thought', while its responsibilities in Scotland were divided between two 'east and west' committees. At one level the organization merely reworked older themes raised by the PRC. The subject of the 'beastly Hun' was revisited by the publication of the 'German Crimes Calendar' in which one German atrocity was portrayed for every month, with the dates on which they were committed circled in red.[64] From another angle, the public was reminded that the war could only be won with the total commitment of British workers and British industry. In posters women were exhorted to 'learn to make munitions'; and workers were told that their endeavours were an essential prop of the war effort. Messages were spread across a diversity of mediums. At its simplest were the publication of cartoons, picture postcards, designs for cigarette cards and banners for meetings (flags lent out on request), Christmas cards, and 25 sketches offered at £25 each; these were supported by the publication of posters, leaflets and pamphlets. Posters such as 'Huns Ancient and Modern' sought to play on popular anti-German feelings; others were entitled 'Liberté! Egalité! Fraternité!' and had a symbolic figure of France standing firm at the centre, while two crossed swords of Britannia and America emphasized the patriotic message.[65]

Different themes were highlighted when the NWAC was co-opted by other government departments to manage their propaganda drives. The War Savings Committee, for example, used the NWAC apparatus to publicize its War Loan schemes. Patriotism through thrift was the message spread from a series of posters. Designs included 'Make every penny do the work of two', aimed specifically at women; 'Turn your silver into bullets', depicting a handful of coins melting into bullets; and 'Buy National War Bonds and protect your home', against a background of a ruined Belgian cottage. This drive culminated in December 1917 when a 'tank bank' was set up in Trafalgar Square, earning nearly £320,000 in one week by selling War Bonds and War Savings Certificates. Leaflets were seen as especially valuable. Some intended for foreign audiences were commandeered for domestic use. Others, such as those intended for local preachers, accentuated an 'ethical point of view'. Otherwise, pamphlets were published reproducing notable speeches from prominent figures, including Lloyd George (of course!), the American President Woodrow Wilson and respected literary figures, including Rudyard Kipling and Arthur Conan Doyle. The NWAC supplemented these outpourings by publishing its own series of leaflets, *Realities and Searchlights*, employing the services of 38 paid contributors and dispersed nationally using the distribution network of the newsagents W.H. Smith.[66]

The main thrust of NWAC activity, however, was through the public meeting. Face-to-face was considered to be the most effective of all mediums. Between August and October 1917 a formidable 3,192 gatherings were arranged and sponsored by the NWAC, occasionally as mass meetings, such as those seen in Blackpool and Newcastle in 1918, or public rallies held in holiday resorts, industrial areas, London parks, town halls and village squares, sometimes enlivened by brass bands, stalls distributing propaganda literature and music hall artists reciting popular patriotic songs. Speakers came in two classes. For the 'really important meetings', major figures would be engaged, such as Lloyd George, Asquith and members of the War Cabinet, to address large-scale gatherings in major industrial cities or centres of armaments production. More commonly, however, local committees were able to call upon specially trained 'staff' speakers from the NWAC to address smaller meetings. In some instances these would include 'eye-witnesses' from the front or devastated areas, or even survivors from U-boat attacks.

American speakers were also included, once the United States of America had entered the war. Perhaps the pinnacle of NWAC patriotic activity was the 'Win the War' mass meeting held in Birmingham in September 1918. Here, a procession of volunteers was gathered who, led by a tank, marched through the city centre accompanied by Boy Scouts handing out pamphlets, topped off with the dropping of 250,000 leaflets by aeroplane.[67]

Less clear was the application of film technology to propaganda. Since its origins at the turn of the century, the cinema had burgeoned into a cheap, accessible and essentially modern form of entertainment, functioning mainly as a fairground attraction with its audience paying money to watch themselves in crowd scenes, or be entertained by short comedies and melodramas. In comparison with the American-produced large-budget 'feature films' of Charlie Chaplin and the director D.W. Griffith, the British film industry was tiny. But it had quickly become an established part of popular culture. Twenty million cinema tickets were being sold weekly by 1916. Films succeeded because they appealed to the illiterate as well as the educated and no formal instruction was required for understanding; they worked both as mass entertainment and works of art. Yet the government was slow to realize their potential.[68]

Officials' resistance was rooted in cultural snobbery. Film was regarded as trivial and rather pernicious by the educated elite: a cheap way of entertaining the ignorant – 'a sort of moving edition of the "Penny Dreadful"'.[69] Whitehall's distaste for this technological modernity was not shared, however, by Charles Masterman, whose initial interests arose from his fear of German film propaganda affecting opinion in the Balkans and Asia, where 'their immense illiterate populations' made literature practically useless.[70] Masterman's keenness in using film as a propaganda tool was matched by the industry's conviction that there was a mass market for authentic front-line footage for a domestic audience that had been denied any direct reporting of the war. Initial War Office doubts were soothed by two agreements, one with Wellington House, which allowed the shooting for a single film; the other struck with the cinema industry's representative body, the Trade Topical Committee, which gave filming at the front official blessing.[71]

These aspirations were realized to an extent by Wellington House's first official propaganda film, *Britain Prepared*, released on 29th December 1915 amidst much publicity, depicting rather mundane images of munitions making and military and naval training. After its showing in London cinemas, the film was subsequently distributed across 61 towns, and booked for another 50. But this was the high point. *Britain Prepared*'s success was not repeated in the ensuing 27 short films released on similar topics between December 1915 and the summer of 1916.[72] It seemed that filming the more banal features of army life had lost its appeal to the paying public.

Masterman and his contemporaries were still determined that films had to be factual, expressing as one source saw it 'the actual likeness of events'. So the reality film took a step further when Wellington House commissioned a series of so-called 'battle' films produced between 1916 and 1917. The first, and most successful, *Battle of the Somme*, was released in August 1916 (a time when the battle was far from over) and immediately captured the public imagination. The film opened in 34 cinemas simultaneously, was shown to an estimated audience of over 20 million people and attracted reactions that ranged from shock and outrage to stunned admiration. To be sure, *Battle of the Somme* was pioneering. For once, the Army was openly co-operative in allowing two official cameramen, Geoffrey Malins and J.B. McDowell, to film the preliminary build-up, the artillery bombardments and the opening day. Filming continued until 10th July, and the first rushes were shown in London two days later. In some respects, *Battle of the Somme* settled into familiar propaganda grooves by including scenes of smiling British Tommies, but it was the images of soldiers going into action, men going 'over the top', and graphic portrayals of casualties, both wounded and dying, that proved to be the most enduring. The sequence showing men from the Lancashire Fusiliers assembling in a sunken road on the first day of the battle, strained faces and anxious eyes staring at the camera before they went 'over the top', still has the power to move modern audiences.[73] Other sequences, however, were deliberately faked. Historians' suspicions have been raised about the authenticity of Malins's two 'over-the-top' scenes, where men scramble out of a trench into smoke, with several men falling as others pick their way over barbed wire towards enemy lines. Some claim that such scenes were shot in training trenches, well behind the lines, two or three days before the battle, highlighting how the soldiers filmed were unsuitably equipped for the fighting and with one of the 'casualties' crossing his legs and smiling at the camera.[74] Such deception does threaten the integrity of *Battle of the Somme* but, in another sense, duplicity was forced upon the film-makers, as shooting footage of front-line scenes was discouraged by Army High Command out of concern for the cameramen's safety. As Stephen Badsey has commented, '[a]ctual combat ... was beyond the power of the film-makers to record'.[75] On the other hand, contemporaries argued that the film shook the British public out of their complacency, stimulating a sense of admiration for the soldiers' courage. Films that exposed the chaos and carnage of battle, and the brutal inhumanity and barbarity of war, swung public opinion, according to Nicholas Reeves, 'towards reconfirming existing convictions that Britain's cause was just'.[76]

Other films, however, became victims of an increasingly fickle public. Subsequent productions (*The Battle of Ancre and the Advance of the Tanks* and *The German Retreat and the Battle of Arras*, released in June 1917) were played to smaller audiences, with exhibitors complaining of losing money on screenings. The situation was worsened by the Army's unwillingness to allow filming of vivid scenes showing the wounded and dying. Old habits emerged as footage of casualties in 'Battle films' were now removed.[77] The slump in popularity prompted Lord Beaverbrook (proprietor of the *Daily Express*), who had taken charge of the War Office's Cinematograph Committee in May 1916, into a policy review.[78] The factual war film was thus renewed as a 'newsreel', in a style similar to the French-produced *Gaumont Graphic* and *Pathé Gazette*. The British version, *The Topical Budget*, first screened in May 1917, was not wholly successful, despite having access to front-line footage and exclusive rights to the French official newsreel. Its first series focused mainly on troops from the colonies and Britain's Allies; the second was a series of 'regimental films' depicting scenes of happy soldiers and the Navy in action, alongside films of the Royal Family.[79]

The newsreel format was supplemented by a series of weekly magazine films, which became more refined by the addition of short 'tag' films, produced when the Ministry of Information took over responsibility for film propaganda in March 1918. Usually made by its own staff of professional film-makers on behalf of individual government departments, such productions were characteristically between two and ten minutes in length and shown between feature-length films in cinemas. 'Tag films' strove to inform, browbeat and shame viewers into approved types of behaviour. The content often adopted a storyline using prominent actresses like Ellen Terry to dramatize a variety of messages, from exhorting women to join the Land Army, to persuading audiences to buy war bonds or to save coal, or highlighting the patriotic virtues of signing up for munitions work, or encouraging food economy.[80] *A Day in the Life of a Munitions Worker*, for example, filmed an attractive young girl's skill in filling and fusing a shell, with detailed depiction of medical examinations and health and safety activities. *Father and Lather* was a comedy relating the profligate use of a family's soap bar by the head of the household and his subsequent shaming into economizing by his wife and daughters. In a similar format, *The Secret* offered audiences the worthiness of using potatoes instead of flour in dumplings, as a message to 'grow your own vegetables'.[81]

None of this, however, succeeded in regenerating the audience enthusiasm of the *Battle of the Somme*. So, if people were reluctant to view official films in cinemas, then the films would come to them. In February 1918 the ministry attempted to stimulate public interest in official films by launching 'cine-motor' tours, where free film shows would be projected from the backs of specially adapted lorries, either on to a 25-foot screen or the gable ends of houses. The initial experiment in Wales proved enough of a success to persuade propagandists that the idea was viable, and two major tours were undertaken in April and May, and September and October, 1918, attracting audiences averaging 163,000 – a far cry from the millions who paid to watch *Battle of the Somme* just two years earlier.[82] The cinema trade press criticized the films as lacking human interest and cohesion. Future productions, they said, should emulate the feature-length films with strong story lines whose success was amply demonstrated in Charlie Chaplin's film, *Shoulder Arms*, released towards the end of the war.[83] Captured by both its style and content, the NWAC subsequently attempted to produce a feature-length 'story'-type propaganda piece of its own. *The National Film* aimed at rekindling anti-German hatreds and tackling the unpatriotic behaviour of strikers through the fictional tale of a successful German invasion of Britain. But the film ran into expensive production problems and, although the interjection of the Ministry of Information helped push the film to completion in October 1918, by then the war had swung decisively in the Allies' favour and the message of the film looked decidedly redundant and inappropriate.[84] This forced the ministry's Cinematograph Department (which had now assumed control over the production of all British propaganda film output) to adopt a new policy whereby the origin and attribution of propaganda films would be hidden from audiences. The aim was to deflect the cinema trade's hostility and viewers' indifference whilst giving the ministry scope to develop a more furtive approach in producing film with propaganda content. Apparently, film as a subtle and discreet tool of managing opinion was now a legitimate pursuit.[85]

Resisting the resisters

Covert propaganda was not confined to film-makers. When Edward Carson took over responsibility for all government propaganda in August 1917, ministers could no longer be certain of the public's commitment to the war. They looked hard at the reports of the Industrial Unrest Commissions; became restive at the Army's failure to achieve its much-vaunted 'breakthrough' on the Western Front; and concluded that dangers of war-weariness and popular discontent were almost palpable. The possibility that the cries of the peace movement would now take root amongst industrial workers was given added urgency by the Russian Revolution and the Bolshevik government's subsequent withdrawal from the war, under the terms of the Brest-Litovsk treaty, in March 1918. The War Cabinet concluded that 'for the vigorous prosecution of the war, a contented working-class was indispensable'.[86]

The government was lucky in that the pacifist voice was a disparate one. Intellectual to its core, the movement comprised many anti-war groups, but remained largely on the political fringe and lacked a central authority. The most prominent, the Union of Democratic Control (UDC), formed in 1914 by disillusioned Liberals Arthur Ponsonby and C.P. Trevelyan, included Labour Party leader Ramsay MacDonald and the writer Norman Angell amongst its membership. The UDC's criticism of the government's war policies had been constant, but its calls for a negotiated peace, particularly after the Somme, now appeared to chime with other political and religious groups, including the Independent Labour Party and the Quakers, and it joined hands with activists in the No-Conscription Fellowship and women's peace organizations, such as Sylvia Pankhurst's East London Federation of Suffragettes. It was Pankhurst's newspaper, the *Workers' Dreadnought*, that had been first to publish Siegfried Sassoon's outburst against the war in 1917.[87] However, the pacifists', cause received a significant boost with the publication of Lord Lansdowne's letter in the *Daily Telegraph* on 29th November 1917. As a leading senior Conservative, Lansdowne, horrified at the appalling losses at the Somme, advocated a negotiated settlement, and his correspondence restated his comments made in a Cabinet memorandum in 1916, that 'we are slowly but surely killing off the best of the male population of these islands'.[88] Lansdowne's anxieties spoke less to the working classes than to his aristocratic and upper-class brethren. But the fact that Lansdowne's declared anti-war stance now placed him in alliance with the likes of Ramsay MacDonald and feminist socialists suggested the formation of an all-party pacifist alliance that was positively alarming.

The government reacted in two ways: one private; one public. In private, the NWAC, together with the Home Office, embarked on a programme of subterfuge and black propaganda in an attempt to discredit the various pacifist groupings. Home Office and Scotland Yard agents set out to collect 'information' on the movement's activists. Thomas Cox, secretary to the NWAC, agreed with Basil Thomson (in charge of Scotland Yard's newly formed Special Branch) to supply details of pacifist meetings 'in order that we may get our local committee machinery going'.[89] Thomson called the strategy a 'counterblast', as lectures, public meetings, mass demonstrations and pro-war speeches were organized to put the government's case. NWAC propaganda then launched a concerted campaign to smear the movement by claims that it was being funded by the Germans. Carson argued that there was a grain of truth in this, although Thomson failed to find any evidence, suggesting that the movement was receiving subscriptions from 'cranks'. The Home Office briefly dallied with the notion of censoring pacifist publications, though the implications of this for the future of free speech were too much for Lloyd George to sanction. All pamphlets, therefore, were to be submitted to the Press Bureau for official approval before publication.[90]

All the same, Lansdowne's letter did finally compel Lloyd George into publicly declaring Britain's war aims in January 1918: a recognition that simply relying on the public's innate patriotism to keep them fighting was no longer tenable. After more than three long years of war there was now a public yearning for peace, and the need to rally a tired, confused and war-weary people made it necessary to make this propaganda message particularly powerful. After endless discussions with the Cabinet, and even consultations with old Liberal colleagues Asquith and Edward Grey, Lloyd George formulated a series of war aims that included the restoration of Belgian independence; reparations for war damage; self-determination for the peoples under Turkish and Austrian rule and living in the German colonies; the re-establishment of 'the sanctity of treaties'; and the securing of all future territorial settlements on the basis of the right of self-determination and the 'consent of the governed'. Lloyd George finished by urging the creation 'of some international organization to limit the burden of armaments and diminish the probability of war'.[91]

The fact that Lloyd George delivered his speech to an audience of trade unionists at Caxton Hall was significant. The morale and mood of the industrial workforce were essential if the war was to be won, yet its attitude to the conflict, and that of the labour movement overall, was unknown and, without a system to accurately gauge the temper of workers' opinion, unknowable. The rush of strikes and industrial unrest that had disrupted war production in 1917 was evidence enough of workers' discontent, yet the findings of the Industrial Unrest Commissions, as we have seen, had played down their revolutionary character in favour of more multifarious factors of localized complaints about working and housing conditions, rising prices and food shortages. However, ministers, their minds filled by the constant weekly reports of Basil Thomson (whose network of agents now began to report back details of the revolutionary potential of trade union and labour organization meetings), viewed almost every strike, walkout, protest meeting and publication as potentially revolutionary. The NWAC, for example, despatched speakers to industrial areas (Wigan and Hull were two areas earmarked for such treatment) where unrest and pacifist influence had threatened to spread amongst the workforce.[92] Edward Carson received Cabinet approval to arrange visits of parties of workers to the front.[93] Cabinet memoranda were prepared on 'revolutionary agitation on Clydeside'.[94] And Lloyd George's press office prepared a dossier on the background, role and utterances of almost every prominent Labour Party politician and industrial 'troublemaker' across the country.[95]

Ministers were tired; the constant worries of the war had shot their nerves to pieces. Keith Middlemas commented that 'Ministers did not exactly deceive themselves, but by creating a machine for surveillance they highlighted the things they feared.'[96] Anxious ministers thus took note of official memoranda that stated, 'For the purpose of steadying public opinion and allaying labour unrest, propaganda in the form of a direct appeal to patriotism is not nearly so effective as the publication in an attractive form of information and instruction about the war.' They approved measures aimed at combating what they saw as pacifist and revolutionary propaganda through techniques of mass persuasion, channelled primarily through the press. Newspapers were supplied with articles, letters and features that stated the government's position, but without revealing their sources. Recommendations were made to establish a Publicity Office at the NWAC under an editor to furnish the press with material favourable to the government. The organization was already claiming that it supplied leading articles and editorial notes to 400 newspapers through one agency, and '189 through another'. In addition, the NWAC declared that about 150 newspapers had taken printed articles and news paragraphs.[97] From 1917 the War Cabinet began to make frequent references to the importance of the press in conveying favourable publicity for the government, with newspapers being oiled with large sums of money. Auckland Geddes went to great lengths to 'prime' London press editors with claims of broken pledges by the Engineering Unions or government refutations of British Socialist Party propaganda.[98] Thus, striking workers in Coventry could be labelled 'anti-patriotic'; ex-servicemen were cheerily volunteering for strike duty; and Oliver Stanley, a minister at the Board of Trade, could meet the press 'confident that their attitude would be in accord with Government policy'. Propaganda as opinion-manipulation now came with tacit government sanction.[99]

In this sense, three points are worth making about the British propaganda effort. First, it should perhaps be understood more as a case made than case proven. Keith Middlemas has argued that Lloyd George and his cohorts deliberately attempted to create a climate of favourability towards the coalition. Lloyd George's bid to gain control of the British press (his unsuccessful attempt to purchase *The Times* should be counterbalanced with his successful takeover of the liberal *Daily Chronicle*), the enticing of major press proprietors (Northcliffe, Rothermere and Beaverbrook) with offers of ministerial posts and access to secret information, and the use of coalition money, state intelligence services and government secrets simply 'smacks of dictatorship': moves not all that far removed from the flag-waving, drum-beating, Hun-hating, behaviour-influencing nature of 'official' government propaganda.[100] Yet, second, as some historians assert, questions remain as to how effective the propaganda product was in swaying public opinion. People did not believe everything they read in the papers. The public appeared to be quite capable of mobilizing themselves during the first two years of the war, often taking the press and propaganda agencies with them. The onset of war-weariness, the understandable sense of frustration and anger at the interminable nature of the war, the scale of casualties and the worsening conditions on the Home Front inevitably spilled over into strikes and civil unrest that worn-out jittery ministers misinterpreted as revolutionary. By the spring of 1918 the shock of the German spring offensive on the Western Front, the capitulation of the Bolsheviks and the collapse of the British Fifth Army had combined to reawaken public memories of the war's early days. The prospect of German armies marching across Europe once more united the nation with an intensity that owed little to the propagandists. Government propaganda remained one step behind a public mood that was being shaped by an even greater determination to defeat the enemy, and increasingly defined by a revival of the xenophobic hatreds that persisted until the end of the war and spilled over into the first days of peace.[101] By then, finally, the government had become almost embarrassed about its propaganda machine. Perhaps recalling Stanley Baldwin's comment that 'Propaganda is not a word that has a pleasant sound in English ears ... the Englishman dislikes talking about himself and dislikes advertising what he has done', the government hastily set about dismantling the apparatus of wartime propaganda following the Armistice.[102] The Ministry of Information was closed in December 1918; the NWAC and the Press Bureau were abolished in April 1919.[103] It is often said that Britain's propaganda effort was much admired by the Nazi party. But, for the country's governors, the foray into manipulating the public's wartime consciousness had taught a powerful lesson: complacency and ignorance of the people's thinking was no longer acceptable in the new mass democracy that was to come. The propaganda question had clarified what had already been evident: public opinion and the need to gauge it accurately was now a critical determinant of political behaviour, attitude and the making of policy.

Notes

1 Cate Haste, *Keep the Home Fires Burning*, London: Allen Lane, 1977, pp. 1–2.
2 Gary S. Messinger, 'An Inheritance Worth Remembering: The British Approach to Official Propaganda During the First World War', *Historical Journal of Film, Radio and Television*, vol. 13, no. 2, 1993, pp. 117–27.
3 *The Times*, 7th August 1914.
4 *The Times*, 28th August 1914, 20th September 1914; Cate Haste, *Keep the Home Fires Burning*, op. cit., p. 24.
5 See Adrian Gregory, *The Last Great War: British Society and the First World War*, Cambridge: Cambridge University Press, 2008, p. 37.
6 *The Times*, 18th September 1914.
7 *The Fight for the Right Movement*, London: T. Fisher Unwin, 1916, IWM Pamphlet, 6089 K, p. 5; cited also in Cate Haste, *Keep the Home Fires Burning*, op. cit., p. 25.
8 George Bernard Shaw, *Common Sense About the War*, London: The Statesman Publishing, 1914, p. 3; Harold Owen, *Common Sense About the Shaw: Being a Candid Criticism of Common Sense About the War, by George Bernard Shaw*, London: Allen & Unwin, 1915; George Robb, *British Culture and the First World War*, Basingstoke: Palgrave, 2002, pp. 132–33.
9 Trevor Wilson, ed., *The Political Diaries of C.P. Scott, 1911–1928*, London: Collins 1970, p. 95; Adrian Gregory, *The Last Great War*, op. cit., p. 37; Cate Haste, *Keep the Home Fires Burning*, op. cit., p. 25.
10 Adrian Gregory, *The Last Great War*, op. cit., p. 37; Cate Haste, *Keep the Home Fires Burning*, op. cit., p. 27; Samuel Hynes, *A War Imagined: The First World War and English Culture*, London: The Bodley Head, 1990, p. 69.
11 *Daily News*, 14th August 1914. See also D.G. Wright, 'The Great War, Government Propaganda and English "Men of Letters", 1914–16', *Literature and History*, no. 7, Spring, 1978, pp. 70–100.
12 University of Oxford, Faculty of Modern History, *Why We Are At War: Great Britain's Case*, Oxford: Clarendon Press, 1914, ch. 6; Arthur Marwick, *The Deluge: British Society and the First World War*, 2nd edn, Basingstoke: Macmillan, p. 95.
13 Richard van Emden and Steve Humphries, *All Quiet on the Home Front: An Oral History of Life in Britain During the First World War*, London: Headline, 2003, p. 110.
14 Adrian Gregory, *The Last Great War*, op. cit., p.159. Gregory is the one historian who analyses the role of British religiosity during the Great War in depth.
15 Richard van Emden and Steve Humphries, *All Quiet on the Home Front: An Oral History of Life in Britain During the First World War*, op. cit., p. 110.
16 Adrian Gregory, *The Last Great War*, op. cit., p. 174.
17 Trevor Wilson, *The Myriad Faces of War: Britain and the Great War, 1914–1918*, Cambridge: Polity Press, 1986, pp. 178, 740.
18 Alan Wilkinson, *The Church of England and the First World War*, 2nd edn, London: SPCK, 1996, p. 217; Adrian Gregory, *The Last Great War*, op. cit., pp. 168, 327.
19 William Temple, *Church and Nation*, London: Macmillan, 1915; Adrian Gregory, *The Last Great War*, op. cit., pp. 162–65.

20 Eric Field, *Advertising: The Forgotten Years*, London: Benn, 1959, pp. 28–29; Cate Haste, *Keep the Home Fires Burning*, op. cit., pp. 51–52.

21 James Duane Squires, *British Propaganda at Home and in the United States from 1914 to 1917*, Cambridge: Harvard University Press, 1935, pp. 16–25.

22 See Roy Douglas, 'Voluntary Enlistment in the First World War and the Work of the Parliamentary Recruiting Committee', *Journal of Modern History*, vol. 42, no. 4, Dec. 1970, pp. 564–85; Cate Haste, *Keep the Home Fires Burning*, op. cit., p. 53.

23 Frank Gardner, 'The Sounds of Flanders', BBC Radio Four broadcast 'The Archive Hour', 24th November 2007.

24 Maurice Rickards, *Posters of the First World War*, London: Evelyn, Adams & Mackay, 1968, p. 14; Philip Dutton, 'Moving Images? The Parliamentary Committee's Poster Campaign 1914–16', *Imperial War Museum Review*, 1989, pp. 43–58.

25 Carol Acton, 'Best Boys and Aching Hearts: The Rhetoric of Romance as Social Control in Wartime Magazines for Young Women', in Jessica Meyer, ed., *British Popular Culture and the First World War*, Leiden: Brill, 2008, pp. 173–93; Cate Haste, *Keep the Home Fires Burning*, op. cit., pp. 55–57; Joanna Bourke in Frank Gardner, 'The Sounds of Flanders', BBC Radio Four broadcast 'The Archive Hour', 24th November 2007.

26 See Stephen Koss, *The Rise and Fall of the Political Press in Britain*, vol. II, London: Hamish Hamilton, 1984, pp. 238–49.

27 Nicholas Hiley, 'Lord Kitchener Resigns; The Suppression of "The Globe" in 1915', *Journal of Newspaper and Periodical History*, vol. 8, 1992; Colin Lovelace, 'British Press Censorship During the First World War', in George Boyce, James Curran and Pauline Wingate, eds, *Newspaper History from the Seventeenth Century to the Present Day*, London: Constable, 1978, p. 307.

28 Colin Lovelace, 'British Press Censorship During the First World War', op. cit., p. 309.

29 Phillip Knightly, *The First Casualty: From the Crimea to Vietnam: The War Correspondent as Hero, Propagandist and Myth Maker*, op. cit., p. 69.

30 See M.L. Sanders and Philip Taylor, *British Propaganda During the First World War, 1914–18*, Basingstoke: Macmillan, 1982, pp. 20–24.

31 *Hansard Parliamentary Debates*, 5th series, vol. 65, cols 2153–56, 7th August 1914.

32 M.L. Sanders and Philip Taylor, *British Propaganda During the First World War, 1914–18*, op. cit., pp. 20–24.

33 See Phillip Knightly, *The First Casualty: From the Crimea to Vietnam: The War Correspondent as Hero, Propagandist and Myth Maker*, op. cit., pp. 75–76; Cate Haste, *Keep the Home Fires Burning*, op. cit., pp. 33–34.

34 Colin Lovelace, 'British Press Censorship During the First World War', op. cit., pp. 311–12.

35 Ibid., p. 315; M.L. Sanders and Philip Taylor, *British Propaganda During the First World War, 1914–18*, op. cit., pp. 22–23.

36 Sir Ernest Swinton and Earl Percy (8th Duke of Northumberland), *A Year Ago: Eye-Witness's Narrative of the War from March 30th to July 18th 1915*, self-published, 1915.

37 Phillip Knightly, *The First Casualty: From the Crimea to Vietnam: The War Correspondent as Hero, Propagandist and Myth Maker*, op. cit., p. 78.

38 Phillip Knightly, *The First Casualty*, p. 79.

39 Gerard DeGroot, *Blighty: British Society in the Era of the Great War*, Harlow: Longman 1996, p. 185.

40 Phillip Knightly, *The First Casualty*, op. cit., pp. 79–80.

41 Philip Gibbs, *Adventures in Journalism*, London: Heinemann, 1923, p. 231.

42 See Alice Goldfarb, 'Words as Weapons: Propaganda in Britain and Germany During the First World War', *Journal of Contemporary History*, vol. 3, no. 3, 1978.

43 Philip Gibbs, *The Battles of the Somme*, London: William Heinemann, 1917, pp. 16–17. Also cited in Cate Haste, *Keep the Home Fires Burning*, op. cit., pp. 68–69.

44 Paul Fussell, *The Great War and Modern Memory*, Oxford: Oxford University Press, 1975, pp. 115–16.

45 Adrian Gregory, *The Last Great War*, op. cit., p. 66.

46 See James Morgan Read, *Atrocity Propaganda 1914–1919*, New Haven: Yale University Press, 1941, pp. 78–103; Hew Strachan, *The First World War*, London: Simon & Schuster, 2003, pp. 50–51.

47 *The Times*, 12th September 1914; Cate Haste, *Keep the Home Fires Burning*, op. cit., pp. 84–85; *Daily Mirror*, 25th August 1915; see also Alice Goldfarb, 'Words as Weapons: Propaganda in Britain and Germany During the First World War', op. cit.; Cate Haste, *Keep the Home Fires Burning*, op. cit., p. 88.

48 See 'Germans and Their Dead', in *The Times*, 17th April 1917.

49 See Arthur Ponsonby, *Falsehood in Wartime*, London: Allen & Unwin, 1928, pp. 102–13; Phillip Knightly, *The First Casualty*, op. cit., pp. 89–91; Adrian Gregory, *The Last Great War*, op. cit., pp. 41–42.

50 See Adrian Gregory, *The Last Great War*. op. cit., pp. 57–63.

51 *Report of the Committee on Alleged German Atrocities*, London: HMSO, 1915; *Appendix to the Report of the Committee on Alleged German Atrocities*, London: HMSO, 1915; Trevor Wilson, *The Myriad Faces of War*, op. cit., p. 189. See also Gary S. Messinger, *British Propaganda and the State in the First World War*, Manchester: Manchester University Press, 1992, pp. 70–84.

52 See Trevor Wilson, *The Myriad Faces of War*, op. cit., pp. 183–91; James Morgan Read, *Atrocity Propaganda 1914–1919*, op. cit., pp. 201–09; Trevor Wilson, 'Lord Bryce's Investigation into Alleged German Atrocities in Belgium 1914–15', *Journal of Contemporary History*, vol. 14, no. 2, 1979; Gerard DeGroot, *Blighty*, op. cit., pp. 189–90; Adrian Gregory, *The Last Great War*, op. cit., pp. 67–68; Cate Haste, *Keep the Home Fires Burning*, op. cit., pp. 93–95.

53 See Adrian Gregory, *The Last Great War*, op. cit., pp. 57–63.

54 *The Times*, 29th July 1916; James Morgan Read, *Atrocity Propaganda 1914–1919*, op. cit., p. 223; Neil Oliver, *Not Forgotten*, London: Hodder & Stoughton, 2005, pp. 200–03.

55 James Morgan Read, *Atrocity Propaganda 1914–1919*, op. cit., pp. 210–15; Cate Haste, *Keep the Home Fires Burning*, op. cit., pp. 89–90; Harold D. Lasswell, *Propaganda Technique in the World War*, London: Kegan, Paul, Trench, Trubner: 1927, p. 32; comments by Gerard DeGroot, *Blighty*, op. cit., p. 180; Trevor Wilson, *The Myriad Faces of War*, op. cit., pp. 744–45.

56 Trevor Wilson, *The Myriad Faces of War*, op. cit., pp. 92–93; James Morgan Read, *Atrocity Propaganda 1914–1919*, op. cit., pp. 199–201; Adrian Gregory, *The Last Great War*, pp. 61–62, 68; Cate Haste, *Keep the Home Fires Burning*, op. cit., pp. 101–02; Gerard DeGroot, *Blighty*, op. cit., p. 180.

57 See Gary S. Messinger, *British Propaganda and the State in the First World War*, op. cit., pp. 85–98, 24–52.

58 M.L. Sanders and Philip Taylor, *British Propaganda During the First World War, 1914–18*, op. cit., pp. 247–49.

59 Cate Haste, *Keep the Home Fires Burning*, op. cit., p.40.

60 M.L. Sanders and Philip Taylor, *British Propaganda During the First World War, 1914–18*, op. cit., pp. 247–49.

61 See Stephen Badsey, 'Press, Propaganda and Public Perceptions', in *A Part of History: Aspects of the British Experience of the First World War*, London: Continuum, 2008, pp. 27–35.

62 NA, CAB 24/13, GT.774, 'Propaganda at Home: Memorandum by the Director, Department of Information', 18th May 1917; M.L. Sanders and Philip Taylor, *British Propaganda During the First World War, 1914–18*, op. cit., pp. 66–67.

63 M.L. Sanders and Philip Taylor, *British Propaganda During the First World War, 1914–18*, op. cit., pp. 62, 65–70. See also Cate Haste, *Keep the Home Fires Burning*, op. cit., pp. 40–41.

64 M.L. Sanders and Philip Taylor, *British Propaganda During the First World War, 1914–18*, op. cit., p. 141.

65 NA, Ministry of Information papers (hereafter, 'INF') 1/317, 'Home Publicity During the Great War: The National War Aims Committee', prepared for the Ministry of Information, 1939. See also Cate Haste, *Keep the Home Fires Burning*, op. cit., pp. 42–43.

66 NA, INF 1/317, 'Home Publicity During the Great War: The National War Aims Committee', prepared for the Ministry of Information, 1939. See also Cate Haste, *Keep the Home Fires Burning*, op. cit., pp. 42–43; M.L. Sanders and Philip Taylor, *British Propaganda During the First World War, 1914–18*, op. cit., pp. 139–42, 149–51; S. Colclough, 'No Such Bookselling Has Ever Before Taken Place in This Country: Propaganda and the Wartime Distribution Practices of W.H. Smith & Son', in Mary Hammond and Shafquat Towheed, eds, *Publishing in the First World War*, Basingstoke: Palgrave: Macmillan, 2007.

67 NA, INF 1/317, 'Home Publicity During the Great War: The National War Aims Committee', prepared for the Ministry of Information, 1939.

68 NA, CAB 27/17, 'Cinema Industry and Its Relation to the Government', memorandum by T.L. Gilmour, 13th October 1917; Nicholas Reeves, *The Power of Film Propaganda: Myth or Reality?* London: Continuum, 1999, p. 22. See also Nicholas Reeves, 'Official British Film Propaganda', in Michael Paris, ed., *The First World War and Popular Cinema*, New Brunswick: Rutgers University Press, pp. 27–50.

69 NA, CAB 27/17, 'Cinema Industry and Its Relation to the Government', memorandum by T.L. Gilmour, 13th October 1917; NA, INF 4/6, 'Minute on the Cinema Industry and Its Relation to the Government', 8th June 1918.

70 Cited in Nicholas Reeves, *The Power of Film Propaganda*, op. cit., p. 23.

71 Nicholas Reeves, *The Power of Film Propaganda*, op. cit., pp. 23–24.

72 Nicholas Reeves, *The Power of Film Propaganda*, op. cit., pp. 23–24. See also Nicholas Reeves, *Official British Film Propaganda During the First World War*, London: Croom Helm, 1986, pp. 56–57, 142–45; M.L. Sanders and Philip Taylor, *British Propaganda During the First World War, 1914–18*, op. cit., pp. 126–27.

73 Nicholas Reeves, *Official British Film Propaganda During the First World War*, op. cit., pp. 101–3, 225–38.

74 See Roger Smither, 'A Wonderful Idea of the Fighting: The Question of Fakes in The Battle of the Somme', *Imperial War Museum Review*, no. 3, 1988; Kevin Brownlow, *The War, the West and the Wilderness*, London: Secker & Warburg, 1979, pp. 64–65; Alastair H. Fraser, Andrew Robertshaw and Steve Roberts, *Ghosts on the Somme: Filming the Battle, June–July 1916*, Barnsley: Pen & Sword, 2009, pp. 163–71. For a rather implausible contradictory account, see Lieut. Geoffrey Malins, *How I Filmed the War*, London: Imperial War Museum, 1920 (introduction by Nicholas Hiley, 1993), pp. 162–68.

75 Stephen Badsey, 'Battle of the Somme: British War Propaganda', *Historical Journal of Film, Radio and Television*, vol. 3, no. 2, 1983, pp. 99–115.

76 Nicholas Reeves, *The Power of Film Propaganda*, op. cit., pp. 35–36.

77 Nicholas Reeves, 'Official British Film Propaganda', op. cit., pp. 39–40.

78 Nicholas Reeves, *The Power of Film Propaganda*, op. cit., p. 27.

79 Nicholas Reeves, *The Power of Film Propaganda*, op. cit., pp. 27–30.

80 Cate Haste, *Keep the Home Fires Burning*, op. cit., pp. 46–47.

81 IWM, Film Collection, 'A Day in the Life of a Munition Worker', production date, July 1917, no. 510; 'Father and Lather', production date, May 1918, no. 1122; 'The Secret', production date, May 1918, no. 549–1. See also Nicholas Reeves, *Official British Film Propaganda During the First World War*, op. cit., p. 192.

82 See Nicholas Reeves, 'Film Propaganda and Its Audience: The Example of Britain's Official Films During the First World War', *Journal of Contemporary History*, vol. 18, no. 3, 1983, pp. 463–94.

83 J.M. Winter, 'Propaganda and the Mobilization of Consent', in Hew Strachan, ed., *The Oxford Illustrated History of the First World War*, Oxford: Oxford University Press, 1998, pp. 221–23.

84 Nicholas Reeves, *The Power of Film Propaganda*, op. cit., p. 30.

85 Nicholas Reeves, *The Power of Film Propaganda*, op. cit., p. 31.

86 NA, CAB 23/3, War Cabinet Minutes, Meeting 190 (1), 19th July 1917.

87 Cate Haste, *Keep the Home Fires Burning*, op. cit., pp. 145–47. See also Martin Ceadel, *Pacifism in Britain: The Defining of a Faith*, Oxford: Clarendon Press, 1980; Marvin Swartz, *The Union of Democratic Control in British Politics During the First World War*, Oxford: Clarendon Press, 1971.

88 NA, CAB 37/159/32, Lord Lansdowne Memorandum, 13th November 1916.

89 NA, HO 45/10743/263275/265, Thomas Cox to Secretary Home Office, 15th November 1917, cited in Cate Haste, *Keep the Home Fires Burning*, op. cit., pp. 170–71.

90 NA, HO 45/10743/263275/265, op. cit.

91 *The Times*, 7th January 1918; John Grigg, *Lloyd George: War Leader, 1916–1918*, Harmondsworth: Penguin, 2003, pp. 378–82.

92 NA, INF 1/317, 'Home Publicity During the Great War: The National War Aims Committee', prepared for the Ministry of Information, 1939.

93 NA, CAB 23/4, War Cabinet Meeting 253 (4), 19th October 1917; NA, CAB 24/28, GT.2268, 'Suggested Visit of Workers and Others to Theatre of War', 12th October 1917.

94 NA, CAB 24/44, GT.3838, 'Revolutionary Agitation in Glasgow and Clydeside', 5th March 1918.

95 See Keith Middlemas, *Politics in Industrial Society: The Experience of the British System since 1911*, London: Andre Deutsch, 1979, pp. 130–31.

96 Keith Middlemas, *Politics in Industrial Society*, op. cit., pp. 132–33.

97 NA, CAB 24/39, GT.3360, 'Use of the Press for Propaganda Purposes', 16th January 1918; NA, CAB 23/5, War Cabinet, 328 (18), 22nd January 1918; NA, CAB 24/40, GT.3412 'Home Propaganda', 21st January 1918.

98 NA, CAB 23/5, War Cabinet, 328 (18), 22nd January 1918; Keith Middlemas, *Politics in Industrial Society*, op. cit., p. 131.

99 Keith Middlemas, *Politics in Industrial Society*, op. cit., p. 131.

100 Keith Middlemas, *Politics in Industrial Society*, op. cit., pp. 351–52.

101 George Robb, *British Culture and the First World War*, op. cit., p. 124; Nicholas Reeves, *The Power of Film Propaganda*, op. cit., pp. 19–20.

102 Quoted in Gerard DeGroot, *Blighty*, op. cit., p. 176.

103 M.L. Sanders and Philip Taylor, *British Propaganda During the First World War, 1914–18*, op. cit., pp. 247–48.

9   War culture

British cultural life during the war was a place of mixed feelings. Writers, dramatists, painters and poets produced work that was deeply informed by the conflict, where the familiar, essentially conservative language of patriotism, heroism and romanticism was set against the newer voices of disenchantment, rage and realism. Greater certainties about the conflict were expressed in the cultural dialogue of the 'common people'. Here, the nature and purpose of the war were understood through a vocabulary of valour and pluck, and an unquestioning acceptance of Britain's struggle, where culture was an unashamedly commercial enterprise. In their efforts to understand British wartime culture, historians have been inclined to divide its substance into the 'high' and 'low': where the 'elite' intellectual pursuits of poetry, literature, classical music and painting rubbed shoulders with the 'popular culture' of the people, as expressed in popular song, theatrical revue and cheap novelettes. This dual view of British 'conflict' culture still has some validity, but the war blurred its boundaries. During these years the response of the elite appeared to parallel that of the masses, all sharing a common of experience. Indeed it could be argued that the war *became* British culture.

The war of the arts

Samuel Hynes, highlighting the year 1912, spoke of Edwardian culture as a 'variety of things'. That year London saw the first production of Chekhov's *The Seagull*, the publication of H.G. Wells's *Marriage*, the first performance of Schoenberg's atonal *Five Pieces for Orchestra* at the Queen's Hall and the second exhibition of paintings from the post-Impressionists.[1] The war, however, brought this flirtation with modernism to a temporary halt. To his relief, Edmond Gosse, critic and editor, saw the war as a 'purifier ... the sovereign disinfectant' that would clear 'the clotted channels of the intellect' and put an end to the political upheaval, intellectual bickering and the pernicious foreign influences that had corrupted British culture.[2] For sure, the war reawakened British cultural insularity and traditional suspicions of intellectualism. Scholars, critics and audiences fell into the popular outburst of patriotism and anti-German fever that swept the country in 1914. Beethoven's music was scorned; Goethe's writings were ridiculed; some London book-shops banned Nietzsche's works; the discordant unmelodic music of Richard Strauss was shunned.[3] Indeed, the innate superiority of British culture was resurrected with the linguistic brilliance of Shakespeare and the rustic idyllic beauty of Wordsworth and Keats held high: an attitude that was confirmed when news of the German army's burning of the ancient library at Louvain became known. As the war progressed, public lectures were held across the country to commemorate the three hundredth anniversary of 'the Bard's' death, and soldiers were given patriotic broadsheets from *The Times* con-taining extracts from Dickens, Macaulay, Wordsworth and Kipling, to comfort them as they marched to the front.[4]

British wartime culture was full of tensions. The practicalities of viewing art, for example, became more difficult. The government's decision in 1916 to close the major museums and galleries, in spite of record attendances, was universally condemned by the arts community but, against the backdrop of national sacrifice and battlefield slaughter, art somehow seemed frivolous and ephemeral. Shaw damned such attitudes as 'war delirium'.[5] But British art had its own dilemmas. Some pre-war painters struggled to break free from the representational formats (where subjects are depicted as they appear to the eye) and allegorical styles that dominated Victorian art. In 1910, Roger Fry staged the first exhibition of paintings by a group of French, Russian and English artists whom he identified as the 'post-Impressionists', whose works rejected the 'naturalistic' impulses of the French school in favour of depicting a more solid 'art of the museums', highlighting the earlier works of Cézanne, Gaugin and Matisse. In a similar vein, Walter Sickert's Camden Town Group drew its influences from the American artist Whistler, with the focus on depicting urban themes and painting from photographs.[6] But the more radi-cal movements of Cubism (which deconstructed its objects and recomposed them from various concurrent points of view) and Futurism (an art form that soaked itself in the modern world of industrial technology, speed, movement, machines and violence), which provoked a strong reaction from the arts establishment, had only a limited impact on the public mind.[7] Modernists, however, had welcomed the war, arguing that the conflict would sweep aside the orthodoxies of establishment culture. Percy Wyndham Lewis, an *avante-garde* writer and abstract painter (along with his fellow advocates Edward Wadsworth and the free verse poet Ezra Pound) attacked the nostalgia and traditionalism of British art and hoped that the war would destroy its 'cul-tural philistinism' and replace it with 'Vorticism' (a British version of Futur-ism), the painting of forms as geometric abstract shapes. Vorticists, in opposing sentimentalism and romanticism, looked to the more primal instincts of energy, clear thought and purity, with a desire to emphasize the mechanical over the naturalistic.[8]

Yet only those who wanted to listen heard Wyndham Lewis's battle cry for modernism. His manifesto for tomorrow became lost amongst the rising tide of nationalistic bellicosity that gripped the country in the autumn months of 1914. Modernism failed to dent the popularity of 'establishment' artists – John Charlton, Lady Elizabeth Butler, Christopher Clarke and Richard Caton-Woodville (to name but four) – who retained traditional contexts and narratives in their work. From the moment the 'Some Modern War Pictures' exhibition opened in London's Bond Street during October 1914 it was clear that one narrative of war art was determined to depict heroism and glory: battles and soldiers, set not in the trenches, but in the age of Wellington, Napoleon and Waterloo. Ships of the Royal Navy, Britain's 'hearts of oak', storming the enemy amongst the crashing foam, and generals surveying battle-scenes were omnipresent themes, each emphasizing the rhapsody and thrill of war: arms and armaments were romantic; military leaders were heroic. The unrealistic cavalry attack of Allen Stewart's *The Charge of the Scots Greys at St Quentin* (1915) and Lucy Kemp-Welch's *Forward!* (1916, pasted into a poster image) or, later, *Forward the Guns* (1917) are good examples of the genre. This impulse to restate older views ignored newer realities, but was still in evidence as late as April 1918, when the magazine *The War Illustrated* could depict a valiant cavalry charge or one plucky British Tommy capturing an entire enemy trench single-handed.[9]

The deception was intentional, in some respects. Traditionalists recognized the need for idealization. Elizabeth Butler warned that 'the painter should be careful to keep himself at a distance, lest the ignoble and vile details under his eyes should blind him irretrievably to the noble things that rise beyond'.[10] Thus, the durability of older narratives determined that depictions of limbless, shattered corpses were not good for public morale. James Clarke's *The Great Sacrifice*, a painting which appeared in *The Graphic* at Christmas 1914, shows a young, handsome, yet very dead British soldier, lying peacefully at the foot of a crucifix, caught as in an endless sleep. Sentiment and inspiration were the sub-themes of Frederick Roe's *The Foster Parent*, which depicted a kilted Scottish soldier taking care of a sleeping infant in a French farmhouse, Fortunino Matania's *The Last Message* (1917), where a dying soldier whispers his last goodbyes into the ear of his comrade, and Richard Caton Woodville's melodramatic *When Night Sets In*, where a soldier, blinded in battle, sits alone in a garden, while images of all the activities that are now denied him – a tennis match, riding a horse, playing cricket – circle around.[11]

Such imagery played well in the wartime public eye. The paintings were widely disseminated as postcards, magazine illustrations and propaganda posters and were consumed by a nation who appeared to want its war served up in this manner. Yet the pictures of Clarke, Roe, Butler and Caton-Woodville *et al.* expressed an imagined war: an idea of conflict that belonged in the Edwardian and Victorian drawing room. In this sense, they shared some common ground with the modernists, for they also relied on art as a concept: as intellectual interpretation rather than optical clarity. But the point of departure was fixed in the experience of war. None of the 'war pictures' produced by the traditionalists came from artists with any direct experience of the front; they were practitioners of an absentee tradition whose limits had been clearly exposed by the gruesome nature of the First World War. Mark Gertler's *Merry-Go-Round* (1916), produced at the height of the war, hinted at a changing mood. Gertler's soldiers and civilians ride together on a fairground carousel that spins ever faster, never ending and without meaning. Its shocking imagery moved the novelist D.H. Lawrence, who came across a photograph of the painting in October 1916, to comment, 'I *do* think that in this combination of blaze, and violent mechanical rotation and complex involution, and ghastly, utterly mindless human intensity of sensational extremity, you have made a real and ultimate revelation.'[12] Gertler's work was representative of a move amongst younger painters to make more sense of the war, yet some interpreted this new mission as more about changing the emphasis of war art through the 'direct experience' of Flanders mud. This newer artistic style would parallel that of the traditionalists until 1918, but would supersede them in the 1920s once the public itself began looking for meaning from the war.[13]

The alternative view of war art emerged slowly. The move towards a more truthful vision of the conflict appears to have originated in the volume of violent cartoons by Dutch artist Louis Raemark. Raemark's disturbing images caught the eye of Charles Masterman at the Official Propaganda Bureau in Wellington House. Masterman well understood the power of imagery as a propaganda tool: showing the war 'in its truest form' was a way to 'present facts and general arguments based upon those facts' to foreign audiences. Unfortunately, the Bureau's attempts to sponsor and distribute photographs of the war through its Pictorial Propaganda Department ran up against Army opposition, so Masterman turned to painting as the only alternative. In July 1916 the Bureau appointed Frances Dodd to produce portraits of military figures and Muirhead Bone (an 'etcher' and successful printmaker) to travel to France and create drawings based on his observations. Bone's appointment saved him from conscription, but it did not save him from the front. When he arrived in Flanders in August 1916 his new commission as war artist took him straight into the Battle of the Somme.[14]

Bone arrived at the front in the role of detached observer with a preference for landscapes. His depictions of foreign views leant heavily towards the English romantic tradition. Two hundred of Bone's pictures were eventually published, in ten monthly instalments, sponsored by Wellington House and reproduced through the magazine *Country Life*. They reflect Bone's wanderings behind the lines, sketching ruined churches, distant landscapes and cratered roads. His depiction of the Battle of the Somme featured a dark land mass punctuated by plumes of smoke and whiffs of explosions set at a distance from the viewer. The battle is seen as a tangential detail to the landscape. Later Bone admitted that the work was 'limited' and 'prosaic', but it suited the propaganda purposes of Wellington House perfectly.[15] Here were real images of a real battle, but without the suffering and destruction.

Soldiers, however, viewed Bone's 'Somme Pictures' as ludicrous. Though strong in representational form, they lacked a moral commentary on the hideous and horrific nature of war. In short, Bone's pictures were out of their depth. Bone's traditionalist instincts meant that his war was depicted within an older context, but without the narratives of heroism and sense of noble sacrifice. His style was already being supplanted when C.R.W. Nevinson exhibited his 'Paintings and Drawings of War' at London's Leicester Galleries in September 1916.[16]

The dynamism of Futurist art had made a deep impression on Nevinson. His limited experience of Western Front warfare, gained first as an ambulance driver for the Red Cross and then as an orderly in the Medical Corps, convinced Nevinson that the conflict was now 'dominated by machines, and that men were mere cogs in the mechanism'. These beliefs drove him to inject into his work the machinery, energy and brutishness of industrialized combat.[17] Nevinson's rise to prominence was initially thanks to the favourable reception his paintings received at the London Group's exhibition in March 1915, where the futuristic *Returning to the Trenches* was first seen. The success of the Leicester Gallery's show brought Nevinson to the attention of Masterman, and the young artist was incorporated into the Wellington House Official War Artists scheme. When the scheme was more systematically organized with the creation of the Department of Information in 1917, Nevinson, alongside Paul Nash and Eric Kennington, formed a group of young modernist painters who were all trained artists with experience of military service, but who had either been sent home wounded or invalided out of the Army. The new regime took their brief from Masterman: no paintings to be related to the orthodox images of war art. Masterman told Nevinson to paint 'anything you please'.[18] As a consequence, these artists began to construct a new visual language of war. The influences of Cubism, Futurism and Vorticism were clearly visible in their work, but not as pure imitation, rather as the application of a method, where the narratives of geometric distortions were applied to industrialized warfare, and the reduction of human beings to robots or tiny figures in huge shattered landscapes. Before the war, modernism had extolled machines, speed and violence; now the war gave these forces a new reality. 'This is war', declared Nevinson, 'as I understand it.'[19]

The war gave Nevinson a sense of mission; his early war paintings depicted the conflict as the soldier-poets would write it: in a narrative that expressed compassion for its victims and anger at its futility and destruction. Nevinson's work as an official war artist, however, became much more subdued, as if the artist had consciously assumed that his official status was a call to censor himself and to dilute his anger. Masterman later commented that Nevinson had 'actually abandoned his own metier in order to produce official (perhaps tame) pictures'.[20] Even so, Nevinson's war art resonates with the grim and unforgiving nature of industrial war. Arguably, his work was at its most effective in its depiction of human faces: the wounded soldiers being treated at a casualty station in *The Doctor* (1916), for instance, cry in agony, their bloody wounds clearly displayed; the grim faces of soldiers handling a huge machine gun in *The Mitrailleuse* (The Machine Gunners, 1915), a dead comrade by their side; the exhausted faces of *French Troops Resting* (1916); the gaunt, shabby and dour expressions of the women depicted in *The Food Queue* (1918); the determined, unsmiling faces of workers, dwarfed by machinery and conveyor belts in *Building Aircraft* (1917).[21]

Eric Kennington visualized the pain of war through his depictions of the experience of front-line soldiering in his most famous work *The Kensingtons at Laventie* (1915) where tired and scruffy men stand in the ruins of a shelled village, and in the anguished and painful faces of injured infantry men on stretchers in *Gassed and Wounded* (1918).[22] Paul Nash, on the other hand, saw the war as a blasted, blighted landscape. He was not as able as other front-line artists at painting human figures, but in a way this was not necessarily a problem. Nash regarded his talents as better directed at 'Going in for nature'. He told his friend Gordon Bottomley in 1912 that he preferred to paint trees 'as tho [*sic*] they were human beings ... because I sincerely love and worship trees and know they *are* people and wonderfully beautiful people'.[23] As David Boyd Hancock has commented, if Nevinson's work portrayed the war as a brutal, merciless machine, Nash saw the war as an assault on nature. If Nevinson's paintings were softened by his role as an official war artist, Nash's work, by contrast, was 'vigorously emboldened' by the war. Drawn by Nevinson to the pointed 'zigzag' style of Futurism and Vorticism, just as he was abandoning it, Nash's war art is that of 'devastated woods and disembowelled hillsides'.[24] Soldiers are bent double, or are reduced to mice-like figures picking their way through shell holes, coils of barbed wire, pools of mud and stagnant water, and shattered tree stumps, as in *The Field of Passchendaele* (1917–18) or, more famously, *The Menin Road* (1919), *Wire* (1918–19) and the savage, almost haunting beauty of *The Ypres Salient at Night* (1918).[25] Nash was an angry courier. 'I am no longer an artist,' he complained to his wife, 'I am a messenger ... who will bring back word from the men who are fighting to those who want the war to go on forever. Feeble, inarticulate, will be my message, but it will have a bitter truth, and may it burn their lousy souls.'[26]

By 1918 the number of artists at the front had expanded quite considerably, chiefly under the auspices of Beaverbrook's British War Memorials Committee within the new Ministry of Information. Beaverbrook desired a greater volume of battlefield art work, and artists recruited included Wyndham Lewis; John Duncan Ferguson a Fauvist (a style of painting that emphasized the use of colour in a non-naturalistic manner: its chief protagonist was the French artist Matisse); Wyndham Lewis's fellow Vorticist David Bomberg; Stanley Spencer (whose attention was focused on the war in the Middle East); and Bernard Adeney. Among the more notable were the internationally renowned John Singer Sargent and the establishment artist William Orpen, who was appointed as official war artist in 1917.[27] Orpen's initial works were taken up with portraits of senior military figures: Douglas Haig, for example, formed his subject matter in 1917; the Commander of the French forces, Marshal Foch, a year later; and a sketch of a tank in action was, perhaps, a tribute to British military technology. Alongside this, however, Orpen stretched himself towards depicting front-line scenes along a modernist narrative, if not necessarily following the style. A cadaverous soldier, rifle in hand, uniform in shreds, stares bleakly at the viewer in *Blown Up* (1917), for example; *Dead Germans in a Trench* (1918) is self-explanatory; a pensive Tommy squats upon a mound beside a trench in *The Thinker on the Battle of Warlencourt* (1918), leaving the audience to speculate on the subject's thoughts; a dead soldier lies sprawled beside a flooded shell crater in the work *Zonnebeke* (1918).[28] Whilst Sargent was an enthusiastic participant in the war art scheme, he struggled to depict the reality of front-line combat. His moment of revelation came when he encountered hundreds of men afflicted by temporary blindness following a gas attack in 1918. He worked upon the scene to produce the moving and intensely emotional *Gassed* (1919), where medical orderlies lead queues of blinded soldiers out of a battle zone. *Gassed* went on to become one of the most popular and famous wartime paintings of the period.[29]

Was modernist war art a progression in the depiction of conflict? The movement certainly had its advocates. Modernist exhibitions were popular and attracted international attention; Orpen was knighted for his endeavours, an honour that eluded his counterparts. But the new modernist prominence in war art was not enough to see off the traditionalists, whose work continued to capture the popular imagination. Magazines, newspapers and war journals never tired of the stuff; it satisfied a public appetite. And Nevinson ran into trouble with the military authorities when his painting of weary, hard-faced troops in his *Group of Soldiers*, was suppressed by the censor as 'not worthy of the British Army'. Nevinson's later picture, *Paths of Glory* (1918), an ironic 'Wilfred Owen'-like comment on notions of military heroism with his depiction of two dead British soldiers lying prostate beneath coils of barbed wire, also fell foul of the authorities. The painting was forbidden from exhibition in March 1918. Nevinson indignantly rehung the picture with a paper banner marked CENSORED stretched across its face. He had, however, misinterpreted the 'official' view of showing the war dead. Orpen, for instance, explored a similar topic in his *Dead Germans* painting, which was exhibited successfully a few months later. In the censor's eye, depicting enemy dead was fine; showing British dead was harmful to public opinion.[30] But perhaps it was Nevinson and the modernists who had the final say. Our view of the First World War, as pointless death, mass slaughter and trench warfare, is their view. Who remembers the Charltons, Caton-Woodvilles and Elizabeth Butlers now, for all their wartime popularity? Still, modern art had its uses. Naval commander Norman Wilkinson applied the geometric patterns of modernist work to ships' camouflage. Painting hulls in the 'dazzle' technique made an excellent deterrent against submarine attack.[31]

Music and words

The war of the artists rippled into the world of music, though the intellectual angst and passions aroused were not quite as severe. Patriotism still formed a strong reference point. In 1914 a Music in Wartime Committee was formed to safeguard the interests of British musicians. Those of Austrian or German descent found themselves out of a job as orchestras, hotels and restaurants divested themselves of 'alien' influences. Arguments raged over the banning of German music. The works of Wagner, Strauss and even Beethoven were fair game, but the position of Handel and Mendelssohn was more ambiguous. Even so, the conductor Thomas Beecham organized patriotic concerts that rejected all forms of German-originated scores. At the Proms, Henry Wood substituted the traditional 'Wagner Night' with an evening of Russian music. German operas were now sung in English. Patriotic concerts of French, English and Russian music were hurriedly arranged and very well attended. Composers, too, felt the patriotic tug on their sleeves. Sir Charles Stanford and the country's most popular poet, Sir Henry Newbolt, collaborated on *Song of the Sea*, which was performed at the Proms in October 1914. More famously, Sir Hubert Parry's aptitude for choral writings was revealed when his music to Blake's words in the rendering of 'Jerusalem', which extolled 'England's green and pleasant land', produced a hymn-like tune that was almost an alternative English anthem, whilst *Songs of Farewell* exemplified his talent for finding texts from unusual sources. The pain of war, however, was deeply felt by Gustav Holst and Edward Elgar. Holst, who had been turned away from the Army because of ill health, was working on 'Mars: the Bringer of War': a violent, bestial and all too apposite opening to his most celebrated work, 'The Planets' suite. Holst continued working on the piece right through to 1917, and the work reflects the changing atmosphere of wartime Britain.[32] Elgar, on the other hand, succumbed initially to the war's drumbeat. As the composer of 'Pomp and Circumstance' marches (written between 1901 and 1907) and another national hymn in 'Land of Hope and Glory' (1902), Elgar's patriotic credentials were impeccable. And his composition *Carillion*, which set music to a Belgian war poem, sat so perfectly in the patriotic musical menu that it became a war anthem. *Carillion* was welcomed by first-night audiences. Its musical complexity, however, reflected Elgar's discomfort with the war. In composing patriotic music, Elgar was undoubtedly acting from a sense of duty: making music *his* contribution to the war effort. But he also recognized the need to express the sense of grief in war. The success of *Carillion* set Elgar working on similar compositions – 'Le Drapeau Belge', 'Une Voix dans le desert' and the Laurence Binyon poems 'To Women' and 'For the Fallen' (1914), a piece that echoes across the generations:

> They shall not grow old as we who are left grow old:
> Age shall not weary them nor the years condemn.
> At the going down of the sun and in the morning,
> We will remember them.

But Elgar's heart wasn't in it. In April 1915 he confessed to a friend that, although the public demanded popular, patriotic music, 'well, they do not want me and never did. If I work at all it is not for them.'[33] Elgar made war music, yet he yearned to dissociate himself from its sentiments. A complex and emotional man, Elgar's true feelings about his life, his loves and even the war perhaps were encapsulated in the haunting miniature 'Sospiri' (meaning 'sighing'), written before the war, but first performed ten days after its declaration. 'Sospiri' is an anguished melody, a lament for the passing of the 'Pomp and Circumstance' of pre-war Britain, and perhaps reveals itself to the modern listener as a musical prophecy of the sorrows that were to come. Elgar could find no feelings to express a Britain gripped by patriotic fever in the summer of 1914. Perhaps he felt some of Virginia Woolf's pain when she complained to Duncan Grant about a concert of patriotic music at the Queen's Hall in 1915 that 'the ... sentiment was so revolting that I was nearly sick'.[34]

The literary world, too, went through an assortment of moods during the war: exultation, doubt and disillusion. Masterman's gathering of the glittering authors of the Edwardian pre-war era at Wellington House in September 1914, which included Thomas Hardy, John Masefield, G.K. Chesterton, Henry Newbolt and Anthony Hope Hopkins, was essentially a call-up of the old. Few of those at the meeting were young enough to qualify for military service. Yet many formed the backbone of the 'official' literature of the war, expressing a government view of its causes, its morality, its continuation and purpose. Twenty-five of the group signed the famous 'Author's Declaration' that appeared in *The Times* just after the outbreak. By then, the group had been joined by four prominent women authors – Jane Ellen Harrison, May Sinclair, Flora Annie Steel and Mrs Humphrey Ward – although Hardy was already beginning to break ranks.[35] Prominent counterpoints to the official view were represented by the philosopher Bertrand Russell (who found it hard to understand the war) and the favourable attitudes of his fellow thinkers. Russell openly demonstrated his pacifism by his membership of the No-Conscription Fellowship. He was later fined and imprisoned 'for statements likely to pre-judice the recruiting and discipline of His Majesty's Forces'. Russell's teaching post at Trinity College, Cambridge, was withdrawn. Bernard Shaw, by contrast, favoured the prosecution of the war, but then poked fun at Britain's role in it. Initial reactions to his November 1914 manifesto *Common Sense about the War* were favourable, but the general reaction that it created was inevitably hostile. H.G. Wells described it as 'Like an idiot child screaming in a hospital'. Friends shunned him, his letterbox became crammed full of abusive correspondence, he was turned away from his clubs and newspapers were forbidden to report on his meetings. Undeterred, Shaw would later criticize the conduct of the war, support the introduction of trade unionism into the Army and speculate on the instigation of a 'hegemony of peace'.[36]

The path from delight to dread and disenchantment was most visibly trod by H.G. Wells. In *The World Set Free*, published in the spring of 1914, Wells prophesied the arrival of the atomic bomb and a world parliament. The book coincided with turbulences in Wells's personal life as he waited for the birth of his illegitimate son with the feminist writer Rebecca West (he already had two older sons within his marriage), which just seemed to add to the tensions reverberating in Europe.[37] The arrival of his child and the outbreak of war were two influences that drove Wells to write his 'The War that Will End War' article, but he was already by then a jumble of contradictions. He could equally speak of a war without revenge, and peace without passion, sprinkled with liberal doses of jingoism. By the time he published *Mr Britling Sees It Through* (1916), Wells's attitude towards the war had become more certain, if bleaker. Set in the village of Matching's Easy (a pseudonym for his own village, Easton Glebe), Mr Britling, the central character, is clearly Wells himself. Britling travels through the mental complexities of disbelief, fear and expectancy to a sense of despondency. He criticizes the government; his aunt is killed in an air raid; and Britling's eldest son dies in the trenches (a death that occurs almost simultaneously with the death of his son's German teacher). Britling's attempt to correspond with the tutor's family in Germany represents Wells's own struggles to overcome the inner turmoil of war that divides peoples but reunites them in death. Described as 'the outstanding literary record of the war', Wells's novel appeared to chime well with the darkening national atmosphere. *Mr Britling* was published through 13 reprints between October and December 1916 and received acclaim in the United States of America.[38]

Wells's tussle with his progressive politics, gut-reaction patriotism and the cataclysms of war was shared in the work of May Sinclair. As a suffragist and well-regarded author, Sinclair found it impossible to write a novel that supported the war and did not shy away from criticizing the military and political leadership. An early wartime short story 'Red Tape' depicted the war as an agent of social change and broadening people's domestic horizons. A Sinclair novel, *The Tree of Heaven* (1917), dwelt on the mixed fortunes of the Harrison family, who welcome the war at the beginning only to see the conflict strike down many of their loved ones. In spite of the tragedy, however, the Harrisons reconcile themselves to the war as the harbinger of a new world of altruism and selfless classless communities.[39]

The wartime novels of Wells and Sinclair played on themes that linked them with more mainstream, but less highbrow, works: the impact of war on the lives and understanding of ordinary people and their attempts to locate their own personal space and role within its enormity. Many Home Front novels thus interpreted the war in ways that were intelligible to the public, with an emphasis on domestic virtues and the overturning of material decadence by a higher sense of spiritual values. Some works interpreted this through an essentially middle-class, southern-England-based rural obsession. Agnes Castle's *Little House in Wartime* (1915) offers a good example of an idealized, sentimental view of family conditions, located in a Surrey village in scenes that pre-date Flora Robson's *Lark Rise to Candleford* (1939). A deep love of the countryside preoccupies the villagers of a Sussex farming community in Sheila Kaye-Smith's *Little England* (1918). It drives some to sacrifice themselves for their country.[40] Such essentially patriotic 'hearth and home' themes were repeated outside the rural genre. The idealization of essentially middle-class home-life was reflected in *The Smiths in War Time* (1917) by Howard Keble. An elderly, comfortably off couple, Mr and Mrs Smith, make every effort to strive for wartime economies. They move to a small cottage after renting out their suburban villa; they encourage their maid to take on war-work; they observe meatless days and eat less bread. The 'front' in this domestic bliss is a distant feature: it intrudes only when the Smiths are informed of their missing grandson, who is later reported to be safe and sound. Another notion of sacrifice is raised in Annie Jamieson's *War-Time in Our Street* (1917), which focuses its attention on families in a working-class neighbourhood, with a series of uplifting stories of hope and resilience in the face of adversity. Jamieson again acknowledges 'the heroes of the home front' in *The Silent Legion* (1918), where the Simpson family endure a series of tragedies. A son is killed at the front; their business falls into bankruptcy; the daughter Barbara offers to sacrifice her nursing career to care for her sick mother. Mrs Simpson, however, forgoes her needs for the greater national good. She refuses her daughter's help – she is needed at the front to care for wounded soldiers. Margaret Sherwood's *The Worn Doorstep* (1917) depicts the war in a series of letters written by the central character to her deceased sweetheart, a victim of the war, informing him of her help to Belgian refugees, war orphans and stray animals.[41]

Such works settled within the comfort zones of the domestic readership. Tales of endurance and determination chimed well with the sympathies of the average wartime reader. Those who broke away from these narratives failed to appeal in the same way. Booksellers and libraries were reluctant to stock anything that was too controversial, and publishers fought shy of releasing work that fell outside accepted genres. However, overtly anti-war novels did begin to find an audience by 1916. First, Mary Hamilton's *Dead Yesterday* (1916) expressed socialist beliefs behind a tale that attacked the war as a waste of money – a conflict that sacrificed the more urgent needs of social reform and assistance for the poor. Second, Rose Macauley's *Non-Combatants and Others* (1916) placed a sympathetic, charismatic and peace-loving heroine as the central character, pouring scorn on popular conceptions of war as heroic and thrilling. Criticizing the war was the pre-occupation of a novel by Arthur Machin, *The Terror* (1917), set in rural Wales, where the mysterious violent deaths of local munition workers, miners and farmers are initially put down to German agents. Until, that is, the revelation that the workers have been killed by animals rebelling against their human masters in an Orwellian-style plot. *The Coming* (1917) by John Snaith explores the same theme, this time as a fantasy, where a village carpenter, John Smith, brings suspicion upon himself with his refusal to enlist and go to church. Here the idea of Christ living amongst us is deployed to criticize wartime patriotism as essentially un-Christian. Smith's behaviour is so abhorrent to the local vicar that the carpenter begins to hear voices in his head and is eventually confined to an asylum. None of this, however, plumbed the depths as much as Rudyard Kipling's controversial *Mary Postgate*, which appeared in the magazine *The Century* in 1915. Appalled when an air raid on her village kills a young girl, Mary stumbles across a mortally wounded German pilot in her back garden; rather than offer him succour, she instead ignores his cries for help, stands back and oversees the pilot's death. The war brutalized Mary Smith, as perhaps Kipling himself had been brutalized.[42]

The people's literature

Patriotic sentiments were reflected more clearly in popular literature. Since the beginning of the war, the book-publishing industry had become ensnared in a small crisis of its own. Wood pulp being siphoned off for explosives manufacture had created a paper shortage, and demands for men to join up had given rise to a dearth of writers. Though the most critically renowned authors of the day – Arnold Bennett, H.G. Wells and May Sinclair – could command quite respectable sales in the nation's bookshops, they failed to achieve anything like the profits returned by the 'penny novelettes' that had long been the publishing business's stock-in-trade. But the war stiffened the popularity of the formulaic 'thriller'-type novel, typified by Ernest Hodder-Stoughton's innovative Yellow Jacket series in 1917, which went on to dominate this part of the trade for the next 40 years.[43] Cheap, easily read and appreciated, and occasionally well-written books such as Nat Gould's *The Rider in Khaki* (1917) simply rehearsed the same plot lines, with the war as an additional extra. Yet thrillers could come in several guises.

One of the best known authors of the day, Cyril McNeile (pen name: Sapper), and creator of the Bulldog Drummond character (a man 'who found peace dull'), achieved considerable success with action-packed 'adventure' stories. *Men, Women and Guns* (1916), *No Man's Land* (1917) and *The Human Touch* (1918) all drew inspiration from McNeile's front-line experiences as an army Royal Engineer. McNeile's success was replicated (although to greater critical acclaim) by Ian Hay, in reality Captain John Hay Beith of the 10th Argyll and Sutherland Highlanders. Hay's *The First Hundred Thousand* was a novel that dramatized the New Armies for domestic readers. It gave, according to Samuel Hynes, an 'imaginative reality to the life of the young men who had volunteered, but a *cheerful reality*, full of humour and good-fellowship, that the families at home must have found reassuring'.[44] Not for Hay the intellectual angst about war. *The First Hundred Thousand* eulogized conservatism and patriotism. The politics of Ulster Protestant unionism was celebrated; and Suffragettes, Bernard Shaw and Liberal politics were treated as 'small nuisances of peacetime'.[45] Hay had many imitators. A. Neil Lyons's *Kitchener Chaps* (1916) and Boyd Cable's *Between the Lines* (1917) were just two. And the formula could be easily distilled and reshaped to apply to different times and different contexts. Hodder-Stoughton's own *Jack Cornwall V.C.*, one of his company's more profitable titles, set the action in the Battle of Jutland, with liberal doses of a 'boys own' tale of derring-do and heroic endeavours.[46]

Thriller writing was also a genre that reached through the generations and the sexes. Adventure stories for boys restated the war as heroism and dewy eyed patriotism. Albert Lee's *At His Country's Call* (1916), for instance, features a Boy Scout, Maurice Millard, who is despatched to France on first-aid duties. Once there, Millard is captured by the enemy when delivering a secret message behind the lines, but escapes by stealing an airplane and then launches a bombing raid on German defences. Other titles in the genre were characteristically titled *The Khaki Boys*, *The Boy Volunteers* and *The Navy Boys*. Robert Drake's series of *Boy Allies* novels proved immensely popular, chronicling the adventures of an English boy, Jack Templeton, and his American chum, Frank Chadwick. Female authors, too, made a considerable impact in the genre. Drawing from their experiences as army nurses and military auxiliaries and of munitions and other war work, women, particularly those who had seen front-line action, retold their experiences in an 'adventure' format. Two of the best examples are Sister Martin-Nicholson's *My Experiences on Three Fronts* (1916) and Flora Sandes's *An English Woman Sergeant in the Serbian Army* (1916). Other examples include Brenda Girvin's *Munition Mary* (1918), where the heroine discovers a spy ring in a defence establishment, and Martha Trent's *Alice Blythe: Somewhere in England* (1918), where Alice first drives an ambulance in France, then manages to pilot a plane and eventually captures a German spy.[47]

Finally, thrillers explored the underside of war. The spy novel was a tried and tested formula: very familiar to pre-war readers, and highly profitable for publishers. Such novels followed a common plot line: a hero discovers a nest of enemy spies or plans of hidden espionage; rebuffed by his superiors, the hero becomes a fugitive, pursued by deadly assassins; all this culminates in a spectacular final scene, where 'our man' proves his suspicions, while he evades or kills the enemy agents. This was certainly the style of John Buchan's *The Thirty-Nine Steps* (1915) and John Ferguson's *Stealthy Terror* (1917). These are novels of heroic and charismatic men, doing *manly* things, displaying *manly* courage. Women are portrayed as beautiful, seductive enemy agents, as fictional Mata Haris, 'devilish dangerous … [but] really pretty and fascinating', as Buchan writes in his novel *Greenmantle* (1915).[48] Female readers, meanwhile, could seek their own solace and entertainment in the 'romance' novel. The genre had a long pre-war history of success and, like thrillers, its plotlines and formulaic storylines could be readily adapted to war themes. Women's magazines and journals had proved enormously successful in producing a format of home hints and romantic tales, and the themes appeared to be sufficiently robust to reach across the age and class barriers.[49] Some girls' magazines, such as *Girl's Own Paper* and *Girl Guides' Gazette*, had tried to break out of the wartime straightjacket of enduring sorrows in silence or knitting 'comforts' for soldiers, by portraying women in a more heroic frame, featuring stories of the 'Red Cross Girls' or the 'Khaki Girls', which emphasized a more active wartime role for women. Specifically 'women's novels', however, towed a more orthodox line. *The Long Road to Happiness* (1915) and *Invalided Out* (1918), written by Ruby Ayres, placed the war as a backdrop to courtship and romance. One of the more popular authors was Berta Ruck, whose output of romantic stories and tales of young love (typical titles included *The Bridge of Kisses* (1917) and *The Lad with Wings* (1915)) achieved lasting fame with *The Girls at His Billet* (1916), which portrays three bored young ladies living on the English east coast, whose lives are transformed when they become involved with dashing young army officers billeted at a nearby army camp. In others, romance is interwoven with adventure, as in Dorothy Black's *Her Lonely Soldier* (1916), a story where a heroine discovers her lost love whilst serving as a Red Cross nurse on the front. Another best-seller was *Love of an Unknown Soldier* (1918) which tells its tale through the correspondence of a British Officer and Red Cross nurse found in a trench after he is killed. The novel has an Arthurian feel of knights and fair maidens.[50]

The endless poetry ...

If the novelists were busy, the poets were even busier. Samuel Hynes notes that poems became a regular adornment in much of the British press, often appearing as regularly as leader columns. (*The Times* reported that it was receiving as many as 100 poems daily in the autumn of 1914.) Publication of anthologies began to appear with increasing regularity: three in September 1914, three more in November, twelve in 1915 and another six in 1916.[51] The modern reader may be forgiven for assuming that 'war poetry' was something delivered by the soldier-poets. The elevation of Sassoon, Sorley, Graves, Owen, Rosenberg and others to 'genre' status occurred only during the postwar years, when the war was more grimly remembered. But war as 'tragedy' was not recognized by the wartime reader. Anti-war poetry was read, but the mass of poetry was overwhelmingly patriotic and supportive of the war. A bibliography of English war poetry reveals that, of 3,000 works by 2,225 poets, less than a quarter were written by soldiers, a quarter were authored by women, and over half were written by male civilians, a traditional source of war poetry.[52] The poets who were read substantially included the most eminent and popular writers of the day: John Oxenham (the war's most popular poet), Thomas Hardy, Rudyard Kipling, G.K. Chesterton, Robert Bridges (then poet laureate) and Maurice Hewlett. But equally admired were the scribes whose names have now been largely forgotten – Harold Begbie, Henry Chappel, Jessie Pope: these were all war poets as much as their soldier counterparts.

Hence old rhetorics sat with the new, if rather uneasily. The soldier-poets' rejection of the older forms of language, tradition and style flew in the face of something that was respected, venerated and deployed by other poets. At a time of fear and great uncertainty, many drew comfort from the familiar. Much of First World War poetry was framed in the heroic verse of wars past, written in the lyric of the Romantics, Wordsworth, Shelley and Coleridge, a love of the 'English' countryside, a devotion to Christian piety and notions of noble sacrifice and dogged fortitude. Thus, John Masefield's highly respected, pitiful but essentially patriotic work 'August 1914' writes of an 'England' not located in city streets, but in leafy lanes and green fields:

> How still this quiet cornfield is to-night
> By an intenser glow the evening falls
> Bringing, not darkness, but a deeper light
> Among the stooks a partridge covey calls ...
> These homes, this valley spread below me here,
> The rooks, the tilted stacks, the beasts in pen,
> Have been the heartfelt things, past-speaking dear
> To unknown generations of dead men ... .

Masefield would later supplement this lyrical view with a dash of sadness for what the war had become:

> Then sadly rose and left the well-loved Downs,
> And so by ship to sea, and knew no more
> The fields of home, the byres, the market towns,
> Nor the dear outline of the English shore,
> But knew the misery of the soaking trench,
> The freezing in the rigging, the despair
> In the revolting second of the wrench
> When the blind soul is flung upon the air.[53]

Rupert Brooke also leant heavily on pastoral sentiments. Seen as the embodiment of early war idealism and naivety, Brooke's most famous sonnet 'The Soldier' ('If I should die, think only this of me: That there's some corner of a foreign field, That is forever England')[54] was popularized by the Dean of St Paul's when quoted in a sermon of Easter 1915. Brooke's verse lent the conflict a sense of idealism and was still being recited in 1918. Robert Bridges joined the rural theme and pastoral imagery in his equally popular *Poems of Today*, where nearly a third were celebrations of 'England' and its landscape. For some, this is what Britain went to war to defend.[55] Yet the rural overtones of the early war poetry should not be seen as crowding out the verses that voiced more visceral feelings. John Oxenham, whose pre-war collection of poems, *Bees in Amber: A Little Book of Thoughtful Verse*, ran into 14 editions, penned lines that spoke with optimism and a sense of religious zeal about the war:

As sure as God's in His Heaven
As sure as He stands for Right
As sure as the Hun this wrong hath done,
So surely we win this fight.

Oxenham went on to produce the characteristic *All's Well! Some Helpful Verses for the Dark Days of War* in 1915, claiming that to die 'Fighting for God, and Right and Liberty', was synonymous with 'Immortality'.[56] In the book, *Poems of the Great War*, published for the Prince of Wales' Relief Fund a year earlier, Oxenham collected the best (or the worst!) of the patriotic outpourings from Britain's best-known poets of the day. Robert Bridges, for example, wrote:

Thou careless, awake!
Thou peacemaker, fight!
Stand, England, for honour,
And God guard the Right!

Henry Newbolt, a man who wanted to 'keep the Nelson touch', extolled:

Then let memory tell thy heart;
'England! What thou wert, thou art!
Gird thee with thine ancient might,
Forth! And God defend the Right!'

They were joined by Owen Seaman:

England, in this great fight to which you go
Because, where Honour call you, go you must,
Be glad, whatever comes, at least to know
You have your quarrel just.[57]

Patriotism occasionally came in disguise. John McCrae's poem 'In Flanders Fields', which was published anonymously in *Punch* on 6th December 1915, has often been interpreted as a haunting theme of remembrance. But seldom is the full verse heard:

In Flanders fields the poppies blow
Between the crosses, row on row,
That mark our place; and in the sky
The larks, still bravely singing, fly
Scarce heard amid the guns below.
We are the Dead. Short days ago
We lived, felt dawn, saw sunset glow,
Loved and were loved, and now we lie
In Flanders fields.

Take up our quarrel with the foe:
To you from failing hands we throw
The torch; be yours to hold it high.
If ye break faith with us who die
We shall not sleep, though poppies grow
In Flanders Fields.[58]

None of this, however, could match the strident tones of Rudyard Kipling's drum-beating 'For All We Have and Are', published in 1915 to aid the recruitment drive:

For all we have and are,
For all our children's fate,
Stand up and meet the war
The Hun is at the gate![59]

Kipling's strident patriotism shared its audience with the equally popular, but more populist, poets who were not afraid to revert to a more readily understood music hall mode. Jessie Pope's call for recruits, for instance, was not all that far in stylistic terms from the narratives of the literary celebrities. Called by one historian 'the high priestess of humiliation', Pope's 1915 cry for recruits came with a large slice of condescension:

Who's for the khaki suit–
Are you, my laddie?
Who longs to charge and shoot –
Do you, my laddie?
Who's keen on getting fit,
Who means to show his grit,
And who'd rather wait a bit –
Would you, my laddie?[60]

Harold Begbie, now thankfully forgotten, but widely read in his day, tried to instil similar emotions in reluctant soldiers:

What will you lack, sonny, what will you lack,
When the girls line up in the street,
Shouting their love to the lads come back
From the foe they crushed to beat?
Will you send a strangled cheer to the sky
And grin till your cheeks are red?
But what will you lack when your mate goes by
With a girl who cuts you dead?[61]

Those who did respond to the calls of the patriotic poets could perhaps be happy in the knowledge that, if the worst came to the worst, they would be venerated as heroes. At least this was according to the Sussex bard Thomas Baker, who had few doubts about the honour of being killed in battle:

> He valued not his life
> So much as right and truth
> A champion was there
> He died while but a youth
> Sweet consolation this,
> For those who for him weep
> He died as die the brave
> And calmly doth he sleep
> Their tears will quickly fall
> Their hearts with grief will swell
> But joy comes with the words
> Fighting in front he fell.[62]

There was a lot of poetry of this sort during the war: written because the British public was happy to read and appreciate it. Yet, amidst the clarion calling, there was still room for dissent. One poet writing in the journal *The Egoist* had decided that enough bad poetry was enough:

> At the sound of the drum
> Out of their dens they come, they come,
> The little poets we hoped were dumb,
> The little poets we thought were dead,
> The poets who certainly haven't been read
> Since Heaven knows when, they come, they come
> At the sound of the drum, of the drum, of the drum.[63]

Thomas Hardy, who was in his seventies when war broke out, wrote, perhaps more to oblige his many readers than from any personal conviction, 'Men Who March Away', in September 1914:

> Hence the faith and fire within us
> Men who march away
> Ere the barn-cocks say
> Night is growing gray,
> Leaving all that here can win us
> Hence the faith and fire within us
> Men who march away.[64]

Hardy's rhythmic marching form should not be over-estimated. Hardy sees the war grimly, rather than favourably, and his verse strikes an effective counterpoint to Rupert Brooke's lyricism.[65] Edith Sitwell, by contrast, unhappy at the banality of Home Front life, attacked those who made merry while soldiers suffered. Her poem 'The Dancers' is an acerbic comment on her fellow Britons' insensitivity to front-line suffering:

> We are the dull blind carrion-fly
> That dance and batten. Though God die
> Mad from horror of the light–
> The light is mad, too, flecked with blood, –
> We dance, we dance, each night.[66]

But there was room for social commentary. Nina MacDonald, too, referred to wartime deprivations, albeit in a strictly middle-class context, yet penned with a sense of humour, and told through the eyes of a child:

> Sing a song of war-time,
> Soldiers marching by,
> Crowds of people standing,
> Waving them 'Good-bye',
> When the crowds are over
> Home we go to tea,
> Bread and margarine to eat,
> War Economy!
> ...
> Mummie does the house-work,
> Can't get any maid,
> Gone to make munitions,
> 'Cause they're better paid,
> Nurse is always busy,
> Never time to play,
> Sewing shirts for soldiers,
> Nearly ev'ry day.[67]

Jessie Pope (again!) offered this tribute to the women war workers, which shows a hint of social progress, though with its feet firmly stuck in older attitudes:

> There's the girl who clips your ticket for the train
> And the girl who speeds the lift from floor to floor,
> There's the girl who does a milk-round in the rain
> And the girl who calls for orders at your door
> Strong, sensible and fit,
> They're out to show their grit,
> And tackle jobs with energy and knack.
> No longer caged and penned up,
> They're going to keep their end up
> Till the khaki soldier boys come marching back.[68]

It is perhaps convenient to speak of a double culture in British war poetry: the verse of the masses who saw war as duty, heroism and patriotism; and the voices of the soldier-poets, waist-deep in mud, blood, futility and tragedy, and busy constructing a new rhetoric for war poetry, one that, in confronting 'the ugly and stupid side of war' repudiated the idealistic and unrealistic voices of the traditional and popular.[69] But though it is their voice that rings through history, it was the 'people's poetry' that formed and shaped the war for the mass readership. This reinforced a language of understanding that relied heavily on traditional styles, and was accessible to the less educated (but not necessarily less intelligent). Oxenham and Pope could sell volumes of texts when Sassoon, Rosenberg and Owen could hardly register a whisper. Brooke, on the other hand, rose above them all. His book of collected poems, published in 1918, sold over 300,000 copies. The soldier-poets had to wait until time and public taste caught up with them. They, in the end, would have their say.

Theatres and music

Unlike the war poems, much popular literature was rooted and stayed within its time. Its flights of fancy helped the Home Front population engage with the conflict in ways that rendered both meaning and purpose to their individual experience of war. Soldiers would complain that its cosy narratives insulated civilians from knowing the true nature of the war, but nevertheless there were points of unity between them. On one side, the Library Fund, which supplied books for soldiers in camps, hospitals and the trenches, revealed soldiers' favourite authors included the popular Nat Gould, Jack London, William Le Queux and Rudyard Kipling.[70] On another side, soldiers' sense of belonging, rooted in local cultures and run through voluntary associations, neighbourhoods and workplaces, in cities, towns and villages up and down the country, was often powerfully expressed through staged entertainments. Soldiers knew that the plays, revues and songs of the music hall softened the reality of war for their domestic audiences, but it reminded them of a life they had left behind and to which they would return. As Jay Winter put it, 'In song and stylized stage buffoonery, millions of soldiers saw the "before" and dreamed of the "after".'[71]

Not that this was an easy task. 'Going out' became more difficult and expensive during the war. Alcohol regulations took a slow grip on the pub trade. Opening hours were shortened for the sake of munitions production; beer was being taxed and diluted. Theatres and music halls were controlled and restricted; professional football matches were suspended for the duration of the war; and all paid entertainments were subject to a burdensome Amusement Tax after 1916, often doubling the cost of entry. Some families retreated to the home and listened increasingly to the patriotic songs on their gramophones, such as Stewart Gordon's 'Our United Front', 'Songs of Old Britannia' and the 'Little Mother'.[72] Recordings of more satirical 'soldier songs' inspired amusement but generated less interest. The ironic brilliance of the song 'Oh! What a Lovely War!, recorded in 1917 by Courtland and Jeffries, cast light on the soldier's condition without delving into the bitter stanzas of the soldier-poets:

> Come to the cookhouse door boys,
> Sniff the lovely stew,
> Who is it says the Colonel gets better grub than you?
> Any complaints this morning?
> Do we complain, not we
> What's the matter with lumps of onion floating around your tea?[73]

Those without the means or the inclination to indulge in this new technological amusement sought their enjoyments in theatres, music halls and cinemas. 'Picture houses' were fast becoming the entertainment phenomenon of the era. As discussed in Chapter 8, over 4,000 cinemas were in full operation by 1917 entertaining thousands of regular customers.[74] However, wartime economic constraints limited the output of domestic film companies, whilst those that persisted produced a familiar fare of the patriotic and melodramatic. Tears were likely if the average citizen sat down to watch *Christmas without Daddy* (1914); anger was expected if *The Kaiser's Spies* (1914) was viewed; pride in the armed services and faith in the virtue of women may be aroused if *Saving the Colours* (1914) or *They Called Him Coward* (1915) were seen. Few of these films, however, could match the popularity of American imports. By sheer scale alone Hollywood films, which were still in their relative infancy in 1914, offered a far superior product. British films could not compete with the likes of Cecil B. DeMille's *The Little American* (1917) which starred Mary Pickford, or the effervescent comedies of Charlie Chaplin, whose Little Tramp character blended irreverent humour with mockery of authority and seemed to strike a chord with both ordinary citizen and soldier.[75]

Conversely, British theatre had its problems. Actors and backstage staff fell foul of military conscription. All productions were subject to censorship. No criticism of the armed forces was permissible; scenes deemed to be harmful to public morale had to be removed. One play that portrayed an Indian spying for Germany was censored on the grounds that it was insulting to colonial troops. Drunken sailor scenes were deleted from another production. This left many theatre managers with little option but to produce entertainments that emphasized national loyalty and militarism. Major theatres hurried to stage plays with a strong military theme. Shakespeare's *Henry V* was revived and performed to packed houses. King Harry's battlefield speech, 'We few, we happy few, we band of brothers', seemed to resonate clearly with the outgunned and outnumbered BEF in France during 1914. For the patriotic wartime theatre-goer there was no shortage of opportunities to wave the flag. It became customary to play the national anthem at the close of all performances. 'Recruiting' plays also became widespread in the early months of the war. Productions with such titles as *Soldiers' Honour* and *England Expects* were events that highlighted patriotic songs and recitations, usually with a recruiting sergeant loitering in the wings. Music halls, catering for the less sophisticated audience, performed comic-book routines that made great play of caricature – all German soldiers were fat, for instance, they all had strings of sausages protruding from their pockets and answered to the name Little Willy. These were accompanied by songs subtly entitled 'To Hell with the Kaiser' and 'Gilbert the Filbert, the Colonel of the Nuts'.[76]

Despite Bernard Shaw's criticism of shows with 'silly jokes, dances, and brainlessly sensuous exhibitions of pretty girls', the public wanted escapist entertainment.[77] After two or three hours of harmless but enjoyable (and psychologically necessary) fun, to the serious world they would return. Musical revues such as *Chu Chin Chow, aid of the Mountains* and *The Bing Boys Are Here* (which featured George Robey and the song, 'If You Were the Only Girl in the World') sold out most nights when a Zeppelin raid was thought to be unlikely. *Chu Chin Chow*, a fantasy set in the Far East, ran for 2,000 performances in London's West End, featuring troupes of dancing girls and portrayals of harems amidst a splattering of light-hearted tunes, including one of the war's most popular, and unashamedly sentimental, songs, 'Roses of Picardy', with a verse ripe for an audience sing-a-long:

Roses are shining in Picardy,
In the hush of the silvery dew,
Roses are flowering in Picardy,
But there's never a rose like you!
And the roses will die with the summertime,
And our roads may be far apart
But there's one rose that dies not in Picardy!
'Tis the rose that I keep in my heart![78]

The success of such songs inspired the music industry to produce an avalanche of imitations to be performed in music halls and bought as sheet music for home entertainment around the 'joanna' (rhyming slang for piano). Titles ranged from the stridently patriotic, 'The Bulldog's Bark', 'Stick to Your Guns', 'We'll Fight Till We Win or Die', to the comedic, 'Sister Suzie's Sewing Shirts for Soldiers', and 'When an Irishman Goes Fighting', whilst leaving room for the sentimental and the romantic, 'Brave Women Who Wait' and 'Khaki Boy'. Such material was outshone, however, by the enormously popular ballads, 'Roamin' in the Gloamin', 'Annie Laurie' and Jack Judge's strident 'Tipperary' (though written in 1912, it became popular with the soldiers of the New Army as a marching song) and Ivor Novello's poignant and tearful 'Keep the Home Fires Burning' (1914), a song that became an enduring popular anthem for Home Front War:

Keep the home fires burning,
While your hearts are yearning,
Though your lads are far away
They dream of home.
There's a silver lining
Through the dark cloud shining,
Turn the dark cloud inside out,
Till the boys come home.[79]

Songs of course need singers, and their popularity owed much to the rising prestige and esteem of those entertainers who made their names in the Edwardian music hall and theatre. Music hall comediennes, Nellie Taylor, Phyllis Dare and Marie Lloyd made great play of the 'recruiting' song, a heady blend of light-hearted banter and sexual innuendo. Lloyd in particular had long been regarded as the Queen of the Music Hall, but she had a notoriously 'racy' reputation. Her version of the song, 'Now You've Got Your Khaki On' included the verse lines:

I didn't like you much before you joined the Army, John;
But I do like you cocky now you've got your khaki on.

Equally infamous was the provocative 'I'll Make a Man of You':

On Sunday I walk out with a soldier
On Monday I'm taken by a tar,
On Tuesday I'm out with a baby Boy Scout,
On Wednesday with a Hussar,
On Thursday I gang out with a Scottie,
On Friday the captain of the crew,
But on Saturday I'm willing, if you'll only take a shilling,
To make a man of any one of you![80]

Perhaps the most famous music hall 'star' of the day was Harry Lauder. An artist who enjoyed international celebrity, Lauder's trade-mark persona was as a kilted Scots vaudeville minstrel-style singer, complete with a crooked walking stick. His name was made through the rendition of songs such as 'I Love a Lassie', 'A Wee Deoch-an-Doris' and 'Keep Right on Till the End of the Road' (written following his son's death at the front in December 1916). In 1916–17 his London revue finished with the song 'The Laddies Who Fought and Won', complete with the appearance of a battalion of the Scots Guards. Lauder divided his time between his London shows and entertaining the troops in France. His performance in Arras in June 1917 brought out an audience of 5,000. With their patriotic messages and calls to see the war through to victory, Lauder's songs and jokes were cultural letters to the British people that were intended to encourage and maintain popular support for the war without the use of state-sponsored propaganda.[81] M.W. Pope would comment later, 'it was at the halls you learnt your patriotism, were told you had a navy, a British navy, which kept your foes at bay, that a little British Army went a damned long way, that the soldiers of the [King] always won, and that you couldn't beat the boys of the bulldog breed who made Old England's name. And you believed it all.'[82]

As Jay Winter writes, cultural history 'is a messy subject, full of unevenness and inconsistencies'.[83] It is hard not to agree, given the scale, diversity and vitality of Britain's wartime cultural life. Perhaps it is for these reasons that historians cannot agree on its historical legacy. Some scholars like to see British war culture as a series of discontinuities. The binary divide between the sophisticated, 'elite' and 'middle-brow' cultures of the wealthy and educated, and the more simplistic popular 'mass' culture of the less schooled and less wealthy. Paul Fussell and, to a lesser extent, Samuel Hynes argue that the scale of suffering, the destruction and the trauma of war were beyond the extant forms of language and narrative and almost demanded the creation of a new war rhetoric, initiated chiefly by the soldier-poets, to relate the horror of the trenches to present and future generations. And it is this 'modern memory' that informs and shapes contemporary understanding of the war. Modern generations still search for meaning in the devastation and upheavals of the First World War; in the works of the soldier-poets and protesting writers, they think they have found it. But students should be careful to understand the war through the eyes of the generation that fought it. The voices of the *avante garde* were only dimly heard. Whatever its forms, there was arguably a unity in British culture during the war. Whether elite, middle rank or popular, its messages of consensus, patriotism and belief in the national cause cut across the class barriers, brought the country together and created a bond between civilian and soldier. Though British culture helped fulfil the government's propaganda purpose, it sprang not from the state, but from within its own public and commercial structures, with a reputation for money-making business and entrepreneurial endeavour. Perhaps this is why the consent of Britons to the war remained more or less unbroken throughout its 1,500 fearful days. At the very least, British culture's sublimity and banality helped to create what one historian has called a 'commonality of purpose', as the nation entered the worrisome final months of the war.[84]

Notes

1 Samuel Hynes, *A War Imagined: The First World War and English Culture*, London: The Bodley Head, 1990, p. 5.
2 Edmund Gosse, 'War and Literature', *Edinburgh Review*, vol. 220, October 1914, p. 313.
3 See Samuel Hynes, *A War Imagined*, op. cit., pp. 67–87.
4 George Robb, *British Culture and the First World War*, Basingstoke: Palgrave, Macmillan, 2002, pp. 130–31.
5 See Richard Cork, *A Bitter Truth: Avant-garde Art and the Great War*, London, New Haven: Yale University Press, 1994, p. 138.

6 Frances Spalding, *British Art since 1900*, London: Thames & Hudson, 1986, pp. 37–48.

7 See Ian Dunlop, *The Shock of the New: Seven Historic Exhibitions of Modern Art*, London: Weidenfeld & Nicholson, 1972; Robert Hughes, *The Shock of the New: Art and the Century of Change*, revised and enlarged edn, London: BBC, 1991; Richard Cork, *Vorticism and Abstract Art in the Modern Age*, London: Gordon Fraser, 1976, ch. 2.

8 Karin Orchard, 'A Laugh Like a Bomb: The History and the Ideas of the Vorticists', in Paul Edwards, ed., *Blast*, Aldershot: Ashgate, 2000, pp. 14–23; William Wees, *Vorticism and the English Avant-garde*, Manchester: Manchester University Press, 1974; see also Samuel Hynes, *A War Imagined*, op. cit., pp. 58–67.

9 Samuel Hynes, *A War Imagined*, op. cit., p. 33; Peter Harrington, 'Early Paintings of the Great War', *Imperial War Museum Review*, vol. 7, 1992; Richard Cork, *A Bitter Truth: Avant-garde Art and the Great War*, op. cit., pp. 72–73; George Robb, *British Culture and the First World War*, op. cit., p. 138.

10 George Robb, *British Culture and the First World War*, op. cit., p. 138.

11 Joanna Bourke, *Dismembering the Male: Men's Bodies, Britain and the Great War*, London: Reaktion, p. 213; Peter Harrington, 'Early Paintings of the Great War', *Imperial War Museum Review*, op. cit.; George Robb, *British Culture and the First World War*, op. cit., p. 138.

12 Quoted in David Boyd Haycock, *A Crisis of Brilliance: Five Young British Artists and the Great War*, London: Old Street, 2010, pp. 257–58. See also Frances Spalding, *British Art since 1900*, op. cit., p. 47.

13 Samuel Hynes, *A War Imagined*, op. cit., p. 34.

14 See Sue Malvern, 'War As It Is: The Art of Muirhead Bone, C.R.W. Nevinson, and Paul Nash, 1916–17', *Art History*, vol. 9, no. 4, December 1986, pp. 487–515; Michael Sanders and Philip Taylor, *British Propaganda During the First World War, 1914–1918*, London: Macmillan, 1982, pp. 122–23; Gary S. Messinger, *British Propaganda and the State in the First World War*, Manchester: Manchester University Press, 1992, p. 42.

15 Sue Malvern, 'War As It Is: The Art of Muirhead Bone, C.R.W. Nevinson, and Paul Nash', op. cit.

16 Samuel Hynes, *A War Imagined*, op. cit., pp. 159–61.

17 Samuel Hynes, *A War Imagined*, op. cit., p. 162. See also Karin Orchard, 'A Laugh like a Bomb', op. cit., pp. 14–23; Richard Cork, *A Bitter Truth: Avant-garde Art and the Great War*, op. cit., ch. 3–5.

18 Samuel Hynes, *A War Imagined*, op. cit., p.195.

19 Lucy Masterman, *C.F.G. Masterman: A Biography*, London: Nicholson & Watson, 1939, p. 287; Sue Malvern, 'War As It Is: The Art of Muirhead Bone, C.R.W. Nevinson, and Paul Nash', op. cit.; *Daily Express*, 25th February 1915.

20 See David Boyd Haycock, *A Crisis of Brilliance*, op. cit., pp. 271–72.

21 IWM Collections, Art, 691(a), 725, 840. See also Richard Cork, *Vorticism and Abstract Art in the First World War*, vol. I, *Origins and Development*, London: Gordon Fraser, 1976.

22 IWM Collections, Art, 15661; Frances Spalding, *British Art since 1900*, op. cit., pp. 57–58.

23 Quoted in David Boyd Haycock, *A Crisis of Brilliance*, op. cit., p. 128.

24 David Boyd Haycock, *A Crisis of Brilliance*, op. cit., pp. 275–79.

25 IWM Collections, Art, 1145, 2242, 2705; Sue Malvern, 'War As It Is: The Art of Muirhead Bone, C.R.W. Nevinson, and Paul Nash', op. cit.

26 Richard Cork, *A Bitter Truth: Avant-garde Art and the Great War*, op. cit., p. 198; Robert Hughes, *The Shock of the New: Art and the Century of Change*, op. cit., p. 59.

27 George Robb, *British Culture and the First World War*, op. cit., pp. 143–44.
28 Robert Upstone *et al.*, *William Orpen: Politics, Sex and Death*, London: Philip Wilson for the Imperial War Museum, 2005, pp. 34–46.
29 IWM Collections, Art, 1460.
30 Samuel Hynes, *A War Imagined*, op. cit., p. 198.
31 George Robb, *British Culture and the First World War*, op. cit., p. 144.
32 John Ferguson, *The Arts in Britain in World War I*, London: Stainer & Bell, 1980, pp. 23–24, 60–63.
33 Samuel Hynes, *A War Imagined*, op. cit., pp. 36–39.
34 From Nigel Nicolson and Joanne Trautmann, eds, *The Letters of Virginia Woolf*, London: Hogarth Press, 1976, p. 57.
35 See Helen Small, 'Mrs Humphrey Ward and the First Casualty of War', in Suzanne Raitte and Trudi Tate, eds, *Women's Fiction and the Great War*, Oxford: Clarendon Press, 1997, pp. 18–46.
36 Samuel Hynes, *A War Imagined*, op. cit., p. 26; John Ferguson, *The Arts in Britain in World War I*, op. cit., pp. 30–33.
37 H.G. Wells, *The World Set Free*, London: Macmillan, 1914; John Ferguson, *The Arts in Britain in World War I*, op. cit., p. 33.
38 H.G. Wells, *Mr Britling Sees It Through*, London: Cassell, 1916; John Ferguson, *The Arts in Britain in World War I*, op. cit., pp. 47–48; Samuel Hynes, *A War Imagined*, op. cit., pp. 130–33.
39 See Trudi Tate, *Women, Men and the Great War: An Anthology of Stories*, Manchester: Manchester University Press, 1995, pp. 202–09; Laura Stempfel Mumford, 'May Sinclair's *Tree of Heaven*: The Vortex of Feminism, the Community of War', in Helen M. Cooper, Adrienne Munich and Susan Merrill Squier, eds, *Arms and the Woman: War, Gender and Literary Representation*, North Carolina: Chapel Hill, 1989.
40 See Nicola Beauman, 'It is Not the Place of Women to Talk of Mud: Some Responses by British Women Novelists to World War I', in Dorothy Goldman, ed., *Women and World War I*, Basingstoke: Macmillan, 1993; George Robb, *British Culture and the First World War*, op. cit., p. 152.
41 George Robb, *British Culture and the First World War*, op. cit., p. 152.
42 Rudyard Kipling, 'Mary Postgate', *The Century*, September 1915; Trudi Tate, ed., *Women, Men and the Great War: An Anthology of Stories*, Manchester: Manchester University Press, 1995, pp. 256–67; George Robb, *British Culture and the First World War*, op. cit., pp. 151–54.
43 Jay Winter, 'Popular Culture in Wartime Britain', in Aviel Roshwald and Richard Stites, eds, *European Culture in the Great War: The Arts, Entertainment and Propaganda 1914–1918*, Cambridge: Cambridge University Press, 1999, pp. 327–28.
44 Samuel Hynes, *A War Imagined*, op. cit., p. 49. See also George Robb, *British Culture and the First World War*, op. cit., pp. 161–62.
45 Ian Hay, *The First Hundred Thousand*, Edinburgh: Blackwood, 1916, p. 84; George Robb, *British Culture and the First World War*, op. cit., p. 161.
46 Jay Winter, 'Popular Culture in Wartime Britain', op. cit., p. 338.
47 George Robb, *British Culture and the First World War*, op. cit., pp. 164–77.
48 George Robb, *British Culture and the First World War*, op. cit., p. 163.
49 See Carol Acton, 'Best Boys and Aching Hearts: The Rhetoric of Romance as Social Control in Wartime Magazines for Young Women', in Jessica Meyer, ed., *British Popular Culture and the First World War*, Leiden: Brill, 2008, pp. 173–93.
50 Jane Potter, 'A Great Purifier: The Great War in Women's Romances and Memoirs, 1914–18', in Suzanne Raitte and Trudi Tate, eds, *Women's Fiction and the Great War*, op. cit., pp. 85–106; George Robb, *British Culture and the First World War*, op. cit., p. 165.

51 Samuel Hynes, *A War Imagined*, op. cit., p. 28; George Robb, *British Culture and the First World War*, op. cit., p. 145.

52 Samuel Hynes, *A War Imagined*, op. cit., p. 29.

53 John Masefield, 'August 1914', *English Review*, vol. 18, September 1914, p. 145. See also John Masefield, *The Collected Poems of John Masefield*, London: William Heinemann, 1924, pp. 374–76.

54 From Jon Stallworthy, *Anthem for Doomed Youth*, London: Constable & Robinson, 2002, p. 20; Jon Silkin, *The Penguin Book of First World War Poetry*, 2nd edn, Harmondsworth: Penguin, 1981, pp. 81–82; Geoffrey Keynes, ed., *The Poetical Works of Rupert Brooke*, London, Faber & Faber, 1946, p. 23.

55 Robert Bridges, *Poetical Works*, 2nd edn, Oxford: Oxford University Press, 1936.

56 John Oxenham, 'Victory Day', in *All's Well: Some Helpful Verse for These Dark Days of War*, London: Methuen, 1915, p. 64.

57 John Ferguson, *The Arts in Britain in World War I*, op. cit., pp. 17–18.

58 Jon Silkin, *The Penguin Book of First World War Poetry*, 2nd edn, op. cit., p. 85. See also Paul Fussell, *The Great War and Modern Memory*, Oxford: Oxford University Press, 1975, pp. 248–50.

59 Rudyard Kipling, 'For All We Have and Are', in *The Times Recruiting Supplement*, 3rd November 1914.

60 Gerard DeGroot, *Blighty: British Society in the Era of the Great War*, Harlow: Longman, 1996, p. 51; see also Catherine Reilly, ed., *Scars Upon My Heart: Women's Poetry and Verse of the First World War*, London: Virago, 1981, p. 88.

61 William J. Reader, *At Duty's Call: A Study in Obsolete Patriotism*, Manchester: Manchester University Press, 1988, p. 116; Martin Taylor, 'You Smug-faced Crowds: Poetry and the Home Front in the First World War', *Imperial War Museum Review*, no. 3, 1988, pp. 87–96.

62 *The Observer and West Sussex Recorder*, 21st October 1914.

63 Samuel Hynes, *A War Imagined*, op. cit., pp. 28–29. See also Martin Taylor, 'You Smug-faced Crowds: Poetry and the Home Front in the First World War', op. cit.

64 David Wright, ed., *Selected Poems of Thomas Hardy*, Harmondsworth: Penguin, 1978, pp. 280–81.

65 Samuel Hynes, *A War Imagined*, op. cit., p. 103.

66 From Catherine Reilly, ed., *Scars Upon My Heart: Women's Poetry and Verse of the First World War*, op. cit., p. 100.

67 From Catherine Reilly, ed., *Scars Upon My Heart: Women's Poetry and Verse of the First World War*, op. cit., p. 69.

68 Jessie Pope, 'War Girls', from Catherine Reilly, ed., *Scars Upon My Heart: Women's Poetry and Verse of the First World War*, op. cit., p. 90.

69 Samuel Hynes, *A War Imagined*, op. cit., p. 31.

70 See T.W. Koch, *Books in Camp, Trench and Hospital*, London: J.M. Dent, 1917, p. 13.

71 Jay Winter, 'Popular Culture in Wartime Britain', op. cit., p. 332.

72 Jay Winter, 'Popular Culture in Wartime Britain', op. cit., p. 333.

73 Max Arthur, *When This Bloody War is Over: Soldiers' Songs of the First World War*, London: Piatkus, 2001, pp. 47–48.

74 John Stevenson, *British Society 1914–45*, Harmondsworth: Penguin, 1984, p. 382.

75 J.M. Winter, 'Propaganda and the Mobilization of Consent', in Hew Strachan, ed., *The Oxford Illustrated History of the First World War*, Oxford: Oxford University Press, 1998, pp. 221–44.

76 George Robb, *British Culture and the First World War*, op. cit., pp. 166–68.

77 George Bernard Shaw, *Heartbreak House, Great Catherine and Playlets of the War*, London: Constable, 1927.

78 Dorothea York, ed., *Mud and Stars: An Anthology of World War Songs and Poetry*, New York: Holt, 1931, pp. 200–220; L.J. Collins, *Theatre at War*, Oldham: Jade, 2004, p.12.

79 George Robb, *British Culture and the First World War*, op. cit., p. 167; Samuel Hynes, *A War Imagined*, op. cit., pp. 36–37.

80 Trevor Wilson, *The Myriad Faces of War*, Cambridge: Polity Press, 1986, p. 706; R. Mander and J. Mitchenson, *British Music Hall*, 2nd edn, London: Gentry, 1974; Midge Gillies, *Marie Lloyd: The One and Only*, London: Gollancz, 1999; George Robb, *British Culture and the First World War*, op. cit., p. 166.

81 Gordon Irving, *Great Scot: The Life Story of Sir Harry Lauder, Legendary Laird of the Music Hall*, London: Leslie Frewin, 1968, pp. 88–94.

82 See J.G. Fuller, *Troop Morale and Popular Culture in the British and Dominion Armies, 1914–1918*, Oxford: Oxford University Press, 1990, p. 37.

83 Jay Winter, 'Popular Culture in Wartime Britain', op. cit., p. 343.

84 Jay Winter, 'Popular Culture in Wartime Britain', op. cit., p. 348.

10 After rejoicing

Almost everyone agreed that 1917 had been the worst year of the war, regardless of the United States of America's entry into the conflict against Germany in April: it was the year of many losses in the U-boat campaign, upheaval in Russia, the bloodbath of Passchendaele and few signs of Field Marshal Douglas Haig's prophesied collapse of the German army.[1] At home, there were food queues, shortages of coal, cigarettes and paper, dimmed street lights and fresh waves of bombing raids from the Germans' new Gotha heavy aircraft. The Cabinet began planning for a conflict that would continue into 1919 (Churchill thought 1921 was a more accurate date).[2] The year 1918 had opened with gales and snowstorms pummelling southern England with many fallen trees and some damage to shipping, though fine weather had been reported in Scotland. There were even accounts of a decline in drunkenness.[3] By June, however, the country was bracing itself as the first outbreaks of the Spanish Influenza, or 'the plague of the Spanish Lady', were being reported. Rumoured to be spread by American soldiers, the disease displayed a virulence hitherto unknown and was thought by medics to be another form of malaria. Schoolchildren sang of 'Enza':

> I had a little bird
> Its name was Enza
> I opened the window
> And in-flu-enza.

Lloyd George was struck down (and nearly died) with the disease in September, and was incapacitated for two weeks in Manchester Town Hall, where he had just delivered a speech. Lloyd George recovered well, but the disease went on to kill 228,917 Britons before it lost its strength in the summer of 1919.[4]

For some, the war appeared endless. At his home in Cobham, Surrey, Frederick Robinson, assiduously writing his diary as he had done since the war's beginning, pleaded, 'When is this awful nightmare to end? ... The country is getting tired out, people no longer talk of war, they are saturated with it, it enters into their every thought and action, it is part of our flesh and of their bone. When are we again to live our proper lives?'[5] But peace came suddenly. After the surprise launch of the German army's spring offensive, which drove British and French forces back some 40 miles in its first few days, the Allies regrouped around a unified military command structure, secured a resounding victory at Amiens in August, and began to push the Germans back through France and Belgium. In October, representatives of the German government contacted the American President, Woodrow Wilson, to negotiate a peace settlement on the basis of his 'fourteen points'.[6] By that time, Germany was collapsing from within. In the cities her people were starving; social unrest had broken out in several urban centres; and her allies were leaving the war. On 30th October the Ottoman Empire had agreed a peace deal with the British; on 3rd November, Austria–Hungary signed an armistice with the Italians. A mutiny in its navy, the abdication of the Kaiser and the installation of a new socialist government in Berlin eventually brought German representatives into an early morning rendezvous on 11th November in a railway carriage at Rethondes outside Paris, to sign an armistice agreement with the Allies. The Armistice was to come into force at 11 a.m. The fighting (if not the war) was over.[7]

Lloyd George, having spent the evening of 10th November at his home at Walton Heath in Surrey, was woken at 6 a.m. by a phone call informing him that the Armistice had been signed. At 9.30 a.m. he addressed a hastily convened meeting of the War Cabinet, where the decision was taken for the military authorities to fire guns, sound bugles, ring church bells and let loose their marching bands. The wraps were taken off the striking mechanism of Big Ben; its bells would ring for the first time since war had been declared four years earlier. At 10.55 a.m., Lloyd George appeared on the steps of the Foreign Office. 'At eleven o'clock this war will be over', he declared. 'We have won a great victory and we are entitled to a bit of shouting.' Lloyd George then beat a path back to his garden, laughing. He probably didn't stop all day.[8]

The 11th November fell on a Monday: the 1,568th day of the war, yet few Britons considered turning in for work. London, the *Daily Express* wrote, was in 'the throes of jubilation'.[9] As Lloyd George spoke, large crowds had already begun to spread into London's streets, parks and squares in an outburst of spontaneous celebration. The country seemed mad with relief and joy. Street lamps were lit for the first time since 1915. Dancing became a public craze; couples copulated in doorways. Bonar Law, Milner, Smuts and other members of the War Cabinet struggled to make their way through the crowds to offer the Prime Minister their congratulations. Winston Churchill, driving in his car with his pregnant wife, Clementine, was stopped short of Downing Street after being surrounded by the cheering thousands.[10] Georgina Lee, an educated, middle-class woman who had spent much of the war at her home in Chelsea, wrote in her diary:

[I]t was curious to see the awakening of London to enthusiasm and excitement. People ran about, flags began to appear at all the windows; women from the aeroplane and munitions factories poured into the streets, standing in big groups, cheering and shouting. In an hour the streets were transformed ... . We went down Constitution Hill where motor cars festooned with flags, filled with servicemen and women made a continuous stream towards the Palace, and the crowds all converged there too. Once in front of the Palace we found thousands of people there, the monument in front black with human beings who had climbed on to the heads and behind the wings of the marble figures.[11]

Across the country, the revelry was the same. Spontaneous fancy-dress parties were thrown in Sunderland. Groups of servicemen commandeered a beer lorry in Leith Street, Edinburgh, and broke it open on the street to the delighted amazement of onlookers. In Blaina, South Wales, 'practically every house exhibited a flag'.[12] Some, however, celebrated less than others. The reactions of Wilfred Owen's mother, who received news of her son's death on 11th November, can perhaps be readily surmised. Phylliss Illiff, whose fiancé was killed in France, could find in 11th November nothing but the tragic. She wrote, 'the day when this war has ended that has wrecked my life and altered my own character ... what does it mean to us who have lost all in this fight, a

Figure 10.1 It's over! WRAFs celebrate the Armistice

fight which has not yet been won [?]'[13] Florence Younghusband found herself on the top deck of a bus when the guns fired the first signals for national jubilation. Seated in front were two soldiers, one whose face was 'horribly scarred'. 'He looked straight ahead and remained stonily silent; the other just bowed his head in his hand and burst out crying. The omnibus conductress dropped into the vacant seat … leant her head on her shoulder and cried too. "I lost my man two months ago, I *can't* be happy today".'[14]

Representing the people

As the celebrations continued, the coalition government found itself contemplating the need for a long overdue general election. The House of Commons had been *in situ* since 1910, and Lloyd George was not alone in his view that the social changes wrought by the war almost demanded the modernizing of British politics. Yet, at the same time, maintaining national unity through the continuation of the coalition was the only sensible mechanism for managing reconstruction, the threat of unrest and the uncertain politics of organized labour. Lloyd George needed a mandate from the voters and quickly.[15] His haste was tempered by the unpredictability of the new electoral landscape. Under the provisions of the Representation of the People Act, passed by Parliament in February 1918, the character of the voting public had changed irrevocably. The act had originated from Asquith's move to initiate a House of Commons Speaker's Conference, an all-party body of MPs chaired by James Lowther. Their brief was to reform the old 'householder-based' electoral rolls (where voting rights were given to men over the age of 21 who had resided at the same address for at least one year) which had been thrown into chaos by the mass movement of people into war work and the armed services, leaving thousands of workers and soldiers effectively disenfranchised. The Conference report, when delivered to Lloyd George in January 1918, made three recommendations: the reduction of the residency requirement to six months, an expansion of the electorate and an overhaul of the entire voting system.

Whilst MPs accepted, without a murmur, changing the residency requirement and enfranchising all adult males over the age of 21, consensus on extending the vote to women was far from solid. In the parliamentary debates on the Bill, some Conservative MPs, still mindful of the pre-war suffragette outrages, opposed enfranchising women on principle. Others were concerned that women voters would somehow rebalance the electoral topography to the detriment of their party, amid fears that a working-class majority inherent in a larger voting population would ensure that future parliaments would be dominated by left-leaning parties or even revolutionaries. In the event, given their vital contribution to the war effort, women's case for the franchise had been put beyond debate. Yet, by wedging it within a household franchise and higher age requirement, Conservative MPs showed that their primal fears of women voters had not escaped them.[16]

It was Lloyd George, however, who was most discomforted by the Conference's arguments, particularly if future parliaments were to reflect the opinions of voters more closely, then proportional representation (PR) had to be introduced. Specifically, in single-member constituencies, where the number of candidates exceeded two, polling should be conducted on an 'alternative vote' system. In urban constituencies, consisting of a number of parliamentary seats, a single-transferable vote should function. The Conservatives viewed PR as a way of preventing possible infiltration by left-wing extremist candidates resulting from the adoption of universal suffrage; Labour members felt that the alternative vote system would benefit their candidates standing in rural, Tory-dominated constituencies. But Lloyd George, the great progressive, the radical campaigner and the self-styled People's Champion resisted. In the Commons, the Prime Minister refused to lend his support to the proposals, and his lack of enthusiasm rubbed off on some of his fellow MPs, who eventually voted down the proposal by just seven votes. Caught between a reluctance to surrender the authority of government to the power of the Commons and the lack of time to consider the scheme more carefully, the reasons for Lloyd George's failure to embrace PR are still unclear. But it was a decision that he and his fellow Liberals would come to regret.[17]

The Act, then, was already mired in controversy by the time the Prime Minister rose to launch the election campaign before an audience in Wolverhampton just two days after the Armistice. Faced with the addition of two million, mainly working-class, young men and six million women (all aged over 30, and qualified by virtue of their owning or occupying premises with a rateable value of not less than £5) with no political roots and no party affiliations, Lloyd George attempted to stress the importance of the peace settlement and the coalition's social reform programme, pledging his future government to building 'habitations fit for the heroes who won the war'. He was met with shouts of 'hang the Kaiser'.[18] From then onwards campaign narratives emphasized maliciousness rather than magnanimity as candidates attempted to placate a vengeful public not yet attuned to peace and determined to make Germany pay for the hardships, the killing and the atrocities.[19]

Vote counting began two weeks after the election, giving time for the soldiers' ballots to arrive. In contrast to the 80 per cent turnouts of the 1910 elections, only 57.6 per cent of the new electorate went to the polls (only one in four servicemen cast a vote). As expected, the coalition won handsomely: polling 5,091,528 votes and claiming 526 MPs out of 707 Commons' seats. With 374 MPs, the Conservatives were by far the largest party. They were joined by 133 of Lloyd George's supporters (the Lloyd George Liberals), with ten MPs from the National Democratic Party. Opposition folded under the weight of the coalition's victory. Though the Labour Party's vote had increased from 400,000 to 2,374,000, Labour MPs now totalled only 59, a very modest growth from its pre-war total of 42. And the party had lost several of its leading figures. War sceptics Ramsay MacDonald and Philip

Snowden had been defeated; party godfather Arthur Henderson also lost his seat, leaving William Adamson, a little known Scottish former miner, to lead the parliamentary party. Labour's disappointments were accentuated by the practical disappearance of Asquith's Liberals. From its landslide victory of 1906 the party now had just 28 MPs, huddling together under the token leadership of Donald Maclean. Asquith failed to secure his constituency, as did Charles Hobhouse and McKinnon Wood.[20] Parliament now became home for the Conservative battalions: company directors and men with a background in finance and commerce. It was a chamber of 'hard faced men', in Stanley Baldwin's embarrassed view, 'who looked as if they had done well out of the war' and who stood on the brink of a 20-year domination of British politics.[21] Even Nancy Astor (returned in 1919 as the only woman MP in the House of Commons following a by-election) took the Conservative whip, taking her place in history as one of the first women to be elected to Parliament alongside Sinn Fein MP Lady Constance Markiewicz, who refused to take her seat.

In its legacy the election of 1918 revealed less about the politics of war and more about the politics of the future. Lloyd George's position as Prime Minister had been affirmed, but the landscape of electoral politics was different. Political opinion was divided across three main parties, Conservative, Labour and Liberal, a division which was to form the spine of the British electoral structure for the remainder of the twentieth century and beyond. The immediate future for the Conservatives looked bright, illuminated by the benefits of a weakened opposition, an atmosphere of public bellicosity and voters' apparent inclination to take comfort in the familiar. Liberalism, however, looked dangerously dated. The party, torn as it was between its two leading personalities, Asquith and Lloyd George, was leaking its social democrat supporters to the Labour Party and its older, right-wing Whig supporters (including Churchill) to the Conservatives. What remained was a rump of old free-traders and idealistic social reformers. Liberalism as a political force was spent (though liberalism as an intellectual force was far from dead). Not that Labour was in any better shape. Despite the party fielding a record number of candidates and its electoral 'war chest' being boosted by trade union funding, 60 per cent of its potential working-class constituency had failed to support the party. Expecting a breakthrough, Labour had thus been forced back into its electoral heartlands of Scotland, South Wales and the industrial districts of northern England, home of the skilled, heavily unionized and essentially male workforce. Future progress would depend on how far the party could capture the minds of younger voters, women, wobbling Liberals and wavering middle-class Tories.[22]

Confrontations

Lloyd George's new government had little time to consolidate its victory. Demobilization was one issue fraught with difficulties. Ministers shrank with dread at the prospect of releasing a surge of war veterans back into the country without any promise of a job. Mass unemployment held the menace of civil unrest. Instead, it was reasoned that demobilization had to be controlled in line with economic adjustment to peacetime production and the absorption of this influx of manpower. Under plans drawn up by the Ministry of Reconstruction, demobilization was handcuffed to the needs of industry, dividing servicemen into categories: the 'pivotal' (those who were most likely to create jobs swiftly – skilled engineers and company managers, for example), followed by the 'slip men' (a reference to the detachable section of the civil employment document that needed to be shown to a commanding officer to provide proof of guaranteed employment), who could qualify for controlled release in accordance with their importance in relation to the country's industrial priorities, and 'nonslip' men, some of whom possessed the skills necessary for immediate employment in essential industries, and others of whom did not.

The scheme offered administrative process over social justice but, to the soldiers anxious to return home, it appeared that economic expediency took precedence over human interest – giving men who had recently joined the services, and were more likely to have fresh contact with their employers, priority over those who had volunteered much earlier. 'Last in, first out' appeared to be a remarkably unjust way of handling a shrinking army, and trouble soon broke out. Complaints at the slow start of demobilization were perhaps justified – the process only effectively began on 9th December, a month after the Armistice. And, as Lloyd George reminded the troops, without a peace settlement, technically the country was still at war. But frustrations boiled over in January 1919 when 12,000 soldiers in camps at Dover and Folkestone demonstrated against their ordered re-embarkation to France, and 8,000 men paraded their discontent in Brighton. The protests spread to London on 6th January, when three separate demonstrations paraded the length of Whitehall in lorries with placards declaring, 'We want civvies suits', 'We won the war. Give us our tickets' and 'Promises not pie crust'.[23] Lloyd George attempted to answer the protests by appointing Eric Geddes to oversee and co-ordinate demobilization across the government departments most affected. Geddes introduced a 'contract system' in which soldiers who could prove a definite offer of employment could be released, no matter the length of service. These adjustments, however, did not offset unrest in the camps. Winston Churchill reformed the system by arranging a more equitable release scheme with the Army. Men who had enlisted before 31st December 1915, or were over the age of 37 or had three 'wound stripes' now became eligible for immediate demobilization. That still left 1.3 million disqualified soldiers, from which 400,000 could be released as 'pivotal men', or on grounds of hardship, and 900,000 who formed the occupying army on the Rhine, or could be available for home front service. Henceforth, demobilization proceeded rapidly. Within a year, over four million men had been released into 'civvy street'. The government only just escaped from this trap with its integrity intact.[24]

Any crumbs of comfort could be found in the booming post-war economy. On the surface, Britain's economic position was weak – burdened by heavy foreign debt (the country owed the United States of America £1,037 million and Canada £73 million, among others), the loss of overseas investments and a large balance of payments deficit. In tackling the debt, the government adopted a 'dash for growth' strategy, unleashing the wealth of untapped investment funds that had accumulated since 1914 through an easing of fiscal policy, while borrowing heavily to fund the reconstruction programme and redeploying funds from the rapid sale of surplus war material. By the end of 1919, what *The Economist* called a 'craze for speculation' had emerged across the country, reflected initially in the rapid growth of new companies (from 7,425 in 1913 to 11,000 in 1920), alongside a spate of mergers and acquisitions that created a number of huge 'combine' companies across the engineering, mining, cotton and steel industries whose capital value was far less than the money spent in their formation.[25]

Debt, especially of the finance-capital kind, created the illusion of easy prosperity. But, for the industrial working classes, the inflationary economic boom revealed itself in the dwindling value of their weekly wages. As during the war, and as in 1910, many working-class families found themselves afflicted by rising prices. The pound that could buy 8s 8d (approximately 43p) in food and groceries in 1914 was worth, in 1920, 7s 9d (approximately 39p).[26] Trade unions, who until now had been actively lobbying the government for the nationalization of the coal and the railway industries, now reverted to more traditional causes. A wave of industrial action, beginning in the unlikely guise of two police strikes in London (August 1918) and Liverpool (August 1919), intensified across the railway industries in September 1919, and there were simultaneous strikes amongst Lancashire cotton operatives and iron-moulders.[27] The unrest peaked in Glasgow, where economic grievances moulded with radical politics. Following the call of the by now infamous Clyde Workers' Committee for a general strike on 27th January 1919, a mass meeting of some 30,000 people, who had gathered outside St Andrew's Hall, decamped to George Square, where the red flag was hoisted on the Glasgow Corporation's flagpole. The government responded by ordering troops with tanks and machine guns to surround and occupy the city, quell the disturbance and arrest ringleaders William Gallacher, Emanuel Shinwell (who later became a member of Labour's 1945 government) and David Kirkwood.[28] The revolutionary threat, however, reared its head again a year later when a dispute over wages in the coal industry resurrected the old pre-war Triple Alliance, as the railway and transport unions joined hands with the miners in calling for a general strike. Lloyd George conceded to the miners' demands in March 1920, but a further wage claim in the autumn was met with a more determined attitude from the government. The dispute reached a climax when a 'datum line' stoppage of miners began on 16th October, prompting the railway unions to call a strike for 24th October. Lloyd George now offered the velvet glove of further negotiations, wrapped around the iron fist of the Emergency Powers Act, and the secretive formation of a Supply and Transport Committee to maintain essential services in the event of a national emergency. The Act, passed in 1920, gave ministers the right to declare a state of emergency if industrial action deprived the nation of the essentials of life. The legislation was effectively a post-war Defence of the Realm Act, giving the government widespread powers of requisition and enforcement of civil order, with troops if necessary. In the event, the disputes were quickly resolved, albeit temporarily.[29]

Declaring civil war on the working classes was not something Lloyd George's liberal politics could accommodate. Even though the resurgence of industrial unrest had been more economic than political in character (a visible signal that organized labour was seeking to defend its financial interest against a newly confident and assertive industrial class), this was not the post-war future that Lloyd George had sought to bring about. In conversation with his friend George Riddell in September 1919, the Prime Minister stated his belief that 'coalition' meant a 'fusion' of conflicting parties, achieving a symmetry of outlooks between Capital and Labour, where the interests of the 'haves' and 'have-nots' were evenly balanced.[30] Industrial confrontation was a clear threat to such aspirations, but it failed to shake Lloyd George from his longer-term goal. If discontent could be managed, then the state had to incorporate the aims and interests of warring parties through a series of forums for settling differences on the one hand, and by instituting a fully formulated social reform programme on the other: what one historian summarized as 'killing discontent by kindness'.[31]

For heroes …

The government's initial efforts were promising. Its convening of a National Industrial Conference with 500 workers' representatives and 300 employers in February 1919 at Caxton Hall, Westminster, emphasized the need for a 'mutuality of interest'. The Minister of Labour, Robert Horne, expressed the government's desire to settle difficulties arising from the transition to peace, and conference resolutions spoke ambitiously of fixing the hours of the working week, measures to offset unemployment by organized short-time working, housing schemes, public works programmes, together with more generous benefits for the sick and workless. Delegates spoke ambitiously of establishing the conference on a permanent basis as a means of finding some common ground between workers and employers.[32] But the conference collapsed amidst much acrimony in 1921, revealing, according to one historian, that there was 'no broad industrial basis for consensus in the immediate post-war years'. Indeed, Elie Halévy noted, the forum simply shifted the class struggle onto a formal footing.[33]

Two more efforts were made to establish a worker–employer consensus. The Industrial Courts, for example, brought into existence in 1919, created a permanent forum of arbitration as a means of settling disputes. But the court lacked the power to enforce its decisions. Marginally more successful were the Whitley Councils. Emerging out of a need to absorb the growing influence of the shop stewards' movement, a government-appointed committee under the leadership of Liberal MP J.H. Whitley proposed the creation of national industrial councils for every industry in Britain, with a myriad of similar local and district bodies working under them, each comprising employers and trade unionists, to negotiate jointly over the everyday problems of pay and working hours, as well as handling the larger issues of training, welfare and production methods. This state-sponsored behemoth eventually embraced some 56 joint industrial councils by the 1920s, with bodies spread across flour milling, pottery, chemicals, manufacturing, road transport and the printing, wool and textile industries. But the bigger industries stayed aloof. Mining, railways, shipbuilding, cotton and engineering were disinclined to partake in this early attempt at industrial democracy. And many such councils eventually became victims of the inter-war economic depression.[34]

Amelioration through social reconstruction appeared to be a better way of pacifying working-class feelings. As a programme, reconstruction had many origins. In its initial form it was more a policy of economic rather than social security. When Asquith formed the first 'reconstruction committee' in 1916 (an administrative body that grew in true Asquithian style, with nine sub-committees publishing reports on issues ranging from forestry to industrial and commercial policy),[35] Cabinet members spoke openly of a policy that would continue an economic war against Germany if military efforts failed to defeat her. Facing a Germany that was still economically strong, and able to undercut British manufacturers in world markets, reconstructing the conflict as a trade war was possible. However, by 1918 the emphasis had changed. In view of the disruption and turmoil of an untidy peace and fears of a resurgent Germany, the reconstruction problem had become one of securing Britain's access to supplies at Germany's expense: in other words gaining an advantage in world markets while the foe remained weak. This spilled over into concerns about readjusting the economy out of its wartime footing. Shortages of basic essential commodities and the prospects of economic depression and mass unemployment, combined with the problems of re-integrating millions of homeward-bound soldiers and laid-off munition workers, would place enormous social and economic strains on the country, with a possible breakdown in civil order. Reconstruction would thus mean a continuation of state controls and intervention, possibly in the form of tariffs on foreign imports, constraints on labour, food and prices, and the control of trade.[36]

Yet by now ministers' dread of social upheaval lent reconstruction a different meaning. Against a backdrop of industrial unrest, uncertainties over the temper of labour and fears of the consequences of the Russian Revolution, reconstruction became a question of widespread and fundamental social reform.[37] The ingredients of a successful reconstruction programme were already in place. Food rationing had proved that active and benign state intervention was possible without encountering opposition; the high taxes needed to pay for it had been widely accepted by the public. Moreover, it gave a sense of the post-war future for returning soldiers and played upon Lloyd George's social unity ambitions with the possibility of political dividends. To Lloyd George, there seemed no time like the present.[38] A Ministry of Reconstruction was thus formed in 1917, under the charge of Christopher Addison, one of Lloyd George's most devoted admirers and fresh from his troublesome time as Minister of Munitions. Addison was a busy man. His department was less a ministry than an 'idea factory': hovering over the government, circulating reports around its separate offices of state and developing half-baked conceptions into proposals for legislation.[39] The number of reconstruction committees ('panels' as Addison labelled them) was innumerable. Reports were published on many matters including local government, transport, electricity, women in industry and agricultural concerns. For Addison, the priorities of reform resided in areas that rose above the sectional interests of party politics: health, unemployment insurance, education and housing. But the minister underestimated the powers of resistance amongst his Cabinet colleagues, administrative practices and outside vested interests.

Health was particularly problematic. The case for reform was all too apparent. The First World War had exposed the continuing problems of poor health and poverty amongst the poorer classes and the gross deficiencies in infant and maternity care. (In spite of the efforts of reformers following the Boer War, the Army was still reporting large numbers of working-class men who were unfit for military service during the conflict.)[40] Moreover, treating the large numbers of disabled soldiers now drifting back from France was proving too much for the existing structure. Medical care was administered and financed by a scattering of different agencies, education authorities, Poor Law guardians, insurance commissioners and municipal public health authorities. As a medic of considerable repute, Addison had been manoeuvring for a Health ministry (with support from Lord Rhondda) even before his move to reconstruction.[41] But the opposition of friendly societies and insurance companies, fearful of a catastrophic loss in revenue, and an obstructionist Local Government Board, who were wary that a new ministry would smother their efforts to reform the Poor Law, succeeded in delaying the establishment of the new department until 1919. Addison was its first minister.[42]

Education presented a similar case. The Board of Education's Annual Report in 1918 admitted that the war had shown 'the defects and shortcomings of our system'. Levels of school funding varied widely. Being largely dependent upon the ability of local authorities to raise sufficient monies through the rates, adequate provision in poorer areas was always a struggle. School attendances fluctuated. Secondary school rolls fell by 1,000 in 1914–15, but improved thereafter, touching 9,000 by 1916. The pull of war work undoubtedly brought a premature end to many young juveniles' school careers, and a high proportion of younger children were still 'half-timing', a problem most apparent in agricultural areas. Police reports of rising incidences of juvenile delinquency exposed the need for post-school education and training.[43] The best education was still to be had in the public schools. The appointment of H.A.L. Fisher (historian and vice-chancellor of Sheffield University) as Minister of Education in 1916, was an open recognition by the government of the need for reform, but the gap between aspiration and implementation remained considerable. Fisher regarded education as a crusade. He drew large audiences to rallies held across the country in 1917, and his first Education Bill, brought before Parliament in the same year, proposed sweeping and fundamental changes to the system, only to be defeated by the concerted opposition of the local education authorities.[44]

When Fisher reintroduced a diluted version of the Bill a year later, it was evident why his proposals had incited so much opposition. He intended that all future educational provision should be administered and financed by the state. All fees paid to secondary schools were to be abolished, and local authorities across the country were now required to submit plans for comprehensive schemes covering all aspects of education in their areas, from nursery to secondary schools. The school-leaving age was raised to 14, and Fisher was keen to create the opportunity of post-school education by introducing 'continuation classes' for juveniles. Half-time schooling was eradicated; teachers' salaries were increased; and government grants to local education authorities were raised. Fisher envisaged a complete education system across all ages and all social classes, and many of his proposals predated the more famous Education Act of 1944. But such moves were costly and Fisher's lofty claims of investing in the country's future did not sit well against the more pressing economic concerns.[45]

The core of Addison's reconstruction programme lay in two critical areas of social security: unemployment insurance and housing. In the short run, the government knew that introducing a comprehensive scheme of financial relief to meet the expected onset of mass unemployment resulting from demobilization was imperative. The contribution principle, whereby a proportion of workers' wages was diverted into an insurance fund that could be drawn upon in times of distress, had been successfully initiated under the National Insurance Act of 1911, but covered only workers employed in industries vulnerable to fluctuations in activity – engineering, building and shipbuilding. However, the near absence of unemployment during the war and the extension of the Act's provisions to include wartime munitions had boosted the scheme's operating surplus to over £21 million by 1918: sufficient, it was thought, to cover any possible emergency. But the scheme's patchy coverage posed considerable political and administrative difficulties. It was too small to cope with an economic crisis and the growth of mass unemployment, and many idle workers would be forced to seek relief through a system of 'doles'.[46]

Unfortunately, with the abrupt ending of the war, Addison was forced to run in just such a direction. The first of his initiatives, the 'out of work donation', proposed in the autumn of 1918, was devised to cover the thousands of demobbed soldiers and civilian workers rendered jobless from the forced closure of war industries. As a direct state payment, without contribution, funded by taxation and levelled at what the authorities deemed to be a subsistence payment, the donation established an important precedent. Another involved the inclusion of dependants' allowances to the scheme, similar to the wartime separation payments, which exceeded anything being paid under the Poor Law system or the existing state insurance schemes. Both principles were enshrined in the Unemployment Insurance Act which was stampeded through Parliament in 1920, and successfully extended the 1911 scheme to embrace all workers earning up to £250 a year. But it also threatened to pull the state into the bottomless pit of poor relief.[47]

Housing, on the other hand, presented the most pressing issue of the day: one that was laden with high expectations and public demands for swift action. In the election campaign many words had been expended on the general dearth of affordable and good-quality accommodation. Yet the scale of the ministry's task was formidable. Estimates of the overall shortage ranged from 300,000 to 805,000 by 1921.[48] Rent controls had deterred many landlords from investing in new housing, and the post-war building industry was in a sorry state, beset by bankruptcies, loss of labour to the armed services and high costs of materials. Wartime house building had been undertaken by the Ministry of Munitions, resulting in the construction of 2,800 temporary cottages, with some 10,000 permanent houses erected on 38 sites across the country.[49] Yet Addison correctly surmised that the country's housing dilemmas went much deeper. The general shortage of accommodation was partly a function of the large numbers of slums and unfit housing that still required clearing and improvement. This was a task that had been only partially tackled before the war and still required urgent attention. An equally pressing issue, however, was the imminent expiry of the rent controls legislation, which raised the frightening vision of hyper-inflation in house-rent levels, with possible dangers to civil peace.[50] Addison took a long-term and a short-term view of the problem. The longer-term option was to expand state activity in housing as 'a temporary expedient': to bridge the gap between the existing infrastructural shortcomings of the private housing industry and public need. The priority was to make good the shortages, restore the conditions that would enable the private individual to resume investment in working-class housing and, eventually, bring house rents down to equitable levels whilst encouraging landlords to repair and renovate their dilapidated properties. In the meantime, a new rent act would be required to extend the period of controls to allow a normal housing market to be restored. But there was one other, and potentially more awkward, factor. Public expectations of better-quality municipal accommodation had been raised by the publication of Sir John Tudor Walters's report on housing standards (largely shaped by the garden-city architect Raymond Unwin), which recommended that the Victorian terrace-type building favoured by the industry before the war be succeeded by a new rural-cottage style house, furnished with a parlour, equipped with all modern facilities, set in gardens front and back and arranged in culs-de-sac or stylized winding country lanes. Garden-city reformers visualized the high-quality, 'cottage-style' dwellings of Letchworth being applied on a national scale – these were indeed the 'homes for heroes' that many hard-pressed families anticipated as a reward for their wartime sacrifices. But the financial support required to build such houses in such numbers effectively placed the entire programme in the hands of a Treasury that was much more concerned with reducing the country's war debts. Perhaps Addison guessed that the gap between social expectancy and economic priority was unlikely to be bridged.[51]

Addison confronted these problems, first, by pushing through Parliament a new act extending rent controls for a further three years and, second, by agreeing new government housing subsidy rates with the Treasury. Local authorities, who had been empowered to build houses under a housing act of 1890, were assigned the task of taking over house building and slum clearance until the construction industry was back on its feet. Under the terms of Addison's Housing and Town Planning Act of 1919 all local authorities were required to conduct a housing needs survey in their districts and to prepare and enact new schemes accordingly. In return they would receive a subsidy in the form of a payment guarantee that could cover any housing expenditures met by raising local taxation rates by one penny: a 'blank cheque' incentive offered by the ministry to ensure that much-needed houses would be built and let at relatively cheap rents, regardless of the costs of construction.[52] The struggle to revive the post-war building industry, shortages of labour and materials (in 1918 the Tudor Walters Committee had estimated that the building of 300,000 houses in one year would require 421,000 men, 5,431,330,140 bricks, 15,748 tons of nails and 5,175,000 cubic feet of cow dung for chimney flues), and continuing disputes with the Local Government Board (the government department through which local councils were answerable to ministers) over areas of responsibility ensured that the programme made a slow start. Nevertheless, between the summer of 1919 until it finally expired in 1928, the Addison Housing Act had brought into existence over 170,000 new council homes; of these 80,000 were completed in 1922 – the second largest number of houses completed under government sponsorship in any year before 1939 (the largest being in 1928).[53] But prices continued to rise. The construction of an average three-bedroomed property in 1914 at £250, had by October 1919 risen to £704; by August 1920 the costs had spiralled to £930, peaking in 1921 at £1,250 – expenditures that were not met by incomes.[54] Houses that should have commanded 30s in weekly rents could not be let for more than 12s 6d. Addison tried hard to overcome such difficulties. His department encouraged local authorities to hire their own builders rather than contracting schemes out to private construction firms. Experiments were made with different forms of house building, using new and cheaper materials – concrete and steel – rather than the ubiquitous and more expensive brick, and a series of Housing Bonds was launched to entice members of the public to invest in council housing.[55] This, however, did little to stem rising state expenditure on house building, which by 1920 had begun to take on the characteristics of a runaway horse.

Housing in fact represented the central problem within reconstruction. Total government expenditures by 1919 were touching £9.7 million, and total government deficits were touching £7,000 million. These had to be serviced in the same way in which the government had financed the war effort, by borrowing through the issue of government bonds on the home and international markets. The loss of foreign investments in the USA, Russia and central Europe made significant dents in Britain's ability to reduce her borrowing by selling overseas assets, but the scale of the debt owed to foreign lenders, particularly the United States of America, put into question the British economy's capacity to continue living on credit.[56] In August 1918 a committee of Treasury representatives and Bank of England officials, led by Lord Cunliffe, published an interim report that called for early reductions in public expenditure and government borrowing, in order to create the surplus necessary to repay the country's huge wartime debts, balance the budget and restore London's position as the centre of world finance. Though Cabinet action along these lines did not emerge until the autumn of 1919, an alarmed Bank of England, on its own volition, decided to take action on managing the government's £1,000 million floating debt by raising the bank rate to 6 per cent in November 1918. Although this reduced the debt by approximately one-half by the following spring, the rationing of credit by the banks limited the government's ability to refinance the remainder at prevailing interest rates. Accordingly, the Bank of England raised domestic interest rates to 6.5 per cent on 15th April 1920 and then to 7 per cent the following day.[57] The sudden volte-face in the government's economic policy placed a very hard brake on the inflationary post-war boom. Prices began to fall, company orders dwindled, and workers were being laid off. By 1921 unemployment stood at 13.5 per cent of the insured workforce, with totals of over a million, a figure from which they would not drop until 1940.

Almost overnight, reconstruction moved from being a social imperative to an unaffordable extravagance. Addison now became the target of a strident 'anti-waste' campaign conducted by the *Daily Mail* and *The Times*. He was held up as the most conspicuous example of 'squandermania'. Lord Rothermere even formed an Anti-Waste League, which won three by-elections between January and June 1921 at Dover, St George's Westminster and Hertford. Lloyd George, fearful that his Minister of Health had now become a political liability, moved Addison at the end of March 1921 to the more nebulous and politically harmless post of Minister without Portfolio.[58] The material damage to the programme was inflicted by a financial committee set up by Lloyd George to investigate the opportunities for budgetary cutbacks under the chairmanship of Sir Eric Geddes. Not surprisingly, Geddes discovered economies of around £87 million. Addison's housing programme was practically halted; Fisher's education budget was reduced by £18 million. Only fear of the social and political consequences protected the Unemployment

Insurance Fund from similar treatment; instead, it was extended to manage the rising numbers of jobless families and contain the very real prospects of widening poverty and destitution. Lloyd George's desire for a social and economic future driven by a programme of social amelioration and domestic harmony between Capital and Labour was no longer possible. Class conflict was resumed, as workers sought to extract what they thought were deserved rewards, while industrialists looked to restore profits to pre-war levels.[59]

Once the ashes had settled it became evident that anti-waste and economy campaigns were hiding several agendas. Many historians have noted that the central idea of reconstruction held differing interpretations; reconstruction of a new and better world was markedly different for those who saw the idea as a restoration of the old. The enormous growth of the wartime state (ten new ministries and 160 Boards and Commissions had been created, and hardly a person in the country had not been touched by it) was welcomed by progressives as an agency of social betterment in the post-war world. But the advocates of state action were equalled, if not outnumbered, by those who regarded state intervention as a necessary but essentially short-term measure during a national emergency. Such attitudes were not confined to the political camps. Trade unionists disliked state involvement in the workplace as much as company managers; Liberal thinkers feared for the future of voluntarism. Certainly, an 'old ways' mentality was a central motive for the financial retrenchment of the 1920s. Government ministers and City financiers saw the future as a restoration of the past: orthodox economics supporting a laissez-faire society. High taxes and so much state spending in the economy had distorted 'normal' business practices and loaded the country with too much debt. Governments of the inter-war period were convinced that keeping the state's economic profile to a minimum, maintaining a tight grip on public expenditures and moderating tax levels would create the conditions for recovery through normal business activity and the operation of the free market. Despite the huge economic and social tensions of the 1920s and 1930s, ministers of all political shades clung hard to such notions.

The socialist intellectual R.H. Tawney explained this resurgence of orthodoxy as if an 'intellectual conversion' to state intervention during the war had not taken place. Once the crisis had passed, Tawney argued, the ethos and reality of state intervention became 'exposed to the attack of the same interests and ideas as, but for the war, would have prevented its establishment'.[60] Thus reconstruction suffered from an ideological missing link. The introduction of state measures in wartime was accepted as necessary, but not as a template for the future. Thus, a society and economy run on laissez-faire principles was seen as the norm, rather than a post-war aberration. Company bosses wanted an immediate restoration of pre-war freedoms; returning soldiers wanted their old jobs back; and the public wished a return to old spending habits. The voluntary ethic in social policy was defended as much as the expectation that individuals should take responsibility for their own welfare. A return to familiar ways, therefore, could be easily explained and accepted. It was the advocates of state control who needed to justify their argument.

Hence the government's headlong rush to decontrol. The Ministries of Food, Munitions and Shipping had been dismantled by March 1921. The Central Liquor Board was abolished by the Licensing Act of August that year. Trade union calls for the nationalization of the railways and coal mines were refuted. Returning the British economy to the market so quickly brought different fortunes to different industries. Without the comfort of guaranteed markets and prices, the older 'staple' industries of the northern regions faced bleak prospects. The growth of new manufacturing economies in the Far East, particularly Japan, the loss of old export markets in Europe and India, the rise of competition from the United States of America and the lack of modernization in infrastructure and production methods brought on successive crises in profitability. Rectifying the problems drove company owners first into cutting wages, particularly in mining (a move that eventually brought trade unions into the General Strike of 1926) and, second, into closing plant and sending thousands onto the dole queues. As older industries faltered, the subtle changes in economic conditions made a fundamental restructuring of the British economy possible by the end of the 1920s, dominated by the rise of the new 'consumer' industries (car, wireless and consumer goods), with manufacturing plants powered by electricity and now located mainly in the Midlands and south of England.[61]

The desire to put back the pre-war world was reinforced by the treatment of women workers. The notion that women's efforts in wartime industries would lead to an increase in employment opportunities after the Armistice was knocked aside in the unseemly stampede to remove women from the workplace. Under the provisions of the Restoration of Pre-War Practices Act, women had few means with which to defend their position. Within a year of the Armistice, almost 750,000 women had been forced out of work. Women workers at Woolwich were losing their jobs at the rate of 1,500 a week.[62] Women's reactions to the rapid changes in their position were mixed. Many women accepted their lot. Martin Pugh reports that, although some expressed widespread regret at their leaving work, a majority welcomed the break; others married and retreated to the home, whilst others chose, or were forced though loss of income, to find other jobs.[63] Many younger women, however, proved extremely reluctant to return to their 'traditional' trades – domestic service, laundry, millinery and dressmaking – until the threat of poverty and destitution inevitably forced their hand.[64]

With the long trek out of the workplace came the unwelcome return of traditional attitudes. Women were praised as heroes during the war, but peace saw them being condemned as selfish parasites who were keeping men on the dole. This reassertion of older mores expressed itself clearly in the lower weekly payments for women under the Out of Work Donation scheme, just 20s to men's 24s, and the London County Council's denial of granting a pay award to its women teachers when it was granted to their male colleagues.

The press encapsulated the mood of retrenchment. The *Daily Sketch* attacked the 'Scandal of Proposed Retention of Flappers while Ex-Soldiers Cannot find Jobs', in a leader of 28th June 1919. The *Daily Mail* encouraged its readers to inform them of examples of 'unoccupied women'. By 1922 new regulations excluded women from claiming out-of-work benefit unless their family income fell below 10 shillings a week. Women instead were marched back into their traditional role of mother and housewife in a reassertion of family life around 'the home' and domesticity. In the 1920s a raft of new magazine titles appeared, *Woman and Home*, *My Home*, *Modern Woman*, *Modern Wife and Home*. The new journal, *Good Housekeeping*, saw house-work as the new avenue of emancipation, campaigning on elevating the status of housewife into household manager as part of a 'great feminine awakening'. With the decline of domestic service and the increasing numbers of women controlling their pregnancies and occupying a pivotal role in the drift into suburban living in the 1930s, perhaps there was some substance in the claim.[65]

All the same, there was some progress. Some of the barriers inhibiting entry to the professions, for example, were lifted by the Sex Discrimination (Removal) Act of 1919. And the interior design of the new post-war state housing was profoundly influenced by the work of the Women's Housing subcommittee which canvassed thousands of working-class housewives for suggestions about improving the living and working space within the newly built cottages. Contemporaries noted how the presence of women voters (universal female suffrage was achieved in 1928) had somehow 'domesticated' inter-war political debate. Writing in 1921, when female suffrage was still only partial, the Conservative Party's Principal Agent drew attention to the underlying change:

> The woman's vote is having a narrowing effect upon politics, making them more parochial and is, at the moment, reducing them to bread and butter politics and the cost of living ... their votes will probably be given on purely home questions ... while Imperial and foreign issues will leave them cold.[66]

Such changes have left us with an impression, not of unemployment and domestic 'duty', but of the emancipated 'flapper' girl, a product both of pre-war feminism and the war, attracted into the newer consumer goods factories which grew rapidly in the later 1920s, working where no union agreements existed, and for less pay than men. They were independent, unattached, daring to enter public houses for a drink, smoking cigarettes in public, dressed in long, cylindrical-style outfits, with sloping shoulders, hair cut short into an 'Eton bob', with a social life split between attending parties and cinema-going. Whatever the motives for the collapse of the reconstruction programme, and the reassertion of financial orthodoxy, the industrial and eco-nomic changes wrought by the conditions of the later 1920s produced two of the most prominent images of the inter-war years: the flat-capped unemployed man, made redundant from his job in heavy industry in the north, and the lip-sticked young woman employed in the new factories further south, obsessed with fashion and, in J.B. Priestley's phrase, 'looking like actresses'. These were caricatures, but they were rooted in actualities, and enough to remind us that post-war Britain was undergoing a profound, yet essentially modernizing, era of change.[67]

In memory …

Despite the rise of the 'bright young things' of the youthful upper classes, the frivolous jazz and dance crazes of the 1920s and the desire of some writers to withdraw from the world, the war was difficult to forget. Its immediate and obvious impact was the huge numbers of dead and wounded. The total number of casualties has been a bone of contention amongst scholars. Some put the total at 550,000; others at around 1.1 million. Jay Winter, after some deep and exhaustive enquiries, places the total war dead at the more reliable figure of 722,785, with the total number of wounded reaching 1.6 million. This excluded the 15,000 deaths among the passengers and crews of merchant and fishing vessels lost at sea, or the 1,266 civilian fatalities of air raids or coastal bombardments.[68] Yet, it was also difficult to escape the visibility of suffering. The presence of limbless and disabled men on the streets and in public places was a constant reminder of hideous times past. Some spoke of a 'lost generation'. Over half of the British Army's losses on the Western Front in 1918 had been soldiers of under 19 years of age. Death rates amongst the elite were reputed to be proportionately greater than those of any other social class. Oxford and Cambridge undergraduates, the 'officer class' of the Army, were calculated to be 19.2 and 18 per cent, respectively (as against the 11.5 per cent total death rate for the armed forces). For those who graduated between 1910 and 1914, the figures were even higher: 29.3 per cent killed from Oxford and 26.1 per cent from Cambridge. Comparable figures occurred amongst those who were recruited from the elite public schools: 19 per cent aged under 50 failed to return. Pointing to the ordinariness of inter-war politicians, intellectuals like Vera Brittain (and others) argued that the war had robbed the country of its brilliant generation of future political leaders, thinkers, poets and scholars. Intensive investigation of longer-term demographic trends has led modern scholars to dismiss the lost generation as either largely mythical (96 per cent of infantry casualties were from the working classes), or an upper-class whimsy as the elite classes fed their angst into literary outpourings while struggling to come to terms with the new mass democracy and the intellectually bankrupt popular culture of the 1920s.[69] Moreover, such arguments ignore the struggle of thousands of bereaved and war-affected families to come to terms psychologically with the war – the magnitude of loss, the scale of sacrifice and the need to understand its

Figure 10.2 The cost of war. Young mourners, *c.* 1917

meaning and purpose. Out of these mental dilemmas emerged the dynamic of commemoration.

Adrian Gregory identifies this amongst the significant majority of families whose sons, fathers and brothers returned from the war, where a collective sense of guilt and incomprehension about survival fed a need to commemorate as balm for a stricken conscience. Death in this, more than any other war perhaps, had been a lottery. Survival was a question of fate, not logic, and to remember the fallen was to understand their own survival. Gregory cites the case of a teacher, Robert Saunders from Fletching in Sussex, whose six sons, having served in the war, all survived. In a letter to his son on 16th November 1918, Saunders felt that:

> I can see so many tragedies in families I know well and I can see so many of my old boys who are dead or wounded, or dying of consumption and recall them as boys at school where I used to urge on them the duty of patriotism, so that at present it doesn't seem right that those who have escaped shall give themselves to joy days ... I have suggested to the Vicar that when our boys return we should have a special Reunion service for those who have escaped death. He quite agrees and also wishes to have another memorial service for all those who have fallen, for although we have already had one, others of our Boys have fallen and there is an

almost universal feeling through the country that Honour should be rendered to the dead and sympathy to the bereaved.[70]

In some places the process of remembrance had already taken root. In Hull 'shrines' to the fallen had begun to evolve from the Roll of Honour tablets that appeared in some working-class districts of the city from 1914, celebrating the city's menfolk who had volunteered for armed service. After 1916, the concept of honour took on a different meaning. Families who had lost loved ones at the front began to set their grief in wooden memorial plaques placed on walls and adorned with flowers and bunting as symbols of popular remembrance.[71] Others closer to the front had also been memorializing. Red Cross worker Fabian Ware took time to locate and record the graves of soldiers in a War Registration Commission, recognized by the War Office in 1915 and evolving into the Imperial War Graves Commission in 1917. For the War Office, the dead represented a logistical problem. The corpses from Wellington's victory at Waterloo had simply been shovelled into mass pits (to prevent the spread of disease) and commemorated in plaques and memorials in regimental churches.[72] In 1916 the decision was taken that no soldiers' bodies should be returned home, but they should be buried where they fell in specific military graves marked with a single wooden cross. With the destruction of these makeshift affairs from continued fighting over the same territory, the military changed its policy to digging long trenches before each major offensive, which were filled as the battles wore on.

The moves towards official remembrance originated within a report from two of the nation's leading architects, Sir Edwin Lutyens and Herbert Baker, concerning the cemetery question in France. They made two recommendations. First, that all graves should be marked with a single uniform headstone, made from Portland stone, identifying the name of the soldier (where possible), with no special adornments for officers, and arranged in single neat rows in a manner that suggested both military efficiency and equality of sacrifice. The stones were secular in character, bearing standard inscriptions of a regimental badge with the inscription of name, rank, regiment and date of death, but still showing some evidence of religious conviction, if desired. Relatives of the deceased could purchase permission for an individual inscription as their funds permitted. Each cemetery was to be deeded in perpetuity to the Imperial War Graves Commission and fronted by two monuments: a Great War stone raised upon three steps and a Cross of Sacrifice upon which a bronze sword would be placed, inscribed with Kipling's suggested epitaph 'Their name liveth for evermore', taken from the Bible chapter Ecclesiasticus. Second, Lutyens was subsequently commissioned to design a national memorial to the war to be situated back in London. Lutyens's design – the Cenotaph, initially intended as a temporary structure – was a classical representation of an 'empty tomb'. A stark and plain structure, the Cenotaph was decorated solely with stone wreaths and carried the inscription, 'The Glorious Dead', and was unveiled by the King in Whitehall at the

Peace Celebrations of 19th July 1919. The war was blessed with official meaning.[73]

The date 19th July marked the starting point for the 'ritual of remembrance'. On that day, church bells were rung across the country, firework displays were held in the evening and there was an abundant presence of military men. Some 18,000 troops marched in London, led by the most prominent wartime commanders, Haig, Robertson, Pershing and Foch: troops saluted the Cenotaph as they marched past. Thousands of grieving families made pilgrimages to Whitehall and laid wreaths at Lutyens's temporary memorial. The overwhelming response of the public to these celebrations prompted the government and military to institute the commemoration as a permanent event. Henceforth, remembrance became a parade of symbols. As the empty tomb, the Cenotaph became the tomb of everyone; those who had died in foreign fields could become, once again, part of official London, and part of their nation. The following year the Cenotaph was remodelled as a permanent memorial in stone, the anniversary of the Armistice was chosen as Remembrance Day (although this was a matter of some debate amongst government ministers) and, on the suggestion of Sir Percy Fitzpatrick, ex-High Commissioner in South Africa, a 'pause' was introduced, a silence of two minutes to allow the population its own personal tribute.[74] The ritual of memory was then enshrined by the commissioning of a Tomb of the Unknown Warrior – another symbol of national sacrifice framed within a militarized rhetoric. In 1920 the unidentifiable corpse of a Western Front soldier was exhumed in France, brought to London and buried in Westminster Abbey.[75] Over the following week more than a million people paid homage: a point of focus for those families who had no body to weep over, a symbol of the thousands of missing anonymous soldiers yet to be found and unearthed from the Flanders battlefields.[76]

Samuel Hynes has identified such rituals as one of two rhetorics within the remembrance of the First World War.[77] It fulfilled a public need to memorialize and record the dead, to express a sense to the living that their relatives had not died in vain, rendering meanings of the war within an older 'official' language of heroism and glory. This indeed was the language displayed in the inscriptions on thousands of local war memorials which, sponsored by public donation, were erected in towns, cities and communities across the United Kingdom over subsequent years.[78] It formed the framework for the reintegration of British soldiers into society without becoming sucked into revolutionary or right-wing protest movements. It meant that the disabled could be nursed under the auspices of the British Legion, formed in 1921 as an amalgam of a diversity of servicemen's charities, and whose appeal for donations, through the purchase of red paper poppies (which often flowered in No Man's Land, in spite of all the destruction), became universally respected.[79] And yet Hynes identified one other 'anti-monumental' rhetoric of remembrance that became the imperative of returning soldiers. More obliquely, this found partial expression in Thomas Cook's hugely popular battle-site tours of the 1920s, where 'pilgrimages' of bereaved families glimpsed the war in its aftermath.[80] This could also explain the popularity of spiritualism: families attempting to contact their dead relatives as they 'lived' in the spirit world.[81] Yet the impulse for truth-telling, already residing in the graphic bitterness of soldier-poetry, would emerge later in the spate of veterans' biographies published towards the end of the 1920s, finding a new and receptive readership.[82]

The tension between these two rhetorics, the heroic and the official, the tragic and the real, has since become wrapped around the remembrance ritual, sometimes in conflict, but at other times inhabiting the same cultural space. In the early post-war period, they occasionally prevented cultural producers from making their own sense of the war. In 1919 the artist William Orpen was commissioned by the Imperial War Museum to paint three pictures of the peace conference in Versailles. Orpen managed to complete two canvasses of the delegates, or in his eyes 'frocks', but the third found Orpen descending into his own intellectual crisis over the war. He explained, 'It all seemed so unimportant somehow. In spite of all these eminent men, I kept thinking of the soldiers who remained in France for ever.' Orpen's original canvass of the 'frocks' posing in the Hall of Peace was painted over and replaced by the depiction of a single coffin, draped in the Union Jack, being guarded by two ghostly soldiers, oddly with a pair of cupids drifting over their heads. The soldiers too were scratched out in the finished work. Orpen struggled to settle on a representational meaning of the war. The constant rethinking, redrawing and erasure of the painting almost rendered the picture meaningless, although with a powerful resonance to the modern eye. Truth to the reality of war prevented Orpen from reaching a simple solution. But it was still very well received by the public when shown at the Royal Academy's exhibition of 1923.[83]

Perhaps the same conflict is with us still. The social and cultural memory of the war has become, in recent years, a new and fruitful branch of historical enquiry.[84] Dan Todman, writing in 2005, suggests that the memory of the First World War is a continuum, a multi-vocal experience in which each generation brings is own values and attitudes to the war and draws its own conclusions. Our current view, that of horror, official stupidity, futility and carnage is a relatively new orthodoxy from the 1960s, argues Todman, though its antecedents lay in the inter-war period when the war was re-enacted in print using the narratives of waste and destruction that were formulated, mainly by the poets, during the war.[85] Recently a clutch of 'new-generation' scholars has attempted to confront the 'tragic' history of the First World War, by emphasizing that the conflict was indeed an Allied victory, and a vindication of liberal democracy over autocracy and militarism. Such views are not intended to undermine prevailing public perceptions of the war, but to emphasize the fact that, for this particular generation, in spite of the losses, there was something of a triumph to celebrate.[86]

How these debates apply to remembering the Home Front nation that endured the war is open to question. Yet the generation that fought the war from the factories, fields and farms has also had to grapple with the vagaries of history. If the narrative of the Home Front generation of the Second World War is heroic and noble – a valiant defiance in the face of a tangibly evil foe – then the innocently naive and gullibly patriotic domestic veterans of the First World War walk under a very large cloud. No doubt their place in the 'honourable' history of Britain has yet to be found. Yet, as the innumerable scholars who have ventured to study this period have found, this was a post-Victorian generation in its final throes, determined and tough, one that was not known or understood by the politicians, afflicted with worry about their loved ones at the front, but that, through it all, remained broadly loyal to the cause and stayed as determined to see the war to a victorious end as their Second World War successors. In the end, the Home Front people of the First World War were, and have been, poorly rewarded, their efforts and achievements under-acknowledged, their existence brushed away, as subsequent generations justifiably weep for and pity the soldiers. Perhaps it is time that *this* wartime generation was brought in from the cold.

Notes

1 Keith Middlemas, ed., *Thomas Jones: Whitehall Diary*, vol. I, *1916–25*, London: Oxford University Press, 1969, p. 18.
2 David French, *The Strategy of the Lloyd George Coalition, 1916–1918*, Oxford: Clarendon Press, 1995, p. 183.
3 Malcolm Brown, *The Imperial War Museum of 1918: Year of Victory*, London: Sidgwick & Jackson, 1998, p. 1.
4 See Mark Honigsbaum, *Living with Enza: The Forgotten Story of Britain and the Great Flu Pandemic of 1918*, London: Macmillan, 2009. See also Malcolm Brown, *The Imperial War Museum Book of 1918: Year of Victory*, op. cit., pp. 168–73; *The Times*, 24th October 2008 (see also the book review of 'Living with Enza' by Joanna Bourke).
5 IWM, 11335-P401–2, Private Papers of Frederick Arthur Robinson, diary entry for 1st January 1918.
6 This was Wilson's vision for the post-war world. The plan included the need for open diplomacy, the removal of economic barriers, freedom of navigation on the seas in both peace and war and reduction of armaments 'to the lowest point consistent with domestic safety', together with the creation of a 'League of Nations'. See David Stevenson, *1914–1918: The History of the First World War*, London: Allen Lane, pp. 389–91.
7 David Stevenson, *1914–1918*, op. cit., chs 16–17; Hew Strachan, *The First World War*, London: Simon & Schuster, 2003, chs. 9–10.
8 John Grigg, *Lloyd George: War Leader 1916–1918*, London: Penguin, 2003, p. 639, 'Afterword' by Margaret MacMillan.
9 Adrian Gregory, *The Last Great War: British Society and the First World War*, Cambridge: Cambridge University Press, 2008, p. 251.
10 John Grigg, *Lloyd George: War Leader 1916–1918*, op. cit., p. 639.
11 Gavin Roynon, ed., *Home Fires Burning: The Great War Diaries of Georgina Lee*, Stroud: Alan Sutton, 2006, p. 276.
12 Adrian Gregory, *The Last Great War*, op. cit., p. 251.
13 Adrian Gregory, *The Last Great War*, op. cit., p. 251.

14 Gavin Roynon, ed., *Home Fires Burning: the Great War Diaries of Georgina Lee*, op. cit., p. 277.

15 John Turner, *British Politics and the Great War: Coalition and Conflict 1915–1918*, New Haven and London: Yale University Press, 1992, p. 317.

16 See Martin Pugh, *Electoral Reform in War and Peace 1906–18*, London: Routledge, 1978, pp. 148–54.

17 See Martin Pugh, *The Making of Modern British Politics 1867–1945*, 3rd edn, Oxford: Blackwell, 2002, pp. 156–57; Martin Pugh, *Electoral Reform in War and Peace 1906–18*, op. cit, pp. 183–84; Gerard DeGroot, *Blighty: British Society in the Era of the Great War*, Harlow, Longman, 1996, p. 320; John Grigg, *Lloyd George: War Leader 1916–1918*, op. cit., pp. 105–09.

18 *The Times*, 13th November 1918, 18th November 1918.

19 Martin Pugh, *The Making of Modern British Politics 1867–1945*, op. cit., p. 161.

20 Martin Pugh, *The Making of Modern British Politics 1867–1945*, op. cit, pp. 161–64; Charles Loch Mowat, *Britain Between the Wars*, London: Methuen, 1955, pp. 6–7.

21 Charles Loch Mowat, *Britain Between the Wars*, op. cit., p. 7. See also John Maynard Keynes, *The Economic Consequences of the Peace*, London: Macmillan, 1919.

22 See John Turner, *British Politics and the Great War*, op. cit., pp. 445–48; Duncan Tanner, *Political Change and the Labour Party 1900–1918*, Cambridge: Cambridge University Press, 1990, pp. 426–42; Paul Adelman, *The Decline of the Liberal Party 1910–1931*, 2nd edn, Harlow: Longman, 1981, pp. 28–29; Martin Pugh, *The Making of Modern British Politics 1867–1945*, op. cit., pp. 163–64; Andrew Thorpe, *A History of the British Labour Party*, 2nd edn., Basingstoke: Palgrave, 2001, pp. 41–42.

23 *The Times*, 7th January 1919.

24 *The Times*, 8th January 1919; NA, CAB 33/12, 'War Cabinet: Post War Priority and Demobilisation Committees, 1918–19'. See also Stephen Richards Graubard, 'Military Demobilization Following the First World War', *Journal of Modern History*, vol. 19. no. 4, 1947; Gerard DeGroot, *Blighty*, op. cit., pp. 253–57.

25 *The Economist*, 6th December 1919; Charles Loch Mowat, *Britain Between the Wars*, op. cit., pp. 25–26; E.V. Morgan, *Studies in British Financial Policy, 1914–25*, London: Macmillan, 1952, pp. 317–31; Peter Dewey, *War and Progress: Britain 1914–1945*, Harlow, Longman, 1997, pp. 43–46.

26 See A.L. Bowley, *Prices and Wages in the United Kingdom, 1914–20*, Oxford: Clarendon Press, 1921, pp. 10–31, 70–71; Labour Research Department, *Wages, Prices and Profits*, London: The Department, 1922, pp. 87–89, 106–10. See also NA, CAB 24/93, GT 168, 'Report on Revolutionary Organizations in the United Kingdom: No. 30', 20th November 1919.

27 NA, CAB 27/59, 'Industrial Unrest, 1919'; *The Times*, 27th September–7th October 1919; Charles Loch Mowat, *Britain Between the Wars*, op. cit., pp. 38–43.

28 Charles Loch Mowat, *Britain Between the Wars*, op. cit., pp. 24–25; *The Times*, 28th January 1919, 30th January 1919, 3rd February 1919; William Gallacher, *Revolt on the Clyde*, London: Lawrence & Wishart, 1936, pp. 217–42; David Kirkwood, *My Life of Revolt*, London: Harrap, 1935, pp. 9–10.

29 Keith Middlemas, *Politics in Industrial Society: The Experience of the British System since 1911*, London: Andre Deutsch, 1979, p. 153; Keith Jeffrey and Peter Hennessy, *States of Emergency: British Governments and Strikebreaking since 1919*, London: Routledge, 1983, chs 1–2.

30 George Riddell, *Lord Riddell's Intimate Diary of the Peace Conference and After 1918–1923*, London: Gollancz, 1933, p. 127, diary entries, 20th September 1919; see also Bentley B. Gilbert, *British Social Policy 1914–1939*, London: Batsford, 1970, p. 39.

31 John Turner, *British Politics and the Great War*, op. cit., p. 387.

32 *The Times*, 5th March 1919.

33 Charles Loch Mowat, *Britain Between the Wars*, op. cit., pp. 36–37; Rodney Lowe, 'The Failure of Consensus in Britain: The National Industrial Conference, 1919–21', *Historical Journal*, vol. 21, no. 3, 1978, pp. 649–75; Gerard DeGroot, *Blighty*, op. cit., p. 317.

34 Ministry of Reconstruction, *Industrial Councils: The Whitley Scheme*, London: HMSO, 1919; Committee on Relations Between Employers and Employed, *Report on the Establishment and Progress of Joint Industrial Councils Set up in Accordance with the Recommendations of ... the 'Whitley' Committee, 1917–1922*, London: HMSO, 1923; Charles Loch Mowat, *Britain Between the Wars*, op. cit., pp. 36–37.

35 Paul Barton Johnson, *Land Fit for Heroes: The Planning of British Reconstruction, 1916–1919*, London: University of Chicago Press, 1968, p. 10.

36 See Peter Cline, 'Winding Down the War Economy: British Plans for Peacetime Recovery, 1916–19', in Kathleen Burk, *War and the State: The Transformation of British Government 1914–1919*, London: Allen & Unwin, 1982, pp. 157–81.

37 Derek Fraser, *The Evolution of the British Welfare State*, 2nd edn, London: Macmillan, 1984, p. 178.

38 *The Times*, 7th March 1917. See also Bentley B. Gilbert, *British Social Policy 1914–1939*, op. cit., pp. 5–6.

39 Bentley B. Gilbert, *British Social Policy 1914–1939*, op. cit., p. 9.

40 See Adrian Gregory, *The Last Great War*, op. cit., pp. 281–83.

41 See Christopher Addison, *Politics From Within, 1911–18*, vol. II, London: Jenkins, 1924, p. 55; NA, CAB 24/9, GT 361A, 'The Urgent Need for a Ministry of Health', 4th April 1917.

42 Bentley B. Gilbert, *British Social Policy 1914–1939*, op. cit., pp. 98–137; NA, CAB 24/74, GT 6734, 'Ministry of Health Bill', 3rd February 1919; Christopher Addison, *Politics From Within, 1911–18*, vol. II, op. cit.

43 See NA, HO 45/10790/301145, 'Juvenile Offences: paper read at Conference at Portsmouth, 16th November 1916'.

44 *The Times*, 27th February 1917; Trevor Wilson, *The Myriad Faces of War: Britain and the Great War 1914–1918*, Oxford: Polity Press, 1986, pp. 814–16; Geoffrey Sherington, *English Education, Social Change and the War, 1911–1920*, Manchester: Manchester University Press, 1981, pp. 30–32.

45 Derek Fraser, *The Evolution of the British Welfare State*, op. cit., p. 183; Trevor Wilson, *The Myriad Faces of War*, op. cit., pp. 817–19.

46 Ministry of Reconstruction, *Report of the Insurance Sub-committee*, February 1918.

47 Bentley B. Gilbert, *British Social Policy 1914–1939*, op. cit., pp. 54–85; Derek Fraser, *The Evolution of the British Welfare State*, op. cit., pp. 184–85; see also NA, CAB 24/88, GT 8123, 'Unemployment Insurance', 5th September 1919.

48 *Housing in England and Wales: Memorandum by the Advisory Housing Panel on the Emergency Problem*, Cmnd 9087, London: HMSO, 1918, p. 1; Marian Bowley, *Housing and the State 1919–1944*, London: Allen & Unwin, 1945, pp. 15–33. See also NA, CAB 24/44, GT 3877, 'Housing', 11th March 1918.

49 See NA, *Official History of the Ministry of Munitions* (1922), vol. V, part 5, 'Provision for the Housing of Munitions Workers'. See also S. Pepper and Mark Swenarton, 'Home Front: Garden Suburbs for Munitions Workers 1915 to 1918', *Architectural Review*, vol. clxiii, no. 976, June 1978, pp. 366–75; NA, CAB 27/89, CP 1593, 'Housing Committee: Report by the Chairman of the Committee' September 1920.

50 See Marian Bowley, *Housing and the State 1919–1944*, op. cit., p. 10.

51 See *Report of the Committee appointed by the President of the Local Government Board ... to Consider Questions of Building Construction in Connection with the Provision of Dwellings for the Working Classes in England and Wales and Scotland,*

and Report Upon Methods of Securing Economy and Despatch in the Provision of Such Dwellings (The Tudor Walters Report), Cmnd 9191, 1918. See also John Burnett, *A Social History of Housing 1815–1985*, 2nd edn, London: Routledge, 1986, pp. 222–26.

52 NA, CAB 24/71, GT 6497, 'Housing of the Working Classes: Memorandum by the President of the Local Government Board', December 1918; Charles Loch Mowat, *Britain Between the Wars*, op. cit., p. 44.

53 Marian Bowley, *Housing and the State 1919–1944*, op. cit., p. 271; *A National Housing Policy*, Report of the National Housing Committee, London, 1934, p. 46.

54 *Second Annual Report of the Ministry of Health 1920–1921*, Cmnd 1446, London: HMSO, 1922, p. 62.

55 Ministry of Health, *Housing: New Methods of Construction*, Cmnd 426, 1919; Mark Swenarton, *Homes Fit for Heroes: The Politics and Architecture of Early State Housing in Britain*, London: Heinneman, 1981, p. 125; NA, CAB 24/97, CP 545, 'Housing Bonds: Memorandum by the Minister of Health', 28th January 1920.

56 Peter Dewey, *War and Progress*, op. cit., p. 46.

57 *First Interim Report of the Committee on Currency and Foreign Exchanges After the War*, Cmnd 9182, 1918, paras 16 and 17; Susan Howson, 'The Origins of Dear Money 1919–20', *Economic History Review*, vol. 27, no. 1, February 1974, pp. 88–107; Bentley B. Gilbert, *British Social Policy 1914–1939*, op. cit., pp. 156–57.

58 Kenneth and Jane Morgan, *Portrait of a Progressive: The Political Career of Viscount Christopher Addison*, Oxford, Oxford University Press, 1980, pp. 122, 132, 138.

59 Gerard DeGroot, *Blighty*, op. cit., pp. 328–29; Andrew McDonald, 'The Geddes Committee and the Formulation of Public Expenditure Policy, 1921–22', *Historical Journal*, vol. 32, no. 3, 1989, pp. 643–74.

60 R.H.Tawney, 'The Abolition of Economic Controls 1918–21', *Economic History Review*, vol. 13, nos 1–2, 1943, pp. 1–30.

61 Charles Loch Mowat, *Britain Between the Wars*, op. cit., pp. 28–29; see also Peter Dewey, *War and Progress*, op. cit., p. 46 and ch. 5.

62 Martin Pugh, *Women and the Women's Movement 1914–1999*, 2nd edn., Basingstoke: Macmillan, 2000, p. 80; Gerry R. Rubin, 'Law as a Bargaining Weapon: British Labour and the Restoration of the Pre-war Practices Act', *Historical Journal*, vol. 32, no. 3, 1989, pp. 925–45.

63 Martin Pugh, *Women and the Women's Movement 1914–1999*, op. cit., p. 82.

64 For a more detailed analysis on this topic, see Gail Braybon and Penny Summerfield, *Out of the Cage: Women's Experiences in Two World Wars*, London, Pandora, 1987, pp. 137–43.

65 Martin Pugh, *Women and the Women's Movement 1914–1999*, op. cit., pp. 82–87.

66 Martin Pugh, *Women and the Women's Movement 1914–1999*, op. cit., p. 103.

67 J.B. Priestley, *English Journey*, London: Heinemann, 1934, p. 140. See also Robert Graves and Alan Hodge, *The Long Week-end: A Social History of Great Britain 1918–1939*, London: Hutchinson, 1940, pp. 36–49; Charles Loch Mowat, *Britain Between the Wars*, op. cit., pp. 212–14; Judy Giles and Tim Middleton, eds, *Writing Englishness 1900–1950*, London: Routledge, 1995, p. 106; 'The Long Summer', Channel 4 TV broadcast, 6th June 1993, 'Lightbulbs and Lino'.

68 J.M. Winter, *The Great War and the British People*, 2nd edn, Basingstoke: Macmillan, 2003, p. 71.

69 See J.M. Winter, *The Great War and the British People*, op. cit., pp. 65–99; Gerard DeGroot, *Blighty*, op. cit, pp. 273–74.

70 Adrian Gregory, *The Last Great War*, op. cit., p. 251.

71 Neil Oliver, *Not Forgotten*, London: Hodder & Stoughton, 2005, pp. 29–35.

72 Samuel Hynes, *A War Imagined: The First World War and English Culture*, London: The Bodley Head, 1990, pp. 270–71; Gerard DeGroot, *Blighty*, op. cit., p. 284.

73 Samuel Hynes, *A War Imagined: The First World War and English Culture*, op. cit., pp. 271–72.

74 Adrian Gregory, *The Silence of Memory: Armistice Day 1919–1946*, Oxford: Berg, 1994, pp. 8–9.

75 For a fuller story, see Adrian Gregory, *The Silence of Memory: Armistice Day 1919–1946*, op. cit., pp. 24–28. See also 'The Unknown Warrior' in http://www.collections.iwm.org.uk.

76 Adrian Gregory, *The Silence of Memory: Armistice Day 1919–1946*, op. cit., pp. 25–28; see also Jay Winter, *Sites of Memory, Sites of Mourning*, Cambridge: Cambridge University Press, 1995, pp. 102–05; Penelope Curtis, 'The Whitehall Cenotaph: An Accidental Monument', *Imperial War Museum Review*, vol. 9, 1994, pp. 31–41.

77 Samuel Hynes, *A War Imagined: The First World War and English Culture*, op. cit., p. 283.

78 See Alex King, *Memorials of the Great War in Britain: The Symbolism and Politics of Remembrance*, Oxford: Berg, 1998; Catherine Moriarty, 'Private Grief and Public Remembrance: British First World War Memorials', in Martin Evans and Kenneth Lunn, eds, *War and Memory in the Twentieth Century*, Oxford: Berg, 1997.

79 Adrian Gregory, *The Silence of Memory: Armistice Day 1919–1946*, op. cit., pp. 93–104.

80 Gerard DeGroot, *Blighty*, op. cit., pp. 286–87; David W. Lloyd, *Battlefield Tourism: Pilgrimage and the Commemoration of the Great War in Britain, Australia and Canada 1919–1939*, Oxford: Berg, 1998.

81 Jay Winter, *Sites of Memory, Sites of Mourning*, op. cit., pp. 54–77; David Cannadine, 'War and Death, Grief and Mourning in Modern Britain', in J. Whaley, ed., *Mirrors of Mortality: Studies in the Social History of Death*, London: Europa, 1981, pp. 187–219; Jennifer Hazelgrove, 'Spiritualism after the Great War', *Twentieth Century British History*, vol. 10, no. 4, 1999, pp. 404–30.

82 See Modris Eksteins, 'Memory and the Great War', in Hew Strachan, ed., *The Oxford Illustrated History of the First World War*, Oxford: Oxford University Press, 1998; Modris Eksteins, *Rites of Spring: The Great War and the Birth of the Modern Age*, Boston: Houghton Mifflin, 1989; Nicoletta Gullace, 'Memory, Memorials and the Postwar Literary Experience: Traditional Values and the Legacy of World War I', in *Twentieth Century British History*, vol. 10, no. 2, 1999, pp. 235–43.

83 Samuel Hynes, *A War Imagined: The First World War and English Culture*, op. cit., p. 295. See also 'The Long Summer', Channel 4 TV Broadcast, 16th May 1993, 'After Mourning'.

84 See, for example, Jay Winter, *Remembering War: The Great War Between Memory and History in the Twentieth Century*, New Haven and London: Yale University Press, 2006; J.M. Winter and Emmanuel Sivan, eds, *War and Remembrance in the Twentieth Century*, Cambridge: Cambridge University Press, 1999, pp. 1–39.

85 Dan Todman, *The Great War: Myth and Memory*, London: Hambledon, 2005, pp. 221–22. See also Nicholas Hiley, 'The News Media and British Propaganda, 1914–18', in J.J. Becker and Stephan Audoin-Rouzeau, eds, *Les Sociétés Européennes et la Guerre de 1914–1918*, Paris: Université de Paris, 1990; Nicholas Hiley, 'Kitchener Wants You and Daddy, What Did *You* Do in the Great War?', *Imperial War Museum Review*, vol. 11, 1997; Gary Sheffield, *Forgotten*

Victory: The First World War: Myths and Realities, London: Headline Review, 2002, pp. 1–24.

86 Brian Bond, *The Unquiet Western Front: Britain's Role in Literature and History*, Cambridge: Cambridge University Press, 2002, pp. 94–101; Gary Sheffield, *Forgotten Victory: The First World War: Myths and Realities*, op. cit., pp. 258–63.

Index